Southern Illinois University Press
Carbondale and Edwardsville

# William S. Burroughs

# At the Front

## Critical Reception, 1959–1989

Edited by

## Jennie Skerl

and

## Robin Lydenberg

Printed in the United States of America
Designed by Katherine E. Swanson
Production supervised by Natalia Nadraga
94  93  92  91    4  3  2  1


Library of Congress Cataloging-in-Publication Data

William S. Burroughs at the front : critical reception, 1959–1989 /
    edited by Jennie Skerl and Robin Lydenberg.
        p.   cm.
    Includes bibliographical references.
    ISBN 0-8093-1585-8. — ISBN 0-8093-1586-6 (pbk.)
    1.  Burroughs, William S., 1914–   —Criticism and interpretation.
    I. Skerl, Jennie.   II. Lydenberg, Robin, 1947–
    PS3552.U75Z93   1991
    813'.54—dc20                                                    90-9403
                                                                       CIP

Photograph of William S. Burroughs by Kate Simon

The paper used in this publication meets the minimum requirements of
American National Standard for Information Sciences—Permanence of
Paper for Printed Library Materials, ANSI Z39.48-1984.♾

# Contents

Introduction

# Points of Intersection

## *An Overview of William S. Burroughs and His Critics*

Robin Lydenberg and Jennie Skerl

T he reception of William Burroughs' work has tended toward extremes—from "UGH . . . ," the title of the *Times Literary Supplement* review that provoked the longest exchange of letters in that publication's history, to Norman Mailer's oft-quoted statement that the author of *Naked Lunch* was "possessed by genius." Critics generally break down into two groups: those who reject Burroughs on the basis of traditional humanist moral and aesthetic values and those who, from a variety of critical perspectives, are receptive to his basically antihumanist art. In fact, Burroughs' work acts almost as a litmus test of a reader's response to the contemporary avant-garde, or what we now call postmodernism. Criticism of Burroughs has been further complicated by extraliterary factors: the censorship of *Naked Lunch*, the legend surrounding his life and personality, his involvement in popular culture, his early association with the Beats, his expatriation, and the fragmentation of his critical audience. These factors are also the source of extreme emotional responses that have often prevented critics from looking at the work itself.

## 1950s

In the 1950s, Burroughs published only *Junky* (1953), which went unnoticed, and produced several unpublished manuscripts: "Queer"; "In Search of Yage," a manuscript of about one thousand pages that later became the basis of *Naked Lunch* and portions of the subsequent novels; and an extensive correspondence that contained fragments of his fiction. Throughout the 1950s he was acquiring an underground reputation, largely created by his friends Allen Ginsberg, Jack Kerouac,

Alan Ansen, and others associated with the Beat movement. Burroughs was fiction-
alized in Kerouac's *The Town and the City* (1950) and *On the Road* (1957), and the
as-yet-unpublished *Naked Lunch* was mentioned in Ginsberg's dedication to *Howl*
(1956). At the end of the decade, a portion of *Naked Lunch* was published in the
censored little magazine *Big Table,* leading to the novel's publication by the somewhat disreputable Olympia Press in Paris, and then to subsequent publication in the
United States and England in the 1960s.

Alan Ansen's essay, which opens our collection, reflects Burroughs' underground
reputation and the sensibility of the end of the decade: Ansen sees Burroughs as a
spiritual hero, and calls his essay a kind of hagiography. His biographical approach
to the fiction is one that has been sustained throughout the decades by many other
critics, some of whom, like Ansen, are responding to Burroughs' own aesthetic
challenge to break down the boundary between life and art, and some of whom simply
want to read the texts as autobiography.[1] We have also included as representative of
this early period in Burroughs' reception John Ciardi's *Saturday Review* piece. His
reaction to the postal censorship of the *Big Table* issue that contained the *Naked
Lunch* excerpts reflects the oppression that artists and intellectuals felt at the time.
Ciardi, like Ansen, interprets Burroughs' extravagant fiction as a form of spiritual
protest. This theme in Burroughs criticism continues in the 1960s: Norman Mailer,
for example, called Burroughs "a religious writer" in his testimony at the censorship
trial in 1965.

## 1960s

Critical response in the 1960s was influenced by the censorship of *Naked Lunch,*
the publication of the three subsequent cut-up novels, and the Edinburgh Writers
Conference in 1962. *Naked Lunch* was the last literary work in the United States to
be censored by the academy, post office, customs, and state and local governments.
The book was banned in Britain until 1964 and was not cleared by the Massachusetts
Supreme Court until 1966. By the time *Naked Lunch* was published in the United
States in 1962 and in England in 1964, Burroughs had also published *The Soft
Machine* (Paris, 1961), *The Ticket That Exploded* (Paris, 1962), *Nova Express* (New
York, 1964), and many shorter experimental cut-up pieces. He was also involved
in a variety of multimedia, film, and cut-up experiments with Brion Gysin, Antony
Balch, and others from the mid- to late 1960s. As a consequence, the reception of
*Naked Lunch* was influenced by readers' awareness of other (cut-up) works.

Burroughs participated in the Edinburgh conference in 1962 as part of the American delegation that also included Mary McCarthy, Norman Mailer, and Henry
Miller. But he also became a subject of the conference in what became a battle
between the ancients and the moderns, and between a conservative British literary
establishment and the Americans. McCarthy stunned everyone by declaring that
Burroughs was one of the most interesting and important new writers she had read
recently, and Mailer referred to his "vast talent." The audience and those who read

news reports of the conference were startled to hear such high praise from these literary lions for a writer whom almost no one had heard of and whose book was unavailable in the United States or England. Burroughs himself gave two presentations, one on censorship, and one on the future of the novel in which he discussed the cut-up technique which was the focus of his work at the time. His conservative dress and demeanor and his well-reasoned analysis of the issues inspired respect, but his explanation of the cut-up technique also aroused consternation and debate. The events of the conference brought to the fore several critical issues that would be debated in Burroughs criticism from the 1960s on: high praise by other writers producing incomprehension and resentment in some literary critics, the morality issue, the use of montage and collage techniques in the fiction, and the drawing of battle lines between the traditionalists and those in favor of freer experimentation in the novel.

The Massachusetts censorship trial of *Naked Lunch* in 1965 focused on issues that also entered the critical debate, such as whether the moral or "socially redeeming" significance of the work justified the revolting images of sex and violence, and whether Burroughs had deliberately chosen the montage structure because it would allow the insertion of pornographic passages. Thus, the aesthetic issue of coherence, unity, and structure was actually an element in assessing moral intention. Consequently, major literary figures testifying at the trial, such as Norman Mailer, John Ciardi (then editor of the *Saturday Review*), and Allen Ginsberg, as well as professors from Harvard, Wellesley, and M.I.T., defended the novel as an important moral and social document, and all defended the structure of the book as artistically justified and having an underlying unity. These questions of morality, artistic structure, and authorial control occupied critics throughout the 1960s.

*Naked Lunch* was widely reviewed in the United States and England. Many reviewers praised the book for its power and serious purpose, and Burroughs was compared to other writers in the modern tradition. But *Naked Lunch* received strong negative reviews as well. The most notable of these protests, because of the correspondence it generated both pro and con, was the unsigned review entitled "UGH . . ." in the *Times Literary Supplement* (1963). The review (now acknowledged by its author John Willett) and a portion of the correspondence are included in this volume. The passionate invective of Burroughs' attackers was striking: *Naked Lunch* was deeply offensive to certain readers who found the surreal portrayal of forbidden forms of sexuality, combined with the kaleidoscopic effect of montage, too outrageous for calm critical reflection. The "UGH . . ." reviewer, for example, indulged in a shallow diatribe along the lines of "Glug glug. It tastes disgusting." Contributing to the rejection of Burroughs' work was the author's status as a legendary founder of the Beat movement, which, throughout the late 1950s and early 1960s, was constantly under attack by the popular media and conservative culture critics. The fact that Burroughs writes openly as a homosexual was also a factor (largely unacknowledged) in the intense revulsion his work inspired in some. Leslie Fiedler, for example, accused Burroughs, among others, of endangering

American culture by leading the young into an antimale, antihumanist dead end.[2] In addition, negative critics were often resentful of Burroughs' acclaim, and a petulant tone seems to pervade many of their reviews.

Throughout the 1960s, Burroughs' works were seen by attackers and defenders alike as somehow emblematic of the times. In an early review of *Naked Lunch,* Herbert Gold predicted that "many will be disgusted, snobs will say it's a masterpiece, but they miss the relevance to our times."[3] The perception of Burroughs as the writer of the moment was most forcefully asserted in the essay by Marshall McLuhan that we have reprinted here. He interprets *Naked Lunch* and *Nova Express* as illustrations of how the contemporary technological environment shapes consciousness. Calling Burroughs a prophet who describes the new electric environment and warns against its dangers, McLuhan concludes that critics' attempts to evaluate Burroughs' work in strictly literary terms are "a little like trying to criticize the sartorial and verbal manifestations of a man who is knocking on the door to explain that flames are leaping from the roof of our home." This line of praise tended to obscure Burroughs as a writer and elevate him as a social commentator or prophet of doom.

The main focus of both attacks and counterattacks on Burroughs' work in the 1960s was the question of morality. Many critics claimed that there was no moral content to the obscene imagery in the works, and that Burroughs had an immorally ambivalent stance toward the world of violence, sexuality, and drugs he portrays. Many reviewers, like John Wain, mistakenly perceived him as a promoter or romanticizer of drugs, and *Naked Lunch* was identified as a series of visions produced while under the influence of narcotics.[4] Burroughs was seen as a life-denying nihilist who actually enjoyed the destruction and degradation in his work. The fact that Burroughs' fiction does not affirm any positive value was seen as a major flaw even by those who praised him. Ihab Hassan, for example, discussed Burroughs sympathetically in several essays in the early 1960s, but, as in the 1963 piece published here, he ultimately concluded that Burroughs is a lesser writer than Joyce, Mann, Kafka, or Faulkner because he is too nihilistic and loves too little. Most of these critics did not analyze Burroughs' form and style, but they did claim that a clear and consistent moral point of view could not be put forth through a collage structure having no single authoritative point of view.

This difficulty in identifying Burroughs' moral position led the conservative critics to deny that Burroughs could be considered a satirist along the lines of Jonathan Swift, a comparison Burroughs himself had invited in his introduction to *Naked Lunch*. David Lodge's review of *Naked Lunch* and *Nova Express,* included in our collection, best sums up the traditional humanist "objections to Burroughs." Lodge states that Burroughs fails as a moralist because he is deeply confused and nihilistic and also fails as an innovator because he is repetitious and lazy. He ranks him lower than modernist experimentalists like Joyce and Eliot because his work lacks continuity, unity, discipline, and control. This particular debate continued throughout the 1970s.[5]

Burroughs' defenders, rather than questioning the moral terms of the debate, responded from within the same traditional humanist point of view. They asserted that Burroughs made use of taboo subject matter to criticize the postwar social order and to express the contemporary mood of spiritual alienation. Burroughs was seen as the outcast in revolt, the underground man, the voice of outrage against the degeneration of the human race and against a consumer society diseased with bureaucracy—the drug addict as social critic.[6] "Outrage" was a key positive spiritual term for Burroughs' admirers, finally becoming an existential metaphor in Hassan's "The Subtracting Machine." Theodore Solotaroff's review of *The Ticket That Exploded*, included in this volume, identifies in Burroughs' work the voice of the native American underground, and compares him to stand-up comedian and social satirist Lenny Bruce. Mary McCarthy was also among those who admired Burroughs as an effective social satirist whose deadpan factual style was indeed comparable to Swift and other eighteenth-century writers. McCarthy also pointed out that classical satirists, like Burroughs, were often so carried away by savage indignation and wild humor that a clear moral position was lost.

While Burroughs' attackers wished to dismiss his work as the vile outpourings of a drug addict, his admirers praised its importance on the grounds that Burroughs had given an accurate account of the addict's life, and had brought the truth back from hell. Burroughs was defended as a courageous reporter, scientist, or anthropologist for his unromanticized representation of the alienation of the addict. Some reviewers pointed out that addiction in *Naked Lunch* and the later works expands in meaning from personal experience to social satire and finally to a metaphorical and even allegorical status, and some also gave similar metaphorical readings of Burroughs' sexual scenes.[7] In response to misreadings of *Naked Lunch*, Burroughs himself publicly stated his opposition to drugs in essays and interviews throughout the 1960s. He also became increasingly didactic and explicit in the cut-up novels that followed *Naked Lunch*, clarifying his position against all addictions, whether to drugs or to the sexual "Garden of Delights."

While critical attention in the 1960s was focused mainly on the content of Burroughs' fiction and the moral issues it raised, there were those even among the early reviewers and critics who insisted on the literary nature of his work, particularly those reviewers who were fellow novelists. They urged us to read Burroughs not for meaning or moral message but for the sheer pleasure of his distinctive voice, as a scientist of literature, or as an anthropologist of language. They asserted that Burroughs' focus was on the repressive nature of language, not on morality.[8] We have chosen for this volume the most important essay by another novelist, that of Mary McCarthy, published in *Encounter* and in the first issue of the *New York Review of Books* in 1963. McCarthy was one of the few early critics who examined Burroughs' comedy in some detail and stressed that *Naked Lunch* was a new kind of novel. She devotes her analysis to Burroughs' style, especially his comic techniques, and to his ideas, rather than to the morality issue. It was many years before other critics began to develop her insights and, like her, to look at Burroughs' fiction primarily as an art form.

Two of the best academic essays of the period—those by Ihab Hassan and Frank

D. McConnell that are included in this collection—also focused on the literary significance of Burroughs' work. In his early (1963) overview of several of Burroughs' works, Hassan places Burroughs in the line of modern literature from Rimbaud to Beckett, pointing out that Burroughs' fiction goes beyond social revolt to a metaphysical critique of reality and language. Similarly, McConnell refuses to limit *Naked Lunch* to the status of a social document and links Burroughs to the Romantic literature of drugs. He sees addiction as the basis for Burroughs' powerful antisymbolic literary vision, and *Naked Lunch* as a talking cure for our addiction to the image itself, particularly to those images of Western civilization that form the basis of our humanism.

The publication of the cut-up trilogy produced a shift in attention from content to style, and the more radical experimentalism of these novels called attention to the technique of *Naked Lunch* as well. But in the decade of the 1960s, the positive assessments of Burroughs' cut-ups were rare. A few critics saw them as producing a "brutal poetry" stripped of sentimentality and illusion. Some saw the potential power of the cut-up style, the energy of disgust and compulsive repetition, the possibility of altering consciousness. But most saw cut-ups as boring or repellent— an experimental dead end. Almost everyone, including Burroughs' publishers, his editors, his critical supporters, and his friends, were uncomfortable with cut-ups, urging Burroughs to return to what now seemed the more continuous narrative style of *Naked Lunch*. It remained for critics of the 1970s and 1980s to take cut-ups seriously and to explicate in detail their purpose, structure, and effects. The poststructuralist revolution in literary studies led to a rereading of Burroughs' fictions as texts rather than messages and justified the very techniques that had previously met with incomprehension and disapproval.

## 1970s

In the next decade, the publication of *The Wild Boys* (1971), *Exterminator!* (1973), and *Port of Saints* (1975) showed Burroughs using experimental techniques more sparingly and moving gradually toward a more simplified narrative style. However, other works published during the 1970s, such as *The Last Words of Dutch Schultz* (1970) were still highly experimental, and, in *The Third Mind* (Paris, 1976; New York, 1978), Burroughs explained the procedure and results of his cut-up collaborations with Brion Gysin in the 1960s. The 1970 publication of *The Job*, a collection of interviews with Daniel Odier, provided a helpful resource for those interested in Burroughs' theories. Although the mass media reviews of this period were almost entirely negative, Burroughs' popular audience was growing, and it was during the 1970s that his reputation as the grand old man of the avant-garde and the pioneer of the space age was consolidated. During this decade, Burroughs became associated with the youth culture and the rock scene in England and America. Upon his return to the United States in 1974, he began a schedule of frequent readings and taught writing at the Naropa Institute, activities which put him in touch with his younger audience. Two major events were held in his honor in the late 1970s: the Colloque de Tanger in Geneva, Switzerland, in 1976, and the Nova Convention in New York in 1978.[9] At both events, a mixed group of critics, avant-garde writers, and artists confirmed Burroughs' status as an important leader of the transatlantic avant-garde.

In the academic arena, the appearance of four bibliographies of Burroughs' work and critical responses to it and a growing number of dissertations contributed to his further recognition as a writer of major significance.[10] Three important publications of this period provided overviews of Burroughs' entire body of work from *Junky* through the cut-up trilogy and beyond.[11] Several critical surveys of contemporary fiction devoted entire chapters to Burroughs' contribution, and his work became the subject of sophisticated textual analysis attending more to issues of form and theory than to historical context.[12]

Eric Mottram's *WILLIAM BURROUGHS: The Algebra of Need* (Buffalo, NY, 1971; London, 1977) provided the first thorough coverage of Burroughs' published and unpublished work through the mid-1970s. Mottram set Burroughs within a tradition of radical thought and social criticism, focusing particularly on his exploration of sexuality and religion in the West, and drawing many parallels between Burroughs and other dissident voices in the Western tradition. We have included in this collection Mottram's discussion of *The Last Words of Dutch Shultz* in which he explicates the relationship between Burroughs' fiction and the art of film. John Tytell's *Naked Angels: The Lives and Literature of the Beat Generation* (1976), a study of Burroughs, Ginsberg, and Kerouac, devoted two chapters to Burroughs, placing him in the context of post-World War II American fiction and social change. The excerpt we have chosen for this volume is the introductory chapter from his book in which he examines the social criticism and visionary mythology that united Burroughs with other Beat writers.[13] While Mottram and Tytell gave more attention to Burroughs' form and style than did most earlier critics, both still saw him primarily as a moralist and social critic. Tony Tanner's chapter on Burroughs in *City of Words: American Fiction, 1950–1970* (1971) turned in a more literary direction, focusing on the role of language in Burroughs' mythology. Tanner's essay, a portion of which is included here, led the way toward greater understanding of the theoretical basis of Burroughs' fiction in the 1970s, and in particular to the greater acceptance of cut-ups.

While earlier critics had often praised Burroughs for championing the spontaneity of the individual against the repressions of society, in the 1970s critics recognized his more radical challenge to the notion of identity itself. Adopting a psychoanalytic perspective, some critics accounted for the unresolved oppositions in Burroughs' content and the absence of any unified voice or identity in his style as evidence of his "schizophrenic" state of mind. Although most psychoanalytic readings of his fiction treated Burroughs as a patient, he saw himself in the role of doctor or analyst, proposing a "talking cure" for the diseases of Western civilization. In the psychoanalytic essay we have selected for this volume, Neal Oxenhandler proceeds cautiously, reminding the reader that he is engaged in literary analysis, not clinical assessment. Focusing on infantile fantasies of violence and perversion in Burroughs' work, Oxenhandler sheds light on the psychic ambivalence that many critics have noted. Although not psychoanalytic in orientation, Alfred Kazin's review of *The Wild Boys,* which we have also included here, sees Burroughs' fiction in psychological terms: as reverie, dream, sexual fantasy, and narcissistic obsession with the self. Kazin also stresses, however, that Burroughs translates his sexual fantasy into literary energy, and has high praise for him as a writer.[14]

As critics in the 1970s looked more closely at Burroughs' experimental writings, some turned their attention toward themselves as readers, and toward Burroughs' manipulation and transformation of the reading process. The development of reader response criticism during this period undoubtedly contributed to this shift in Burroughs scholarship. Cary Nelson, in the essay reprinted here, analyzes the experience of reading the cut-up texts as an encounter that denies readers the reassuring continuity of time and identity. The relationship between reader and narrator in *Naked Lunch* was also explored in detail by Anthony Hilfer.[15]

In the 1970s then, Burroughs criticism turned from a preoccupation with the visceral content of the author's fiction and its moral purpose to an assessment of its theoretical and stylistic power. Critics discussed not only his social criticism, but his affinity with similar aesthetic innovations in film, music, and painting. We have included here, for example, an essay by Anne Friedberg in which she discusses Burroughs' collaborations with an artist, a filmmaker, and a recording engineer and reviews two films by Antony Balch that were based on Burroughs material. Burroughs' continued collaborations with artists during this period, such as with Robert F. Gale on *The Book of Breeething* and with Brion Gysin on *The Third Mind,* demonstrated that, for him, the connection between word and image is literal as well as theoretical.

## 1980s

In the 1980s, Burroughs published a second trilogy consisting of *Cities of the Red Night* (1981), *The Place of Dead Roads* (1984), and *The Western Lands* (1987). These novels renewed critical interest in his writing, providing the occasion for reassessments of his career, and reviews became generally more positive with the publication of each book in the trilogy. Burroughs, who had been elected to the American Academy and Institute of Arts and Letters in 1983, was being granted his official place in the pantheon of American writers. (He was also made a Commandeur de l'Ordre des Arts et Lettres in France, an indication of his wider recognition abroad.) Victor Bockris' 1981 portrait through interviews, *With William Burroughs;* Howard Brookner's 1984 film biography, *Burroughs: The Movie;* the 1984 William S. Burroughs number of the *Review of Contemporary Fiction;* and Ted Morgan's 1988 biography, *Literary Outlaw: The Life and Times of William S. Burroughs,* contributed to a consolidation of Burroughs' reputation as an important literary and cultural figure. As part of this fuller documentation of Burroughs' career, Viking Press began publishing early material still in manuscript: the novel *Queer* in 1985 and a collection of early pieces under the title of *Interzone* in 1989.

Major critical publications of the decade included books on Burroughs by Michael

B. Goodman, Jennie Skerl, and Robin Lydenberg. Goodman's *Contemporary Literary Censorship: The Case History of Burroughs' Naked Lunch* gave a meticulous account of the censorship of *Naked Lunch,* and all the legal and literary issues raised by the novel's publication. Skerl's *William S. Burroughs* was a comprehensive overview of his life and work that explored Burroughs' relationship to hipster philosophy, the international avant-garde, and a postmodern vision of popular culture. Skerl defined Burroughs' "artwork" as a new kind of fiction that criticizes the structures of reality and creates a new form of consciousness through a merging of high and low culture. Lydenberg's *Word Cultures: Radical Theory and Practice in William S. Burroughs' Fiction* focused more narrowly on *Naked Lunch* and the cut-up trilogy, examining the theoretical basis of Burroughs' efforts to explode conventional notions of language, the book, reality, and the self. Lydenberg maintained that the work of such theorists as Barthes, Derrida, and Kristeva provides the framework within which Burroughs' work can best be understood and evaluated.

Although critics in the 1980s were able to view Burroughs' work and its reception retrospectively, they often chose once again to see him as emblematic of the current decade. As he was the quintessential postwar or Beat writer to critics in the 1960s, he was now perceived as an exemplary model of postmodernism. In the larger debate over the difference between modernist and postmodernist aesthetics, Burroughs' writing was often used to clarify the distinction. Many earlier critics had compared Burroughs either favorably or unfavorably to the high modernism of writers like Kafka or Joyce. In this decade, instead of criticizing Burroughs as a failed modernist for his lack of continuity and organic wholeness, some critics celebrated his breakdown of conventions, his dissolving of individual identity and voice, as a postmodern victory.

While modernism tended toward ultimate resolution, postmodernism and Burroughs' fiction produced deliberately discontinuous texts that challenge the notion of the artist as unique producer and owner of his work. The tradition of collage, both verbal and visual, was often seen as the basis for this collective postmodern aesthetic, and some critics noted that Burroughs had often emphasized collage and collaboration as integral to his creative process.[16] We have included here two essays that explore Burroughs' relationship to the collage tradition. Oliver Harris' essay, appearing for the first time in this collection, is part of his longer critical study of the evolution of Burroughs' experimental writings. Looking at the most recent direction Burroughs has taken into painting and collage, James Grauerholz examines biographically and aesthetically the influence on Burroughs of various art movements from surrealism to postmodernism. His essay, reprinted here, offers particularly valuable insights into Burroughs' collaborations with Brion Gysin.

The collage aesthetic evident in the historical avant-garde and postmodernism often involves an innovative use of technology, and the relationship of man to machine is frequently a feature of the content as well as the style and production of these works. Burroughs' attitude toward technology has been a significant issue for critics since Marshall McLuhan's essay in the 1960s, and we follow this question into the 1980s with the inclusion of essays by Nicholas Zurbrugg and Wayne

Pounds. While Zurbrugg has suggested that Burroughs exemplifies postmodernism's optimistic attitude toward technology as a tool for artistic innovation, Pounds stresses the dystopian and dehumanizing power exposed by Burroughs' technological myths. Both critics agree, however, that it is crucial to situate Burroughs aesthetically and politically within the modernist/postmodernist debate.

The 1960s disagreement over the moral or amoral intentions of Burroughs' work was displaced in the 1980s by a debate about politics, and much of the political discussion focused on Burroughs' postmodernist incorporation of popular culture into his work.[17] Burroughs' use of popular genres in *Cities of the Red Night* and *Place of Dead Roads* was seen by many critics as a stylized nostalgia for the past, a nostalgia condemned by Marxist critics like Eagleton and Jameson as antithetical to any political consciousness. Critics disagreed about whether Burroughs assimilates popular culture and the mass media as forms for the reshaping of human consciousness or whether he condemns them as dangerous parasitic structures that drain or displace reality. Critical division on Burroughs' relationship to popular culture often took the form of disagreement on the utopian or dystopian nature of his fiction. We have included here three essays dealing with this issue. In her 1984 article from the *Review of Contemporary Fiction*, Jennie Skerl discusses Burroughs' inclusion of utopias as well as dystopias in the works from 1971 on, and the significance of Burroughs' "retroactive utopia" in *Cities of the Red Night* as an anarchist ideal opposed to the dystopian present. In his essay on *Place of Dead Roads*, David Glover argues that Burroughs never offers us conventional models for utopia, but rather generates a sheer narrative energy that might propel us toward utopia. But, as Lydenberg points out in her review of *The Western Lands*, Burroughs is never deluded about the possibility of reaching the promised Western Lands of immortality, and never blind to the danger that achieving utopia would lead only into stasis and death. The goal of Burroughs' postmodern politics, then, might be seen as the production of a state of perpetual revolution, continuous process, and quest—a different concept of utopia which evolves throughout the second trilogy.

The concept of postmodernism is only one aspect of a broader discourse in contemporary theory about the nature of language, culture, reality, and the self. Burroughs criticism, like most criticism of this period, was marked by poststructuralist ideas either explicitly or implicitly. The collision of literature and critical theory in the 1980s was less violent in Burroughs' case because his own theoretical assumptions are so close to those of writers like Derrida, Barthes, and Baudrillard. Charles Russell pointed out very early in the decade (using Burroughs as a prime example) that postmodern literature and criticism involved a similar recognition of intertextuality.[18] Several critics also saw in Burroughs' work a poststructuralist attack on such binary oppositions as subject/object, presence/absence, and reality/illusion. By 1986, a reviewer in the *Village Voice* could refer casually to the obvious parallels between deconstruction and Burroughs' notions of the work as virus and the death of the author.[19] In the wake of Burroughs' recent trilogy, the accumulation of nonfiction books, and explicitly theoretical statements in interviews, critics were reevaluating Burroughs as a thinker and as a theorist rather than as a survivor of outrageous experiences.[20] Steven Shaviro's essay on *Cities of the Red Night*, revised for this collection, is an example of how poststructuralist theory has led critics to look at Burroughs' deconstruction of binary oppositions in the recent novels.

* * *

This volume of criticism is meant to be representative of the responses to Burroughs' work for the past thirty years, while also including some of the best criticism. In our final shaping of the book, several excellent essays were omitted, but we have acknowledged their importance in this introduction. Although our concentration on Burroughs' reception in England and America did not permit their inclusion in the volume, we have also drawn attention to significant critical studies in French and German. We wish to thank William Burroughs for his generosity and encouragement, James Grauerholz for his sharing of files and information, and the many scholars and students of Burroughs' work from around the world who corresponded with us. Thanks also to Lois Brown for research assistance, to Elaine Gottlieb for her editorial assistance and preparation of the manuscript, and to Boston College for several generous research grants. At Southern Illinois University Press we thank Curtis Clark for his support of our project and Stephen W. Smith for his meticulous copyediting.[21] We hope that this overview and gathering of essays, some of them from widely scattered or inaccessible sources, will stimulate and broaden critical scholarship on this important writer and man of ideas.

As for Burroughs, the creative process continues vigorously to the present—he writes every day, pursues his new venture into the visual arts with his paintings, and lives his life. Just as his fiction has been signing off for over thirty-five years with sad farewells or strident warnings against imminent apocalypse, so critics and reviewers have been summing up his career with every new "last" book. It seems only fitting to offer Burroughs the last word in this volume: his own assessment of the critical reception of his work during the past three decades.

## Notes

1. Ansen later incorporated the *Big Table* essay into his monograph, *William Burroughs* (Sudbury: Water Row, 1986).

2. Leslie A. Fiedler, "The New Mutants," *Partisan Review* 32 (1965): 505–25.

3. Herbert Gold, "Instead of Love, the Fix," *New York Times Book Review* (25 Nov. 1962): 4, 69.

4. John Wain, "The Great Burroughs Affair," *New Republic* (1 Dec. 1962): 21–23. Wain's review, like the "UGH . . . " review in *TLS*, inspired a lively correspondence for several weeks afterward.

5. Lodge himself reconsidered his earlier response to Burroughs' work in *Modes of Modern Writing: Metaphor, Metonymy and the Typology of Modern Literature* (Ithaca: Cornell UP, 1977).

6. See Gold; Edward Dorn, "Some Notes More or Less Relevant to Burroughs and Trocchi," *Kulchur* 7 (1962): 3–22; Richard Kostelanetz, "From Nightmare to Serendipity: A

Retrospective Look at William Burroughs," *Twentieth Century Literature* 11 (1965): 123–30; and E. S. Seldon, "The Cannibal Feast," *Evergreen Review* (Jan.–Feb. 1962): 110–13.

7. Some examples of both literal and figurative readings of Burroughs' depictions of drugs and sex can be found in Kostelanetz; Robert A. Lee, "William Burroughs and the Sexuality of Power," *20th Century Studies* 2 (1969): 74–88; Gilbert Sorrentino, "Firing a Flare for the Avant-garde," *Book Week* (3 Jan. 1965): 10; and Terry Southern, "Rolling Over our Nerve-endings," *Book Week* (8 Nov. 1964): 5, 31.

8. See Anthony Burgess, "Yards and Yards of Entrails," *Observer* (13 Feb. 1966): 27; Joan Didion, "Wired for Shock Treatments," *Book Week* (27 Mar. 1966): 2–3; Stephen Koch, "Images of Loathing," *Nation* (4 July 1966): 25–26; and Michael Moorcock, letter to *TLS* (21 Nov. 1963).

9. The proceedings of the Geneva conference were published in *Colloque de Tanger,* ed. Gérard-Georges Lemaire (Paris: Bourgois, 1976), and the Nova Convention was recorded by Giorno Poetry Systems (New York: 1978 [records], 1986 [cassettes]).

10. Bibliographies published in the 1970s are Michael B. Goodman, *William S. Burroughs: An Annotated Bibliography of His Works and Criticism* (New York: Garland, 1975); Joe Maynard and Barry Miles, *William S. Burroughs: A Bibliography, 1953–1973* (Charlottesville: UP of Virginia, 1978); Miles Associates, *A Descriptive Catalogue of the William S. Burroughs Archive* (London: Covent Garden, 1973); and Jennie Skerl, "A William S. Burroughs Bibliography," *Serif* 11 (1974): 12–20. The bibliographies by Goodman and by Maynard and Miles were in the process of being updated in the 1980s. Dissertations on Burroughs in the 1970s are by Michael J. Bliss (Univ. of Minnesota, 1979), Lemuel B. Coley (SUNY—Stony Brook, 1979), Michael B. Goodman (SUNY—Stony Brook, 1979), Harry G. Polkinhorn (New York Univ., 1975), and Robert M. Whitelaw (Univ. of Massachusetts, 1970).

11. The 1970s also saw the first critical book on Burroughs published in France: Philippe Mikriammos, *William S. Burroughs* (Paris: Seghers, 1975).

12. Surveys of contemporary American fiction published in the 1970s that include a substantial discussion of Burroughs' work are Jerry H. Bryant, *The Open Decision: The Contemporary American Novel and Its Intellectual Background* (New York: Free, 1970); Josephine Hendin, *Vulnerable People: A View of American Fiction Since 1945* (New York: Oxford UP, 1978); Alfred Kazin, *Bright Book of Life: American Novelists and Storytellers from Hemingway to Mailer* (Boston: Little, 1973); and Tony Tanner, *City of Words: American Fiction, 1950–1970* (New York: Harper, 1971), a selection from which is included in this volume. Studies including Burroughs in a larger context are Cary Nelson, *The Incarnate Word: Literature and Verbal Space* (Urbana: U of Illinois P, 1973), selection included in this volume; Richard Pearce, *Stages of the Clown: Perspectives on Modern Fiction from Dostoevsky to Beckett* (Carbondale: Southern Illinois UP, 1970); and Alvin Seltzer, *Chaos in the Novel: The Novel in Chaos* (New York: Schocken, 1974).

13. The German critic Jürgen Ploog published *Strassen des Zufalls: über William S. Burroughs und für eine Literatur der 80er Jahre* (Bern: Lichtspuren, 1983), which discussed Burroughs in the Beat context.

14. On Burroughs and schizophrenia, see John Vernon, *The Garden and the Map: Schizophrenia in Twentieth Century Literature and Culture* (Urbana: U of Illinois P, 1973). For a Lacanian psychoanalytic approach, see Serge Grunberg, *A la recherche d'un corps: Langage et silence dans l'oeuvre de William S. Burroughs* (Paris: Seuil, 1979).

15. Anthony Channell Hilfer, "Mariner and Wedding Guest in William Burroughs' *Naked Lunch,*" *Criticism* 22 (1980): 252–65. A detailed analysis of reading cut-ups can be found in

Michael Skau's overview of Burroughs' work, "The Central Verbal System: The Prose of William Burroughs," *Style* 15 (1981): 401–14; and Craig Hansen Werner offers a rare close reading of a section of *The Ticket That Exploded* in *Paradoxical Resolutions: American Fiction since James Joyce* (Urbana: U of Illinois P, 1982) 96–119. These three critical studies published in the early 1980s reflect the intensified critical focus on the reading process in the previous decade.

16. See Laszlo K. Géfin, "Collage, Theory, Reception, and the Cutups of William Burroughs," *Literature and the Other Arts: Perspectives on Contemporary Literature* 13 (1987): 91–100; and Laurent Jenny, "Sémiotique du collage intertextuel: ou la littérature à coups de ciseaux," *Revue Aesthétique* 31 (1978): 165–82. Oliver C. G. Harris' unpublished dissertation, *The Last Words of William Burroughs* (Oxford, 1988), gives the most thorough analysis of Burroughs' relationship to collage techniques.

17. On Burroughs and popular culture see David Glover, "Utopian Fantasy in the Late 1960's: Burroughs, Moorcock, Tolkien," in *Popular Fiction and Social Change*, ed. Christopher Pawling (London: Macmillan, 1984): 185–211; Luc Sante, "The Invisible Man," *New York Review of Books* (10 May 1984): 12–15; Christopher Sharrett, "The Hero as Pastiche: Myth, Male Fantasy and Simulacra in *Mad Max* and *The Road Warrior*," *Journal of Popular Film and Television* 13 (1985): 82–91; and Jennie Skerl, "William S. Burroughs: Pop Artist," *Sphinx* 11 (1980): 1–15.

18. Charles Russell, "Individual Voice in the Collective Discourse: Literary Innovation in Postmodern American Fiction," *Sub-stance: A Review of Theory and Literary Criticism* 27 (1980): 29–39. See also Robin Lydenberg, "Cut-Up: Negative Poetics in William Burroughs and Roland Barthes," *Comparative Literature Studies* 15 (1978): 414–30; and Nicholas Zurbrugg, "Burroughs, Barthes, and the Limits of Intertextuality," *Review of Contemporary Fiction* 4.1 (1984): 86–107.

19. See C. Carr, "Hollow Man," *Voice Literary Supplement* (Oct. 1986): 20–22; and Gérard-Georges Lemaire, "23 Stitches Taken," in *The Third Mind*, Burroughs and Gysin (New York: Viking, 1978) 9–24. On Burroughs' undermining of binary opposition see Clive Bush, "Review article: An anarchy of new speech: notes on the American tradition of William Burroughs," *Journal of Beckett Studies* 6 (1980): 120–28; Michael Leddy, "'Departed have left no address': Revelation/ Concealment Presence/Absence in *Naked Lunch*," *Review of Contemporary Fiction* 4.1 (1984): 33–39; and from the same issue (pp. 64–74) Steven Shaviro's "Burroughs' Theater of Illusion: *Cities of the Red Night*," included in this volume.

20. For readings of Burroughs as a man of ideas, particularly in *The Third Mind*, see Regina Weinreich's "Dynamic Déjà Vu of William Burroughs," *Review of Contemporary Fiction* 4.1 (1984): 55–58; and Jeff Bryan, "William Burroughs and His Faith in X," *West Virginia University Philological Papers* 32 (1986–87): 79–89. The increased interest in Burroughs' ideas also led to the discussion of misogyny as an emerging issue in Burroughs criticism in the 1980s. Carr, Pounds, Sante, and Skerl all deal with misogyny in their overviews of Burroughs' artistic project. An early essay by Catharine R. Stimpson discussed Burroughs' misogyny in the context of Beat attitudes toward women: "The Beat Generation and the Trials of Homosexual Liberation," *Salmagundi* 58–59 (1982–83): 373–92. Readings of Burroughs in relation to feminist theory are offered by Françoise Collin, "Coupes/coupures," in *Colloque de Tanger*, ed. Lemaire, 63–72; Alice Jardine in *Gynesis: Configurations of Woman and Modernity* (Ithaca: Cornell UP, 1985); and Lydenberg in *Word Cultures*.

21. We have left undocumented essays in their original form and standardized all documentation in the remaining essays.

# 2

# The Book Burners
# and Sweet Sixteen

## John Ciardi

T he *Chicago Review* is a literary quarterly published by the University of Chicago. Last fall, as the editors were preparing their winter issue, a columnist on one of the Chicago newspapers attacked the fall issue as "filthy." The charge called forth a prompt reaction from Chancellor Lawrence A. Kimpton. In a memorable blow for academic freedom, Chancellor Kimpton summoned then Editor-in-Chief Rosenthal and announced that the material submitted for the winter issue was definitely not to be published. The issue, as Rosenthal reports the Chancellor's instructions, was to be completely "innocuous and noncontroversial" and it must contain "nothing which [*sic*] would offend a sixteen-year-old girl."

When has the true role of the American university been more profoundly enunciated? Its intellectual content is to be harmless and innocuous; its final test of moral values is to reside in the sensibilities of a sixteen-year-old girl. The petty-minded may insist that there is still some question as to exactly which sixteen-year-old girl Chancellor Kimpton may have had in mind, but in general, all men of learning and good will must certainly be grateful to Chancellor Kimpton for the depth and courage of his intellectual leadership.

The student editors of the *Review*, however, showed no sign of gratitude, and six out of seven of them promptly resigned over so trivial a matter as intellectual freedom. Some of the six thereupon managed to raise private funds, and founded a new magazine called *Big Table*, the first issue of which published intact the material suppressed by Chancellor Kimpton.

Now, as if to confirm Chancellor Kimpton's standing in the company of men of taste and learning, the scholar-inspectors of the Post Office Department have entered the picture by seizing 400 copies of *Big Table #1*. A hearing scheduled for early

John Ciardi, "The Book Burners and Sweet Sixteen," *Saturday Review* (27 June 1959): 22, 30. Copyright © 1959 by John Ciardi, and 1989 by Judith Ciardi. Reprinted by permission of Judith Ciardi.

June will already have been held by the time this issue reaches the newsstands, and the charge will in all probability have been that there exists obscenity in two of the works featured in *Big Table #1,* specifically, in "Old Angel Midnight," by Jack Kerouac, and in "Ten Episodes from *Naked Lunch,*" by William S. Burroughs. The third featured author, Edward Dahlberg, will probably not have been charged.

The immediate issue, therefore, is the charge of obscenity brought against two specified works.

There have been many court rulings on obscenity in the last two decades, and the tests are by now clearly established. Obscenity cannot be determined by any isolated word or passage but only by the total intent of a particular work. That total intent cannot be found to be obscene unless there is reasonable likelihood that it will stimulate to lewd and lustful excitement a man of average sexual instincts— *l'homme moyen sensuel,* as Judge Woolsey labeled him in the 1933 decision that cleared Joyce's *Ulysses* of the charge of obscenity.

A further test of obscenity is in the social importance of the work. As Judge Horn ruled in 1957 in clearing Allen Ginsberg's *Howl:* "If the material has the slightest redeeming social importance it is not obscene because it is protected by the First and Fourteenth Amendments of the United States Constitution." Various other tests have been applied by the courts, but the legal ground is substantially covered by these three principles: total intent, *l'homme moyen sensuel,* and "the slightest redeeming social importance."

I am no admirer of Kerouac's assaults on near-prose. But the issue here is legal and not aesthetic, and to argue an esthetic disagreement cannot imply in any remotest legal sense that Kerouac's writing is not immensely serious in its conceived intent, and that it is in fact a life-consuming attempt to describe what the writer sees as the place of value in a world fractured by disorder. Nor, in either a legal or an aesthetic sense, could one argue that Kerouac is not a writer of substantial gift, however much the gift may be smothered by indiscipline.

The impulse toward censorship can only arise from failure to understand the intent. True, an excessively literal-minded man may easily become suspicious of the surfaces of Kerouac's writing. Nor is it hard to imagine that excessive literal-mindedness is a survival characteristic in Post Office bureaucracy. But the test of literature cannot reside in men of such mind, neither in the aesthetic nor legal sense.

What Kerouac has written is a series of Joycean improvisations (no less!) on the nature of irreality as created by a slangy and polyglot god once named Old Angel Midnight. What the reader ends up with is thirty-five pages of free association in several languages (of which Kerouac is no certain master) and in gibberish (of which he recognizably is). Add a random of bilingual puns. Add four-letter words at will. Add even—here and there—a glimpse of orderly perception in the whirling chaos. What one comes out with (minus the four-letter words) runs:

> God's asleep dreaming, we've got to wake him up! Then all of a
> sudden when we're asleep dreaming, he comes and wakes us up—how
> gentle! How are you Mrs. Jones? Fine Mrs. Smith! Tit within Tat—

Eye within Tooth—Bone within Light, like—Drop some little beads
of sweetness into the stew (O Phoney Poetry!)—the heart of the
onion—That stew's too good for me to eat, you!—

Or:

Sor god denoder pie your pinging lief bring Ida Graymeadow Wolf
babe oo brooding in the is-ness seastand graygog magog bedonigle
bedart ooo

In fairness one must add, against the pressure of space limits, that such excerpt-lifting cannot help but make for some distortion. In this sort of writing *tone* is a major vehicle of communication. The writing, moreover, goes by something like musical principle, with basic themes recurring and being varied. Thus any number of details may be lost in transit, and the reader may still succeed in identifying, if only behind a veil of verbiage, at least the area of the writer's intent.

On the legal question of whether such writing could conceivably be held to be obscene, however, there is no need to lean over backwards. Mix as many blasphemies and obscenities as you like into this sort of mish-mash, and it is still impossible to conceive how any average man can go on reading the stuff, let alone be corrupted by it. Certainly its intent is serious. But how can a man put to sleep by the reading become lewdly and lasciviously excited by it? I would suggest to our guardians in the Post Office Department, as a ponderable principle of law, that dullness precludes excitation of the centers, and that by the test of dullness, Kerouac's writing is as unimpeachable as Federal prose.

When, moreover, writing of this experimental nature appears in what must be roughly classified as a "highbrow literary quarterly" that sells at $1 a copy, and that almost exclusively by subscription, it is very unlikely that the four-letter words will ever pass before the eyes of any but literary sophisticates. That sixteen-year-old girl, here and hereinafter known as The Sweetheart of Chicago U, is safe forever. The Statue of Liberty's torch continues to burn high and clean. And why don't you just go on about the business of getting my mail to me in time, gentlemen?

The ten episodes from William S. Burroughs' *Naked Lunch*, on the other hand, is writing of an order that may be cleanly defended not only as a masterpiece of its own genre, but as a monumentally moral descent into the hell of narcotic addiction. As in Kerouac's blurt, the writing does, to be sure, contain a number of four-letter words, but the simple fact is that such obscenities—if obscenities they are—are inseparable from the total fabric and effect of the moral message. No less a writer than Dante made it a principle of harmonious style deliberately to coarsen the writing when dealing with debased characters as his subject matter. And in what shall a man have sinned in applying the lessons of a great master?

What Burroughs has written is a many-leveled vision of horror. At times the surfaces of the writing seem to be coldly reportorial:

The body knows what veins you can hit and conveys this knowledge
in the spontaneous movements you make in preparing to take a shot.
. . . Sometimes the needle points like a dowser's wand. These
messages from the blood are infallible, literally always right.
Sometimes I must wait for the message, but when it comes I always
hit blood.
        [. . .] Running out of veins and out of money.

Bit by bit the undertone of self-consuming horror leaps free of even surface realism and begins to develop through more fanciful perceptions:

She seized a safety pin caked with blood and rust, gouged a great hole
in her leg which seemed to hang open like an obscene, festering
mouth waiting for unspeakable congress with the dropper which she
now plunged out of sight into the gaping wound.

By the end, the horror emerges in a surrealistic montage of dramatic scene and dramatic hallucination. Even the physical lineaments of the body are absorbed into the lust for drugs. The lust becomes a kind of green ooze that sucks the body into itself. Burroughs' portrait of The Buyer is certainly one of the most memorable (and, ultimately, most moral) horrors of surrealistic writing.

And only after the first shock does one realize that what Burroughs is writing about is not only the destruction of depraved men by their drug lust, but the destruction of all men by their consuming addictions, whether the addiction be drugs or over-righteous propriety, lasciviousness or sixteen-year-old girls. Burroughs is not only serious in his intent, but he is a writer of great power and artistic integrity engaged in a profoundly meaningful search for true values. Neither of the works cited could conceivably be held to be obscene by a reasonable court.

One is not dealing here with reason, however, but only with the Post Office Department. The postal inspectors can read the law as clearly as can the next man, but it is evident by now that the Post Office is not interested in the law but only in its own kind of harassment. The history of the Department's book seizures has consistently justified the assumption that it will deal in every sort of moral sneak-play rather than make a clean declaration of principle. Dr. Kinsey, in gathering books and other materials for his sex studies, endured seizure after seizure by the Post Office, and tried for years to engage the Department is a test case. In every instance the Post Office backed down and delivered the seized material at the threat of a courtroom test, only to begin the whole mindless routine over again at the next opportunity. Or could it be that the boys in the Inspector's office just liked peeking into Dr. Kinsey's mail, and what then of *l'homme moyen sensuel,* and by whom defined?

Many American men of letters have filed their protests against this seizure. If the Post Office does not back down in the face of that expert opinion, funds will certainly be raised by public appeal, a court action will be initiated, and the Post Office will eventually release *Big Table #1*. That much is certain.

But the question is not one of the eventual release of the magazine. Rather, it is of the official harassment of a small, imperfect, but serious literary magazine that is trying to operate on a necessarily tight budget. Who pays for the letters that must be written to established writers to request their support? Who pays for the trip to Washington and for counsel? And when the editors have won the release of *Big Table #1*, what assurances have they that it will not begin all over again with *Big Table #2?* Is this the true intent of the Post Office Department: to force a safe and sane sixteen-year-old sweetheart conformity upon all writing, by making it financially disastrous to venture beyond the literary standards of a postal inspector, who yet seems to enjoy peeking into other people's more promising mail?

In matters of art, what is official is always inhuman. Neither the barbarians of the Book of Regulations nor the barbarians of sweet-sixteen have any business between the minds of a serious writer and a serious reader. Nor can they be tolerated there. All censorship is a disaster that begins in ignorance and seeks to culminate in demagoguery. No occasion in the turbulences of a complex but still hopefully democratic society calls for stronger language in rebuttal. A curse on all of them as faithless men. Or worse, as men who have subverted faith to expedience. There can be no compromise with the book burners. There is only the duty to hold them in disgust, and the hope that they can be made to understand the scorn of freer and better men.

# 3

# Anyone Who Can Pick Up a Frying Pan Owns Death

Alan Ansen

A gatha Christie, somewhere, making fun of the plot of a hypothetical modern play, says that the young hero is actually a sort of saint: he robs, he commits mayhem, he kills, and then finally he performs a miracle. She spoke better than she knew; for in the burgeoning American potlatch of yummy cholesterol, high-priced protein, and the infinitely extensible falsie only some sharp delinquency, whether a private needle or a public bomb, seems capable of reminding us that we live perpetually with heaven and hell.

What William S. Burroughs gives us, in his life and his writings, is the example of a deeply committed personality totally uninterested in culture as information, in a surface of "nice" people, in all those time-wasting activities with which even the most earnest hen-track makers seek to beguile the specter.

Picture a young man brought up in St. Louis descended from the founder of one of America's great industrial enterprises. The depression reduces the family fortune but by no means completely wipes it out. At Harvard during the first New Deal administration he impresses his contemporaries with the force underlying his political intelligence, his serious studies in poetry and ethnology, his experiments with Yogi. A year or so in corrupting Europe and back to Harvard for graduate study in anthropology.

And now the break. An early traumatic experience has resulted in a rough love life and, even more important, in a loss of confidence in his family. Psychoanalysis removes fear but not a sense of isolation. Self-contrived rejection by the Army after the fall of France strengthens that sense. All of us who failed to participate in the war effort owing to one form of unclubbability or another have, I think, felt the

Alan Ansen, "Anyone Who Can Pick Up a Frying Pan Owns Death," *Big Table* 2 (Summer 1959): 32–41. Copyright © 1986 by Alan Ansen. Reprinted by permission of the author.

necessity to conduct private wars of our own. Even pacifists and enemy sympathizers participate dialectically; the outsiders feel they need the danger even if they and the purpose find each other mutually dispensible. In addition Burroughs has the need for commitment, which odd jobs—exterminator, private detective, bartender—cannot give, since a small trust fund effactually excludes him from basic concern. This commitment he finds in addiction to narcotics, an addiction which swallows up his income and gives him a new grim interest in the economy.

However gratifying the sense of urgency and the solidarity of weakness he finds in criminals, their stupidity gets on his nerves. After the war, establishing himself in the vicinity of Columbia University, he becomes the guide, philosopher, and friend of a group of young college boys including Allen Ginsberg and Jack Kerouac, a role he has continued to play for many of us ever since with great success and to our great spiritual profit.

After a period in New Orleans Burroughs heads for Mexico with his wife and two children. There things are possible, living cheaper, dope with less trouble, boys ditto.

At the age of thirty-five, under the prodding of Ginsberg, Burroughs begins writing his first and as yet only published book, *Junkie,* an account of his life as an addict in the United States and Mexico as well as "Queer," a further account of his Mexican adventures.

After a stay in East Texas helping to run a farm, he accompanies an anthropological expedition through Colombia and visits Peru on a quest for Yage, a drug which induces hallucinations and purportedly endows its users with telepathic powers. Out of this quest comes a series of letters to Ginsberg called "In Quest of Yage," now part of his novel, *Naked Lunch.*

Then Tangier, his base of operations from 1954 to the beginning of 1958, when he moves to Paris in search of further psychiatric revelations. This period, given to "steeping himself in vice," to use his own words, is devoted to the composition of "Interzone," the latest and longest section of *Naked Lunch*. The first half of this period is marked by increasing seclusion, by the horrors of long drawn-out and ineffective junk withdrawals and eventually by a cure in England. The second is distinguished by a frenzy of marijuana-stimulated composition and a progressive loosening of ties with Tangier culminating in the definitive move to Paris. Tomorrow India? Greece? Mexico again? Who knows? What we do know is that whatever the scene an incorruptible eye will enjoy its fissures and sustain its strengthlessness.

I first had the great good luck to meet Burroughs in New York through Allen Ginsberg just before he sailed for Tangier. At the moment I was at a loose end, housebound out of inertia, unwilling to travel for fear of enrollment in a gaggle of jabbering queens. Meeting this totally autonomous personality gave me the courage to get up off my ass without worrying about what I was conforming or non-conforming to, and I can never thank him enough.

A tall ectomorph—in Tangier the boys called him El Hombre Invisible—his persona constituted by a magic triad of fedora, glasses, and raincoat rather than by a face, his first presence is that of a con man down on his luck. But that impression soon gives way to the feeling that, whatever his luck may be, yours has been very good. A cracker accent and use of jive talk fail to conceal incisive intelligence and a frightening seriousness. "No one owns life," says Burroughs, "but anyone who can pick up a frying pan owns death."

A distinguishing feature is the mania for contacts. One sometimes feels that for him drugs and sex exist only to provide opportunities for making appointments. It is a revealing clue to his tremendous isolation.

He is an indispensable indication that it is possible to be vicious without being slack. How many addicts one knows incapable of more than a sob or a monosyllable, how many queers who seem to have no place in life except the perfume counter at Woolworth's or the economy price whorehouse. To use drugs without losing consciousness or articulateness, to love boys without turning into a mindless drab is a form of heroism. With some writers drugs take the place of the excitement of composition; with Burroughs they are rather succedanea for the beatific and malefic visions.

Burroughs' attitude toward property is most austere—living quarters tantamount to the worst inn's worst room and no more personal possessions than what can be packed into a handbag or worn on his back plus a portable typewriter. His motives are partly prudential—one never knows when a spot of bother may render a fast departure mandatory; the less substance involuntarily abandoned, the slighter the pang—and partly self-lacerating; but primarily the renunciation of possessions is the necessary consequence of his nonattachment to inessentials.

Beneath the tics and through the awareness of misery there exist a wholeness and devotedness of personality that create repose for Burroughs and instill it in others. I know of no one with whom it is such a delight to share an apartment. Not only awareness, not only psychic generosity, but a calm of spirit that can tame even the most fidgety poltergeist.

Why so much biography in the discussion of a literary figure? First, because of his importance as mentor and example in the lives and works of those writers, Ginsberg and Kerouac particularly, who are trying to recapture American poetry and prose for the total personality. Secondly, because, if, as they and I believe, writing is more than a matter of cerebrally selective craftsmanship, is, in fact, the total and continuous commitment of a given history, the raw materials of that history have public importance and back up the testimony of the work. And, in the case of Burroughs, the writing is a byproduct, however brilliant, of a force. What I am writing is not only a paean to a writer: it is also a variant of hagiography.

Seen in this light, Burroughs' closest parallel is Genet. His emergence into a sense of reality out of coddled conformity is comparable to Genet's triumph over misery and degradation through consciousness.

*Junkie* is a flat, cold narrative interspersed with factual lectures. In the ecological pattern of the drug addict the narrator is reduced to a cipher in the crowd, and the use of the first person is almost a mockery. People's actions and relations only point up the basic isolatedness of each; and the individual's sense of his own existence takes on the bleak unreality of an unloved newspaper paragraph. New York, Lexington

Penitentiary, New Orleans, and Mexico City pass by in a uniform chill that accurately differentiated topography and characterization somehow make chillier. It is Riesman's lonely crowd with the factitious warmth of convention replaced by the real if forbidding warmth of—junk. But that isn't enough warmth to export; in fact, the sense of physiological self-sufficiency it imparts blocks all other relations. Meanwhile the tireless lecturer keeps telling us the facts in season and out, medical, legal, anthropological, with an angry impatience. The truth may make you miserable, but it is the truth.

The thirteenth and fourteenth chapters of *Junkie* overlap "Queer"; and the thirteenth, particularly, figures a new subjective approach to the theme of isolation. A sick spirit tortures its helpless body to their respective limits. If the isolation of narcotics expresses itself in an aggregate of responseless units, the isolation of homosexuality brings out a unique internality. Bare hard narrative continues in the recitation of environments, of fixes and their sexual equivalents. The conversation, however, is much less clipped than in *Junkie* and in the mouth of the narrator turns into a new form, the routine. The first routine in "Queer," the life and times of the ideal oilman, reveals a double parentage, the lecture and the Tom Sawyer handstand meant to impress the work's *blaue Blume*, Eugene Allerton. Amid the dust and the abjection there is a disturbing hint of the atmosphere of the Platonic dialogue told from the point of view of a dispirited Socrates rather than an admiring disciple. The other major routines in the work—a self-lacerating True Confession, the story of Reggie the British agent, the madman's history of chess, and the explorer's account of his caravan—are parodies toppling over into outrageousness and are all addressed to Allerton. Only the caravan routine is spoken alone, but it is the outgrowth of an earlier routine to which Allerton refuses to go on listening, and in its description of the relations between the explorer and his hired boy menacingly announces the actual trip on which Burroughs takes Allerton in the second half of the book. They go through Panama and Ecuador formally in search of Yage, but for Burroughs it is the tantalizing but perpetually unsuccessful search for the perfectly spontaneous, perfectly responsive companion. Themes that exfoliate in "Interzone," particularly the erotic basis of theories of political power, first appear here in a more intimate form: it is the saddest course in *Naked Lunch*.

In "Yage," Burroughs is alone again. He recounts his travels through the horrors of Panama and much more briefly Ecuador, through the political noxiousness of Colombia, where, a member of an anthropological expedition, he first tries Yage, through the confined joys of Peru, where life is easy, and he steeps himself in the drug. The actual discovery of the drug plays a relatively small part in the work; at the center are the anthropologist's field report and Burroughs' life in Yage. The formal novelty of the work is expansion of the routines and their increasing independence of an erotic context. Only one has even an imaginary reference to Allerton, the presentation of the relation between a jealous lover and his beloved in terms of a loan company calling on a delinquent debtor. Two others, the death of Billy Bradshinkel, a parody of a slick paper magazine story, and Roosevelt after Inauguration, a violent and obscene account of the imaginary horrors in Washington following the triumph of the New Deal, continue at greater length the pattern of humorous exaggeration established in the routines of "Queer" as does the Zen Routine, in which a Mahatma devoted to what Burroughs likes to call "fact," that is, the maximum consciousness of reality, teases and instructs a disciple too prone to take words for things. The most ambitious routine of all, however, Yage City, is neither parody nor erotic philosophy but a vision of "The Composite City where all human potentials are spread out in a vast silent market."

And that brings us to "Interzone," the cold observer in abeyance, the horrid scene and the boisterous routines at the prow. Here, to sketch a progression is pointless, since the work is conceived as a total presence. The various luckless environments come together seeking refuge from unimaginative totalitarianisms that their own maniacally passional selfishnesses have created. Only the Seven Stages section of Auden's *Age of Anxiety* affords an equal example of "their own disorder as their own punishment."

Hitherto omnipresent, "Lee," Burroughs' *nom de guerre,* is here reduced to a sufferer in a hospital and a noncommittal witness to the evils of the County Clerk and the manias of Dr. Benway. Beyond that he fulfills his role as Tiresias, the passive clairvoyant, by disappearing into what he sees. In fact, Lee, the cold if concerned observer, gives way to Dr. Benway, the conscious and impassioned lecturer who shares his patients' weaknesses, as the author's principal mask. Interzone, the superficially bothered resort of individuals on the lam from amalgamation, is over against Freeland, the superficially generous trap for the surrenderers of their individuality, where everything is permitted and nothing ever gets to happen.

The anthropological survey radiates out of Tangier in the Panorama and Market sections of the work. A.J.'s Annual Ball and Hassan's Rumpus Room are expanded routines trembling on the verge of such sheer free fantasy as Voices, which filter to Lee's sickchamber. Islam Inc. provides the political organization and theory that is speeding Interzone toward total calamity first through the presentation of its directorate: A.J. the large extrovert, Hassan the slinky go-between, and Clem and Jody the professionally hateful Americans; and second through a description of the parties of Interzone: the Senders, whose only interest is to exercise power with no thought of its consequences, the Liquefactionists, greedyguts who want to absorb all the richness of all other lives into themselves, the Divisionists, who create ideal responsive friends (see "Queer") by cutting off bits of their own bodies, and the Factualists, who rejoice in the variety of existence. In this world politics derive from the data of acquaintanceship and romance: only the Factualists are living. Finally, there is Word, in which the author, all masks thrown aside, delivers a long tirade, a blend of confession, routine, and fantasy ending in "a vast Moslem muttering."

And now? There are rumors of a work dealing with the night of prehistory. In his last letter to me the author says: "complete satisfaction with everything I have done in writing . . . Unless writing has the danger and immediate urgency of bullfighting it is nowhere to my way of thinking . . . I am tired of sitting behind the lines with an imperfect recording device receiving inaccurate bulletins . . . I must reach the Front."

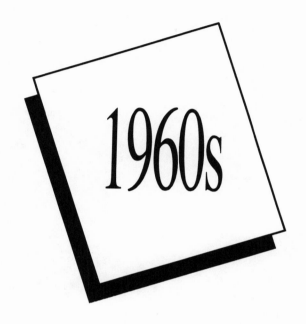

4

# Burroughs'
# *Naked Lunch*

## Mary McCarthy

L ast summer at the International Writers' Conference in Edinburgh, I said I thought the national novel, like the nation-state, was dying and that a new kind of novel, based on statelessness, was beginning to be written. This novel had a high, aerial point of view and a plot of perpetual motion. Two experiences, that of exile and that of jet-propelled mass tourism, provided the subject matter for a new kind of story. There is no novel, yet, that I know of, about mass tourism, but somebody will certainly write it. Of the novel based on statelessness, I gave as examples William Burroughs' *The Naked Lunch*, Vladimir Nabokov's *Pale Fire* and *Lolita*. Burroughs, I explained, is not literally a political exile, but the drug addicts he describes are continually on the move, and life in the United States, with its present narcotics laws, is untenable for the addict if he does not want to spend it in jail (in the same way, the confirmed homosexual is a chronic refugee, ordered to move on by the Venetian police, the Capri police, the mayor of Provincetown, the mayor of Nantucket). Had I read it at the time, I might have added Günter Grass' *The Tin Drum* to the list: here the point of view, instead of being high, is very low— that of a dwarf; the hero and narrator is a displaced person, born in the Free City of Danzig, of a Polish mother (who is not really a Pole but a member of a minority within Poland) and an uncertain father, who may be a German grocer or a Polish postal employee. In any case, I said that in thinking over the novels of the last few years, I was struck by the fact that the only ones that had not simply given me pleasure but interested me had been those of Burroughs and Nabokov. The others, even when well done (Compton-Burnett), seemed almost regional.

Mary McCarthy, "Burroughs' *Naked Lunch*," from *The Writing on the Wall and Other Literary Essays* (New York: Harcourt, Brace & World, Inc., 1970): 42–53. [Originally published in *New York Review of Books* 1.1 (1963): 4–5.] Copyright © 1963 by Mary McCarthy. Reprinted by permission of Harcourt Brace Jovanovich, Inc., and the estate of Mary McCarthy.

This statement, to judge by the British press, was a shot heard round the world. I still pick up its reverberations in Paris and read about them in the American press. I am quoted as saying that *The Naked Lunch* is the most important novel of the age, of the epoch, of the century. The only truthful report of what I said about Burroughs was given by Stephen Spender in *Encounter,* October 1962. But nobody seems to have paid attention to Spender any more than anyone paid attention to what I said on the spot. When I chided Malcolm Muggeridge in person with having terribly misquoted me in the *New Statesman,* he appeared to think that there was not much difference between saying that a book was one of two or three that had interested you in the last few years and saying that it was one of the "outstanding novels of the age." According to me, the age is still Proust, Joyce, Kafka, Lawrence, Faulkner, to mention only the "big names," but to others evidently the age is shrinking to the length of a publishing season, just as a literary speaker is turned into a publisher's tout. The result, of course, is a disparagement of Burroughs, because if *The Naked Lunch* is proclaimed as the masterpiece of the century, then it is easily found wanting. Indeed, I wonder whether the inflation of my remarks was not at bottom malicious; it is not usually those who admire Burroughs who come up to me at parties to announce: "I *read* what you said at Edinburgh." This is true, I think, of all such publicity; it is malicious in effect whatever the intention and permits the reader to dismiss works of art and public figures as "not what they are cracked up to be." A similiar thing happened with *Dr. Zhivago,* a wonderful book, which attracted much hatred and venom because it was not Tolstoy. Very few critics said it was Tolstoyan, but the impression got around that they had. Actually, as I recall, the critics who mentioned Tolstoy in connection with Pasternak were those bent on destroying Pasternak's book.

As for me, I was left in an uncomfortable situation. I did not want to write to the editors of British newspapers and magazines, denying that I had said whatever incontinent thing they had quoted me as saying. This would have been ungracious to Burroughs, who was the innocent party in the affair and who must have felt more and more like the groom in a shotgun literary wedding, seeing my name yoked with his as it were indissolubly. And the monstrousness of the union, doubtless, was what kept the story hot. In the end, it became clear to me that the only way I could put an end to this embarrassment was by writing at length what I thought about *The Naked Lunch*—something I was reluctant to do because I was busy finishing a book of my own and reluctant, also, because the whole thing had assumed the proportions of a *cause célèbre* and I felt like a witness called to the stand and obliged to tell the truth and nothing but the truth under oath. This is not a normal critical position. Of course the critic normally tries to be truthful, but he does not feel that his review is some sort of pay-off or eternal reckoning, that the eye of God or the world press is staring into his heart as he writes. Now that I have written the present review, I am glad, as always happens, to have made a clean breast of it. This is what I think about Burroughs.

"You can cut into *The Naked Lunch* at any intersection point," says Burroughs, suiting the action to the word, in "an atrophied preface" he appends as a tailpiece.

His book, he means, is like a neighborhood movie with continuous showings that you can drop into whenever you please—you don't have to wait for the beginning of the feature picture. Or like a worm that you can chop up into sections each of which wriggles off as an independent worm. Or a nine-lived cat. Or a cancer. He is fond of the word "mosaic," especially in its scientific sense of a plant-mottling caused by a virus, and his Muse (see etymology of "mosaic") is interested in organic processes of multiplication and duplication. The literary notion of time as simultaneous, a montage, is not original with Burroughs; what is original is the scientific bent he gives it and a view of the world that combines biochemistry, anthropology, and politics. It is as though *Finnegans Wake* were cut loose from history and adapted for a Cinerama circus titled "One World." *The Naked Lunch* has no use for history, which is all "ancient history"—sloughed-off skin; from its planetary perspective, there are only geography and customs. Seen in terms of space, history shrivels into a mere wrinkling or furrowing of the surface as in an aerial relief-map or one of those pieced-together aerial photographs known in the trade as (again) mosaics. The oldest memory in *The Naked Lunch* is of jacking-off in boyhood latrines, a memory recaptured through pederasty. This must be the first space novel, the first serious piece of science fiction—the others are entertainment.

The action of *The Naked Lunch* takes place in the consciousness of One Man, William Lee, who is taking a drug cure. The principal characters, besides Lee, are his friend, Bill Gains (who seems momentarily to turn into a woman called Jane); various members of the Narcotic Squad, especially one Bradley the Buyer; Dr. Benway, a charlatan medico who is treating Lee; two vaudevillians, Clem and Jody; A.J., a carnival con man, the last of the Big Spenders; a sailor; an Arab called Ahmed; an archetypal Southern druggist, Doc Parker ("a man don't have no secrets from God and his druggist"); and various boys with whining voices. Among the minor characters are a number of automobiles, each with its specific complaint, like the oil-burning Ford V–8; a film executive; the Party Leader; the Vigilante; John and Mary, the sex acrobats; and a puzzled American housewife who is heard complaining because the Mixmaster keeps trying to climb up under her dress. The scene shifts about, from New York to Chicago to St. Louis to New Orleans to Mexico to Malmö, Tangier, Venice, and the human identities shift about too, for all these modern places and modern individuals (if that is the right word) have interchangeable parts. Burroughs is fond too of the word "ectoplasm," and the beings that surround Lee, particularly the inimical ones, seem ectoplasmic phantoms projected on the wide screen of his consciousness from a mass séance. But the haunting is less visual than auditory. These "characters," in the colloquial sense, are ventriloquial voices produced, as it were, against the will of the ventriloquist, who has become their dummy. Passages of dialogue and description keep recurring in different contexts with slight variations, as though they possessed ubiquity.

The best comparison for the book, with its aerial sex acts performed on a high trapeze, its con men and barkers, its arenalike form, is in fact with a circus. A circus travels but it is always the same, and this is Burroughs' sardonic image of modern life. The Barnum of the show is the mass-manipulator, who appears in a series of disguises. *Control,* as Burroughs says, underlining it, *can never be a means to anything but more control—like drugs,* and the vicious circle of addiction is reenacted, worldwide, with sideshows in the political and "social" sphere—the "social" here has vanished, except in quotation marks, like the historical, for everything has become automatized. Everyone is an addict of one kind or another, as people indeed are wont to say of themselves, complacently: "I'm a crossword puzzle addict, a hi-fi addict," etc. The South is addicted to lynching and nigger-hating, and the Southern folk-custom of burning a Negro recurs throughout the book as a sort of Fourth-of-July carnival with fireworks. Circuses, with their cages of wild animals, are also dangerous, like Burroughs' human circus; an accident may occur, as when the electronic brain in Dr. Benway's laboratory goes on the rampage, and the freaks escape to mingle with the controlled citizens of Freeland in a general riot, or in the scene where the hogs are let loose in the gourmet restaurant.

On a level usually thought to be "harmless," addiction to platitudes and commonplaces is global. To Burroughs' ear, the Bore, lurking in the hotel lobby, is literally deadly (" 'You look to me like a man of intelligence.' Always ominous opening words, my boy!"). The same for Doc Parker with his captive customer in the back room of his pharmacy (". . . so long as you got a legitimate condition and an RX from a certified bona feedy M.D., I'm honored to serve you"), the professor in the classroom ("Hehe hehe he"), the attorney in court ("Hehe hehe he," likewise). The complacent sound of snickering laughter is an alarm signal, like the suave bell-tones of the psychiatrist and the emphatic drone of the Party Leader ("You see men and women. *Ordinary* men and women going about their ordinary everyday tasks. Leading their ordinary lives. That's what we need. . . .").

Cut to ordinary men and women, going about their ordinary everyday tasks. The whine of the put-upon boy hustler: "All kinda awful sex acts." "Why cancha just get physical like a human?" "So I guess he come to some kinda awful climax." "You think I am innarested to hear about your horrible old condition? I am not innarested at all." "But he comes to a climax and turns into some kinda awful crab." This aggrieved tone merges with the malingering sighs of the American housewife, opening a box of Lux: "I got the most awful cold, and my intestines is all constipated." And the clarion of the Salesman: "When the Priority numbers are called up yonder I'll be there." These average folks are addicts of the science page of the Sunday supplements; they like to talk about their diseases and about vile practices that paralyze the practitioner from the waist down or about a worm that gets into your kidney and grows to enormous size or about the "horrible" result of marijuana addiction—it makes you turn black and your legs drop off. The superstitious scientific vocabulary is diffused from the laboratory and the mental hospital into the general population. Overheard at a lynching: "Don't crowd too close, boys. His intestines is subject to explode in the fire." The same diffusion of culture takes place with modern physics. A lieutenant to his general: "But chief, can't we get them started and they imitate each other like a chained reaction?"

The phenomenon of repetition, of course, gives rise to boredom; many readers complain that they cannot get through *The Naked Lunch.* And/or that they find it disgusting. It *is* disgusting and sometimes tiresome, often in the same places. The prominence of the anus, of feces, and of all sorts of "horrible" discharges, as the characters would say, from the body's orifices, becomes too much of a bad thing, like the sado-masochistic sex performances—the auto-ejaculation of a hanged man is not everybody's cantharides. A reader whose erogenous zones are more temperate than the author's begins to feel either that he is a square (a guilty sentiment he should not yield to) or that he is the captive of a joyless addict.

In defense, Swift could be cited, and indeed between Burroughs and Swift there are many points of comparison; not only the obsession with excrement and the horror of female genitalia but a disgust with politics and the whole body politic. Like Swift, Burroughs has irritable nerves and something of the crafty temperament of the inventor. There is a great deal of Laputa in the countries Burroughs calls Interzone and Freeland, and Swift's solution for the Irish problem would appeal to the American's dry logic. As Gulliver, Swift posed as an anthropologist (though the study was not known by that name then) among savage people; Burroughs parodies the anthropologist in his descriptions of the American heartland: "the Interior: a vast subdivision, antennae of television to the meaningless sky. [. . .] Illinois and Missouri, miasma of mound-building peoples, groveling worship of the Food Source, cruel and ugly festivals." The style here is more emotive than Swift's, but in his deadpan explanatory notes ("This is a rural English custom designed to eliminate aged and bedfast dependents"), there is a Swiftian laconic factuality. The "factual" appearance of the whole narrative, with its battery of notes and citations, some straight, some loaded, its extracts from a diary, like a ship's log, its pharmacopoeia, has the flavor of eighteenth-century satire. He calls himself a "Factualist" and belongs, all alone, to an Age of Reason, which he locates in the future. In him, as in Swift, there is a kind of soured utopianism.

Yet what saves *The Naked Lunch* is not a literary ancestor but humor. Burroughs' humor is peculiarly American, at once broad and sly. It is the humor of a comedian, a vaudeville performer playing in "One," in front of the asbestos curtain of some Keith Circuit or Pantages house long since converted to movies. The same jokes reappear, slightly refurbished, to suit the circumstances, the way a vaudeville artist used to change Yonkers to Renton when he was playing Seattle. For example, the Saniflush joke, which is always good for a laugh: somebody is cutting the cocaine/ the morphine/the penicillin with Saniflush. Some of the jokes are verbal ("Stop me if you've heard this atomic secret" or Dr. Benway's "A simopath [. . .] is a citizen convinced he is an ape or other simian. It is a disorder peculiar to the army and discharge cures it"). Some are "black" parody (Dr. Benway, in his last appearance, dreamily, his voice fading out: "Cancer, my first love"). Some are whole vaudeville "numbers," as when the hoofers, Clem and Jody, are hired by the Russians to give Americans a bad name abroad: they appear in Liberia wearing black Stetsons and red galluses and talking loudly about burning niggers back home. A skit like this may rise to a frenzy, as if in a Marx Brothers or a Clayton, Jackson, and Durante act, when all the actors pitch in. *E.g.*, the very funny scene in Chez Robert, "where a huge icy gourmet broods over the greatest cuisine in the world": A.J. appears, the last of the Big Spenders, and orders a bottle of ketchup; immediate pandemonium; A.J. gives his hog-call, and the shocked gourmet diners are all devoured by famished hogs. The effect of pandemonium, all hell breaking loose, is one of Burroughs' favorites and an equivalent of the old vaudeville finale, with the acrobats, the jugglers, the magician, the hoofers, the lady-who-was-sawed-in-two, the piano-player, the comedians, all pushing into the act.

Another favorite effect, with Burroughs, is the metamorphosis. A citizen is turned into animal form, a crab or a huge centipede, or into some unspeakable monstrosity, like Bradley the Narcotics Agent who turns into an unidentifiable carnivore. These metamorphoses, of course, are punishments. The Hellzapoppin effect of orgies and riots and the metamorphosis effect, rapid or creeping, are really cancerous onslaughts—matter on the rampage multiplying itself and "building" as a revue scene "builds" to a climax. Growth and deterioration are the same thing: a human being "deteriorates" or grows into a one-man jungle. What you think of it depends on your point of view; from the junky's angle, Bradley is better as a carnivore eating the Narcotics Commissioner than he was as "fuzz"—junky slang for the police.

*The Naked Lunch* contains messages that unluckily for the ordinary reader are somewhat arcane. Despite his irony, Burroughs is a prescriptive writer. He means what he says to be taken and used literally, like an Rx prescription. Unsentimental and factual, he writes as though his thoughts had the quality of self-evidence. In a special sense, *The Naked Lunch* is coterie literature. It was not intended, surely, for the general public, but for addicts and former addicts, with the object of imparting information. Like a classical satirist, Burroughs is dead serious—a reformer. Yet, as often happened with the classical satirists, a wild hilarity and savage pessimism carry him beyond his therapeutic purpose and defeat it. The book is alive, like a basketful of crabs, and common sense cannot get hold of it to extract a moral.

On the one hand, control is evil; on the other, escape from control is mass slaughter or reduction to a state of proliferating cellular matter. The police are the enemy, but as Burroughs shrewdly observes in one passage: "A *functioning* police state needs no police." The policeman is internalized in the robotized citizen. From a libertarian point of view, nothing could be worse. This would seem to be Burroughs' position, but it is not consistent with his picture of sex. To be a libertarian in politics implies a faith in Nature and the natural, that is, in the life-principle itself, commonly identified with sex. But there is little affection for the life-principle in *The Naked Lunch,* and sex, while magnified—a common trait of homosexual literature—is a kind of mechanical man-trap baited with fresh meat. The sexual climax, the jet of sperm, accompanied by a whistling scream, is often a death spasm, and the "perfect" orgasm would seem to be the posthumous orgasm of the hanged man, shooting his jism into pure space.

It is true that Nature and sex are two-faced, and that growth is death-oriented. But if Nature is not seen as far more good than evil, then a need for control is posited. And, strangely, this seems to be Burroughs' position too. *The human virus can now be treated,* he says with emphasis, meaning the species itself. By scientific methods, he implies. Yet the laboratory of *The Naked Lunch* is a musical-comedy inferno, and Dr. Benway's assistant is a female chimpanzee. As Burroughs knows, the Men in White, when not simple con men, are the fuzz in another uniform.

The Naked Lunch, Burroughs says, is "a blueprint, a How-To Book. [. . .] How-To extend levels of experience by opening the door at the end of a long hall." Thus the act of writing resembles and substitutes for drug-taking, which in Burroughs' case must have begun as an experiment in the extension of consciousness. It does not sound as if pleasure had ever been his motive. He was testing the controls of his own mechanism to adjust the feed-in of data, noting with care the effects obtained from heroin, morphine, opium, Demerol, Yage, cannabis, and so on. These experiments, aiming at freedom, "opening a door," resulted in addiction. He kicked the imprisoning habit by what used to be known as will power, supplemented by a non-addictive drug, apomorphine, to whose efficacy he now writes testimonials. It seems clear that what was involved and continues to be involved for Burroughs is a Faustian compact: knowledge-as-power, total control of the self, which is experienced as sovereign in respect to the immediate environment and neutral in respect to others.

At present he is interested in scientology, which offers its initiates the promise of becoming "clears"—free from all hang-ups. For the novel he has invented his cut-out and fold-in techniques, which he is convinced can rationalize the manufacture of fictions by applying modern factory methods to the old "writer's craft." A text may be put together by two or three interested and moderately skilled persons equipped with scissors and the raw material of a typescript. Independence from the vile body and its "algebra of need," freedom of movement across national and psychic frontiers, efficiency of work and production, by means of short cuts, suppression of connectives, and other labor-saving devices, would be Uncle Bill Burroughs' patent for successful living. But if such a universal passkey can really be devised, what is its purpose? It cannot be enjoyment of the world, for this would only begin the addictive process all over again by creating dependency. Action, the reverse of enjoyment, has no appeal either for the author of The Naked Lunch. What Burroughs wants is out, which explains the dry, crankish amusement given him by space, interplanetary distances, where, however, he finds the old mob still at work. In fact, his reasoning, like the form of his novel, is circular. Liberation leads to new forms of subjugation. If the human virus can be treated, this can only be under conditions of asepsis: the Nova police. Yet Burroughs is unwilling, politically, to play the dread game of eugenics or euthenics, outside his private fantasy, which, since his intelligence is aware of the circularity of its utopian reasoning, invariably turns sardonic. Quis custodet custodes ipsos?

March, 1963

# 5

# UGH . . .

## John Willett

[Review of *The Naked Lunch*, *The Soft Machine*, *The Ticket That Exploded*, and *Dead Fingers Talk*]

N ow I, William Seward, will unlock my word horde," warns Mr. Burroughs towards the end of *The Naked Lunch*. Struggling upstream through it is not unlike wading through the drains of a big city. The first shock effects are strong as the rash reader plunges in, then a steady nausea follows which hangs around him long after he has fought his way into the fresh air, finally boredom with the endless monotony as he tries to pick up his stinking feet and skip. Look out: here it comes!

> From the open bronze mold emerged a transparent green shape criss-crossed with pulsing red veins, liquid screen eyes swept by color flashes—a smell of sewage and decay breathing from years of torture films, orgasm death in his black eyes glinting with the slow fish lust of the swamp mud—Long tendril hands penetrated Bradly's broken body caressing the other being inside through the soft intestines into the pearly genitals rubbing centers of orgasm along his spine up to the neck—Exquisite toothache pain shot through his nerves and his body split down the middle—Sex words exploded to a poisonous color vapor that cut off his breath—

On and on it flows, lapping slowly round what soon becomes a stereo-typed debris: ectoplasm, jelly, errand boys, ferris wheels, used contraceptives, centipedes, old photographs, jockstraps, turnstiles, newts, and pubic hairs.

Such is the texture of the grey porridge in which Mr. Burroughs specializes. Three brimming books which he has filled with it for the Olympia Press have already attracted some speculative attention among those who have not read them, partly because of their excellent (though irrelevant) titles, partly because of the respectful admiration of one or two half-stupefied critics, but above all by their blacklisting by

---

John Willett, "UGH . . . ," *Times Literary Supplement* 3220 (14 Nov. 1963): 919. Reprinted by permission of the author.

the British Customs and the U.S. Mails. Now the author himself has fished out an assortment of lumps from all three, stirring the mixture and topping it up to make a fourth, slightly more hygienic bucketful which can be cast before us swine.

Glug glug. It tastes disgusting, even without the detailed but always callous homosexual scenes and the unspeakable homosexual fantasies—pure verbal mastur-bation— that figure so largely in the Olympia Press volumes. Yet there are perfectly intelligent supporters of these books who see them as a deliberate indictment of the society we live in: as a satire on the American Way of Life, a great comic saga of the world below the navel, or a nightmare account of the drug addictions through which the author has passed. How far this can be held to make such a diet agreeable or nutritious is another matter, but it is quite true that Mr. Burroughs' writing gives some insight into the world of drugs, both by islets of straight description (as in the opening of *The Naked Lunch,* which is also the opening of *Dead Fingers Talk*) and by suggesting how the imagination and perceptions are affected. It frequently moves into a kind of farcical high gear, the charadelike style that a number of writers have borrowed from Joyce's Nighttown; while *The Ticket That Exploded* is written partly (though by no means predominantly) as a parody of science fiction. On the strength of such qualities it can be argued, as the *Saturday Review* once put it, that "the obscenities—if obscenities they are—are inseparable from the total fabric and effect of the moral message."

But is there a moral message? And how about if the moral message is itself disgusting? The texture of the passages of farce or satire is in fact very much the same as that of the porridge, even if it is now being chucked around for comic effect; most of them moreover are directed not against the junk world but against the doctors, policemen, psychiatrists, and officials with whom the addict and the homo-sexual have to deal. They are seldom set in the United States, taking place rather in Mexico, Tangier, the Latin American republics, or other areas more closely associ-ated with the expatriate than with the American way of life. Nor do the most shocking episodes seem to be put forward in a particularly satirical spirit: like this relatively printable one from *The Naked Lunch,* for instance:

> Met Marv in front of the Sagasso with two Arab kids and he said:
> "Want to watch these two kids screw each other?"
> "Of course. How much?"
> "I think they will perform for fifty cents. Hungry, you know."
> "That's the way I like to see them." Made me feel like a dirty old
> man but "Son cosas de la vida."

a comment meaning "life's like that." Or take the attitude to the young or relapsed addict, as seen in *The Soft Machine:*

> I handed him two nickels under the table. Pushing in a small way to
> keep up The Habit: INVADE. DAMAGE. OCCUPY. Young faces in
> blue alcohol flame.

At the very least, such things are too uncritically presented, and because the author gives no flicker of disapproval the reader easily takes the "moral message" to lie the other way.

In *Dead Fingers Talk* two of the author's farcical quacks are themselves arguing about the question of disgust:

> SCHAFER: "I tell you I can't escape a feeling—well, of *evil* about this."
> BENWAY: "Balderdash, my boy—We're scientists—Pure scientists. Disinterested research and damned be him who cries 'Hold, *too much!*' [. . .]"
> SCHAFER: "Yes, yes, of course—and yet—I can't get that stench out of my lungs."

There are Benways in the literary laboratory who feel that Mr. Burroughs' characteristic stench is justified by the solemn new "fold-in" technique by which he claims to compose his books. "You can cut into *Naked Lunch* at any intersection point," he says, and again in the same work:

> The word cannot be expressed direct. . . . It can perhaps be indicated by mosaic of juxtaposition like articles abandoned in a hotel drawer, defined by negatives and absence. . . .

What this amounts to is montage, piecing a book together from disjointed chunks that can be satire or parody or else like the unplanned dribbling and splashing of the action painter. Far from having any "total fabric" in mind, the author can reshuffle the pieces and make a "new" book, or the individual chunk can be broken down into phrases and sorted and scattered so that the words come tumbling out in a new order and the already familiar sentences slide out of focus.

This is not a bad way of conveying the mental mists of what Mr. Burroughs terms "the pick-up frontier, a languid grey area of hiatus miasmic with yawns and gaping goof holes" (a zone he clearly knows well), while the repetitiveness to which it leads is only too natural to an author whose best phrases anyway tend to recur (the subway sweeping by "with a black blast of iron," for instance), and whose images and adjectives—like "obsidian"—are often overworked. But it is not always clear whether it is the writing or the writer that is being jumbled, while the air of pretentiousness which surrounds the whole business (aggravated by the author's readings on tape and a ridiculous short film) by no means excuses monotony and impoverishment of style. A yawn is a yawn is a yawn, the reader soon comes to feel. The technique is of a piece with the material all right, but only in the sense that without the shocks and the stench there would be nothing much left.

"Montons la pompe à merde," says the old French army song. Well, now it has been mounted here, to produce lunch for the British. Sample menu:

*The Clear Camel Piss Soup with boiled Earth Worms*

---

*The Filet of Sun-Ripened Sting Ray basted with Eau de
Cologne and garnished with nettles*

---

*The After-Birth Suprême de Boeuf, cooked in drained
crankcase oil, served with a piquant sauce of rotten egg
yolks and crushed bed bugs*

---

*The Limburger Cheese sugar cured in diabetic urine
doused in Canned Heat Flamboyant. . . .*

—as one of the supposedly comic chunks in the new house-trained version has it. A delicious prospect, especially considering the second helpings that another sieving-through of the material might produce. If the publishers had deliberately set out to discredit the cause of literary freedom and innovation they could hardly have done it more effectively. Let us hope that they are left to appreciate the probable impact on their own reputation, and indirectly on that of the other authors on their list, without any interfering body turning them into martyrs. Any juryman can vomit, but only one verdict can clear up the mess: that of the book world itself.

# 6

# Responses to "UGH . . ."

John Calder, Michael Moorcock, Edith Sitwell,
Victor Gollancz, Eric Mottram, and
William S. Burroughs

[Letters to the Editor]

November 21, 1963

S ir, Publishers are not normally in the habit of answering unfavorable reviews of their books, but the long notice devoted to William Burroughs in your issue of November 14 should not really be allowed to pass without comment from us, as it contains a number of extremely dangerous assumptions, not least in the final paragraph when it is apparently seriously suggested that the publication of *Dead Fingers Talk* could discredit the cause of literary freedom and innovation in this country and that it could affect the reputations of other authors on our list. There is admittedly a large measure of involvement between the directors of my company and the type of literature that we publish, but to suggest that the established reputations of Beckett, Robbe-Grillet, and Ionesco, or the currently less established ones of Higgins, Pinget, and Nathalie Sarraute are likely to suffer from appearing in the same catalogue as William Burroughs is nonsense.

John Calder, letter to the editor in *Times Literary Supplement* 3221 (21 Nov. 1963): 947. Reprinted by permission of the author.

Michael Moorcock, letter to the editor in *Times Literary Supplement* 3221 (21 Nov. 1963): 947. Copyright © 1963 by Michael Moorcock. Reprinted by permission of Don Congdon Associates, Inc.

Edith Sitwell, letter to the editor in *Times Literary Supplement* 3222 (28 Nov. 1963): 993. Reprinted by permission of Francis Sitwell.

Victor Gollancz, letter to the editor in *Times Literary Supplement* 3222 (28 Nov. 1963): 993. Reprinted courtesy of Livia Gollancz at Victor Gollancz Ltd.

Eric Mottram, letter to the editor in *Times Literary Supplement* 3222 (28 Nov. 1963): 993. Reprinted by permission of the author.

William S. Burroughs, letter to the editor in *Times Literary Supplement* 3230 (23 Jan. 1964): 73. Reprinted by permission of the author.

Burroughs admittedly deals in unpleasant subject matter; so do Rabelais, Swift, Baudelaire, Dostoevsky, Eliot, and Beckett, to mention only a few authors whom I know have influenced Burroughs' work. There is as much stench of the charnel house and the sewer in Swift as in Burroughs, and I am surprised that your reviewer does not point out the many similarities between these two figures, already pointed out by several other of the "half-stupefied" critics that your reviewer mentions. What other author, except perhaps Beckett, has taken up the challenge to investigate those corners of the mind which have given rise to Auschwitz and to the lesser manifestations of the underground stream that flows towards it: American horror comics, the torture chambers and third-degree rooms of practically every modern country, and the terrible fear and malaise underlying the thin surface skin of society, that (American drugstore counter, fourteen-year-old TV mentality, Hollywood glamour, East-side tough) romanticism which conceals 1984 creeping up on us?

Burroughs is so many-sided that it is possible to defend or attack him from almost every conceivable point of view. Basically, he is a humanist, terrified by his vision of contemporary society and by the nuclear end that he sees as the only possible synthesis of it. Like the other writers that I have cited above, he has a personal preoccupation with the seamy which does not in any way invalidate his humanism. That he has the honesty to put down on paper all that pours through his mind and thereby makes us realize a certain universality in the decadent side of us, is something for which we should be grateful. But the tremendous flow of words, the juxtaposition of images, often on a very high poetic level, the natural gift of phrase, the brilliant, quite uncannily accurate ear for dialogue, making use of exhaustive reading in both literary and scientific spheres, prove quite conclusively that Burroughs is a natural and major writer. I don't personally have very much sympathy with the fold-in technique, which in my personal opinion has so far failed more often than it has succeeded, but Burroughs is a scientist in literature and must be allowed to experiment freely even if his experiments eventually lead nowhere. He considers himself to be doing research along lines originally devised by T. S. Eliot. Only his later work contains much use of fold-in technique, and although there is some of it in *Dead Fingers Talk* which many readers will find boring, they will still find many extraordinary poetic images in these passages and it certainly does not invalidate the drug scenes and the scenes where he creates Freeland, Interzone, Annexia and the other locales that we recognize as our own societies whether we live in the United States, in Russia, or in Britain. Not the least of Burroughs' accomplishments is to make us realize that the same malaise underlies all existing societies, the communist and the capitalist, the democratic, the paternalist, and the despotic. In the same way Burroughs' cast of characters are an analysis of certain tendencies that he recognizes in himself and that are in all of us. Personally, I do not think that Dr. Benway is intended to be a fraud. He is only a slight distortion of the American surgeon, of the atomic scientist, and, in an even slighter degree still, of the German doctors who carried out their researches on concentration camp victims and who are now applying the techniques that they learned on human guinea pigs to the problems of daily medicine, cancer research et al. Just as it is impossible to sit through a performance of *The Representative* at the Aldwych Theatre without a growing sense of guilt and self-disgust, so is it impossible to read any Burroughs without similar feelings. The more we are aware of the antisocial tendencies in us, the more likely we are to do something about them, and I would that I were not Mr. Burroughs' publisher so that I could recommend him more disinterestedly.

It is one thing to criticize an author for his admitted weaknesses, for techniques which often do not come off and for the success or lack of it by which he handles his subject matter, but it is quite another to suggest that the writing or publication of *Dead Fingers Talk* is irresponsible, immoral, or liable to restrict the freedom of other writers to write or publishers to publish, as your reviewer does suggest. I had hoped that we were living in a society which is today adult enough, responsible enough, and intelligent enough to recognize a moralist when it sees one.

John Calder

* * *

Sir, There is a tendency these days to decry the kind of subjective criticism which allowed Ruskin to accuse Whistler of throwing pots of paint at people. Enlightened twentieth-century criticism, so I gather, is supposed to be objective, giving a critic's intellectual appraisal of a book rather than a list of his emotional reactions to it.

Your piece on William Burroughs in the issue dated November 14 is both pompously subjective and thoroughly distasteful. It is also inaccurate.

I had hoped to find a more thoughtful review of Burroughs' books in the *Times Literary Supplement,* something to balance the poorly considered reviews which appeared in the Sunday newspapers, but now I despair. The character of your review was summed up in its title.

Your critic mentions the so-called parody on science fiction in *The Ticket That Exploded.* In your special issue on Science and Art a few weeks ago you featured an article by Mr. Edmund Crispin on science fiction. In this, Mr. Crispin said that SF had little to do with science and more to do with social criticism. This was untrue of the best science fiction (such as J. G. Ballard's *Drowned World*) and is also untrue of Mr. Burroughs' science fiction, for Burroughs is, in his own way, one of the first real writers of SF to emerge to date. These days, it seems to me, critics are capable of reading social criticism into quantum mechanics by stretching a point here and there. I suppose a moral message can be read into Burroughs' work, but this is not its prime concern.

Just as modern physics approaches the metaphysical with each new advancement, so is Burroughs concerned with space and time, its nature, its philosophical implications, the place of the individual in the total universe—the paradox of the individual occupying the universe and the universe occupying the individual. For instance, in *The Naked Lunch:*

"So what you want off me?"
"Time."

> "I don't dig."
> "I have something you want," his hand touched the package. He
> drifted away into the front room, his voice remote and blurred. "You
> have something I want . . . five minutes here . . . an hour someplace
> else . . . two . . . four . . . eight . . . Maybe I'm getting ahead of
> myself. . . . Every day die a little. . . . It takes up The Time. . . . "
> [. . .] "Mister, I don't know what you're talking about."
> "You will, baby . . . in time."

The books are, themselves, something of a scientific as well as a literary experiment. Your reviewer has not noticed how Burroughs conditions the reader to receive
certain impressions from key words which recur throughout the books. He has not
noticed the explicit footnotes actually explaining what Burroughs hopes to do. He
has not noticed very much at all because, it seems likely, he has not read the books
very thoroughly. The "menu" quoted out of context "as one of the supposedly
comic chunks in the new house-trained version" is not revised for *Dead Fingers
Talk* but appears exactly as quoted in *The Naked Lunch*. Preceding this menu
we read:

> Robert's brother Paul emerges from retirement in a local nut house
> and takes over the restaurant to dispense something he calls the
> "Transcendental Cuisine." . . . Imperceptibly the quality of the food
> declines until he is serving literal garbage, the clients being too
> intimidated by the reputation of *Chez Robert* to protest. Sample Menu:

Read objectively nothing in Mr. Burroughs' work should appear "unspeakable"
or "taste disgusting." Your critic seizes passages he doesn't understand and expounds
upon them. For instance the conversation between Schafer and Benway is not to do
with the dog's having been sick on the carpet, but about their feelings in running an
Auschwitz-like "research department." The piece is ironic. The irony which runs
through all the books appears to have escaped your critic's hasty eye.

Luckily, through even the most subjective reviews, Burroughs' large talent
gleams through. Your critic may be young enough to change his mind later. He may
not know just yet what Burroughs' message is, but he will "baby . . . in time."

Michael Moorcock

* * *

Our reviewer writes: To "put down on paper all that pours through his mind," as
Mr. Calder graphically puts it, a writer must have a mind worth respecting. I see no
reason to suppose that Mr. Burroughs has; not only are his books unorganized and
repetitious but they seem quite irrelevant to the ordinary human world except as an
unreasoned gesture against it. The familiar bogy-talk of Auschwitz, torture, bombs,
1984, nameless antisocial tendencies, and vague social malaise is unsupported by
the books; just because his works are nasty there is no reason to assume that they
connect with the much larger and nastier things which really do form part of modern

society—or with those much larger writers, for that matter, who have proved capable of writing effectively about unpopular subjects. The case against William Burroughs is that he is a second-rate writer who would have attracted little critical attention if it were not for his shock effects and his forced inaccessibility. To publish such a man anyway implies a certain confusion of judgment, but when it presents the opponents of literary freedom with a sitting target—a startlingly obscene writer of questionable merit—it can hardly be thought to help the causes for which Mr. Calder might wish to stand.

There is nothing in the idea of freedom—or of objectivity either—to suggest that publishers and critics have no longer got a duty to discriminate. The snag about Mr. Moorcock's attitude is that, "read objectively," nothing tastes at all.

## November 28, 1963

Sir, I was delighted to see, in your issue of the 14th instant, the very right-minded review of a novel by a Mr. Burroughs (whoever he may be) published by a Mr. John Calder (whoever he may be).

The public canonization of that insignificant, dirty little book *Lady Chatterley's Lover* was a signal to persons who wish to unload the filth in their minds on the British public.

As the author of *Gold Coast Customs* I can scarcely be accused of shirking reality, but I do not wish to spend the rest of my life with my nose nailed to other people's lavatories.

I prefer Chanel Number 5.

Edith Sitwell, C.L.

* * *

Sir, Allow me to thank you cordially for "UGH . . . ." The question is not one of pornography, the better sort of which, in a poor secondhand sort of way, is to some degree life-enhancing: like the aroma that might faintly come through to a tramp at the half-open door of an expensive restaurant. I am told, for instance, that *Fanny Hill* can give a mild kind of pleasure to anyone except a puritan.

But the bogus-highbrow filth you attack—and its publication has proliferated horribly—is life-denying; spiritually as well as physically disgusting, and tasteless to an almost incredible degree, it offends against value of any kind (including intellectual value) every bit as much as against public decency. And you are right in suggesting that the current orgy may imperil the freedom of literature by provoking the kind of "authority" that prosecuted *Lady Chatterley's Lover*. This would be a disaster: better an infinity of open drains than a pinpoint of censorship.

Victor Gollancz

* * *

Sir, Since *The Naked Lunch* was published in 1959 and is part of a series of three novels, with a fourth to come, as well as part of a large group of published works since 1953, ranging from an early novel to volumes of experimental pieces, two groups of letters from South America, and numerous articles and fictional episodes, it is a pity that your reviewer saw fit to treat the appearance of *Dead Fingers Talk* as the signal for an unscholarly mockery of William Burroughs, who is a serious writer and recognized as such in a number of critical articles which have appeared both here and in the United States. The new volume is a collation of sections from two of Burroughs' novels, and so at least we ought to have been informed about its construction and its relation to these earlier works. Instead your reviewer offers his own horror at part of Burroughs' chosen materials, those dealing with homoerotic and narcotic experiences. That we have here at least an interesting, perhaps important, satirist, that the plot of all Burroughs' work is exploratory and ironical, that there is no question of him advocating these areas of experience, is not discussed. Admittedly, the reiterations of private obsession become dull in parts of *The Ticket That Exploded,* but your reviewer only exposes a single naïve response, his personal one of disgust. He knows that others have seen the satire in these books but he does not bother to examine that claim thoroughly. He simply jokes it to one side and takes his cue from the *Saturday Review* on obscenity. That there might be a reason for using obscenity as a technique for satire he fails to notice, and it is not all that unusual. The criticism of Dorn, Creeley, Mary McCarthy, and Alan Ansen means nothing to him. He quotes an exchange between what he calls two "farcical quacks," when in fact the passage, as it occurs in *The Naked Lunch,* is part of an extended attack on irresponsible power, those traditional targets of satire the professions and the state controllers. Burroughs carefully shows homosexual and narcotic relationships as metaphors of power relationships. His collage and cutting methods are deliberately built into a program of revolt against authority. His fascination with Mayan ceremonies is part of a satire of religion which includes a strange composite figure called Mr. Bradly Mr. Martin, the Tiresias of this waste land. But your reviewer uses his space to detail a minimal response and quotes only passages of what he loves to hate. This is not criticism: it is—to use his uncritical term for Burroughs—a mess.

E. N. W. Mottram

* * *

Our reviewer writes: Yes, Mr. Burroughs takes himself seriously, and is encouraged in this by a small number of admirers. This does not make him a serious writer, though. Mr. Mottram and others read into his work all sorts of merits which to me are just not there; one reason no doubt is the challenge of a banned author, another the wish to make sense of his confusions, a third possibly that misapplication of the "scholarly" approach with which readers of this journal are becoming all too familiar. They object to my review because I cannot follow them; because I see no reason for anything more than a "minimal response." They do not seem to find the picture wrong so far as it goes.

## January 23, 1964

Sir, It seems to me that any author has a right to expect of his critics an honest attempt to understand and evaluate what he is saying and that this attempt was not made in the review entitled "UGH . . . ." Dismissing the "moral" implications of my work he says, "And suppose the moral message is itself disgusting?" He then cites as an example the relation of the pusher to young addicts: "INVADE. DAMAGE. OCCUPY. Young faces in blue alcohol flame," *Dead Fingers Talk,* and goes on to say, "The author presents these episodes without a flicker of disapproval." Precisely how is a writer expected to "flicker" disapproval? He must announce to the audience whenever a dubious character appears on stage "You understand I don't approve of this man. Just part of the show you know"? This is absurd. My actual views on the junk industry and the infection of young people with the illness of addiction are well known to any one who reads what I have written on this subject. After many years of addiction to morphine I was cured by the apomorphine treatment developed by a London doctor. Since that time I have written a number of articles urging the use of this treatment since in my experience it is the only treatment that works. Two of these articles have been published in the American edition of *Naked Lunch.*

The moral message of *Dead Fingers Talk* should be quite clear to any reader. Quote Inspector J. Lee of the Nova Police: "In all my experience as a police officer I have never seen such total fear and degradation on any planet," or "This is war to extermination. Fight cell by cell through bodies and mind screens of the earth." Speaking of "The Board," a cartel that plans to take over and monopolize space, I say: "Liars cowards collaborator traitors Liars who want time for more lies. Cowards who cannot face your 'human animals' with the truth. Traitors to all souls everywhere." Is this a disgusting message or does it just disgust the reviewer who will perhaps ask whether all this is to be taken seriously and I say it is to be taken as seriously as anything else in my work. It is the critic's job to evaluate what a writer is actually saying not to distort and falsify the writer's obvious intention. This job of evaluation was not done by your reviewer whoever he may be.

William Burroughs

# 7

# The Subtracting Machine
## *The Work of William Burroughs*

Ihab Hassan

To speak is to lie
—William Burroughs

S ome works stand in judgment on the world though the world rules their judgment invalid. Their authors cannot be punished for they have put themselves beyond any punishment the world can dispense. William Burroughs is one of these authors. "I offer you nothing. I am not a politician," Burroughs says.[1] He offers this: the black and bodiless specter of human betrayal, the dreadful algebra of absolute need. He offers a deposition against the human race, a testimony of outrage in the metallic voice of a subtracting machine.

It is not surprising that his testimony is subject to extravagant praise and hysterical denunciation. In the view of some, Burroughs is the underground king of the Beat Movement for which sweet Jack Kerouac is merely the publicist; in that view, *Naked Lunch* (1959) is the secret masterpiece through which the movement is vindicated. There is, of course, some truth in this. Yet the "masterpiece," thanks to the dauntless publishers of the Grove Press, is now public, and the shadowy status of its author is compromised by the encomium he received, at a recent Edinburgh Festival, from Norman Mailer *and* Mary McCarthy! Others, however, remain unimpressed. In a classic snort of common sense, John Wain has said, "From a literary point of view," the novel "is the merest trash, not worth a second glance."[2] Mr. Wain then proceeded, through seven columns of small print, to glance at the novel, comparing it with the work of Miller, Céline, and Sade, in order to prove a very different point, that Burroughs is a partisan of death.

Controversy may profit the sales of Burroughs' works; it will surely dull their terror. We begin to understand that terror when we refuse to accept it exclusively as a literary phenomenon. From Rimbaud to Beckett, a dangerous strain in modern literature has evaded Mr. Wain's "literary point of view." Vision in that strain seems incommensurate with language; experience seems incommensurate with sanity. If

---

Ihab Hassan, "The Subtracting Machine: The Work of William Burroughs," *Critique* 6 (1963): 4–23. Copyright © 1963 by Ihab Hassan. Reprinted by permission.

that peculiar literature retains any form, it is the form of outrage. In the end, outrage is an existential category, a testimony of the self concerning the world in shuddering images. True outrage is autobiography become a universal stutter.

The life of William Burroughs is itself an affront. Born in 1914 in St. Louis to affluent parents—related, presumably, to the Burroughs of the computing machines—he was from the beginning a solitary soul. In his autobiographical work, *Junkie* (1953), written under the pseudonym of William Lee, Burroughs says, "Actually, my earliest memories are colored by a fear of nightmares. I was afraid to be alone, and afraid of the dark, and afraid to go to sleep because of dreams where a supernatural horror seemed always on the point of taking shape. [. . .] I said: 'I will smoke opium when I grow up.' "[3] As a boy, he was fond of hiking and fishing; but he was also a malingerer and a petty criminal, breaking into factories and houses. He was eventually sent to Harvard from which he took a degree "without honors" in English Literature. A trust fund which provided him with one hundred and fifty dollars a month gave him some security during the Depression. He drifted through Europe for a year, returned to the U.S. in 1936. On the surface, these first twenty-two years do not seem eventful. What happened to lead Burroughs since that time through the slums and prisons and hospitals of three continents, forcing him to jostle with hoodlums and pimps and pushers? In two decades, he acquired "the habit" and "kicked" it many times again, shot a wife by accident, cultivated perverts, took the apomorphine cure, exiled himself from civilization only to reemerge as the unregenerate legend of the Beat Movement, the mentor of Kerouac and Ginsberg, author of *Naked Lunch* which Robert Lowell describes, on the dust jacket, as "one of the most alive books written by any American for years!"

The psychiatrist who diagnosed Burroughs as a "schizophrenic paranoid" begs the question, as indeed the question begs itself. We may outlaw madness without comprehending it. But we must still ask: what monition is there in insanity, and how is the affront of crime relevant. The silence of an outlaw remains demonic; the testimony of the damned gives meaning to damnation. Burroughs not only testifies; he also indicts. Burroughs is a didactic writer who affirms his moral passion in the language of denial and derision. Like the later Swift, like Breughel or Hieronymus Bosch, he pushes satire toward the threshold of pathology, claiming from self-hate the hate humanity harbors. Personal outrage may be made into an indictment of history.

The indictment is even larger. "In Naked Lunch The Soft Machine and Novia Express—work in progress—i am mapping an imaginary universe. A dark universe of wounded galaxies and novia conspiracies where obscenity is coldly used as a total weapon," Burroughs writes.[4] And again: "The purpose of my writing is to expose and arrest Novia Criminals."[5] Burroughs does not only map out; he also exposes. His universe is imaginary only in the sense that it is distilled from abstract terrors, dominated by Regulators and Exterminators, by Ovens and Infernal Machines. His universe is as inhuman as interstellar spaces. Yet it swarms with insect people, floats on sentient ooze. The central metaphor of his universe is science fiction, which is the nightmare that our machines dream when they dream of history. The myth of technology, in Burroughs' work, is the dreadful reality of a world in which man makes a last effort to resist nonbeing. In *New Maps of Hell* (1961), Kingsley Amis amiably reads into science fiction the secret aspirations of mankind. Burroughs renders through science fiction the cold apocalypse of the race. The Machine always sounds the rhythm of death. The rhythm of the social mechanism is simple: first mendacity, then control, finally death:

> A POST SCRIPT OF THE REGULATOR
> I would like to sound a word of warning: To speak is to lie. To
> live is to collaborate. Any body is a coward when faced by the Novia
> Ovens. There are degrees of lying collaboration and cowardice. That
> is to say degrees of intoxication. It is precisely a question of
> REGULATION. The Enemy is not Man is not Woman. The Enemy
> exists only where no life is and moves always to push life into
> extreme untenable positions. You can cut the enemy off your line by
> the judicious use of apomorphine and silence. USE THE SANITY
> DRUG APOMORPHINE.
> Signed The Regulator Interstellar Board of Health[6]

This is a long way from autobiography. Outrage expands to embrace the universe. Its dominant metaphor is the machine of death. Three other metaphors, equally life draining, amplify the first: they are sex or obscenity, junk, and money. Each has a social and political correlative.

In Burroughs' work, sex is usually violation. It is sterile, inhuman, malevolent. It is a perversion of the life instinct, an organic process turned mechanical. Sadism, masochism, and pederasty prevail; tenderness, love, and knowledge are absent. Sex is simply the obscene correlative of alienation. Despite the elaborate depiction of homosexuality in Burroughs' work, there is no attempt to understand or justify the homosexual. "A room full of fags gives me the horrors," Burroughs writes. "They jerk around like puppets on invisible strings, galvanized into hideous activity that is the negation of everything living and spontaneous. The live human being has moved out of these bodies long ago."[7] Sex remains the desperate embodiment of an absence, of a lie.

Junk, however, is still a more complete embodiment of the Negative. Burroughs understands that junk wins in a man's life simply by default. Junk is the aboriginal hunger of the cells, the physical correlative of nihilism. The addict himself is bodiless, his ghastly corpse a needle cushion. He is brought back to temporary life by the "kick," a state of pure and solipsistic consciousness defined mainly by its horrible absence. "Kick is momentary freedom from the claims of the aging, cautious, nagging, frightened flesh," Burroughs ruefully says.[8] A freedom of lascivious death! Antonin Artaud saw the point with the dark eye of poetry: "I believe the opium we now have, the black juice of what we call the poppy, is the expulsion of an ancient eradicating power, which man no longer wanted, and those who were weary of the seminal fluid and of the erotic twistings of the self in the fluid of the first offense recoiled toward opium as toward a different lubricity."[9] It is the lubricity of death. Here is Burroughs again, on the terminal addict who sits around "with a spine like a frozen hydraulic jack . . . his metabolism approaching Absolute ZERO."[10]

Sex and junk express for Burroughs the extinction of life. So does money. "Junk is the mold and monopoly of possession," he states. "Junk is the ideal product . . . the ultimate merchandise. No sales talk necessary."[11] Both junk and money are quantitative; both are perversions of work and leisure in a capitalistic society. Money, then, is simply the counter of control, the price of need. It is the gainful term in an equation of degradation and loss. As Burroughs puts it, "the face of 'evil' is always the face of total need."[12] The addict will do anything for junk; the pusher will do anything for money. Hence money always appears in Burroughs' work as the social correlative of exploitation.

Obviously, Burroughs' death machine operates on obscenity, junk, and money. It is the diabolic metaphor of control. Metaphor, however, is the root of language, the very principle of its life. It is natural, therefore, that the language of Burroughs should reflect the quality of the metaphor which animates it. The language is desiccated, automatic. Its final aim is self-abolition. It presupposes the fact of extinction, cooling of novae and abandonment of the earth. The language of testimony testifies even against itself. This is perhaps the most original aspect of Burroughs' work.

Much of that work is rendered in a special language: hipster speech. Its meanings are as restricted as its vocabulary. And as Burroughs himself indicates, hipster words are polyvalent and their meanings are constantly changing.[13] Hipster language confesses its ephemeral character; furthermore, it openly accepts the inability of words to describe felt reality. Referring to *Naked Lunch,* Edward Dorn astutely remarks, "This is probably the first time a book has been written in translation instead of the normally original language."[14] Burroughs' distrust of language, however, is more radical than Dorn implies. To speak is to lie. "I will tell you: 'THE WORD.' Alien Word 'THE.' 'THE' Word of Alien Enemy imprisons 'THEE' in Time. In Body. In Shit. Prisoner, come out. The great skies are open. I Hassan i Sabbah RUB OUT THE WORD FOREVER," he screams.[15] Scream he may, yet write he must. Burroughs is forced to devise ways of circumventing language. His commentary on Jacoubi's "The Night Before Thinking," which Jacoubi wrote under the influence of majoun, a form of hashish jam, is a montage; the account of Jacoubi and the experience of Burroughs with a hallucinogen, "dim-N," are spliced to reveal the "underlying unity of words and images that blossoms like bottle genie from the hallucinogens now open to all the world of The Thousand and One Nights."[16] This technique is carried further in Burroughs' novels. The method, which owes something to the Dadaist antics of Tristan Tzara, is further developed by Brion Gysin, a painter who is a friend of Burroughs:

> Method is simple: Take a page or more or less of your own writing or
> from any writer living or dead. Any written or spoken words. Cut into

sections with scissors or switch blade as preferred and rearrange the
sections. Looking away. Now write out result. . . . Applications of
cut up method are literally unlimited cut out from time limits. Old
world lines keep you in old world slots. Cut your way out.[17]

The aim is to cut oneself out of language, cut oneself *from* language. The aim is
to escape a world made by words and perhaps to discover another. Chance denies
the order we have brought ourselves to accept, an order which Burroughs feels has
viciously betrayed us. The death machine, Burroughs implies, can only be destroyed
by destroying its logic, its logos. But what lies beyond logos? Characteristically,
the answer of Burroughs, the addict saved by apomorphine, is inconclusive. "Yage
may be the final fix," he says at one point.[18] And at another: "LEARN TO MAKE
IT WITHOUT ANY CHEMICAL SUPPORTS."[19] Outrage is its own answer; language is the equivocation of reality. A vision equally uncontaminated by words or
substance beckons him. The vision flashes in rare moments through his work. It is
a broken vision.

## 2

Fugitive and somewhat provisional in its character, the work of Burroughs does
not invite systematic consideration. Its development is obvious from the contrast
between his earliest book, *Junkie,* and a brief experimental work of later date, *The
Exterminator* (1960).[20] The former remains a pungent autobiographical narrative,
written largely in a sparse, naturalistic style. The structure is tight and conventional;
the transitions are clear. The interest of the book lies mainly in its cold depiction of
the sordid and implacable world of addiction.

*The Exterminator,* however, is a jumble of passages and motifs used elsewhere
by Burroughs, a "cut-up" and patched job. It is randomly illustrated with Arabic
script by Brion Gysin who also provides exhaustive permutations of such phrases
as "Kick that habit man," "Rub out the words," and "Proclaim present time over."
The metaphors are those of science fiction, pathology, and politics, and they are all
animated by the sense of revulsion, as if an unspeakable virus were taking over the
whole of life. In the background, a malevolent Control Machine moves to eliminate
all "non-qualitative data." Misogyny and misanthropy blend. "Scientists suggest
That Life on Earth originate and or implemented by garbage shit deposited by Space
Travellers?" (25), Burroughs queries; and elsewhere he states, "Now any American
will admit women are all bitches . . But find an Englishman to call the Queen a
Bitch.?" (22). The violence, indeed the crudity, of the feelings expressed is checked
by bilious humor, restrained by clipped rhythms: "Hook an ape . . When he learns
to say 'Where Is The Man?' He is a sick human junky . . With The Monkey on his
back" (26).

But how authentic is the "cut-up method," and how unique are its effects? "You
can cut the truth out of any written or spoken words," (5) Burroughs claims. The
fact remains that in the first part of this work, which is by far the most effective,

the cut-up method is used cannily and sparingly. Catch phrases acquire force because they are forced into sudden proximity with other slogans. The commentaries on Chessman and on the bombings in Madrid, on sex and on narcotics have a common context which the author slyly provides. The shock of surprise is a contrived shock, and the method turns out, in this case, to be more cerebral than Burroughs admits. Its chief value lies not in atomizing language but rather in disclosing the connections between the separate facts of outrage in our time. In his later trilogy, however, Burroughs worked more wildly.

3

*Naked Lunch,* the first book in Burroughs' unholy trilogy, must be acknowledged as an impressive achievement. The novel, if it can be termed such, is a sequence of dramatic or fantastic episodes without plot or developed characters. The vision is infernal, a glimpse of the abyss which Dante defined in his time by another theology. This is how Burroughs defines his inferno:

> The Word is divided into units which be all in one piece and should
> be so taken, but the pieces can be had in any order being tied up back
> and forth, in and out fore and aft like an innaresting sex arrangement.
> This book spill off the page in all directions, kaleidoscope of vistas,
> medley of tunes and street noises, farts and riot yipes and the
> slamming steel shutters of commerce, screams of pain and pathos and
> screams plain pathic, copulating cats and outraged squawk of the
> displaced bull head, prophetic mutterings of brujo in nutmeg trances,
> snapping necks and screaming mandrakes, sigh of orgasm, heroin
> silent as dawn in the thirsty cells [. . . ]. (229)

The vision is infernal and also satiric in a surrealistic fashion. Burroughs can be misunderstood when he says, "There is only one thing a writer can write about: *what is in front of his senses at the moment of writing. . . .* I am a recording instrument" (221). The recording machine is more accurately described a few lines later: "No matter how tight Security, I am always somewhere *Outside* giving orders and *Inside* this straight jacket of jelly that gives and stretches but always reforms ahead of every movement, thought, impulse, stamped with the seal of alien inspection."

The previous statement explains why, beyond the familiar techniques of distortion and hallucination, *Naked Lunch* refers all its philosophic and political themes to the decayed substance of the human body. The technique is harshly reductive, a reversal of the process of Freudian sublimation; but it serves to debunk the complexities of civilization by thrusting upon us that strange reality which underlies them all: the diseased and obscene flesh. Disease and obscenity are the corporal evidence of our maladies. Most organisms are therefore presented as putrid. The Virus prevails; the Virus "can exhibit living qualities only in a host, by using the life of another—the renunciation of life itself, a *falling* towards inorganic, inflexible machine, towards dead matter" (134). Hence too: "The end result of complete cellular representation is cancer. Democracy is cancerous, and bureaus are its cancer" (134). Likewise, obscenity is used to express outrage. The collector for Friendly Finance turns out to be a toothless Egyptian eunuch; and the procedures of capital punishment are presented in terms of sadistic, homosexual fantasies under the shadow of the gallows.

Burroughs employs other techniques to convey his infernal vision in *Naked Lunch*. Among the more striking is metamorphosis, usually the spontaneous transformation of the human body into lower forms of life. Men turn into crabs or larva. Doctor "Fingers" Schafer, the Lobotomy Kid, witnesses with horror the change in his patient from a Complete All American Deanxietized Man to a monstrous black centipede. The Buyer, a narcotics agent, turns into a noxious blob of jelly which swallows the District Supervisor. The sudden change from realistic to surrealistic narration is terrifying enough. Metamorphosis, however, achieves more than a literary effect of terror. It destroys the objective reality of the world, the identity and separateness of things; it is the actual image of disintegration.

Disintegration is indeed the end of Burroughs' vision. Poetic hallucination and technological fantasy both proclaim, in their different ways, a dark apocalypse. We begin with a fallen world: "America is not a young land: it is old and dirty and evil before the settlers, before the Indians. The evil is there waiting" (11). We end with death or depravity. Dr. Benway, who is in charge of Total Demoralization, states, "Western man is externalizing himself in the form of gadgets" (24). This is mild. From the rooftop of the Reconditioning Center we observe a howling spectacle of the world. "Gentle reader, the ugliness of that spectacle buggers description. . . . Oh Christ what a scene is this! Can tongue or pen accommodate these scandals?" Burroughs asks with mock horror (39 f.). And later we observe the frightful market in the City of Interzone: "A place where the unknown past and the emergent future meet in a vibrating soundless hum . . . Larval entities waiting for a Live One" (109). These apocalyptic scenes, flashed on our consciousness with a hellish projector—"fadeout" is one of the author's favorite directions—fuse the poetic visions of Rimbaud and the lucid nightmares of Orwell into a reel of grotesque malevolence.

The grotesque power of the book is egregious. There are fine scenes, like "The Black Meat," in which the poetic mood predominates; we participate silently in their awesome metaphors. And there are other discursive scenes, like "Benway" or "Islam Incorporated and the Parties of Interzone," in which the satiric content emerges from the vocabulary of pseudoscience. But the quality of Burroughs which sets him apart from both Rimbaud and Orwell is his grotesque humor. Above all, *Naked Lunch* is a parody of evil; it crackles with gargoyle laughter. The revolting sequence on the "talking ass" is one example. This is another:

AMERICAN HOUSEWIFE (opening a box of Lux): "Why don't it have an electric eye the box flip open when it see me and hand itself to the Automat Handy Man he should put it inna water already. . . . The Handy Man is outa control since Thursday, he been getting

physical with me and I didn't put it in his combination at all. . . .
And the Garbage Disposal Unit snapping at me, and the nasty old
Mixmaster keep trying to get up under my dress. . . ." (124)

In satire, the cold passions of Burroughs find release, and the techniques of
outrage find a goal. Satire also defines the range of the author's contempt. The
range is wide. It includes authority, conformity, colonialism, commerce, capital
punishment, café society, patriotism, political parties; it focuses on doctors, policemen, profiteers, gourmets, hipsters, racists, academics, women, and even junkies.
The central motive of Burroughs is, of course, anarchic; his paranoiac fear is of the
Dream Police. Thought control, political exploitation, and social responsibility—
which he usually associates with attachment to women—haunt his dreams. Ostensibly, his desperate wish is for a whole and free man. This is the positive image which
lies behind all the atrocities he depicts, an image of implicit denunciation. Yet what
he sees is only this: "The broken image of Man moves in minute by minute and cell
by cell. . . . Poverty, hatred, war, police-criminals, bureaucracy, insanity, all
symptoms of The Human Virus" (168 f.).

The Virus, it must be concluded, has affected Burroughs more than he realizes.
His denunciation of infamy slips into acquiescence to it; outrage cancels itself by a
partial relish of outrage. One feels of Burroughs, as one does not of the most morbid
moments of Swift, that in some secret part of him he rejoices in the humiliation of
man. "Citizens who want to be utterly humiliated and degraded—so many people
do, nowadays, hoping to jump the gun—offer themselves up for passive homosexual
intercourse to an encampment of Sollubis," he writes (118). The irony of the
statement is limited by the bitter relish of its larger context. In *Naked Lunch,* the
relentless accent on perversion denotes the violation of all human relations; but it
also betrays a compulsive character. The accent on addiction is equally ambiguous.
There is judgment and deprecation and icy pity in Burroughs' statement, "The world
network of junkies, tuned on a cord of rancid jissom . . . tying up in furnished
rooms . . . shivering in the sick morning . . ." (208). But there is also a certain
spite in his statement, "The President is a junky but can't take it direct because of
his position. So he gets fixed through me" (67). Pervert or addict, more often both,
the Outsider exposes the rest of the world even while he envies it. Envy breeds
revenge. The Outsider seeks to revenge himself by abolishing the world. But the
world remains. Burroughs rages at the world for not being a better place, and rages
at it again for not being more completely depraved. The revenge would be perfect
if all men were junkies and women were thrown out of creation!

*Naked Lunch* begins with the narrator's flight from "the fuzz." We meet in
stagnant, imaginary rooms The Vigilante, The Rube, Lee the Agent, A.J., Clem
and Jody the Ergot Twins, Autopsy Ahmed, Hepatitis Hal, Hassan O'Leary the
After Birth Tycoon, The Sailor, The Exterminator, The Buyer, "Fats" Terminal,
and Doc Benway. They vanish again in a green mist. In the end, the narrator pretends
to take the junk cure, and to climb out of that "space-time" which is the junky's death.
Lazarus is back. We have been Nowhere. Narrow, repetitive, secretly diseased, this

extraordinary work still deserves what Burroughs demands for it: *"Naked Lunch* is a blueprint, a How-To Book. . . . Black insect lusts open into vast, other planet landscapes. [. . .] How-To extend levels of experience by opening the door at the end of a long hall. . . . Doors that only open in *Silence*. . . . *Naked Lunch* demands Silence from The Reader. Otherwise he is taking his own pulse. . . ." (224).

## 4

*The Soft Machine* (1961), second book in the trilogy, shows certain differences from the earlier work. The collage technique of *Naked Lunch* yields to the more random effects of composition by a thoroughly cut-up method. All verismilitude vanishes. Moreover, the focus on drug addiction shifts to a vague and pervasive evil which can still be identified, despite the phantasmal setting, by its perverted and excremental character. The limbo depicted by Burroughs proves to be a wasteland no less infernal than his hell. Unfortunately, it also proves to be less interesting.

The claim on the dust jacket of the book is this: "Stroboscopic flicker-lights playing on the Soft Machine of the eye create hallucinations, and even epilepsy. Recurrent flickering of Cut-Up opens up the area of hallucination and makes a map for the human race to invade." These are brave words. More than ever, Burroughs seems determined to alter the human condition. The satirist invokes hallucination because it is more effective in restoring man to his true estate. The theory, no doubt, is attractive. Its results, however, often appear banal or inchoate; and in long stretches of the book gibberish prevails over revelation.

The work is divided into four units which carry the following titles: "Red: Transitional Period"; "Green: Thing Police Keep All Board Room Reports"; "Blue: Have You Seen Slotless City"; and "White: Poison Our Dead Sun in Our Brains." Each unit is composed of episodes with enigmatic subtitles. The routines of Burroughs in these episodes are in many ways similar to his routines in *Naked Lunch:* metamorphosis, parody, distortion, etc. The innovation consists in sketching a portrait or situation early in each unit, and cutting and permutating its components in the sections that follow. The method, of course, heightens the fantasmagoric quality of the work, and, in some cases, it creates fresh contexts and connections which might have been missed in a sequential narrative. Furthermore, the method occasionally permits Burroughs to strip an event from the coils of sentiment or illusion which surround it, rendering it into brutal poetry. More often, however, the effect is quite different. We feel, in the presence of a relentless mechanism, equally repetitive and reductive. All human activities are ground into slogans, compressed into recurrent images. Our imagination is not freed; it is rather constricted by a horrible rhythm of encounters and defeats, by a sinister and inescapable necessity. Permutation produces not variety but sameness. The whole of life seems in the grip of a subtracting machine. What the machine prescribes is not only the ethics of outrage but also the aesthetics of revulsion. Perhaps without realizing it fully, Burroughs seems to have devised in the cut-up method a means not so much of liberating man as of declaring his bondage. For bondage is the central theme of the cryptic episodes which make the book. The hand of necessity lies heavily on sex, commerce, or politics; man is always controlled, diminished, or infected. Explorers of strange and exotic lands, like Carl the Traveller, invariably discover the same degradation which blights their own cities. And Doc Benway is forever engaged in creating cretins or automatons.

The familiar bias of Burroughs is crudely dramatized on the first page. An ugly War Between the Sexes is described. There are Lesbian Colonels and Mongolian Archers in it; what is at stake is The Baby and Semen Market. The Hate Wave disintegrates the sexual Violator in a flash of White Light. "It was a transitional Period because of the Synthetics and everybody was raising some kinda awful life form in his bidet to fight the Sex Enemy," Burroughs states (9). These mutant forms include black centipedes and green newt boys with purple fungoid gills. Other factions are converting to still lower forms of life: "Do not be alarmed citizens of Annexia—Report to your Nearie Pro Station for Chlorophyll Processing—We are converting to Vegetable State—Emergency measure to counter the Heavy Metal Peril! [. . .] 'Citizens of Gravity we are converting all out to Heavy Metal. Carbonic Plague of the Vegetable People threatens our Heavy Metal State' " (12). Meanwhile, the homosexual tandem, "Mr. Bradly Mr. Martin," is preparing to leave earth. As in Annexia, Death in Orgasm prevails in Minraud. "All resident doubles in rooms of Minraud grow living legs for death in orgasm of the Novia Guard" (19). The evil, of course, is traced back to language itself. "Picture the [Novia] guard as an invisible tapeworm attached to word centers in the brain on color intensity beams. . . . The Head Guards are captives of word-fallout only live in word and image of the host," Burroughs explains (17). The solution? "Rub out your stupid word. Rub out separation word 'They' 'We' 'I' 'You' 'The!' Rub out word 'The' forever. . . . Go back to Silence. Keep Silence. K.S. K.S. . . . From Silence re-write the message that is you" (13 f.).

This is Burroughs' eternal theme, and all the permutations of it into sexual attitudes or color imagery add little to it. There are, of course, surrealistic descriptions of the city of Man:

> Border City—Noon Ticker Tape—Fight erupt like sand penned on
> iron—Set Heads bouncing to the void clutching bank notes and
> chemical gardens in rusty "connections"—Distant City is Red Stone
> Mesa—Cut wires a Gambling Fight—Flowers and Jungle shriek for hu-
> mans—Hang anyone they can overpower—Sentries attack the passerby
> with crowds at arbitrary intervals. Down into Present Time and there
> investigate purpose— (22)

There are also grotesque parodies of fertility rites involving the Young Corn God:

> The Priests arrange the initiates into long dog-fuck lines moulding
> them together with green jelly from the Lubricant Tanks. Now the
> Centipede Skin is strapped on each body a segment and The Centipede

whips and cracks in electric spasms of pleasure, writhing in wind
black hair bursts through his flesh great canines tear into gums with
exquisite toothache pain. (50)

Quotation becomes almost pointless. The "soft machine" of the eye can only register horror; the ear always listens to "Phantom jissom in the nettles and dry sound of scorpion" (57); the nose only smells "locker room smell of mouldy jock-straps" (140). The primitive and sensuous roots of life which Lawrence joyfully celebrated are execrated by Burroughs. There is never sacrament; there is always revulsion. Everything must be "cut":

> Cut the Sex & Dream Utility Lines
> Cut the Trak Service Lines
> The paws does not refresh
> Working for the Yankee Dollar?— (74)

Change is regression; contact is torture; property is control; and all desire is addiction. Burroughs is an allegorist—witness his stark events, his epithets and personifications—and he has written the allegory of a mouldy universe. He has chosen technological fantasy as the frame of his allegory to dramatize a vision that could be called puritanical were it not so "obscene." And yet is not obscenity the other face of puritanical outrage? *The Soft Machine* is like a book written in a secret code. When the code is deciphered all the messages read the same: Out!

## 5

Burroughs' trilogy is a grotesque *commedia* which comes to a happy end in *The Ticket That Exploded* (1962). The new setting is sweepingly galactic. The style once again alternates between technical jargon and poetic hallucination. There is, of course, no plot, only a "cut-up" of scenes and images. Some of the earlier characters—Mr. Bradly Mr. Martin, A.J., etc.—reappear. The conspiracy against creation described in the earlier books is finally resolved on a grand scale.

We begin with a dreamy dissolution of reality. A room on the roof of a ruined warehouse, "swept by the winds of time," becomes a space ship. A "blue metal boy" and a "green boy-girl" copulate, twisting "free of human coordinates" (8). A world of acrid ectoplasms and nitrous flakes, of flickering ghosts and mineral silences, unfolds. Newt boys appear, unite, and vanish; nerve patterns become visible in orgasm; a slow, sexual movement ebbs and flows underwater. We are apprised that a certain Bradly explodes the dungeons of the Garden of Delights, releasing all its prisoners, releasing himself from time and human flesh. Hypnotic images lace every page with memories of captive pleasures. We are bewildered; yet we feel that the theme somehow has been stated.

The mood then suddenly changes to satire. A medley of old songs and homosexual fantasies offers a savage parody of sentimental love. But it is not until the sections entitled "Operation Rewrite" and "The Nova Police" that Burroughs reveals his scheme. The galaxy, it seems, is ruled by a Nova Mob which perpetuates every kind of misery and addiction in man; the task of the Nova Police is to break up the Mob. The basic technique of the Mob is to create and aggravate insoluble conflicts. "This is done by dumping on the same planet life forms with incompatible conditions of existence," says Inspector J. Lee of the Nova Police (41). The Nova criminals are a Virus; they feed on human organisms. "The point at which the criminal controller intersects a three-dimensional human agent is known as a 'coordinate point. . . .' Some move on junk lines through addicts of the earth, others move on lines of certain sexual practices and so forth—It is only when we can block the controller out of all coordinate points available to him and flush him out from host cover that we can make a definitive arrest," explains the Inspector (44 f.). The Venusian parasites, for instance, specialize in sexual addicts; those from Uranus, themselves "heavy metal" addicts, specialize in junkies. In other words, the virus or controller is an addict fastening upon a human addict. Inspector Lee continues: "Now you may well ask whether we can straighten out this mess to the satisfaction of any life forms involved and my answer is this—Your earth case must be processed by the Biological Courts— (admittedly in a deplorable condition at this time)" (42 f.). But there is still hope: "The success of the Nova Mob depended on a blockade of the planet that allowed them to operate with impunity—This blockade was broken by partisan activity directed from the planet Saturn that cut the control lines of word and image laid down by the Nova Mob—So we moved in our agents and started to work keeping always in close touch with partisans" (43).

Equally matter of fact and fantastic, Burroughs' scheme comes to focus in his view of love which is the primary concern of *The Ticket That Exploded*. One is compelled by the strangeness of the material to quote at length:

> The Venusian invasion was known as "Operation Other Half," that is, a parasitic invasion of the sexual area taking advantage . . . of an already existing fucked up situation . . . —The human organism is literally consisting of two halves from the beginning word and all human sex is this unsanitary arrangement whereby two entities attempt to occupy the same three-dimensional coordinate points giving rise to the sordid latrine brawls which have characterized a planet based on "The Word," that is, on separate flesh engaged in endless sexual conflict—The Venusian Boy-Girls under Johnny Yen took over The Other Half, imposing a sexual blockade on the planet—(It will be readily understandable that a program of systematic frustration was necessary in order to sell this crock of sewage as Immortality, The Garden of Delights, and LOVE). (37 f.)

And here is Burroughs' conclusion:

> So let us start with one average, stupid representative case: Johnny Yen The Other Half, errand boy from the death trauma—Now look

> I'm going to say it and I'm going to say it slow—Death *is* orgasm *is* rebirth *is* death in orgasm *is* their unsanitary Venusian Gimmick *is* the whole birth death cycle of action—You get it?—Now do you understand who Johnny Yen is? The Boy-Girl Other Half strip tease God of sexual frustration—Errand Boy from the death trauma—His immortality depends on the mortality of others—The same is true of *all* addicts. (39)

The vocabulary of science fiction conceals a radical theory of love, indeed of life. The Mob, which is also The All Powerful Board, controls thoughts, feelings, and flesh with "iron claws of pain and pleasure from birth to death" (15). It uses the division of the sexes, the cant of love or responsibility, the needs of the human body to sustain its control. Above all, it uses the power of Word and Image to exercise its influence. Hence the parallel redemptive functions of the Biological Courts and of the Rewrite Department; the first must refashion the body of man and the second must remodel language. *Ideally, the aim is to make man bodiless and language silent.* Burroughs, we see, has given a terrible twist to the biblical equation of Word and Flesh. His radical hope is to redeem creation by abolishing both.

It is hard to judge whether Burroughs' notion is a consummation of Western nihilism, a rediscovery of Oriental nirvana, or a viciously ironic commentary on our world. Of this we can be more certain: The Mob can call on The Old Doctor, whatever dying, fraudulent god he may be, but it can never call on him Twice. It is later than the Mob thinks, only Minutes to Go, and the Nova Heat of the Police is on. "The separation gimmick that keeps this tired old show on the road" (128) cannot work indefinitely:

> All right, so you sewed up a planet—now unsew it—. . . Reverse all your gimmicks—Your heavy blue metal fix out in blue sky—Your blue mist swirling through all the streets of image to Pan Pipes—Your white smoke falling in luminous sound and image flakes—Your bank of word and image scattered to the winds of morning—Into this project all the way for all to see in Times Square in Picadilly— Reverse and dismantle your machine— Drain off the prop ocean and leave the White Whale stranded—All your word line broken from mind screens of the earth—You talk about "responsibility"—Now show responsibility—Show total responsibility—You have blighted a planet—Now remove the blight—Cancel your "White Smoke" and all your other gimmicks of control—Your monopoly of life, time, and fortune cancelled by your own orders. (129)

Words fall, time falls, body halves are off; the apocalyptic rewriting of creation is nearly complete. Our ticket on this journey through life has exploded. "Won't be much left in the final age of history—Cold empty condom the price on our ticket that exploded" (127). Like Prospero, Burroughs makes his farewell: "Outside East

St. Louis our revels now are ended—These events are melted into air" (131). The epilogue of the book requires "Silence to say goodbye."

*The Ticket That Exploded,* however, is not the programmatic work that this account may suggest. Like its predecessors, it is both satiric and visionary, perhaps more so. Its logic is disrupted by random and transposed scenes or images, fantastic metamorphoses, discursive notes on scientific theory or orgone therapy, calligraphs by Brion Gysin, travelers' diaries, bulletins in newsspeak, parodies of space fiction, dream and delirium sequences, political commentaries, hipster dialogue, and such fleeting characters as Green Tony, Bradly, Sammy The Butcher, Izzy The Push, Hamburger Mary, The Fluoroscopic Kid, and Hassan i Sabbah. Its method, that is, is a constant shifting in the levels of discourse. And its aim is to diffract time, language, and flesh in a crazy kaleidoscopic vision, through which filters a utopian image of man. Like an image track or reel, running intolerably silent and slow, the book blurs all the contours of the visible, the known, world, and dissolves its stationary symbols. Will a new face of reality, then, reveal itself?

6

The question of "reality" in the work of William Burroughs is finally elusive. We know the grounds on which he rejects the world: "Take it from an Old Property, Total Fear and Hate is more of a habit than using."[21] But we are never certain of what he affirms instead. Reality, therefore, is a negative concept where Burroughs is concerned. Despite his apocalyptic gifts, he remains a satirist more than a visionary, an ironist more than a prophet, an allegorist more than a poet. "I offer you nothing," he confesses. He offers more than he pretends, compounding the horrors of our lives with his own grotesque experience. And yet he offers less than the major writers of our century, Mann and Kafka, Joyce and Faulkner, have offered; not because his scope and knowledge are less than theirs, which is indubitably true, but because his love is also smaller. At times, the extent of Burroughs' love—and love is the energy of the soul, the will to life—seems contained in the advice:

> Flesh junkies, control junkies, heavy metal junkies—That's how you
> get caught, son—If you have to have it well you've had it—Just like
> any mark—So slide in cool and casual on the next pitch and don't get
> hooked on the local line: If there is one thing to write on any life form
> you can score for it's this: Keep your bag packed at all times and
> ready to travel on—[22]

Ready to travel on right out of this world. The refrain is, "Man, like goodbye."

In the end, too much is left out. The whole of nature is excluded. An urban writer, Burroughs has inhaled the flowers of evil which have grown on the pavements of every city since the time of Baudelaire. He has tasted or inhaled little else. Like man, nature is corrupt. Nature is out. Society is monstrous. Society is out. All the races and people crowding his books, a vestige, perhaps, of his anthropological interests, bring no virtues that civilization lacks. Mexicans, Arabs, and Chinese are out. Nothing escapes The Subtracting Machine. Again and again, Burroughs turns to the reader belligerently to ask, "Wouldn't you?" That is: "In my place, would you have done otherwise? For once, be honest now!" And again and again the reader wants to answer: "All I know is that many *have* done otherwise."

It is no accident that utopianism and nihilism have often crossed paths in history, and have often shared the same human passions. To neglect that history or suppress these passions is fateful in this moment of our crisis. The work of William Burroughs takes its nauseous sense of life from our moment. It gives a new meaning, however limited, to outrage. Above all, it assaults language savagely, declaring thus its opposition to the deeper assaults which human consciousness suffers. In its respect for silence, it expresses, beyond the cold rage of obscenity, a piteous respect for creation.

## Notes

1. William Burroughs, "Introduction to Naked Lunch The Soft Machine Novia Express," *Evergreen Review* (Jan.–Feb. 1962): 100. Note that the projected work, "Novia Express," appeared under the title *The Ticket That Exploded* (Paris, 1962), and that an augmented and revised edition of *The Soft Machine* (Paris, 1961) is scheduled to appear in Paris in 1963. All three books were first published by the Olympia Press.

2. John Wain, "The Great Burroughs Affair," *New Republic* (1 Dec. 1962): 21.

3. William Lee (Burroughs), *Junkie* (New York: Ace, 1953) 5.

4. "Introduction," *Evergreen Review*, 99.

5. "Introduction," *Evergreen Review*, 102.

6. "Introduction," *Evergreen Review*, 102.

7. *Junkie*, 84.

8. *Junkie*, 149.

9. Antonin Artaud, "Three Letters," *Evergreen Review* (Jan.–Feb. 1963): 60.

10. William Burroughs, "Deposition: Testimony Concerning a Sickness," *Naked Lunch* (New York: Grove, 1962) xiii f. Note that the original edition was published in Paris in 1959.

11. "Deposition," *Naked Lunch*, vi f.

12. "Deposition," *Naked Lunch*, vii.

13. See the Glossary in *Junkie*, 11 ff.

14. Edward Dorn, "Notes More or Less Relevant to Burroughs and Trocchi," *Kulchur 7* (Autumn 1962): 13.

15. "Introduction," *Evergreen Review*, 100.

16. William Burroughs, "Comments on the Night Before Thinking," *Evergreen Review* (Sep.–Oct. 1961): 36.

17. William Burroughs, "The Cut Up Method of Brion Gysin," in *A Casebook on the Beat*, ed. Thomas Parkinson (New York: Thomas Y. Crowell Company, 1961) 105 f.

18. *Junkie*, 149.

19. "Introduction," *Evergreen Review*, 101.

20. William Burroughs and Brion Gysin, *The Exterminator* (San Francisco, 1960) was published by the Auerhahn Press. Subsequent page citations to Burroughs' works are generally given parenthetically in the text.

21. *The Soft Machine*, 127.

22. *The Ticket That Exploded*, 140.

# 8

# Notes on Burroughs

## Marshall McLuhan

T oday men's nerves surround us; they have gone outside as electrical environment. The human nervous system itself can be reprogrammed biologically as readily as any radio network can alter its fare. Burroughs has dedicated *Naked Lunch* to the first proposition, and *Nova Express* (both Grove Press) to the second. *Naked Lunch* records private strategies of culture in the electric age. *Nova Express* indicates some of the "corporate" responses and adventures of the Subliminal Kid who is living in a universe which seems to be someone else's insides. Both books are a kind of engineer's report of the terrain hazards and mandatory processes, which exist in the new electric environment.

2. Burroughs uses what he calls "Brion Gysin's cut-up method which I call the fold-in method." To read the daily newspaper in its entirety is to encounter the method in all its purity. Similarly, an evening watching television programs is an experience in a corporate form—an endless succession of impressions and snatches of narrative. Burroughs is unique only in that he is attempting to reproduce in prose what we accommodate every day as a commonplace aspect of life in the electric age. If the corporate life is to be rendered on paper, the method of discontinuous nonstory must be employed.

3. That man provides the sexual organs of the technological world seems obvious enough to Burroughs, and such is the stage (or "biological theatre" as he calls it in *Nova Express*) for the series of social orgasms brought about by the evolutionary mutations of man and society. The logic, physical and emotional, of a world in which we have made our environment out of our own nervous systems, Burroughs follows everywhere to the peripheral orgasm of the cosmos.

4. Each technological extension involves an act of collective cannibalism. The previous environment with all its private and social values, is swallowed by the new environment and reprocessed for whatever values are digestible. Thus, Nature was succeeded by the mechanical environment and became what we call the "content"

---

Marshall McLuhan, "Notes on Burroughs," *The Nation* (28 Dec. 1964): 517–19. Copyright © 1964 by *The Nation* magazine/The Nation Company, Inc. Reprinted by permission.

of the new industrial environment. That is, Nature became a vessel of aesthetic and spiritual values. Again and again the old environment is upgraded into an art form while the new conditions are regarded as corrupt and degrading. Artists, being experts in sensory awareness, tend to concentrate on the environmental as the challenging and dangerous situation. That is why they may seem to be "ahead of their time." Actually, they alone have the resources and temerity to live in immediate contact with the environment of their age. More timid people prefer to accept the content, the previous environment's values, as the continuing reality of their time. Our natural bias is to accept the new gimmick (automation, say) as a thing that can be accommodated in the old ethical order.

    5. During the process of digestion of the old environment, man finds it expedient to anesthetize himself as much as possible. He pays as little attention to the action of the environment as the patient heeds the surgeon's scalpel. The gulping or swallowing of Nature by the machine was attended by a complete change of the ground rules of both the sensory ratios of the individual nervous system and the patterns of the social order as well. Today, when the environment has become the extension of the entire mesh of the nervous system, anesthesia numbs our bodies into hydraulic jacks.

    6. Burroughs disdains the hallucinatory drugs as providing mere "content," the fantasies, dreams that money can buy. Junk (heroin) is needed to turn the human body itself into an environment that includes the universe. The central theme of *Naked Lunch* is the strategy of bypassing the new electric environment by becoming an environment oneself. The moment one achieves this environmental state all things and people are submitted to you to be processed. Whether a man takes the road of junk or the road of art, the entire world must submit to his processing. The world becomes his "content." He programs the sensory order.

    7. For artists and philosophers, when a technology is new it yields Utopias. Such is Plato's *Republic* in the fifth century B.C., when phonetic writing was being established. Similarly, More's *Utopia* is written in the sixteenth century when the printed book had just become established. When electric technology was new and speculative, *Alice in Wonderland* came as a kind of non-Euclidean space-time Utopia, a grown-up version of which is the *Illuminations* of Rimbaud. Like Lewis Carroll, Rimbaud accepts each object as a world and the world as an object. He makes a complete break with the established procedure of putting things *into* time or space:

> That's she, the little girl behind the rose bushes, and she's dead.
> The young mother, also dead, is coming down the steps. The cousin's
> carriage crunches the sand. The small brother (he's in India!) over
> there in the field of pinks, in front of the sunset. The old men they've
> buried upright in the wall covered with gilly-flowers.

But when the full consequences of each new technology have been manifested in new psychic and social forms, then the anti-Utopias appear. *Naked Lunch* can be viewed as the anti-Utopia of *Illuminations:*

> During the withdrawal the addict is acutely aware of his
> surroundings. Sense impressions are sharpened to the point of
> hallucination. Familiar objects seem to stir with a writhing furtive life.
> The addict is subject to a barrage of sensations external and visceral.

Or to give a concrete example from the symbolist landscape of *Naked Lunch:*

> A guard in a uniform of human skin, black buck jacket with
> carious yellow teeth buttons, an elastic pullover shirt in burnished
> Indian copper [. . .] sandals from calloused foot soles of young
> Malayan farmer [. . .].

The key to symbolist perception is in yielding the permission to objects to resonate with their *own* time and space. Conventional pictorial and literary perception seeks to put diverse objects into the same time and space. Time and space themselves are subjected to the uniform and continuous visual processing that provides us with the "connected and rational" world that is in fact only an isolated fragment of reality— the visual. There is no uniform and continuous character in the nonvisual modalities of space and time. The Symbolists freed themselves from visual conditions into the visionary world of the iconic and the auditory. Their art, to the visually oriented and literary man, seems haunted, magical and often incomprehensible. It is, in John Ruskin's words:

> . . . the expression, in a moment, by a series of symbols thrown
> together in bold and fearless connections; of truths which it would
> have taken a long time to express in any verbal way, and of which the
> connection is left for the beholder to work out for himself; the gaps,
> left or overleaped by the haste of the imagination, forming the
> grotesque character. (*Modern Painters*)

The art of the interval, rather than the art of the connection, is not only medieval but Oriental; above all, it is the art mode of instant electric culture.

8. There are considerable antecedents for the Burroughs attempt to read the language of the biological theatre and the motives of the Subliminal Kid. *Fleurs du Mal* is a vision of the city as the technological extension of man. Baudelaire had once intended to title the book *Les Limbes*. The vision of the city as a physiological and psychic extension of the body he experienced as a nightmare of illness and self-alienation. Wyndham Lewis, in his trilogy *The Human Age*, began with *The Childermass*. Its theme is the massacre of innocents and the rape of entire populations by the popular media of press and film. Later in *The Human Age* Lewis explores the psychic mutations of man living in "the magnetic city," the instant, electric, and angelic (or diabolic) culture. Lewis views the action in a much more inclusive way than Burroughs whose world is a paradigm of a future in which there can be no spectators but only participants. All men are totally involved in the insides of all men. There is no privacy and no private parts. In a world in which we are all

ingesting and digesting one another there can be no obscenity or pornography or decency. Such is the law of electric media which stretch the nerves to form a global membrane of enclosure.

9. The Burroughs diagnosis is that we can avoid the inevitable "closure" that accompanies each new technology by regarding our entire gadgetry as *junk*. Man has hopped himself up by a long series of technological fixes:

> You are dogs on all tape. The entire planet is being developed into
> terminal identity and complete surrender.

We can forego the entire legacy of Cain (the inventor of gadgets) by applying the same formula that works for *junk*—"apomorphine," extended to all technology:

> Apomorphine is no word and no image—[. . .] It is simply a
> question of putting through an innoculation program in the very
> limited time that remains—Word begets image and image IS virus—

Burroughs is arguing that the power of the image to beget image, and of technology to reproduce itself via human intervention, is utterly in excess of our power to control the psychic and social consequences:

> Shut the whole thing right off—*Silence*—When you answer the
> machine you provide it with more recordings to be played back to
> your "enemies" keep the whole nova machine running—The Chinese
> character for "enemy" means to be similar to or to answer—Don't
> answer the machine—Shut it off—

Merely to be in the presence of any machine, or replica of our body or faculties, is to close with it. Our sensory ratios shift at once with each encounter with any fragmented extension of our being. This is a non-stop express of innovation that cannot be endured indefinitely:

> We are just dust falls from demagnetized patterns—Show business—

It is the medium that is the message because the medium creates an environment that is as indelible as it is lethal. To end the proliferation of lethal new environmental expression, Burroughs urges a huge collective act of restraint as well as a nonclosure of sensory modes—"The biological theater of the body can bear a good deal of new program notes."

10. *Finnegans Wake* provides the closest literary precedent to Burroughs' work. From the beginning to end it is occupied with the theme of "the extensions" of man—weaponry, clothing, languages, number, money, and media *in toto*. Joyce works out in detail the sensory shifts involved in each extension of man, and concludes with the resounding boast:

The keys to. Given!

Like Burroughs, Joyce was sure he had worked out the formula for total cultural understanding and control. The idea of art as total programming for the environment is tribal, mental, Egyptian. It is, also, an idea of art to which electric technology leads quite strongly. We live science fiction. The bomb is our environment. The bomb is of higher learning all compact, the extension division of the university. The university has become a global environment. The university now contains the commercial world, as well as the military and government establishments. To reprogram the cultures of the globe becomes as natural an undertaking as curriculum revision in a university. Since new media are new environments that reprocess psyche and society in successive ways, why not bypass instruction in fragmented subjects meant for fragmented sections of the society and reprogram the environment itself? Such is Burroughs' vision.

11. It is amusing to read reviews of Burroughs that try to classify his books as nonbooks or as failed science fiction. It is a little like trying to criticize the sartorial and verbal manifestations of a man who is knocking on the door to explain that flames are leaping from the roof of our home. Burroughs is not asking merit marks as a writer; he is trying to point to the shut-on button of an active and lethal environmental process.

# 9

# Objections to
# William Burroughs

## David Lodge

H ave we come to handle the avant-garde too gently? From the *Lyrical Ballads* to *Ulysses* our literary history is very much a chronicle of revolutionary works hooted and reviled by the literary establishments of their times, appreciated by a small elite of initiates, and belatedly elevated to classic status by succeeding literary establishments. Since the 1920s, however, the time lag between the publication and the public recognition of such works has got shorter and shorter, until now we are, perhaps, more in danger of mistaking than neglecting masterpieces. Part of the reason is the radical change which has overtaken academic criticism in this period: the groves of academe, that were once enclaves of conservative literary taste, are now only too eager to welcome what is new. Another, and perhaps more important reason is that through the development of the mass media and what one might call the boom in the culture market, the "small élite of initiates" which in the past constituted the only audience for experimental art, good and bad, is now able to bring its influence to bear very swiftly and powerfully on the larger public.

Nothing illustrates this latter process more strikingly than the way the reputation of William Burroughs has grown since Mary McCarthy praised *The Naked Lunch* at the Edinburgh Writers' Conference of 1962. (Miss McCarthy has since complained that her words on that occasion were distorted and exaggerated by the press; but it could be argued that writers who participate in such events, which are peculiar to our own cultural era, must expect and accept such treatment.) What is noteworthy about Burroughs' reputation is not so much the encomiums his work has received from such confrères as Miss McCarthy, Norman Mailer ("I think that William Burroughs is the only American novelist living today who may conceivably be

David Lodge, "Objections to William Burroughs," *The Novelist at the Crossroads and Other Essays in Fiction and Criticism* (London: Routledge and Kegan Paul, Ltd., 1971): 161–71. [Originally published in *Critically Quarterly* 8 (Autumn 1966): 203–12.] Copyright © 1971 by Routledge and Kegan Paul, Ltd. Reprinted by permission.

possessed of genius") and Jack Kerouac ("Burroughs is the greatest satirical writer since Jonathan Swift"), as the way in which this body of opinion has acted on the public mind so as to secure the smooth acceptance and accommodation of such books as *The Naked Lunch* and *Nova Express*. It seems to illustrate very well what Lionel Trilling has described as the institutionalization of the "adversary culture" of modernism; and like him, I do not see this process as a symptom of cultural health. *The Naked Lunch,* whatever else it may be, is a very indecent book, and *Nova Express,* whatever else it may be, is a very tedious book. These novels' pretensions to serious literary significance which, if realized, would justify the indecency and the tedium (or rather force us to redefine these qualities) need to be examined rather more rigorously than our present literary climate generally encourages. Before doing so, it may be advisable to attempt a description of these books. I say "attempt" because they both resist any conventional summary of character and action.

## 2

*The Naked Lunch* begins with the first-person narrative of a drug addict who, pursued by the New York police, travels across America with a companion to Mexico; his account of the journey is mingled with reminiscences of various characters from the drugs underworld. In the second chapter the novel parts with actuality and takes on the quality of dream. The action shifts abruptly from place to place, sometimes between mythical states called Freeland, Annexia, and Interzone, which bear a parodic relationship to the actual world. There is no plot, but a general impression of intrigue and pursuit, sometimes on a cops-and-robbers level, sometimes on a political level. The narrative mode shifts from first person to third person to dramatic dialogue. Many of the scenes have a hallucinatory, surrealistic quality reminiscent of the Circe episode in *Ulysses*. The images of the book are primarily of violence, squalor, and sexual perversion. There is a notorious orgiastic sequence in which orgasm is achieved by hanging and finally eating the sexual partner. We seem to be sharing the dream, or nightmare, of an addict—perhaps, as Miss McCarthy has suggested, one who is taking a cure and suffering the agonies of "withdrawal."

In *Nova Express* the dislocation of narrative and logical continuity is much more radical, for here Burroughs has used what he describes as a "cut-up" or "fold-in" technique—that is, a montage of fragments of his own and other people's writings, achieved, for instance, by overlapping two pages of text and reading straight across. Basically the book is a science fiction fantasy based on the premise that the earth has been invaded by extraterrestrial gangsters, the "Nova Mob," whose mission is to infiltrate human institutions and encourage all forms of evil in order to accelerate this planet's progress on the path to destruction. They are pursued by the "Nova Police," who also work invisibly through human agencies, causing, it would seem, almost as much havoc. Only such fantastic suppositions, it is implied, will account for the political lunacy and moral decay of the modern world. That the fantasy is more real than what we take to be actuality is emphasized by such conceits as that life is a "biological movie" created and manipulated in a "Reality Studio" for the control of which Nova factions are competing.

3

Burroughs has, principally, two claims on the attention of serious readers: as a moralist, and as an innovator. On both counts, it seems to me, he cannot be considered as more than a minor, eccentric figure. Undoubtedly he has a certain literary talent, particularly for comedy and the grotesque, but in both precept and practice he is deeply confused and ultimately unsatisfying. *The Naked Lunch* seems to offer an appropriate epitaph on his work: "Confusion hath fuck his masterpiece."

To begin with, there is a deep confusion, not only in Burroughs but in his admirers too, on the subject of narcotics. Much of Burroughs' notoriety derives from the fact that he is a morphine addict, who has been cured, but who still writes very much out of the experience of addiction. He tells us in the Introduction to *The Naked Lunch* that it is based on notes taken during the sickness and delirium of addiction. He is our modern De Quincey; and undoubtedly this accounts for his adoption by the hipster wing of the American literary scene. Herbert Gold has called *The Naked Lunch* "the definitive hip book" and Burroughs tells us that the title was donated by the arch-hipster Jack Kerouac. "I did not understand what the title meant until my recovery. The title means exactly what the words say: NAKED lunch—a frozen moment when everyone sees what is on the end of every fork." These words clearly imply that the drugged state gives access to a special vision of truth—that the junkie, like Conrad's Kurtz, is an inverted hero of the spirit who truly sees "the horror, the horror" that ordinary, conforming humanity refuses to face. But in other places Burroughs undercuts this argument, which alone could justify his distressingly explicit (so much more explicit than Conrad's) descriptions of the horror. In an interview published in the *Paris Review* (35, Autumn 1965) he agreed that "The visions of drugs and the visions of art don't mix"; and both novels contain a great deal of obtrusive propaganda against the use of narcotics and on behalf of the apomorphine treatment by which Burroughs himself was cured. The interviewer challenged him on this point—"You regard addiction as an illness, but also a central human fact, a drama?"—and Burroughs' reply is revealing:

> Both, absolutely. It's as simple as the way in which anyone happens
> to become an alcoholic. [. . .] The idea that addiction is somehow a
> psychological illness is, I think, totally ridiculous. It's as
> psychological as malaria. It's a matter of exposure. [. . .] There are
> also all forms of spiritual addiction. [. . .] Many policemen and
> narcotics agents are precisely addicted to power, to exercising a
> certain nasty kind of power over people who are helpless. The nasty
> sort of power: white junk I call it—rightness [. . .].

It will be noted how Burroughs slides here from a literal, clinical view of addiction to a figurative or symbolic one. Both views are at odds with the assumption behind

*The Naked Lunch* that the junkie's delirium yields truth; and they are also at odds with each other. In the first view addiction is seen as a preventable sickness, in the second it is seen as a metaphor for authoritarianism. On the one hand it is not "psychological," on the other hand it can be "spiritual." In the first place the junkie is a sick man in need of society's protection, in the second place he is a victim of society.

This kind of equivocation is particularly evident in Burroughs' treatment of the police. In *The Naked Lunch* a certain sympathy is generated for the junkies on the run from the police, yet it is difficult to see how the exposure of the individual to drugs, which according to Burroughs is the cause of addiction, could be prevented without the police. In *Nova Express* the Nova Police seem to be the "goodies" as the Nova Mob are the "baddies," but Burroughs, in the interview already cited, says, "They're like police anywhere. [. . .] Once you get them in there, by God, they begin acting like any police. They're always an ambivalent agency." In this case, how are we to read the following passage about the Nova Police:

> The difference between this department and the parasitic excrescence
> that often travels under the name "Police" can be expressed in
> metabolic terms: The distinction between morphine and apomorphine.
> [. . .] The Nova Police can be compared to apomorphine, a regulating
> instance that need not continue and has no intention of continuing after
> its work is done.

The confusion that surrounds these two novels of Burroughs can, I think, be partly explained by the fact that they are very different works which Burroughs is trying to present as in some sense continuous, two stages in a coherent program. *The Naked Lunch* is essentially a nihilistic work and as such it must be granted a certain horrible power; but it is prefaced by an Introduction which seeks to justify it on orthodox moral grounds, and to present its hero as a brand snatched from the burning:

> Since *The Naked Lunch* treats this health problem [addiction], it is
> necessarily brutal, obscene and disgusting. Sickness has often
> repulsive details not for weak stomachs.
>     Certain passages in the book that have been called pornographic
> were written as a tract against Capital Punishment in the manner of
> Jonathan Swift's *Modest Proposal*. These sections are intended to
> reveal capital punishment as the obscene, barbaric and disgusting
> anachronism that it is.

How literature can deal with evil without morally compromising itself is of course a perennial and perhaps insoluble problem, but Burroughs' defense is either näive or disingenuous. The analogy with Swift won't stand up. Whereas in *A Modest Proposal* Swift maintains a constant logical connection between his fable (the monstrous "proposal") and his facts (the miseries of the Irish people), so that in revolting from the former we are compelled to revolt from the latter, it is doubtful whether the uninformed reader would see any connection at all between the Orgasm Death Gimmick and Capital Punishment. It may be that the disgust Mr. Burroughs feels for Capital Punishment has been transferred to the antics of his sexual perverts, but the reverse process which should occur for the reader is by no means to be relied upon. The power of Swift's piece inheres very largely in the tone of calm reasonableness with which the proposal is put forward, so that we feel obliged to supply the emotion which is missing. In *The Naked Lunch,* instead of this subtly controlled irony we have a kinetic narrative style which suspends rather than activates the reader's moral sense, and incites him to an imaginative collaboration in the orgy. Since I do not propose to quote from this particular scene here, I shall illustrate my point with a rather less offensive passage:

> Rock and Roll adolescent hoodlums storm the streets of all nations.
> They rush into the Louvre and throw acid in the Mona Lisa's face.
> They open zoos, insane asylums, prisons, burst water mains with air
> hammers, chop the floor out of passenger plane lavatories, shoot out
> lighthouses, file elevator cables to one thin wire, turn sewers into the
> water supply, throw sharks and sting rays, electric eels and candiru
> into swimming pools [. . .] in nautical costumes ram the *Queen Mary*
> full speed into New York Harbor, play chicken with passenger planes
> and busses, rush into hospitals in white coats carrying saws and axes
> and scalpels three feet long [. . .] .

This is vivid, inventive writing, but it is scarcely satire. There is a note of celebration here, a hilarious anarchism which relishes the mindless destruction it describes; and it extends to the most successfully drawn characters in the book, the brutal surgeon Benway and the inspired practical joker A.J. There *are* patches of effective satire in *The Naked Lunch* (notably a parody of conversation between some "good old boys" of the Deep South—"These city fellers come down here and burn a nigger and don't even settle up for the gasoline"), but the tone and structure of the whole will not support the serious moral significance that is claimed for it. Indeed, the account of the Nova Mob's subversive activities in *Nova Express* seems damagingly appropriate to *The Naked Lunch:* "We need a peg to hang evil full length. By God show them how ugly the ugliest pictures in the dark room can be. [. . .] Take orgasm noises sir and cut them in with torture and accident groans and screams sir and operating-room jokes sir and flicker sex and torture film right with it sir. . . ." Burroughs' reference to himself as an undercover agent of the Nova Police who wrote "a so-called pornographic novel" as a bait to lure the Nova Mob into the open seems an arch evasion of responsibility.

*Nova Express* itself is a much more "responsible" book, much more consistent with the avowed moral intentions of its author—and also much more boring. I find Burroughs more impressive (if no more congenial) as a nihilist than as a moralist, and the sick fantasies of the junkie more interesting than the portentous salvationism of the reclaimed addict. While it is good to know that Mr. Burroughs has been cured of addiction, his attempt to load this private experience with universal significance, equating morphine with evil and apomorphine with redemption, becomes tiresome. But what most makes for boredom in this novel is its technical experiment.

4

First, an example, taken from a chapter vulnerably entitled "Are These Experiments Necessary?":

> Saturday March 17th, 1962, Present Time of Knowledge—Scio is knowing and open food in The Homicide Act—Logos you got it?— Dia through noose— England spent the weekend with a bargain before release certificate is issued—Dogs must be carried reluctant to the center—It's a grand feeling—There's a lot ended—This condition is best expressed queen walks serenely down dollar process known as overwhelming—What we want is Watney's Woodbines and the Garden Of Delights—And what could you have?—What would you?—State of news?—Inquire on hospitals? what?

This seems to be a "cut-up" of English newspapers, advertisements, public notices, etc. One can identify the likely contexts from which the fragments were taken. But does their juxtaposition create any significant new meaning? I think not.

The comparisons which have been canvassed by Burroughs and his admirers between his method and the methods of Eliot and Joyce (Burroughs has described *The Waste Land* as "the first great cut-up collage," and a reviewer in the *New York Herald-Tribune* has likened *Nova Express* to *Finnegans Wake*) will not bear scrutiny. Compare:

> There I saw one I knew, and stopped him, crying: "Stetson!
> You who were with me in the ships at Mylae!
> "That corpse you planted last year in your garden,
> "Has it begun to sprout? Will it bloom this year?
> "Or has the sudden frost disturbed its bed?
> "Oh keep the Dog far hence, that's friend to men,
> "Or with his nails he'll dig it up again!
> You! hypocrite lecteur!—mon semblable—mon frère!"

> riverrun, past Eve and Adam's, from swerve of shore to bend of bay,
> brings us by a commodius vicus of recirculation back to Howth Castle
> and Environs.

What these passages have in common, and what is signally lacking in the Burroughs passage, is continuity. In the Eliot passage it is a thematic and dramatic continuity: the lines, incongruous, anachronistic, and inconsequential as they are, nevertheless all relate to the idea of the "Burial of the Dead" and communicate a very lively sense of the speaker's complex mood of surprise, impudence, admonition, and complicity. In the Joyce passage it is a narrative or descriptive continuity: we hold on tight to the lightning tour of Dublin's topography, while being dimly aware that it is also a tour of human history from Adam and Eve onward according to the cyclic theories of Vico. The more you read each passage the more you get out of it, and everything you get out of it thickens and confirms the sense of continuity and hence of meaning (for in the verbal medium meaning *is* continuity: discrete particulars are meaningless).

Burroughs has much less in common, both in precept and practice, with these modern classics, than with the art which Frank Kermode has dubbed "neo-modernism."[1] Extreme examples of neo-modernism are the tins of Campbell's soup which Andy Warhol signs and sells as *objets d'art,* or the piano piece *4' 33"* by composer John Cage, in which the performer sits before a closed piano in total silence and immobility for the prescribed time while the audience, in theory, becomes aesthetically aware of the noises around them, inside and outside the auditorium. Behind all these experiments is the principle of chance. Chance is allowed to determine the aesthetic product and the aesthetic experience; the artist confines himself to providing an aesthetic occasion within which the random particulars of our environment may be perceived with a new depth of awareness. As Kermode points out, "Artists have always known that there was an element of luck in good work ('grace' if you like) and that they rarely knew what they meant till they'd seen what they said"; but neo-modernism trusts, or tries to trust, completely to luck. Kermode's conclusion seems to me the right one; that neo-modernism, apart from its merely humorous intent and value, is involved in a logical contradiction, for when it succeeds it does so by creating an order of the kind which it seeks to deny. "Research into form is the true means of discovery, even when form is denied existence. So it becomes a real question whether it helps to introduce indeterminacy into the research."

This seems very relevant to Burroughs' experiments, about which he is characteristically equivocal. The cut-up or fold-in technique is clearly designed to introduce a radical element of chance into literary composition. You run two pages of text into one another and allow chance to produce new units of sense (or nonsense). Burroughs defends such experiments (in the *Paris Review* interview) by an appeal to experience. Thus, he describes how he was struck, during a train journey to St. Louis, by the congruence of his thoughts and what he saw outside the window:

> For example, a friend of mine has a loft apartment in New York. He said, "Every time we go out of the house and come back, if we leave the bathroom door open, there's a rat in the house." I look out of the window, there's Able Pest Control.

"Cut-ups," says Burroughs, "make explicit a psycho-sensory process that is going on all the time anyway." Precisely: that is why they are so uninteresting. We can all produce our own coincidences—we go to art for something more. One might guess that Joyce's discovery of a Vico Road in Dublin was a lucky break for him, a coincidence like Burroughs' observation of Able Pest Control (which reappears, incidentally, in a piece of imaginative writing, "St. Louis Return," published in the same issue of the *Paris Review*). But in the case of Joyce we are not aware of it *as* coincidence because it is incorporated into a verbal structure in which innumerable effects of a similar kind are created by means that are palpably not due to luck but to art. I do not mean to imply that we value works of literature solely in proportion to the conscious artifice we are able to impute to the process of composition (though this consideration always has some weight). Rather, that in the experience of successful literature we feel compelled to credit all its excitement and interest, whether this was produced by luck or not, to the creating mind behind it.

There is an essay by Paul Valéry, "The Course in Poetics: The First Lesson,"[2] which deals very profoundly with the difficult problem of indeterminacy in artistic creation. Valéry admits, indeed insists, that "every act of mind is always somehow accompanied by a certain more or less perceptible atmosphere of indetermination." But he goes on to point out that the finished artwork "is the outcome of a succession of inner changes which are as disordered as you please but which must necessarily be reconciled at the moment when the hand moves to write under one unique command, whether happy or not." As a romantic-symbolist, Valéry is prepared to grant the indeterminate a great deal of play—"the dispersion always threatening the mind contributes almost as importantly to the production of the work as concentration itself"—but the dispersion is a threat, concentration is essential. The cut-up method, by which the writer selects from random collocations of ready-made units of discourse, seems a lazy shortcut, a way of evading the difficult and demanding task of reducing to order the personally felt experience of disorder.

Fortunately Burroughs does not always practice what he preaches. Kermode remarks: "Admirers of William Burroughs' *Nova Express* admit that the randomness of the composition pays off only when the text looks as if it had been composed straightforwardly, with calculated inspiration." I would wager that the following passage *was* composed straightforwardly:

> "The Subliminal Kid" moved in and took over bars cafés and juke
> boxes of the world cities and installed radio transmitters and
> microphones in each bar so that the music and talk of any bar could
> be heard in all his bars and he had tape recorders in each bar that
> played and recorded at arbitrary intervals and his agents moved back
> and forth with portable tape recorders and brought back street sound
> and talk and music and poured it into his recorder array so he set
> waves and eddies and tornadoes of sound down all your streets and by
> the river of all language—Word dust drifted streets of broken music
> car horns and air hammers—The Word broken pounded twisted
> exploded in smoke—

Here it does not seem inappropriate to invoke Eliot and Joyce. There is continuity here—narrative, logical, syntactical, and thematic. The language is disordered to imitate disorder, but it is orderly enough to form a complex, unified impression. It is worth noting, too, that the meaning of the passage is a conservative and traditional one—a criticism of those forces in modern civilization that are mutilating and destroying words and The Word, and the values they embody and preserve. The passage thus contradicts Burroughs' protestations (see the *Paris Review* interview) that his experiments are designed to break down our "superstitious reverence for the word."

5

The function of the avant-garde is to win new freedom, new expressive possibilities, for the arts. But these things have to be *won,* have to be fought for; and the struggle is not merely with external canons of taste, but within the artist himself. To bend the existing conventions without breaking them—this is the strenuous and heroic calling of the experimental artist. To break them is too easy.

I believe this principle can be extended to cover not only formal conventions, but also the social conventions that govern the content of public discourse. From the Romantics onwards the revolutionary works have commonly affronted not only their audience's aesthetic standards, but also their moral standards. *Madame Bovary* and *Ulysses,* for example, shocked and dismayed the publics of their respective periods by mentioning the unmentionable. But these works gradually won acceptance because discriminating readers appreciated that their breaches of existing decorums were not lightly or irresponsibly made, and that their authors had substituted for received disciplines and controls, disciplines and controls of their own even more austere and demanding. Much of the work of today's avant-garde, including that of Burroughs, carries no such internal guarantee of integrity. Its freedom is stolen, not earned. The end product is hence startling and exciting on the first impression, but ultimately boring.

*Finnegans Wake* deliberately violates the conventions of language: it seeks to overthrow the law that we can only think and communicate lineally, one thing at a time. Most of us can manage the same trick—we can throw off a Joycean pun once in a while (I offer one free of charge to Mr. Burroughs: "fission chips"). But to produce hundreds and thousands of such puns, as Joyce does, and to weld them all into a complex whole—this is to create not destroy convention, and is a task of staggering difficulty. Similarly, most of us can compose a good obscene joke on occasion, or produce a powerful emotive effect by the use of obscene words; but to give these things authority as public discourse we have to ensure that they will survive the passing of the initial shock—we have not merely to violate, but to re-create the public sensibility, a task requiring precise imaginative control. One can't avoid the conclusion that a lot of Burroughs' most immediately effective writing (e.g., "A.J. the notorious Merchant of Sex, who scandalized international society when he appeared at the Duc du Ventre's ball as a walking penis covered by a huge condom emblazoned with the A.J. motto 'They Shall Not Pass' ") has the short-lived appeal of a witty obscenity; or, in its more grotesque and horrific forms ("Two Lesbian Agents with glazed faces of grafted penis flesh sat sipping spinal fluid through alabaster straws"), amounts to a reckless and self-defeating squandering of the powerful emotive forces that great literature handles with jealous care and economy.

## Notes

1. "Modernisms Again: Objects, Jokes and Art," *Encounter* 26 (1966): 65–74.
2. Reprinted in *The Creative Process,* ed. Brewster Ghiselin (New York: Mentor Books, 1955).

# 10

# The Algebra of Need

Theodore Solotaroff

T *he Ticket That Exploded* was written after *Naked Lunch* and as a sequel to it: "a mathematical extension of the Algebra of Need beyond the junk virus." It is only now being published in revised form in America, having been preceded by *The Nova Express* and *The Soft Machine*. If you have struggled through either of the latter, you are likely to find *The Ticket* to be more of the same "cut-up" account of the Nova Mob, the Nova Police, and the perversions of the future. Being an earlier version, however, as well as a less extreme experiment in pastiche, collage, and electronic writing, about which Burroughs has added a number of passages of commentary, *The Ticket* provides a somewhat clearer sense of what Burroughs is doing in this series of "blue" science fiction novels.

The basis of Burroughs' fiction from *Naked Lunch* forward has been his depiction of the endemic lusts of body and mind which prey on men, hook them, and turn them into beasts: the pushers as well as the pushed. His model of this condition is, of course, drug addiction: the junky being the creature of total need and hence of total vulnerability. He is controlled both biologically and socially—both by the insatiable demands of his body and by the ruthless economy of the drug market. As Burroughs puts it: "Junk is the ideal product . . . the ultimate merchandise. [. . .] The junk merchant does not sell his product to the consumer, he sells the consumer to his product. He does not improve and simplify his merchandise. He degrades and simplifies the client."

Burroughs' experience of this combination of physical and social control, through fifteen years in the cracks and gutters of society, has enabled him to envision a general state of being which, in earlier ages, was known and felt as Hell. In *Naked Lunch* he develops a series of brilliant improvisations, or "bits," in which the more fiendish tendencies that possess men and society are raised to the same power of "total need" as the drug addict's. In these sketches, impersonations, and fantasies, Burroughs acts out an inferno where everyone is turned on, each in his own way;

sex addicts, violence addicts, money addicts, power addicts, and so forth. The result is a species of gallows humor—obscene, ghastly, and timely—of bodily abuse and spiritual death.

Much of Burroughs' manner derives from the caustic mentality and idiom of the carny, the conman, the vaudeville hoofer. Though it wanders across continents, *Naked Lunch* is firmly rooted in the dark side of the American imagination, where the figure of the cracker-barrel hustler has had a complex and vivid career. Burroughs' rural sheriffs, county clerks, and doctors, for example, recall the frontier comedy of Twain, T. B. Thorpe, George Harris, among others. They produced a wild humor, raw and crafty, based on the bodily functions, deformations, and torments. Burroughs brings it up to date, thickens it with other idioms, but it is essentially the voice of the native American underground. There is Dr. Benway's tale of the carny ventriloquist, for example, who taught his bowels to talk:

> After a while the ass started talking on its own. He would go in without anything prepared and his ass would ad-lib and toss the gags back at him every time.
>
> Then it developed sort of teeth-like little raspy in-curving hooks and started eating. He thought this was cute at first and built an act around it, but the asshole would eat its way through his pants and start talking on the street, shouting out it wanted equal rights. It would get drunk, too, and have crying jags nobody loved it and it wanted to be kissed same as any other mouth. Finally it talked all the time day and night; you could hear him for blocks screaming at it to shut up, and beating it with his fist, and sticking candles up it, but nothing did any good and the asshole said to him: "It's you who will shut up in the end. Not me. Because we don't need you around here any more. I can talk and eat *and* shit."

This is also, of course, a brilliant fantasy of anality. Burroughs' grasp of the "Algebra of Need" and the power of his imagination often carry his comedy far into the buried recesses of the psyche. The only other contemporary artist I know of who has been able to spring repressions in this virtually total way and hold up for inspection the maniacal impulses on which all of us sit, some better than others, was Lenny Bruce. It is more than a coincidence that they were both drug addicts, both conversant with the far reaches of fantasy and with the baleful knowledge of how desperate and diabolical men are under the right conditions. Moreover, the addict's special view of the smug inhumanity of society—for example, the fact that some addictions such as nicotine and alcohol are national pastimes while others are criminal offenses— and his natural animus against the authorities and citizens who thrive within the society, provide an aggressive energy and razor edge to their insight. The fact that they are both comedians is also much to the point, for humor is a powerful instrument in mediating the incongruities of the psyche, in giving a structure and power to the dull gibberish that makes up most of the actual content inside our heads. Most of us have had the experience of striking a vein of comic fantasy that goes on and on, cuts deeper and deeper, knits up more and more threads of experience. Burroughs, like Bruce, has the gift, I'd say genius, to do so almost constantly.

Often in *Naked Lunch* Burroughs' imagination of depravity goes so far out that the human fades into the animal and the up-turned, crawling, horrific visions of the unfed junky come into view. Thus, at one point, he writes of "Mugwumps" and "Reptiles":

> Mugwumps have no liver and nourish themselves exclusively on
> sweets. Thin, purple-blue lips cover a razor-sharp beak of black bone
> with which they frequently tear each other to shreds in fights over
> clients. These creatures secrete an addicting fluid from their erect
> penises which prolongs life by slowing metabolism. [. . .] Addicts of
> Mugwump fluid are known as Reptiles. [. . .] A fan of green cartilage
> covered with hollow, erectile hairs through which the Reptiles absorb
> the fluid sprouts from behind each ear. The fans, which move from
> time to time touched by invisible currents, serve also some form of
> communication known only to Reptiles.

In his more recent books, Burroughs has been transmuting the addict vision more persistently in this way. *The Nova Express, The Soft Machine,* and now *The Ticket That Exploded,* all make use of the same futuristic locale as a framework for inventing surrealistic images of virulent life that obey the laws of the "Algebra of Need." For example, there are the "heavy metal" addicts from Uranus (junkies), the "flesh addicts" (homosexuals) from Venus, the hot Crabmen (police), and so forth. At the same time, the pushers, con artists, and other reprobates from *Naked Lunch* have been brought together as the Nova Mob which runs the planet by controlling the mass media—as well as the other channels of addiction—which they use to infect the citizenry with a "word virus" that sustains and exacerbates group conflicts. And in each novel, the Mob is defeated and disbanded by the Nova Police led by Inspector Lee (a reformed addict who is one of Burroughs' surrogates in *Naked Lunch*) along with underground partisans that attack and dismantle the word and image machinery of the "control addicts."

This fable and the commentary about it form a thin thread of continuity through what is becoming the virtually trackless landscape of Burroughs' imagination, which he presents in these books as a kind of dream movie going on in his mind. Just as this "film" is edited to conform to the associative, nonlogical imagery of dream, so the sound track is often "cut-up" and mixed together. Thus, his fantasies of the future often mingle with and dissolve into his memories of the past; monologues, dialogues, and commentary fade in and out; while certain figures and obsessive themes—masturbation and sodomy; hanging, mutilation, and cannibalism; parasitism and plasmic transformations; brainwashing and electronic consciousness, and so forth—loom up and fall away in the maze and haze of the language:

> Naked boy on association line—i stay near right now—be shifted
> harsh at this time of day—The levanto dances between mutual

> erections fading in hand—trails my Summer afternoons—[. . .] My
> number is K₉—I am a Biologic from frayed jacket sitting out in lawn
> chairs with the St. Louis suburb—not looking around—taking away—
> arab drum music in the suburban air—

Some of the sections, to be sure, are a good deal more clear and straightforward
than this; and some of the versions of "cut-up" such as the mingling of popular song
titles and lyrics in a hilarious and gruesome parody of sentimental *"love,"* are very
effective. Moreover, as one goes back over such passages, they become more
intelligible and at times beautiful. But though Burroughs has broken up the syntactical logic of English in order to renovate and heighten its expressiveness, and to
rescue it—and us—from the debased and insidious uses to which it is put—one
finds that the method often lands him in merely a different kind of banality. The
associations that invest the images with significance and tie them together in some
kind of meaning derive from habits of thought and feeling that Burroughs feels free
to indulge, and perhaps has to indulge to keep track of himself. Thus what is gained
in language is lost in content. The result is often arresting fragments of scenes,
characters, thoughts that never develop and merely repeat the same circuit of consciousness—a kind of brilliant merry-go-round of Burroughs' psyche.

Still Burroughs is such a good writer, his imagination works in such original as
well as compulsive ways that one can only reserve judgment about the eventual
outcome of these experiments. Moreover, for all of his acting out of impulse and
cutting up of phrases he is a deadly serious man. If he has one foot in the garish,
corrosive sensibility of the addict, the carny, the lower depths of show biz, the other
is anchored in a moral austerity that is almost Puritanical. However curious or
perverse it may seem, the writer he most reminds me of is T. S. Eliot, whose
language and themes pervade Burroughs' later work far more than those of any other
author and whose own experiments in pastiche and collage such as *The Waste Land*
are a major resource of the modern tradition which Burroughs is attempting to
extend. It is worth noting that both Burroughs and Eliot grew up in the Protestant,
genteel class in St. Louis. (In his essay "St. Louis Return," published in the *Paris
Review,* Burroughs recalls a friend whose mother had been to dancing school with
"Tommy Eliot," and he, characteristically, goes on to muse: "His socks wouldn't
stay up. His hands were clammy. I will show you fear in dancing school.") Both
writers carry in their bones that strain of Puritan refinement that characterized the
WASP elite in America and that often went hand-in-hand with the salty imagination
of the hinterland to produce a certain dry but charged temperament. For all of his
sordid, gray years as an addict, there is still in Burroughs a very visible core of the
aristocrat. Conrad Knickerbocker in his *Paris Review* interview with Burroughs—
a fine and indispensable one—describes him as follows:

> He wore a gray lightweight Brooks Brothers suit with vest, a blue-
> striped shirt from Gibraltar cut in the English style, and a deep blue
> tie with small white polka dots. His manner was [. . .] didactic or

forensic. He might have been a senior partner in a private bank [. . .].
A friend of the interviewer, spotting him across the lobby, thought he
was a British diplomat.

The description could serve for Eliot whose Anglican appearance became so complete in later life that one easily forgets how conversant he was with the wild side
of life in a work like "Sweeny Agonistes." In a way, Burroughs is a sort of Eliot
turned inside out: what Edmund Wilson sees as the buried "rascal," the canny
impersonator in the poet carried to the fore in the novelist, while Eliot's surface of
the man of spiritual austerity is driven deep into Burroughs' nature. But the vision
of the modern world as a wasteland, a gray, ugly soulless place where everything
is permitted, is finally the same. Here is a passage by Burroughs, taken from his St.
Louis essay and put in poetic form:

> Acres of rusting car bodies
> Streams crusted with yesterday's sewage
> American flag over an empty field
> Wilson Stomps Cars—City of Xenia Disposal
> South Hills, a vast rubbish heap
> Where are the people?
> What in the name of Christ goes on here?
> Church of Christ . . . crooked crosses in winter stubble.

I know that it seems odd to compare a writer to Lenny Bruce and T. S. Eliot in one
and the same review. But such are the extremes of experience from which the writing
of William Burroughs derives and draws its energies. He is one of the small group
of American novelists today who are both vital and complex, and though his last
three books seem to me to reach a brilliantly lit dead end they also possess the kind
of genuine innovation that keeps the novel alive and the literary enterprise going.

# 11

# William Burroughs
# and the Literature
# of Addiction

Frank D. McConnell

Then glozening decanters that reflect the street
Wear me in crescents on their bellies. Slow
Applause flows into liquid cynosures:
—I am conscripted to their shadows' glow.
      —Hart Crane, "The Wine Menagerie"

A lthough William Burroughs' *Naked Lunch* has existed as a book for nearly eight years, the best commentary on it is still slight enough to be contained as a preface to the Grove Press paperback edition: I mean the testimony of Norman Mailer and Allen Ginsberg given at the Boston obscenity trial in 1966. That testimony, at least, has the merit of restraint imposed by having to translate a living understanding of the book into the ludicrous terms of the Supreme Court's shibboleths for distinguishing "literary merit" from "obscenity"—the final test being whether "the material is *utterly* without redeeming social value." One has the strong feeling that both witnesses—especially Ginsberg—are "camping" to some extent, putting the court on by answering questions in precisely the sort of schoolmarmish, bad Arnoldian jargon the court obviously requires; and certainly one of the funniest moments in the trial is Ginsberg's reading of a poem on Burroughs' work from his own volume, *Reality Sandwiches,* followed by defense attorney Edward de Grazia's bathetic one-liner, *"No more questions."*

But camp or not, this testimony remains more useful than almost anything else that has been written about *Naked Lunch.* Even bad Arnoldian criticism is better than what has otherwise normally been done with the book, which is to convert it into either the sacred text or the abomination of desolation for the hippie generation, depending on one's age, education, social status, and opinions about drugs versus

Frank D. McConnell, "William Burroughs and the Literature of Addiction," *The Massachusetts Review* 8 (1967): 665–80. Copyright © 1967 by The Massachusetts Review, Inc. Reprinted by permission.

liquor as a relaxant. This is partly the fault of the government itself, of course, in forcing underground a book which, in the last analysis, does not belong there: the generation now reacting so viscerally to *Naked Lunch* is the same generation which only a few years ago was handing surreptitious copies of it around with other such high school delights as clandestine beer or pot and photocopied pornographic cartoons. Naturally this has imposed on the book an aroma which persists after it becomes suddenly "legal," and which determines its meaning as a newly public statement: not necessarily, however, an aroma inherent to *Naked Lunch* itself. Miss Susan Sontag (who is rather a more masculine Tom Wolfe in her espousal of the hippie style) has kind words for Burroughs in *Against Interpretation,* but they are the wrong words. To say that what we must grasp in *Naked Lunch* is "not the 'content,' but the principles of (and balance between) variety and redundancy" is simply to perpetuate the image of Burroughs as an ultimately debased Byron which has already done so much harm to the book and many of its readers. The leitmotif of our new youth may or may not be a euphoric celebration of no-content, but this is certainly not the message of *Naked Lunch,* which shouts from every page the horror of vacuity and the terrible necessity for the rebirth of will. Surely it is one of the most ironic perversions of a text in literary history that an author for whom capitalism is a stronger symbol of imaginative death than for anyone since Brecht should become the hero of a cult revelling in the repeatability of the mass-produced artifact, and have his picture immortalized in a pattern for "psychedelic" wallpaper.[1]

Even more disconcerting than the book's adulators, however, have been its detractors—for the most part older academic critics who should really know better. Accepting *Naked Lunch* along with *On the Road, V.,* and other contemporary novels into the syllabus of modern literature classes is scant recognition indeed, coupled as it usually is with the tacit assumption that Burroughs' book is primarily of sociological interest as a deranged apologia for the drug life—an assumption actually taken over from the wild youngsters, and transvalued by a pose less critical or intellectual than parental in the worst, Theobald Pontifex, sense of the word. The most surprising— and most articulate—expositor of this approach is none other than Leslie Fiedler, a critic to conjure with for almost any American novel written before 1955, but strangely homiletic after that date. In *Waiting for the End,* Fiedler devotes a whole chapter to Burroughs, and it is a disappointing moment in a brilliant career. Beginning with the premise that Burroughs, along with Kerouac, Ginsberg, and Norman O. Brown, is primarily a writer *for* adolescents—not simply one read widely *by* adolescents—Fiedler addresses himself not to the problems of the book itself, but to the pseudoproblems with which the adolescents have surrounded the book. The drug problem, according to Fiedler, is simply another permutation of the American myth of westering, out of which he has gotten so much mileage: a retreat into the last undiscovered territory, the inner space of the mind. And, he tells us, the dilemma from which Burroughs and his tribe of young junkies are fleeing is their love-hate relation to the affluent society, the knowledge that in seeking poverty they are seeking "a state costing someone (usually their absentee parents) . . . a sum equal to that demanded for fairly comfortable living in the years of the depression." These are the tones of a post-New Deal Lord Chesterfield, and they do not improve as the essay progresses: we are finally informed that Burroughs is näive in every conceivable respect, hardly a man any human family would want to acknowledge, and redeemed—if at all—by "only a stupidity monumental enough to be called holy."

*Waiting for the End* was written while *Naked Lunch* was still contraband, and one likes to assume that Fiedler read the book under unfavorable circumstances: the whole essay is very unlike him. At any rate, it is a misuse of the book. Granted that Burroughs' work is intimately related to what is rapidly becoming *the* social problem of the United States, and that the critic has perhaps less right than anyone to abdicate his involvement in such problems (Fiedler has always been a prime exemplar of this duty), there is little to be gained by also abdicating the prerogatives of criticism itself: and in this case that means allowing even a book as "in" as *Naked Lunch* to articulate its own values, which may not be the values of its enthusiasts. Of contemporary critics only Ihab Hassan in such essays as "The Novel of Outrage"[2] has managed to attain this necessary imaginative poise toward Burroughs' work.

We return, then, to the trial testimony of Mailer and Ginsberg, constrained—but refreshingly so—to evaluation rather than polemic. Both men have not only to defend the book, but prior to that, to prove to the court's satisfaction that *Naked Lunch is* a book. Mailer is at his most cogent when he answers de Grazia's questions about the putative "notes" Burroughs is supposed to have made during the most abject stages of his addiction, and which, runs the tale, Ginsberg later collected and edited into *Naked Lunch.* The question of these notes had apparently been brought up earlier by Assistant Attorney General Cowin in his prosecution of the book—and significantly, it is one raised by Fiedler in his very different prosecution of Burroughs. Mailer answers it in a lengthy defense of what used to be called "automatic writing"— the idea that "one's best writing seems to bear no relation to what one is thinking about." He goes on to testify to the strong sense of an underlying structure he has in reading *Naked Lunch,* and to its importance for him as a deeply religious book— "It is Hell precisely." The citation of the book's religious character is important, and we shall return to it later. But in the matter of the book's unity or lack of it— and the folklore that has grown up around the existence of "notes"—the more interesting testimony is given implicitly by Ginsberg, supposedly the *miglior fabbro* of its genesis. In answer to what must be the defense's first question, whether he has read the book entitled *Naked Lunch,* Ginsberg replies "Yes. [. . .] Yes, a number of times," and proceeds to an immensely useful explication of some of its "ideas having social importance" and of the political parties of Interzone, the mythic territory in which the bulk of *Naked Lunch* takes place. It is a tacit recognition of the autonomy of the book, precisely as *Burroughs'* book, and it should serve as an object lesson in reading *Naked Lunch.* Whether or not Ginsberg did collect and arrange snippets of Burroughs' writing, and whether or not, as Burroughs himself says, even the title of the book was suggested by Jack Kerouac and only later understood by the author, the book's unity is a function not of such information but of something at once more simple and more subtle than this: the final fact of its inclusion between covers or, in the most honest terms, its packaging. For we mistake *Naked Lunch* if we read it as anything other than one of our most packaged, consumer-oriented books, and therefore one of our most insidious: set like a depth charge within the inmost form of a cash-and-carry culture, an eminent prefabrication to subvert prefabricators and all their works.

This is something very different from the act of faith we make in the unity of allegory like, for example, Blake's or Swift's: in a radical way, *Naked Lunch* is a stern criticism of allegory. Burroughs is not concerned with objectifying the possible directions of the moral will. He is doing instead something that could not possibly have been done without the precondition of a full-flowered drug traffic: writing a book in which the only alternatives are absolute (and therefore dynamically formless) will or its absolute lack. The question whether Burroughs' talent has been helped or hurt by his long addiction is meaningless: his talent *is*, irreducibly, his addiction and his cure from it, at least at the time of writing the Introduction to *Naked Lunch*. That Introduction, indeed, is an essential and central part of the book, in spite of Grove Press' numbering its pages in lowercase Roman numerals. It is the act of retrospective packaging which gives the book its peculiar and brilliant satiric form, and the key to the basic economic theme in all its ramifications:

> Junk is the ideal product . . . the ultimate merchandise. No sales talk
> necessary. The client will crawl through a sewer and beg to buy. . . .
> The junk merchant does not sell his product to the consumer, he sells
> the consumer to his product. He does not improve and simplify his
> merchandise. He degrades and simplifies the client. He pays his staff
> in junk.

This is the meaning of the title, as Burroughs, always anxious to avoid any allegorizing, tells us: the naked lunch, where everyone really *sees* what is on the end of the fork, where there is no chance left for the allegorical or metaphoric translation (and avoidance) of the alternatives of will and not-will, because the packager-proprietor of *"Bill's Naked Lunch Room"*—has made a commitment to language which involves not less than everything. In a poetic system of this austerity, allegory is a capitulation, metaphor a final temptation to not-will. As Burroughs writes in his later *Nova Express*, "Since junk *is* image the effects of junk can easily be produced and concentrated in a sound and image track. . . ." The presiding genius of *Naked Lunch* is that most antimetaphoric of writers, the Ludwig Wittgenstein of the *Tractatus:*

> Ludwig Wittgenstein *Tractatus Logico-Philosophicus:* "If a proposition
> is NOT NECESSARY it is MEANINGLESS and approaching
> MEANING ZERO."

"And what is More UNNECESSARY than junk if You Don't Need it?"

The party of Interzone with which Burroughs obviously identifies, the Factualists, are the logical positivists of the imagination, dedicated to warfare against the Divisionists, Liquefactionists, and Senders, all of them concerned in some way with the translation of one thing or one person into another, by duplication, annihilation, and control (the Factualists become the Nova Police of the later book). This is why readings—some of them highly laudatory—of *Naked Lunch* which take the book as a relatively straightforward use of drug addiction as a *symbol* for all that is wrong with our society do it an injustice. There is no symbolization (past the sheerly verbal level of naming) at all in the book, and Burroughs would not want us to look for any. Junk *is* image, and therefore image *is* junk: the terrible purity of Burroughs' style will not allow us to extrapolate symbolic matrices because it will not allow terms for the problem other than its own. Any second series of correspondences would be, in the book's own terms, a retreat into image-junk and a final betrayal into addiction.

I am saying, of course, that Burroughs' book operates on probably the most severely minimal linguistic principle out of which poetry can be made at all, and that the critic approaching it is faced at the first turn with the book's internal hostility to the act of explication. After such knowledge, what action? *Naked Lunch* is, I think, undeniably a great book. And its greatness constitutes a very serious challenge to criticism—a perfectly just test of the relevance of its techniques not only to the present of literature but, in fact, to the past which is everywhere and always a function of that present. For in spite of the assertions of some theorists that criticism as a craft is normally ten years or so behind the avant-garde of literature itself, the only alternatives to a criticism able to cope intelligently and productively with what is most vital in the contemporary scene seem, in the last analysis, either the autistic examination of an *a priori* unavailable past or the politely sterile nonstatement of our Sunday Book Reviews.

The minimal poetry of *Naked Lunch* is not, in fact, without precedent. But the tradition to which it belongs, what I have called "the literature of addiction," is one whose importance for our imaginative heritage has never been fully articulated— could not have been, perhaps, before its stark incarnation in Burroughs' book. It is an approximate form and an approximate tradition, developing slowly and for the most part only in flashes in larger works: but it can be identified as primarily an English-American tradition of literature, and as definitively Romantic in its origins and its imaginative direction.

In the simplest terms, of course, the junky himself is an invention of the Romantic era. The disreputable, shabby, compulsive wanderer carrying his mysterious and holy wound is a figure first incarnated in the alcoholic Burns or in the mad Chatterton who so fascinated Wordsworth, and brought to a nearly final development in Coleridge himself, who really died an imaginative death in his addiction, to be reborn as "S.T.C.," defender of Christianity and architect of Victorianism. Burroughs' strange and disgusting characters called Sollubi are a permutation of this archetype:

> (The Sollubi are an untouchable caste in Arabia noted for their
> abject vileness. De luxe cafés are equipped with Sollubi who rim the
> guests while they eat—holes in the seating benches being provided for
> this purpose. Citizens who want to be utterly humiliated and
> degraded—so many people do, nowadays, hoping to jump the gun—
> offer themselves up for passive homosexual intercourse to an
> encampment of Sollubis. . . . Nothing like it, they tell me. . . . In
> fact, the Sollubi are subject to become wealthy and arrogant and lose
> their native vileness. What is origin of untouchable? Perhaps a fallen
> priest caste. In fact, untouchables perform a priestly function in taking
> on themselves all human vileness.)

It is only after the Romantics had taught us, with their strong radical Protestant bent, the impossiblity of a transubstantiation of things from *above*, that the negative eucharist of the outlaw and the sensualist became an aesthetic possibility. And the addict—the nature of the addiction, of course, being of no real importance—was the inevitable celebrant of the new mass, an absolute exile into the world of things in themselves. This is a reaction, finally, neither Byronic nor "Satanic" in the melodramatic sense of Mario Praz' *The Romantic Agony:* it is much closer to the resolute materialism which informs Shelley's finest poems, and to the emotional and intellectual ambivalence about addiction which runs through the first great drug-book, De Quincey's *Confessions of an English Opium-Eater*.

We must distinguish, however, between the literature of addiction proper and the vast number of works in which addiction and the addict serve simply as more or less serious type-cases of sensual exotica or social "problems" in the editorial writer's sense. Wilde's Dorian Gray in the last stages of his degradation feels "the hideous hunger for opium," but we note the fact only as another minor flourish in that masterpiece of titillation. Even less central to what I am talking about is the kind of treatment given addiction in a book like Nelson Algren's 1949 novel, *The Man with the Golden Arm*. That book, which was not as much debased by its movie version as some critics would like to believe, is finally a study in antiheroism in the hard-boiled vein for which addiction as an imaginative, phenomenological fact is of very little importance, as witness the purple prose describing the antihero's first "fix":

> It hit all right. It hit the heart like a runaway locomotive, it hit like a
> falling wall. Frankie's whole body lifted with that smashing surge, the
> very heart seemed to lift up-up-up—then rolled over and he slipped
> into a long warm bath with one long orgasmic sigh of relief.

Whatever the considerable merits of Algren's book, in its treatment of the drug life itself, it is not really much beyond the handling of the "dope fiends" who shuffle around the corners of Dashiell Hammett's mystery novels. In fact, Burroughs' own book, *Junky,* a tough-realistic novel written straightforwardly to make some money, belongs more in this class than in the tradition of Coleridge, De Quincey, Malcolm Lowry, and *Naked Lunch.*

What differentiates that tradition from other, more external treatments of the addict is not so much the element of autobiography in the works I have mentioned—although it certainly exists and is important—but rather the strong ambivalence toward the drug which is present from the real beginning of the tradition, the prefatory note to *Kubla Khan.* It is precisely this ambivalence which has proved so dangerous a component of *Naked Lunch,* leading many to suppose the book is really a defense of drugs rather than a work which transcends the poles of approval or disapproval of addiction. Those who are not addicted should really find *Naked Lunch* no less accessible than those who are—in fact, most of those who prize the book as secret cult-knowledge actually belong to a movement toward the nonaddictive hallucinogens and marijuana which has less to do with the imaginative energy of *Naked Lunch* than the "straight" attitude toward drugs. The "hallucinations" which make up the bulk of the book are not the futuristic and numinous visions reported by users of LSD, but are rather clarified visions of present reality made more terrible by what we have already described as the addict's absolute dependence on real *things* in their aspect of maximum power. Burroughs, in *Naked Lunch* and more blatantly in *The Soft Machine* and *Nova Express,* is a brilliant writer of science fiction (as, in a very different fashion, are John Barth in *Giles Goat-Boy,* Thomas Pynchon in *V.,* and Kurt Vonnegut in *Cat's Cradle*); and science fiction, as should be obvious by now, is the least futuristic of popular genres, attempting as it does a constant purification of the present through the neo-romance landscape of the future.

The ambivalence at the heart of the prefatory note to *Kubla Khan* is Coleridge's central ambivalence toward the Romantic epistemology: his refusal to accept both the full import of the autonomous imagination and, at the same time, the world of untransfigured phenomena. And so addiction and the drug become an aesthetic necessity for the poem: the sunny pleasure-dome, literally what the mind *can do* to the world of things, is transposed into the fictive past of an opium dream and labeled a "fragment." Kubla and the youth with flashing eyes and floating hair are both the new man of the non-numinous universe, and Coleridge fears them both with that orthodox side of his mind which cries "Beware," as much as he identifies with them with another part of his being. So the drug is not the cause of the vision as much as it is, for Coleridge, the inevitable result of vision at all: if the "person from Porlock" had not existed to interrupt the dream (which is probably the case), he would have had to be invented, just as fragmentation is not the actual state but the necessary and sufficient condition for presenting the poem.

Coleridge helps us see the drug life as only the latest permutation of our basic imaginative patrimony, the problem of the sublime, of the world as consumer commodity, and poetry as, literally, the packaging of experience. The expansion of consciousness, achieved with the aid of British sensational philosophy until the mid-nineteenth century and increasingly with the aid of pharmacology after that point, was a poetic difficulty long before it became a social one. But from its beginnings, almost, it was intimately bound up with drugs and with economics. Wordsworth, thinking about Coleridge (then abroad and trying to recover from his addiction) writes, in *Resolution and Independence:*

> But how can he expect that others should
> Build for him, sow for him, and at his call
> Love him, who for himself will take no heed at all?

And De Quincey, remembering the mysterious and celestial-seeming druggist who sold him his first tincture of opium, becomes fascinated by the economics of ecstasy:

> Here was the secret of happiness about which philosophers had
> disputed for so many ages, at once discovered; happiness might now
> be bought for a penny and carried in the waistcoast pocket; portable
> ecstasies might be had corked up in a pint bottle; and peace of mind
> could be sent down in gallons by the mail coach.

A century later, Malcolm Lowry says of his own addiction: "The real cause of alcoholism is the complete baffling sterility of existence as *sold* to you." And with Burroughs, what had begun as *an* aesthetic necessity becomes *the* necessary aesthetic, the addict is finally sold to the addiction, and *Naked Lunch* comes into being as an attempt to retranslate the "ultimate merchandise" of the chemical sublime into meaningful and thereby surmountable fact.

It is no surprise, then, to find at the heart of *Naked Lunch* Coleridge himself, in the guise of his most important creation, the Ancient Mariner: the first great Romantic junky, addicted to the natural world itself. The Professor's lecture on the Campus of Interzone University is perhaps the stylistic matrix of the whole book:

> . . . consider the Ancient Mariner without curare, lasso, bulbocapnine
> or straitjacket, albeit able to capture and hold a live audience. . . .
> What is his hurmp gimmick? He he he he . . . He does not, like so-
> called artists at this time, stop just *anybody* thereby inflicting unsent-
> for boredom and working random hardship. . . . He stops those who
> cannot choose but hear owing to already existing relation between The
> Mariner (however ancient) and the uh Wedding Guest. . . .

It is a remarkable parallel to the moment in that other great modern drug-book, *Under the Volcano,* where the Consul analyzes his alcoholism—and the movement of Lowry's entire novel—under the aspect of another Romantic quester, the poet in Shelley's *Alastor*. But the reference to Coleridge has if anything greater relevance than the invocation of Shelley. For just as the Ancient Mariner's compulsion arises from his never really finding the appropriate language for his experience, so that he must tell his tale again and again *ad infinitum, in exilio,* so the deliberate reduction of linguistic power we have noted in *Naked Lunch* is a desperate attempt to tell the tale truly once for all, and so be rid of it. *Naked Lunch* is, as Mailer implied at the trial, a religious confession: that is, it is not the journal of a cure, but *is* the cure from word-image-junk, a talking cure which makes a striking fictive anticipation of the method used by the organization called Synanon in rehabilitating addicts. The drug, as the option to total not-will, is totally demonic—so totally that possession as a term for it becomes pitifully inadequate. "'Possession' they call it," writes Burroughs toward the end of the book. "As if I was usually there but subject to goof now and again. . . . *Wrong! I am never here.* . . ." And the cure lies inevitably in possessing the demons—in exerting the narrative control which can describe them as "fragmentary," can place them in past time, and can finally achieve the point toward which the whole book moves, the absolutely denotative language of the Appendix, an article by Burroughs published in the *British Journal of Addiction.* The release is the book, the whole book, which without either Introduction or Appendix would be immeasurably crippled, dull, and "unpoetic" as those sections may be in themselves. "I am not," Burroughs writes, "an entertainer."

This is the context in which we must understand the 231 pages of "hallucination." Those hallucinations themselves, however, describe a general movement which is anything but fragmented. Roughly, the first 20 pages are a narrative, "realistic" in flashes, of the problems of obtaining junk and fighting off the police: then with increasing disjunction of narrative time and realistic detail, the story moves toward the central, long vision of "Interzone": the last 20 pages tend again toward "realism," ending with Burroughs' fantasy of killing the narcotics detectives Hauser and O'Brien, only to learn that they do not exist—"Far side of the world's mirror, moving into the past with Hauser and O'Brien." Bracketed between the diminishing realism of the induction and the growing realism of the denouement, the Interzone section is forced inevitably into the *fictive* shape of a withdrawal symptom—whatever Burroughs' actual state at the composition of the episodes. "Interzone" is precisely that—the world between human will and its negation: the point at which, in the absence of the drug, speech at all becomes possible, but correlatively, the point at which the drive toward resumed addiction is at its strongest. The induction ends with the death in Tangier of a girl addict; the denouement concludes with the narrator's first willed act, a killing, however illusive. Between these two deaths, the images of Interzone continually tend toward an allegorization of the drug life (which for Burroughs, the poet, would be, of course, readdiction), and are continually reduced to the antiallegorical, minimal visions which are perhaps the single greatest imaginative triumph of *Naked Lunch.*

Interzone is, in fact, a blasted idyll, where the will projects and then destroys its own suspension in a polysexual, universally addicted junky's reverie. And in this respect, the two episodes which account for by far the lion's share of "shock" in *Naked Lunch,* "Hassan's Rumpus Room" and "A.J.'s Annual Party," are both brilliantly managed and uproariously funny subversions of two of our most cherished myths of escape, "party time" and promiscuity—they are the nearest thing we have, in fact, to Petronius' epochal annihilation of the symposium in the Banquet of Trimalchio.

Angus Fletcher, in his superb study, *Allegory,* has indicated how intimately bound up is the allegorical method with the assumptions of primitive demonism. It is only another sign of Burroughs' masterful control of his work, then, that the intense demonisms of Interzone are so consistently thwarted in their movement to become allegories. The key point of control over this technique is Burroughs' revaluation of "possession" which I have already cited. The master addict is *never* there: the body is not a carrier of demonism, but itself demonic. Burroughs tells us that what the addict craves is the presence of an alien substance in his bloodstream, a possession carried to the ultimate metabolic level of physicality. And in *Nova Express* he develops this motif in one of his most striking correlations of image, junk, and what Whitehead called "the withness of the body":

> What scared you all into time? Into body? Into shit? I will tell you:
> *"the word."* Alien Word *"the." "The" word* of Alien Enemy
> imprisons *"thee"* in Time. In Body. In Shit. Prisoner, come out. The
> great skies are open. I Hassan i Sabbah *rub out the word forever.*

It is under the sign of corporeality itself seen as addictive that the intensely grotesque sexual episodes of Interzone are generated. The process, in fact, is almost Swiftian in its range, a reverse alchemy transmuting semen into excrement in much the same way *The Mechnical Operation of the Spirit* transmutes pneuma into flatulence. And here, too, the pervasive economic orientation of the book is operating. For it is no distortion of the text to see in it the basic economic equivalences of Jungian psychology, semen as an archetype of gold and divinity, and excrement as an archetype of money (nonvaluable currency) and infantilism.

Finally, my reading of *Naked Lunch* leads back, at this level of abstraction, to the Supreme Court's own terms for evaluation: for the last question we can ask about the book *is,* actually, one about its social value (the only substitute for bad Arnoldian criticism being, naturally, better Arnoldian criticism). In one of the finest critical aphorisms of this century, Leslie Fiedler has described America as "a world doomed to play out the imaginary childhood of Europe." It is only appropriate that the literature of addiction, European and Romantic in genesis, should find its fullest articulation in an American novel, just as it is inevitable that America should become the most addicted country in the West, and that only within the last half-century. And the "redeeming social value" of *Naked Lunch,* as a novel written within, and taking advantage of, the predispositions of addicted America, is not anything as simple as an antidrug temperance tract. The "soft flutes of Ramadan," prime image of temperance in Burroughs' work, are heard only at a distance and faintly, disappearing around the corner. For Burroughs, the will to health and cure is fundamentally the will to look directly and honestly at the terms of his exile, and the problem becomes one of revising our characteristic humanist myth, the archetype of the Central Man inherited from Emerson and Whitman.[3] The illusion that one has become God, achieved by Coleridge and De Quincey through the drug, is a basic datum of the American poetic experience, entering our tradition as the birthright of man himself rather than the gift of nature-*cum*-chemistry. It is the indelible achievement of

Burroughs to return this myth to its origins; to give the Whitmanian body which is a part of all that grows and moves its most somber articulation. *Naked Lunch* is the grim and absolutely honest testimony of one who has come back from the last reaches of the Romantic self, the completion, as it were, of one of F. Scott Fitzgerald's most important creations, the monumental alcoholic of "The Lost Decade" ("Jesus. . . . Drunk for ten years"). And miraculously it somehow manages to preserve the fundamental nobility of that vision of the self, even in its revulsion. Burroughs will tell us that it is our duty to will health, but he will also insist that we will it meaningfully, without regression to easy but exhausted versions of the spirit. And as our most seriously Whitmanian novelist, he fittingly gets perhaps his best reading from our most Whitmanian poet, Allen Ginsberg:

> A naked lunch is natural to us,
> we eat reality sandwiches.
> But allegories are so much lettuce.
> Don't hide the madness.

## Notes

1. See Richard and Gwyneth Cravens, "Underground Incorporated," *Mademoiselle* (Apr. 1967): 164.
2. Ihab Hassan, "The Novel of Outrage," *American Scholar* (1965): 239–53.
3. See Harold Bloom, "The Central Man," *Massachusetts Review* (1966): 23–42.

# 12

# Rub Out the Word

Tony Tanner

I t is the possibility of countertactics that has preoccupied Burroughs in his more recent work. He has become interested in methods of *deconditioning* and *decontrol*. In one sense the world of *Nova Express* (1964) is like the world of the earlier books, but there is a more positive appearance of a force attempting to counter the virus which is attacking man. The Nova Mob is made up of various criminals much like the liquefying, devouring, assimilating beasts of his earlier work. But there are also the Nova Police who are moving in on the criminals in order to arrest them. Good enough, one might think, except that when they are called in to rectify the dangerous situation caused by the criminals they are by no means reliable in their activities. In his *Paris Review* interview Burroughs made the point quite clearly: "you've got a bad situation in which the nova mob is about to blow up the planet. So the Heavy Metal Kid calls in the nova police. Once you get them in there, by God, they begin acting like any police. They're always an ambivalent agency. [. . .] For nova police, read technology, if you wish." He clearly concedes that his unique brand of science fiction contains an allegory. And there is a large amount of direct statement in the book. In fact it starts with a long letter full of explicit warnings and admonitions—including the familiar call to *"rub out the word forever."*

Where Burroughs achieves some of his most striking effects is in the merging of biology and contemporary communication media, just as he merges science and science fiction, nightmare and comic strip, carnival, satire, and sexual aberration. Word and image can penetrate us like a virus because, to take another of the cryptic lines from *The Exterminator,* "Only Live Animals have Write Door," and just as the virus literally empties the body and fills it with its own replicas, so word and image eat out consciousness, replacing mind with junk. In this book Burroughs has developed his use of metaphors drawn from film to amplify his vision. There are

---

Tony Tanner, "Rub Out the Word," *City of Words: American Fiction, 1950–1970* (New York: Harper and Row, 1971): 131–40. Copyright © 1971 by Tony Tanner. Reprinted by permission of Harper & Row, Publishers, Inc., and Jonathan Cape Ltd.

constant references to screen, scanning pattern, dark room, and related terms, which are explained by his own statement that, "Implicit in *Nova Express* is a theory that what we call reality is actually a movie. It's a film, what I call a biologic film." The idea is not new: Joyce for instance described modern reality as an "all nights newsery reel." But the way it feeds into Burroughs' overall concerns is effective and in particular it provides him with something specific to resist. It locates, metaphorically at least, the implementors of the virus conspiracy. "There is no true or 'real' reality— 'Reality' is simply a more or less constant scanning pattern—The scanning pattern we accept as 'reality' has been imposed by the controlling power on this planet, a power primarily oriented towards total control." The power remains anonymous; the word is a gesture towards all the manipulators who put out the false film of modern society. And one of the demands that Burroughs is making is for the restoration of an untouched, unsynthesized reality. The inhabitants of the City in his story no longer know what is film and what is not. To combat the manufacturers of the enslaving film we are taught to call reality, man has to develop immunity from the image virus and then attack the place where the film is made. Much of the action of the book, as far as it can be followed, is concerned with a concerted effort to invade the various centers where the alien powers process the kind of false reality with which they narcoticize and dominate the human race. "Storm The Reality Studio. And retake the universe." The recurring cry, "Break through in Grey Room," suggests the possibility that the dark room has been penetrated.

The need to "retake the universe" is made very urgent by the usual graphic images—the metal junkies, the scorpion men, the fish people, the prisoners being broken down into insect forms, the monster crab, the communal immersion tanks which "melt whole peoples into one concentrate,"[1] the Controllers, the Lemurs, the Mongolian Archers "with black metal flesh," as well as the mobsters themselves, all convey a vision of a world very nearly completely taken over already. But of course the trouble with metaphors and analogies is that it is not always easy to establish the terms of application. Is there literally an alien force from another planet taking us over? If not then we have to work out what forces on earth the metaphor applies to. The science-fiction plot and the idea of a virus eating out the independent life of a human host convey an authentic dread. But the potential limitation of such analogies is that as well as vivifying a process or phenomenon in another realm, they may simplify it. The malicious appropriation and exploitation of other people's vitality and individuality of mind and body is a major theme in American literature, for instance in the work of Henry James and Nathaniel Hawthorne, and arguably one learns more about the nature of manipulative evil from the studies of Roger Chillingworth and Gilbert Osmond (for example) than from Burroughs' intergalactic warfare.[2] However, what we do get is a ruthless vision of the ultimate implications of the tenets of our society. To say that the individual is "free" is dangerously untrue in a society in which so much is done to shape our tastes, appetites, and fantasies. Eric Mottram makes the point well when he remarks that Burroughs shows that, "Ultimate freedom means a society constructed of sadist and masochist relationships, fantasy living through pleasure-pain situations of inflicting and receiving. [. . .] The helplessness of the drug addict is the image of free enterprise and its effects." Writing at a moment when scientists have put men on the moon at the same time as they are cracking the code of life, one can find in Burroughs' fused analogies from disparate realms a disturbing relevance.

Burroughs himself has said that he is interested in suggesting a remedy and perhaps the clearest evidence of this comes in a later section entitled "One More Chance?" The question mark reveals the tentative nature of what follows. The notion that man is vulnerable to damaging instructions fed into him as on a tape recorder is countered with the idea that the tape can be wiped clean. Taking some terms from Scientology, a young man explains that in childhood or while unconscious the individual can be imprinted with engrams, words or impressions which store pain that may later be reactivated. This stored pain is called "basic" and basic can be wiped off the tape. "Oh sir *then* that person becomes what they call a *clear* sir." The terms are taken from L. Ron Hubbard, who founded Scientology, which is itself considered by many to be a piece of science fiction. Just how much of Hubbard Burroughs takes seriously it is impossible to say, although the rather effeminate overdeferential accents and "programmed" diction of the speaker suggest that Burroughs is not a true believer.[3]

On the other hand he does seem genuinely interested in the man's account of how they can process a person's responses by beaming words and images at him—"vary the tape sir . . . switch the tape sir . . ."—and the way of ending this subservient state is very much in line with Burroughs' own ideas. "Now all together *laugh laugh laugh* . . . Oh sir we *laugh* it right off the tape sir . . . We *forget* it right off the tape sir." The concluding words of this section—"Do you begin to see there is no patient there on the table?"—suggest a sort of release into invisibility explored in different ways by the other novels we have considered. It seems like a way of referring to that state of being finally "clear" which, whatever the merit of Scientological beliefs, is certainly an abiding American aspiration.

To escape from words into silence and from mud and metal into space is Burroughs' version of a well-established American dream of freedom from conditioning forces. It would perhaps be obtuse to ask what mode of life would be adopted in silent space. We are being given the morphology of an emotion as much as a literal prescription, when Burroughs exhorts us to shed all verbalizations and leave the body behind. But it may be pointed out that escaping into empty space would seem to entail leaving behind that genuinely real nature and that spontaneous free-moving individual life which Burroughs is so keen to protect and warn. Indeed from a remark in the interview it seems as though he is willing to consider changing the human form as we know it. "Mankind will have to undergo biologic alterations ultimately, if we are to survive at all. [. . .] We will simply have to use our intelligence to plan mutations, rather than letting them occur at random." In line with the ambiguity surrounding "randomness," which clearly has its dangers as well as its uses, there is a more problematical ambiguity over the need for "controlling" the individual, a phenomenon which his whole work is written to protest against. Whose intelligence is to plan the mutations? Supposing Dr. Benway is put in charge of biologic alterations!

The point is worth stressing because it draws attention to a basic problem posed by his work. Are the forces of evil and good somehow external to man in their origins? Can white magic (technology) counter black magic (entropy)? Do we need a superhuman doctor to ward off the threat of a superhuman virus? If so, what is the status of the merely human: is he a pawn of embattled demons (or cops and mobs), some benevolent, some malign? This schematization of forces is reminiscent of the old morality play (and Burroughs promises us a Western—which is the American version of the morality play). The morality play was often a graphic medium for showing the bemused situation of man, his vulnerability and plight; but it was, after all, the later dramatists who placed the contending forces deep inside the human individual, who gave us the more penetrating insights into the problems and mysteries of conscious life. It is ultimately harder to write about people than demons. It is easier to plot ways of combating a virus from another planet than to follow a character grappling with a dark impulse welling up from the depths of the individual self.

In terms of Burroughs' developing vision such observations may well seem positively archaic, for in *The Ticket That Exploded* (1967) there is a strong suggestion that the notion of the individual's identity may be another "gimmick" by which man is entrapped by the various virus powers which require fleshly hosts. Two juxtaposed quotations suggest one of the central propositions of the book: "Sex and pain *form* flesh identity"; "sex and pain price of a ticket." The ticket of admission into the exhibition or amusement park or garden of delights or cinema or vaudeville show or penny arcade or circus or game, which are some of the various images in the book for contemporary reality (turnstiles are constantly mentioned), is fleshly identity. This immediately involves one in sexuality and pain, which in turn render one helplessly vulnerable to parasitic takeover and control by all kinds of image-and-symbol systems. The only way out of this trap is to explode the ticket, which also can mean blowing up the fair. The ticket also incorporates the idea that we are all programmed by a prerecorded tape which is fed into the self like a virus punch-card so that the self is never free. We are simply the message typed onto the jelly of flesh by some biological typewriter referred to as the soft machine. To counter this there is a recurrent exhortation, "Why not take over ticket?" "Operation Rewrite" is one of the projects of the familiar Inspector Lee and one of the concerns of the book is to suggest how it might be possible to counter the controlling tape messages being fed into the self, by a special use of tape recorders as defensive machines. The book seems then to embrace two possibilities—the dissolving or exploding of the amusement park of pseudoreality put out by the familiar virus enemy which controls the media to which the state of "flesh identity" is so helplessly open and vulnerable; and also the attainment of the desirable state in which identity is erased and, let us say, "occluded" from the exhibition, a state which can only be reached by passing out of the turnstiles of the fair, getting out of the film.

Modern communications and sexuality are equated as forms of "vampirism." Devourers and parasites abound in the book—like the figure of "Genial," a voice who splices himself in with his lovers on a tape recorder. His words contain a subaudible directive to commit suicide and this way his victims always end their lives. He himself has no identity but is a virus, who may or may not be part of a carefully worked out blueprint for invasion of the planet. There is a good deal of reference to "copy planet," which neatly refers to the repetitive abilities of both literal viruses and the media images, whose intent to enter and discharge themselves in some suitable victim/host is paralleled by the aggressive penetrations and vampirisms of the sexual act. "There are no good relationships—There are no good words—I wrote silences." This is a succinct formulation of a defensive paranoia concerning all forms of communication which is discernible in a large number of recent American novels.

Somewhere at the heart of the book is a feeling that no genuine reality is accessible in present time: "There is no real thing—Maya—Maya—It's all show business." Images crowd in on all sides and from the past, predetermining the present and preempting it of its own reality. Whatever genuine life might appear is molded by old fabrications or sucked out by living corpses. The general atmosphere is a curious combination of desolate wasteland and fading film—reality is rotting or dissolving, a mixture of entropy and evaporation. There is a hint of apocalypse here: "I mean what kind of show is it after everything has been sucked out?" The parasite process has produced a "dead land" and the only solution seems to be to blow up all the existing structures which have been erected to seduce the pliant flesh identity. Burroughs describes modern civilization as a precarious iron city suspended over a void, a city of Ferris wheels and scenic railways as well as planes and cars all in constant motion. This is the whole circus of modern society which takes men in and empties them out. It can be resisted by turning its own weapons on it; camera guns and tape recorders vomit back the destructive input, attacking the source of all the control systems until all control symbols are pounded down to image dust: "The whole structure of reality went up in silent explosions under the whining sirens." This is the success of the combat troops. What people have taken to be reality proves to be a rotting film, a false cover which will disintegrate at a touch.

In Burroughs' view the majority welcome the protected unreality of the film in which they live; but as he sees it, the "reality film" has now become an instrument of monopoly. He notes that anyone who calls the film in question is subjected to punitive pressures by the filmmakers. The punishment the filmmakers threaten is to be forced to live *"outside the film,"* but Burroughs, or Inspector Lee, can see that "The film bank is empty." For those American writers who refuse to accept the fixed reality pictures, "outside the film" is exactly where they feel they want to be. This is why the end of the book once again constitutes a notional abdication from all scripts and structures—a quitting of the exhibition: "So the best minds coolly shut off a switch and went away down a tunnel of flash bulbs and last words [. . .] The Not There Kid was not *there*. Empty turnstile marks the spot—So disinterest yourself in my words. Disinterest yourself in anybody's words . ." This gesture of disengagement from the fouling entanglements of language is part of a larger goodbye to the sort of word-body identity which has been shown to be so vulnerable to assault in the shifting panorama of the book.

"Fading" is one of the most recurrent words in the book and phrases like "Identity fades in empty space" sound a constant leitmotiv. I find a deep, though provocative, ambiguity in the apparent attitude of the author toward the fading of identity. In one sense it is a manifestly desirable thing: it is the escape from the amusement park, the disengagement from the tape and the film versions which are everywhere advocated. In this sense it is analogous to Cabot Wright's escape from media definitions. On the other hand the constant references to the dissolving, disintegrating effects of the agents of decay indicate that they also secure a "fading," in the sense of a melting or sinking of identity. Reducing it to a crude formula it seems that it is a good thing to fade away from identity up into space, but a terrible fate to fade from it downwards into mud. There is, of course, no question of adopting another identity: "the offer of another image identity is always on virus terms." I think we can see again evidence of a profound ambivalence about the very basis of identity. It is manifestly dreadful to be "milked of identity" ("Face sucked into other apparatus"); on the other hand, the body itself (which is the indispensable condition of identity) is at times referred to as an old "overcoat" to be free of which is the highest bliss. In this context it is interesting to note that once again we have a scene connecting the act of vomiting with the experience of release: "Almost immediately i vomited so violently that my body seemed to crack open . . . and i was free of my body." It is also possible that Burroughs intends the suggestion that the sexual fusion to which the flesh identity seems bound to submit might of itself precipitate the fission which will explode all the tickets and release individuals back into air—like Prospero's actors, to whom the book refers.

There is no question of reshaping or reforming the existing molds—only of breaking them wide open to permit the escape and flight of those trapped within: "'So come out of those ugly molds and remember good is better than evil because its nicer to have around you. Its just as simple as that.'" One responds to the directness of the appeal, but it would be fair to make the reservation that the freedom beyond all forms and the goodness which is outside of definitions suggest a degree of disengagement, which, like the peace which passeth all understanding, presages a state approximating death. Since Burroughs is manifestly not writing as a direct advocate of suicide, it seems to be that once again we are confronted by an American writer seeking to establish some third realm—beyond the entrapments and degradations of form and flesh-identity, yet not totally reabsorbed into the unmolding void.

One of the ways in which the image-onslaught is to be resisted is by the tape recorder itself, an apparent paradox which is summed up in the resolution—"Communication must be made total. only way to stop it." The idea is: "Get it out of your head and into the machines." If life is a prerecording, then the one way of introducing a disturbing or fouling factor is to record that prerecording and then play it back, for that playback is the one thing that cannot be allowed for on the prerecording. The book ends by emphasizing the need for the demolition of the playback, which is the world we are subjected to. The strategy is that you record all the ugliness around and then with counterrecording and playback you gradually diminish its power. In a sense this points to a basic paradox in Burroughs' own work. For a writer who finds decay and disintegration so horrific he is unusually immersed in its extremest occasions, just as the interviewer saw the paradox of the writer fighting the word while buried in newspapers. But this is his method. The ugliness has to be recorded, then the recorder (author) can play with it at will, exerting *his* control over *it*. By constantly regurgitating all the foul material, replaying it at his tempo, with his splicings and "inchings," as it were, he is accelerating its disappearance: "the more you run the tapes through and cut them up the less power they will have    cut the prerecordings into air into thin air    ." And there, with no full stop, but the cleanness of a blank page to follow, Burroughs ends the book.

Something of the ambiguity in Burroughs' attitudes may be demonstrated by fragments suggesting the directions in which his recent work has been going. In the *Paris Review* interview he gave a lucid definition of the sort of work he now wants to write: "What I want to do is to learn to see more of what's out there, to look outside, to achieve as far as possible a complete awareness of surroundings. Beckett wants to go inward. First he was in a bottle and now he is in the mud. I am aimed in the other direction—outward." He describes his new, somewhat cumbersome, techniques—writing in three columns what he is doing, thinking, and reading; collecting vast amounts of local data; taking hundreds of random photographs of places. Sounding a different note from the cartoon horrors of his earlier work, this intent seems to hark back to a deliberate sort of inclusiveness of attention to his surroundings reminiscent of Sherwood Anderson or even Whitman. What is different is that much of what he opens out to is the detritus of modern city life. In a short piece called "St. Louis Return," published in the same issue of *Paris Review,* in which he writes about coming back to his birthplace after his years abroad, there is manifest almost a nostalgia, not exactly for the mud, but for the urban desolations of the American landscape. He walks contentedly around the town letting it all flow into his eyes, and his camera:

> "Ash pits—an alley—a rat in the sunlight— It's all here," I tapped my camera, "all the magic of past times like the song says right under your eyes back in your own back yard. Why are people bored? Because they can't see what is right under their eyes right in their own back yard. And why can't they see what is right under their eyes?— (Between the eye and the object falls the shadow)— And that shadow, B.J., is the pre-recorded word."

In just such a way Whitman wanted to sweep back the curtains of old literary styles which he said prevented a direct exposure to reality. Burroughs, with his camera and notebook, and his silent recombinations of fragments, is manifestly a more modern bard, but the underlying affinities are there. He is at least half in love with the tumbling material settings from which he elsewhere exhorts us to extricate ourselves. The end of this short and oddly lyrical piece reveals the author walking back through a setting as haunting as a painting by de Chirico: "back through the ruins of Market Street to the Union Station nudes waiting there in the dry fountain of an empty square—I have returned to pick up a few pieces of sunlight and shadow—silver paper in the wind—frayed sounds of a distant city." The tone is almost elegiac. It is a long way from the nightmares of that room in Tangier in which he himself experienced that going downwards into mud which he repudiates in Beckett but which is everywhere dramatized in his own diagnostic works. Burroughs now can walk through "the City" without being of it or trapped in it. One senses the liberation, and it is to be hoped that he will do some more extended writing on the American landscapes which he so thoroughly knows.

Another recent fragment, published in the *International Times* (August 31, 1967), is called "23 Skidoo Eristic Elite." It dramatizes yet another battle between the powers who control by sending out false images, and the powers who know how to resist and annihilate the image. It ends with the successful capture and destruction of all the tape recordings and films by which the Controlling Board have kept society cowering within a fixed and false fabrication of reality. At the end a vast tapeworm covered with newsprint twists its way out of a lot of microphones set up in the middle of the city square. The watching crowd cheers and tears the worm to pieces. This is their liberation, and the story ends with *"silence . . . et pas de commissions."* Compressed into this short piece are so many images and figures from his earlier work that it reveals that Burroughs has now created a vocabulary—diagnostic and therapeutic—which can engender a theoretically indefinite number of episodes or versions of conflict and victory. This is one of the things that produces that curiously abstract feeling in his prose even when the images are most vivid; one feels the presence of the schematic parable behind the dream images of science fiction, or the shorthand outlines of the strip cartoon. Scanning the apparently turbulent and broken surface one finds a persistent pattern of curious purity.

The end of the piece I have just described points to the underlying theme of all his important work—a dream of being freed from the conditioning forces, of seeing all the tickets explode, of retaking the reality studio. This liberation is envisaged as a liberation into space; at the same time, as demonstrated in such pieces as "St. Louis Return," it is a space from which a sort of total and impregnable perception of "what is really there" is made possible. We should perhaps think in terms of some inner space, remembering that Burroughs himself indicated that the most one could strive for was "inner freedom." This two-way movement—out into reality, up or back into space—is responsible for the strange and unique constitution of his writing which is both deeply immersed in the lowest forms of materiality and serenely withdrawn from them. Using his own term we can call it "sky writing," fading even at the moment of articulation, leaving us with an almost subliminal yet persistent message and dream—*pas de commissions*.

## Notes

1. Oddly enough Henry James referred to American society as the "terrible tank" in *The American Scene*, to make a not dissimilar point about its power to erase individual distinctions. Both terms are probably jokes at the expense of the Melting Pot.

2. Of course from one point of view, the energy and vitality of art lies in its ability to suggest new analogies. In his *Speculations* T. E. Hulme makes the point that there are no

ultimate principles on which all knowledge can be established: "But there are an infinity of analogues, which help us along, and give us a feeling of power over the chaos when we perceive them. The field is infinite and herein lies the chance for originality. Here there are some new things under the sun" (London: Routledge and Kegan Paul, 1960). In America it may be that the pressures are too great, the encompassing realities are too confused, too massed and mobile, to permit of any calm analysis or stable identification of what was behind this threat or that exploitation, or trace to their source the forces of dissolution and misappropriation. The need, then, for new analogues and allegories to give some feeling of "power over the chaos" may be particularly great. From this point of view, William Burroughs' highly original "demonizing" of reality is the most valuable contribution of his fiction.

3. He discusses his attitude to Scientology in interviews with Daniel Odier in *The Job* (New York: Grove, 1970), which appeared after the completion of this essay.

# 13

# He's just wild about writing

## Alfred Kazin

[Review of *The Wild Boys*]

W illiam S. Burroughs is a great autoeroticist—of writing, not sex. He gets astral kicks by composing in blocks, scenes, repetitive and identical memories galvanizing themselves into violent fantasies, the wild mixing of pictures, words, the echoes of popular speech. It is impossible to suspect him of any base erotic motives in his innumerable scenes of one adolescent boy servicing another like a piece of plumbing; nor should one expect a book from him different from his others. Burroughs is the purest writer in Barney Rosset's grove, and not just because in this book he more than ever turns his obsession with cold, callous homosexual coupling into a piece of American science fiction.

The fact is, he is mad about anything that he can get down on paper. He loves, literally, being engaged in the act of writing, filling up paper from the scene immediately present to him. Composition by field, as the Black Mountain poets used to say; plus composition by frenzy and delight, and in any direction. Words, horrid isolate words, those symbols of our enslavement, are replaced by the a-b-c of man's perception of simultaneous factors—the ability to drink up the "scanning pattern." Get it down when it is still hot, vibrant, and wild to your consciousness! The literary impulse is more demonic to Burroughs than sex was to Sade, but can be just as nonconductive to onlookers.

*The Wild Boys* is Burroughs' fifth or sixth or seventh book. The gang of totally sadistic homosexual young Snopeses who come into the book in the last third are not important except as a culmination of the continual fantasy of boys in rainbow-colored jockstraps coldly doffing them; nor are they important to the book. Nothing here is any more important than anything else, except possibly Burroughs' unusually tender memories of adolescent sex around the golf course and locker rooms in his native St. Louis in the 1920s. But the wild boys are apaches of freedom, and so are

Alfred Kazin, "He's just wild about writing" [review of *The Wild Boys*], *New York Times Book Review* (12 Dec. 1971): 4, 22. Copyright © 1971 by The New York Times Company. Reprinted by permission.

different from the "thought-control mob," the narcotics cops, and the despots of the communications monopolies who are the villains of Burroughs' other books—especially *Nova Express*. The wild boys in this book are a positive force for freedom: i.e., they have such an aversion to women (to Burroughs, women are the thought-control mob in infancy) that the boys continue the race by artificial insemination and thus, *Gott zu dank,* a "whole generation arose that had never seen a woman's face nor heard a woman's voice."

This book in texture is like Burroughs' other books—*Naked Lunch, The Soft Machine, Nova Express, The Ticket That Exploded,* and for all I know, *Skirts* and *Who Pushed Paula,* published under a pseudonym and which I have never seen. The book is essentially a reverie in which different items suddenly get animated with a marvelously unexpected profusion and disorder. Anything can get into it, lead its own life for a while, get swooshed around with everything else. Reading it does communicate Burroughs' excitement in composition and in the arbitrarily zany rearrangements that he calls "cut-ups." Actually, he is a cutup who writes in action-prose, kaleidoscopic shifts, spurts, eruptions, and hellzapoppins. But with all the simultaneous and cleverly farcical reversals, noises, revolver shots, sadomasochistic scenes on and off the high wire, the book is inescapably a reverie, the private Burroughs dream state. Whole scenes collide and steal up on each other and break away as if they were stars violently oscillating and exploding in the telescopic eyepiece of an astronomer who just happens to be gloriously soused.

Burroughs became an imaginative force in our self-indulgent literature of disaster with *Naked Lunch*. He was able to turn his addiction to morphine, to "junk," into a really amazing ability to scrutinize the contents of his restlessly bold, marvelously episodic imagination. His aversion to the hallucinogens (LSD and the like) is significant. He did not want to have *his* mind changed—Burroughs does not need inspiration! He wanted, in the tradition which is really his own, for he transcribes sexual fantasy into *literary* energy, to make the fullest possible inventory and rearrangement of all the stuff natural to him. He wanted to put his own mind on the internal screen that is his idea of a book.

More than anyone else I can think of in contemporary "fiction," he showed himself absolutely reckless in writing for his own satisfaction only. And yet he was so inventive, brilliant, funny in his many wild improvisations (he writes scenes as other people write adjectives, so that he is always inserting one scene into another, *turning* one scene into another), that one recognized a writer interested in nothing but his own mind. He was more crazily "dirty" than anyone else (ah, those hanged men having their last involuntary sex thrill) yet one could not put him down as another tiresome Sixth Avenue sex store between covers.

Burroughs from *Naked Lunch* on showed himself a man who had gone very far in his own life and had put just about everything into his system—to please his imagination. He was an addict from 30 to 45. He had an insatiable sort of mind; he was well educated, had a taste for slumming, yet had some marked resemblances to his brilliant grandfather Burroughs, who did not invent the adding machine but thought up the little gadget that kept it steady, and to his uncle Ivy Lee, the public-relations man for old John D. Rockefeller who helped to sweeten that fetid reputation.

Burroughs worked in advertising and, typically, as an exterminator. His travels in Latin America and North Africa show an unmistakably upper-class American taste for practicing discomfort (rather like Theodore Roosevelt proving that he was not a weakling). He has for all his flights into the ether a penetrating common sense about American racketeering, political despotism, police agencies, plus a real insight into how machines work and how the innumerable objects, stimuli, and drugs in contemporary life affect the organism. He has put himself to some ruthless tests, for he has the natural curiosity of a scientist, a fondness for setting up ordeals, and above all an inborn gift for subjecting himself to anything as an experiment. "Experiment" is indeed the great thing in and behind all his work. He is the subject; he is the performing surgeon; he is the paper on which the different stages of the operation are described; he is the result.

Burroughs is indeed a serious man and a considerable writer. But his books are not really books, they are compositions that astonish, then pall. They are subjective experiences brought into the world for the hell of it and by the excitement of whatever happens to be present to Burroughs' consciousness when he writes. There is an infatuation with the storeroom of his own mind that represents a strange lapse somewhere, for Burroughs is smart, perky, courageous, but seems inextricably wired into his adolescence. He believes so screamingly in freedom for himself that one hesitates to admit how boring the wholly personal can be. The self, taken as nothing but itself, its memories, fantasies, random cruelties, is a depressive.

All stream of consciousness writing, in order to rise above the terrible fascination with itself, has to find something other than itself to love. Burroughs is mired in the excitement of writing. A book is something he doesn't really care about. He has invented an instant conduit from his mind to a TV screen before which he sits in perfect self-love. There is no end in sight; hair will grow even in the grave. But what Burroughs has never realized is that a mind fascinated by itself alone is unconsciously lonely, therefore pessimistic.

Burroughs' whole aesthetic and his suspicion of every political idea are the same: let me alone! Even his endlessly fascinated, obsessive recall of homosexual intercourse says—let me alone! There is no love making, no interest in love, not even much interest in the sensation of orgasm. The emphasis is on emission as the end product. The idea is to show in how many different scenes and with how many coldly selected partners one can do it. But repetition, that fatally boring element in Burroughs' "cut-ups," turns the coupling into an obsessive primal scene that never varies in its details. The technical arrangements never vary, but they are described with such unwearied relish that the "wild boys" and their sadistic knives, scissors, gougers, castrators, etc., etc., seem like the embroidery of a cruel dream, not wickedness.

Jean Genet is a hero to Burroughs, but Genet's masturbatory fantasies were undergone in prison, and were in the service of love. Genet is indeed an addict of love, which is why his novels and plays are crowded with people. Burroughs seems to me the victim of solitude. He expresses it in the coldness with which partners are dismissed: "The boy shoved the Dib's body away as if he were taking off a garment." The comic moments in *The Wild Boys* are not situations but jokes: "Bearded Yippies rush down a street with hammers breaking every window on both sides leave a wake of screaming burglar alarms strip off the beards, reverse collars and they are fifty clean priests throwing petrol bombs under every car WHOOSH a block goes up behind them."

No situation, no line, no joke, lasts very long with Burroughs. He once noted that morphine "produces a rush of pictures in the brain as if seen from a speeding train. The pictures are dim, jerky, grainy, like old film." And Burroughs does give the impression of reliving some private scene. Everything turns in on itself. Outside, the planets and constellations reel to prove that life has no meaning, that there is not and cannot be anything else but our own sacred consciousness. Everything outside is *hell*. But as if to prove that life in the United States does imitate art, I open up the *Sunday Times* at random and find an advertisement for the *Capitalist Reporter* that cries out: "Money! Opportunity Is All Around You! . . . American treasures are all around you—attic, church bazaar, house-wrecking yards, thrift shops, etc. Old bottles, obsolete fishing lures, prewar comics. . . . names and addresses of people who buy *everything,* from old mousetraps to dirigibles to *used electric chairs* [author's italics]."

# 14

# The end of the body
## *radical space*
## *in Burroughs*

### Cary Nelson

"I

t is a long trip," Burroughs writes in *The Ticket That Exploded*.[1] "We are the only riders. [. . .] Not that we love or even like each other. In fact murder is never out of my eyes when I look at him. And murder is never out of his eyes when he looks at me" (TX 1). The force of critical invective directed at Burroughs' novels since *Naked Lunch* suggests that the passage describes the reading experience as well. We may ignore both moral outrage and criticism that refuses to deal with Burroughs on his own terms, but we cannot ignore the genuine discomfort of readers trying to empathize. This suggests that frustration is written into the novels deliberately.

Burroughs frequently warns that our enthusiasm for his writing will be qualified, and our pleasure ambivalent: "I offer you nothing. I am not a politician" (I 100). "I am a recording instrument. . . . I do not presume to impose 'story' 'plot' 'continuity.' . . . In sofaras I succeed in *Direct* recording of certain areas of psychic process I may have limited function. . . . I am not an entertainer. . . ." (NL 221). While Burroughs' books do not always entertain, they produce considerable affective response; although deliberately disjunctive and nonlinear, their stylistic presence is unmistakable. Responding to moralistic criticism of his techniques, Burroughs offers methodological and formal constructs that should be obvious to any critic:

> People say to me, "Oh, this is all very good, but you got it by
> cutting up." I say that has nothing to do with it, how I got it. What is
> any writing but a cut-up? Somebody has to program the machine;

Cary Nelson, "The end of the body: radical space in Burroughs," *The Incarnate Word: Literature and Verbal Space* (Urbana: University of Illinois Press, 1973): 208–29. Copyright © 1973 by Trustees of the University of Illinois. Reprinted by permission.

somebody has to *do* the cutting up. Remember that I first made
selections. Out of hundreds of possible sentences that I might have
used, I chose one. (ART 30)
     When the reader reads page ten he is flashing forward in time to
page one hundred and back in time to page one. (CEN 7)

Burroughs states his intentions clearly, and we are encouraged to recognize that our
self-consciousness is generated by specific features of the text. Elevated to critical
judgment, frustration and rage are repressive or pathetic; as responses to the reading
experience, they may even be useful.

     Both Burroughs' more outrageous passages and a variety of explicit devices alert
us to our immediate perceptual situation: "I am reading a science fiction book called
*The Ticket That Exploded*." To support this naked image—the book at the end of
our perceptual fork—he suggests it is not the novel but our own situation which is
fictional: "The story is close enough to what is going on here so now and again I
make myself believe this ward room is just a scene in an old book far away and long
ago" (TX 5–6). Authorial intrusions physically interrupt the illusion of narrative:
"Mr. Burroughs presence on earth is all a joke" (NE 184). He teases the reader
outraged by his sexual extravagances: "My page deals so many tasty ways on the
bed" (SM 54). These techniques effectively challenge our normally continuous sense
of narrative time: "Shift tilt STOP the GOD film. Frame by frame take a good look
boys" (TX 4). In a recent pamphlet he proposes an alternative title, *"Right Where
You Are Sitting Now"* (APO 11), which echoes what he says in *Naked Lunch*: "There
is only one thing a writer can write about: *what is in front of his senses at the moment
of writing*" (NL 221). He also borrows methods now traditional in "objective" verse,
in which the page *does* what the text says:

>            The grey smoke drifted        the grey that stops
>     shift   cut   tangle   they   breathe   medium
>          the   word   cut   shift   patterns   words
>          cut   the   insect   tangle   cut   shift
>          that   coats   word   cut   breath   silence
>          shift   abdominal   cut   tangle   stop   word
>            holes. (NE 69)

The passage short-circuits the perceptual processes we bring to the novel. "The grey
smoke drifted" taunts us with conventional narrative, but the printed page stops our
forward motion. The word "breathe" draws our attention to the altered breath with
which we read this disjunctive passage. We become aware of the unconscious bodily
rhythms which support and sustain the flow of conventional language. Spread out,
the words are eaten away by the "holes" between them; we are drawn out of the
temporal rhythms of speech toward space.

     Engaged in the exact moment of intersection with the text, the reader quickly
discovers assault, seduction, and mimicry in his relation to the printed page: "he
called them and read every word it sometimes took him a full hour by a tidal river

in Mexico slow murder in his eyes maybe ten fifteen years later" (TX 1). Who but the determined critic, generating systems and fabricating historical continuities, fulfills the image of a reader murderously peering at a threatening text. The temptation to reassemble the novels in linear form, evident in all our critical conventions, performs a perfect inversion of Burroughs' writing. Burroughs tells us his novels can be entered anywhere, and he invites us to cut up and fold in our own material. Perhaps embarrassed by the prospect of piously rearranging the novels into narratives susceptible to explication, the critic searches instead for "content" and declarative statement: "One is constantly on the lookout for bits of shipwrecked meaning, searching for glimpses of significant images. One scans the field of words for hints of purposive intent."[2] Even his advocates fail to accept the novels as written: "Apart from the frivolous distractions of cut-ups, Mr. Burroughs, we are reading you loud and clear!"[3]

Such critical disengagement implies a decision to reject the reading experience, to disguise and obfuscate Burroughs' disruption of our humanitarian assumptions. The posture is familiar from critical response to Swift's work. Adverse reaction to the language and form of the novels, which occurs quite apart from an evaluation of their quality, is a defense against what they can *do* to us as human beings. Our uneasiness in confronting Burroughs' art has two sources. The first is an entirely justified suspicion that *Naked Lunch* may be read as a marriage manual, that Burroughs means to reveal the true violent content of our sexuality. The other, confirmed by his later novels, is a fear that Burroughs believes an act of murder is implicit in every human contact.[4]

Both dramas in the psychology of perception are literal rather than thematic—induced not by contact with Burroughs' ideas, but by the inescapable facts of the reading experience. His fantastic imagery of atomic sex and his revelations of unspeakable possession dismiss all questions of verisimilitude. It is the immediate, objective form of the novel—encountered moment by moment—which compresses the mushroom cloud into an emblem for the human head. Burroughs' radical style is designed "to *create* facts that will tend to open biologic potentials" (NE 145), to move us beyond the body toward infinite space. To participate we must first understand Burroughs' unique mythology: "In Naked Lunch The Soft Machine and Novia Express [. . .] i am mapping an imaginary universe. A dark universe of wounded galaxies and novia conspiracies" (I 99). "A new mythology is possible in the space age where we will again have heroes and villains with respect to intentions towards this planet" (CEN 7).

Burroughs' mythology begins in mock-Christian fashion, with the primal word preceding the proliferations of human language. In its original unity, the word occurs at both the beginning and the end of history, for "the end is the beginning born knowing" (TX 10). To his readers' discomfort, Burroughs does not take history on faith; he accepts it only as an antagonist, for "history is fiction" (NE 13). "What we call history is the history of the word. In the beginning of *that* history was the word" (TX 50).

The primary-terminal word is unknown and unspoken; it is antithetical to the circumlocutions of language. Bodiless and silent, the word exists at the opposite ends of history—beyond the limits of human perception: "You were not there for *The Beginning*. You will not be there for *The End*. . . . Your knowledge of what is going on can only be superficial and relative" (NL 220). Our ambivalent and terminal existence cannot enclose the whole of time. We are ignorant not only of history's ultimate form but also of the circumstances underlying the immediate moment. Knowing nothing of the larger theater of action, we cannot act freely in the present.

History—the näive perambulations of language—is bounded by a tautological word excluding all possibility of discourse. The theater of human action becomes the scene of endless talk. "Word is TWO that is the noxious human inter language recorded—And where you have TWO you have odor's and nationalism's word" (NE 98). Human language is the invisible primal word that reproduces itself in time. The word is audible only as a repetitive series of contradictions:

> So I am alone as always—You understand nova is where I am born
> in such pain no one else survives in one piece—Born again and again
> cross the wounded galaxies—I am alone but not what you call
> "lonely"—Loneliness is a product of dual mammalian structure—
> "Loneliness," "love," "friendship," all the rest of it—I am not two—I
> am *one*—But to maintain my state of oneness I need twoness in other
> life forms—Other must talk so that I can remain silent—If another
> becomes one then I am two—That makes two ones makes two and I
> am no longer one—Plenty of room in space you say?— But I am not
> one in space I am one in time—Metal time—Radioactive time—So of
> course I tried to keep you all out of space—That is the end of time—
> (NE 85)

Desperate to feed on the escalating energies of language, the word divided; forgetting their source, the two halves of the word began to interact in the endless combinations of language: "The Word is divided into units which be all in one piece and should be so taken, but the pieces can be had in any order being tied up back and forth, in and out fore and aft like an innaresting sex arrangement" (NL 229).

When the primal word divided in time, its interactions at once achieved the density of matter: "What scared you all into time? Into body? Into shit? I will tell you: *'the word.'* Alien Word *'the.'* *'The'* word of Alien Enemy imprisons *'thee'* in Time. In Body" (NE 12). Human bodies are the accumulated residue of speech. As it exists in time, "Word *is* flesh and word *is* two that is the human body is compacted of two organisms and where you have two you have word and word is flesh" (NE 84). "Your bodies I have written" (NE 139). "When we came out of the mud we had names" (SM 178). Language for Burroughs *is* flesh: "These colorless sheets are what flesh is made from—Becomes flesh when it has color and writing—That is Word And Image write the message that is you on colorless sheets determine all flesh" (NE 36). Language is an illusory dialectic which masks our essential and intolerable doubleness. It proliferates in the endless reproduction of male and female bodies, for flesh is the speech of time: "The human organism is literally consisting of two halves from the beginning word and all human sex is this unsanitary arrangement whereby two entities attempt to occupy the same three-dimensional coordinate points" (TX 52).

There are no mystical unions for Burroughs. Two organisms can occupy the same space only through an explosive fusion that is quite literally, not merely metaphysically, lethal. Like all human interaction, sex is a form of warfare—a series of outrageous violations which occur over and over again. History consequently proceeds in time through the sexual warfare of mutually dependent antagonisms. The word became flesh, permutating in hemispherical, double, warring dialectical forms. Conversing and intersecting, these forms now create history, which is the history of one word and its doubled fleshly variations. What we conceive as reality is merely "A God that failed, A God of conflict in two parts so created to keep a tired old show on the road" (CEN 8).

This complex mythology, where language articulates "planet based on 'the Word,' " that is, on separate flesh engaged in endless sexual conflict" (TX 52), informs every page of Burroughs' work. We know the word only in its double forms of sexual warfare. All identity is oppositional—a conversation, a polar antagonism. The antagonistic doubleness is reproduced on each level of perception. Whether talking, fighting, or making love, all relation merely disguises the narcotic metronome marking time in the human theater—" 'I love you I hate you' at supersonic alternating speed" (NE 180). In his pamphlet *Time,* a cut-up inflicted on "The Weekly Newsmagazine," Burroughs inserts into a story on China (" 'Communism is not love!' cried Mao Tse-tung. 'Communism is a hammer we use to destroy our enemies!' " [T 4]) a series of photographs illustrating proper Victorian etiquette for visiting a woman: "A man calls: The correct handshake, presenting cards, disposition of hat" (T 4). Both the news story and the international relations it reports become as ritualistic and formalized as the photographs. For the "enemy must remain alive exterminated" (T 9), thereby confirming "the necessity of a defense policy at once devious and unyielding firm and elastic so that [. . .] the free world is subject to burst out anywhere" (T 7). The human theater is finally an explosive planet—a double planet or a sphere with cleavage: "The war between the sexes split the planet into armed camps right down the middle line divides one thing from the other" (SM 157).

Rearranged in emotional terms, our tantalized flesh disguises our addiction to reversals of experience generated by verbal associations: "sex and pain words sir . . . vary the tape sir . . . switch the tape sir" (NE 181). As another contemporary author writes, "You are locked into your suffering and your pleasures are the seal."[5] The human body is condemned to time by what Burroughs repeatedly calls the "Orgasm-Death gimmick," the obsessively repeated exposure to extremes of ecstasy and annihilation. Our dreams present torture chambers juxtaposed with the "Garden of Delights" (G-O-D). It is an image of consciousness as an organic form—the brain as the body's eruption into awareness—a two-halved, mushroom-shaped explosion: "Dual mammalian structure—Hiroshima People" (NE 97–98). Our perceptions duplicate the male-female doubleness of our social and sexual roles, and our experience is a complementary alternation of pleasure and pain. Taut with desire and frustration, each single body is really a verbal illusion constructed over an amphibious-hermaph-roditic form. If we stop listening to the flesh language of time, the body is revealed as "two halves stuck together like a mold—That is, it consists of *two* organisms" (TX 159). "Watch what is covering the two halves with so-called human body—Flesh sheets on which is written: 'The spines rubbed and merged' " (TX 160). Tension along the "divide line" keeps the two halves in an alternating state of absolute warfare—a war of sex and pain. Our minds and bodies are ignorant vessels of the primal word bisected into time. Each seeming variation, each apparently new form or illusory synthesis, is nothing more than a trivial variation on the essential conflict, an extension of deception and disguise. The program of complete control, the unvarying life script of the human theater, has been written on flesh sheets by the inflexible authority of word and image: "listen to your present time tapes and you will begin to see who you are and what you are doing here   mix yesterday in with today and hear tomorrow your future rising out of old recordings   you are a programmed tape recorder set to record and play back" (TX 213).

Speech in the biologic theater follows a flesh script of control words with their immediate and repetitive image track. All speech methodically reproduces its atten-dant images, from the most abstract discourse to the preverbal noises that affirm the physical presence of our bodies. To speak is to participate in and augment the biologic theater of control, to preserve the warring polar forms of slave consciousness. All language occurs in association blocks, lethal patterns of image that establish generalized conflict on global and cellular levels. Articulated over centuries, these association blocks force speech into preprogrammed birth-death cycles. They pro-vide inflexible vessels for all illusory variation; they build biologic prisons for the double word incarnate.

"To speak," Burroughs warns us, "is to lie—To live is to collaborate" (NE 15). "The word is spliced in with the sound of your intestines and breathing with the beating of your heart" (TX 50). The word's control lines extend along the divide line of the body, hooked into erogenous zones maintained by sex words in the pleasure-pain syndrome. It simultaneously enforces association on stellar and molec-ular levels. "The word may once have been a healthy neural cell. It is now a parasitic organism that invades and damages the central nervous system" (TX 49). We live on the "word dust planet"; we perceive objects as images linked to conflicting verbal association blocks: "Earth and water stones and trees poured into him and spurted out broken pictures" (TX 93).

"All association tracks are obsessional" (TX 213). Even sex—the traditionally sacred zone of nonverbal experience—is merely controlled rearrangement of image matrices, which are blocks of verbal association: "he came in spasms of light—Silver writing burst in his brain" (NE 165). "The words dissolved—His body twisted in liquid fish spasms and emptied through his spurting penis" (NE 163). "The sex charge is usually controlled by sex words forming an electromagnetic pattern—[. . .] Flash from words to color on the association screen" (NE 169). "Larval erogenous face spurting out through orgasm" (TX 92). The word dust planet is the picture planet, the planet of "bring down word and image" (NE 81). Image, we may economize, is speech. Burroughs, who is even more economical, brutally reproduces the archetype of human encounter: "Talk, Face" (TX 92).

When character is frozen in such obsessive postures of addiction, Burroughs often unmasks an insect parasite hidden beneath the flesh script: "His smile was the most unattractive thing about him [. . .] it split his face open and something quite alien like a predatory mollusk looked out" (TX 2); "In his place of total darkness mouth and eyes are one organ that leaps forward to snap with transparent teeth" (NL 9). Creating a mythological landscape to support this vision, Burroughs extends the metaphor of predatory control across the galaxy, terminating in implacable alien wills. In the Crab Nebula, at once light-years away and immediately beneath the tentative translucence of reality, the Insect Men of Minraud write the flesh history of Earth on their irrevocable tablets of stone. Black beetles, scorpion men with "faces of transparent pink cartilage burning inside—stinger dripping the oven poison" (NE 79), and "red crustacean men with eyes like the white hot sky" (NE 78) surround the ultimate "Controller of the Crab Nebula on a slag heap of smouldering metal" (NE 79). The soulless planet of yellow plains and metal cities does not have "what they call 'emotion's oxygen' in the atmosphere" (NE 77). Requiring Earth's hysteric theater to maintain (by opposition) their alien geometric existence, "The Insect People Of Minraud formed an alliance with the Virus Power Of The Vegetable People to occupy planet earth" (NE 80). Addicted to our oxygen-fed flesh theater of alternating pain and pleasure, the Vegetable People absorb all human and animal experience. Meanwhile, the intractable thought patterns of Minraud control "whole galaxies thousand years ahead on the chess-board of virus screens and juxtaposition formulae" (NE 80). Behind even these alien dramatists, planet junkies manipulating the myriad egg clusters of the galaxy, lurks a radically detached and sentient density: "the ancient white planet of frozen gasses—a vast mineral consciousness near absolute zero thinking in slow formations of crystal" (TX 129).

Against this cosmic background of metallic insect lust, the human body is nothing more than a "soft machine" programmed to satisfy the absolute needs of its controllers—"Paralyzed Orgasm Addicts eaten alive by crab men with white hot eyes or languidly tortured in charades by The Green Boys of young crystal cruelty" (NE 159). *We* are the naked lunch that the universe feeds on; the "frozen moment" (NL xxxvii) is when we see ourselves and our neighbors at the end of every fork. We are all unwitting but slavish "Collaborators with Insect People with Vegetable People. With any people anywhere who offer you a body forever. To shit forever" (NE 12). "Our entire image could be contained within a grain of sand" (NE 57). Our lives are a flesh script written before birth on a soft typewriter. "Postulate a biologic film running from the beginning to the end, from zero to zero [. . .]— Nobody is permitted to leave the biologic theater which in this case is the human body" (NE 16).

As Burroughs' mythology progresses, his tired and violent kaleidoscopic theater becomes a circus of demoniac possession, a virus, an incompatible combination of complete dependence and polar opposition: "There were at least two parasites one sexual the other cerebral working together the way parasites will—That is the cerebral parasite kept you from wising up to the sexual parasite" (TX 144). With explicit social relevance, Burroughs describes the complementary dependence of "Rightness" and "Wrongness":

> The WhiteGodess pays her clean staff in "Rightness" the "White Junk." And naturally the dirtier the work they are called to do the more "Rightness" they need to stay clean. A burning down habit when you start feeding children to the screaming from Carthage to Hiroshima how much "White Junk you need to cover *that*????????
> . . . Now "Rightness" is of course a derivative of "wrongness" "Somebody else to be "wrong expected. After all burning slaves be "wrong." They need more and more slaves to be "wrong" so they can wring "White Junk" out of them: "hospitals" full of "mental cases" stacked up like cord wood. .cells of sick addicts yielding the white no smell of death clean decent "White Junk," millions of prisoners in the vast suburban concentration camps of American and Europe all feeding White Junk to the White Goddess. (APO 4)

The White Goddess is a disguised version of the cerebral parasite, a complex of abstract ideals dependent on mass suffering for her existence. She articulates her idealized and bloodless values by repressing alternative forms of consciousness.

"Rightness" and "Wrongness," identified with their human representatives, develop a symbiotic antagonism. But the opposing forms become continually more extreme. The power of the White Goddess, maintained only by the snowballing warfare of incompatible symbiotic beings, becomes increasingly volatile. Our own history provides an image of the apocalyptic resolution of opposites: "brains armed now with The Blazing Photo from Hiroshima and Nagasaki" (NE 79) commit lethal outrages on their own consciousness. "Incredible forms of total survival emerged clashed exploded [. . .] Desperate flesh [. . .] Transparent civilizations went out talking" (NE 71). "THIS IS WAR TO EXTERMINATION. FIGHT CELL BY CELL THROUGH BODIES AND MIND SCREENS OF THE EARTH" (NE 67).

As every consciousness attempts to supplant the universe, the doubtful structure of reality is suffused with shadowy, improbable life forms. In the human body, cell and planet are simultaneous, superimposed images of microcosmic and macrocosmic violation. Another version of the conflict also achieves its terminal identity in every instant of time: the interstellar war of the sexes is fought in cataclysmic intersections here and now and across the wounded galaxies. Hiroshima screw—atomic sex— "and some of them are consisting entirely of penis flesh and subject to blast jissom right out of their skull" (SM 25). "These bone wrenching spasms emptied me" (SM 21); "sex words exploded to empty space" (TX 88). "Shivering metal orgasms" "vaporized the words" (TX 62, 83). "The dreamer with dirty flesh strung together on scar impressions exploded" (TX 67). "The neon sun sinks in this sharp smell of carrion" (SM 41).

These violent confrontations have infinite variety, for the doubleness creates a self-perpetuating dialectic. But human history does not have time to catalog all the combinations. The doubled flesh of language exists in dependent relation to its progenitor. And the father will finally devour his children. The interacting forms of language escalate to the point of nova; the primal word is reborn in the apocalyptic death of speech. Outside history, the word maintains its unity by feeding on our agonized incarnation in time. Its bodiless and silent presence is addicted to our bodies' talk. But this parasitic word requires increasing doses of our history. The total theater of history is the planet, and the human body is its microcosm. As the level of violence increases, the difference between body and planet ("Globe is self you understand" [NE 177]) becomes functionally irrelevant. Cellular and global conflict are merely rearranged verbal matrices.

These unexpected shifts in perspective contribute to the sense of violation in each encounter. As Burroughs writes, with typically literal irony, "Gentle reader, the ugliness of that spectacle buggers description" (NL 39). Our shock is distinctly physical. Our most sacred biological illusions are threatened when we recognize the body as the residue of talk. The earth is a conglomerate of decaying bodies; talk is the true form of reproduction—reproduction that generates excrement. Speech, the rhythm of our addiction to time, is unveiled as a disguised form of defecation. But the discovery signals an end to talk. Matter, the verbal incarnation of space in time, explodes outward into the universe. Scatology becomes eschatology.

Outraged by the fusion of language and excrement, we purge ourselves of their common product, history—the history of a god of conflict. Writing of this satanic god of word and image, Burroughs describes its revelation in the inverted fusion of orgasm and death: "Gentle reader, we see God through our assholes in the flash bulb of orgasm" (NL 229). "We Are All Shit Eaters . . We Worship A Nameless Asshole . . " (E 25). In a famous incident in *Naked Lunch* a man is taken over by his asshole, which he has trained to talk: "the asshole said to him: 'It's you who will shut up in the end. Not me. Because we don't need you around here any more. I can talk and eat *and* shit' " (NL 132–33).

In the end of time, in the moment of death, we shall know we have been supplanted by our assholes. "In the beginning was the word and the word was bullshit" (TX 198). "Life on Earth originate and or implemented by garbage shit deposited by Space Travellers? . . The Shit wrote out the message that is you [. . .] 'SHIT' was Thee Beginning Word . . And the last word . . Rub out The Word" (E 25). Burroughs' mythology of our present reality begins and ends with the word, but the end is the beginning born knowing.

The whole of this mythology is initiated and fulfilled on every page of Burroughs' work—in each moment of intersection between reader and text. His novels attempt to free us from our present reality. His mythology is the set of assumptions that leads him to write and that makes his writing possible.

Most modern apocalyptic writing moves toward scenes of extreme visionary intensity, and commonly involves the reader in this gradual process. But Burroughs believes linear narrative necessarily defeats the radical potential of a visionary posture. Conventional narrative is an act of domestication, one that enables us to integrate revelation into our established associative channels. It offers the "White

Junk" fix for readers who cannot bear violence and outrage in discrete, total encounters. He pinpoints the lethal palliative of a continuous story: "Why all this waste
paper getting The People from one place to another? Perhaps to spare The Reader
stress of sudden space shifts and keep him Gentle? And so a ticket is bought, a taxi
called, a plane boarded" (NL 218). Burroughs has no interest in a journey he can
plan in advance. He is committed to the end of the world he mythologizes.

This complex of beliefs, perception, and private mythology creates virtually
insoluble problems for verbal communication. All language acts through control
imagery and follows associative channels. Burroughs' own language is equally
capable of taking over a novel and short-circuiting its radical possibilities: "I prefer
not to use *my own words,* I don't like *my own words* because my own words are
prerecorded *on my bare honestie and being dead doe stick and stinke in repetition*
. . . . my words are prerecorded for me as yours are prerecorded for you" (APO
16–17). Nevertheless, Burroughs says, there are degrees of complicity, and his
experiments in literature attempt to break the birth-death cycle enforced by conventional language. Turning the enemy's own weapons against him leads to neither
security nor complacency, but does offer a certain ironic satisfaction (a revolutionary
fifth-column consciousness). Although Burroughs engages in a self-defeating paradox—using a defective instrument for redemptive purposes—he chooses the only
conceivable solution. His assumptions deny us any satisfaction from minor changes
in the flesh script. Language is encouraged to destroy itself: "So he sounded the
words that end 'Word' " (NE 69).

As all of us know, human beings often deal violently with insoluble paradoxes.
Burroughs' cut-up methods extend this understanding to his own prose. As he writes
in *The Exterminator,* a manifesto for his method, "The Word Lines keep Thee In
Slots. . Cut the Word Lines with scissors or switch blade as preferred" (E 5). The
reader comes to realize the switchblade *is* preferred; Burroughs sees his writing as
redemptive violence. But he never conceives his novels as vessels of revelation;
they do not in any sense *contain* the texture of a new landscape. Nor does he wish
us to read his books over and over again in a religious ritual of symbolic annihilation.
The ideal reader would cease to exist in the same time continuum.

The mythology outlined above consequently may describe the universe in which
Burroughs' fiction is written, but it will not provide a handbook for experiencing the
novels as linear narratives. The novels are not in themselves vehicles of revelation,
and they do not, as *Leaves of Grass* and Norman O. Brown's *Love's Body* do, symbolically offer us the visionary body of their author. Burroughs instead continually rewrites
the same book to perfect an instrument of aggression.

As he writes, in a telegraphic prose designed to make its content an event, "CUT
UP AND SPRAY BACK of all minds is switch blade" (E 12). Human consciousness
is a primal act of aggression—the frustrated desire of the two halves of the word to
recombine—and Burroughs tries to infuse the conflict with maximum energy. Describing his fold-in method, he invokes his mythology in its essential context: "The proportion of half one text half the other is important corresponding as it does to the two halves
of the human organism" (TX 65). There is only one landscape in which the event can

occur: the reading (or writing) experience. All Burroughs' work tries to create a radical perceptual situation. When he invites us to fold in our own language, to enter the text at any point, he is not only proposing a specialized activity but also alerting us to what has been happening all the while. For we always randomize a novel's language, diffusing it in our own flesh. Though we carefully protect ourselves from the awareness, each sentence is truly a new entrance, a radical intersection of reader and text. Unlike other writers who share his assumptions, Burroughs does not wish us to reside or even to find temporary repose in a landscape of words.

The novels juxtapose the conflicting male-female human organisms, the double forms of the incarnate word. An absolute juxtaposition would create a miniature nova in the mind of the reader. The state of physical outrage—achieved by our intersection with the printed page—urges us to discover *now* the ultimate form of human history. If we can experience it now—in the conscious reading situation rather than in a self-righteous global war where we die in ignorance—the end of time need not be also the end of consciousness. The alternative apocalypse—already written on the flesh sheets of our bodies—will serve only the needs of our controllers.

Burroughs' fiction attempts to make *this* instant a spatial experience of all time, to make the present a radical implosion of the beginning and the end of time: " 'I was it will be it is? No. It was and it will be if you stand still for it. The point where the past touches the future is right where you are sitting now on your dead time ass hatching virus negatives into present time into the picture reality of a picture planet. Get off your ass, boys. Get off the point' " (TX 196). I spoke earlier of Burroughs' tendency to write as though every human contact were an act of murder. The intent of his style in *Nova Express, The Soft Machine,* and *The Ticket That Exploded* is to make these murders a necessary and inevitable function of the reading experience. Each phrase in the later novels replaces and destroys all preceding phrases, arranging the novel in a new configuration. Each phrase, wholly possessing our attention, acts exclusively to occupy the whole of time in the space of the present.

Burroughs' novels occur in an instant bounded by the beginning and the end of time. The language progresses in an ontology of absolute juxtaposition, from zero to zero. Each communicating particle of language is equivalent to every other particle of language. Each phrase (or group of phrases) resonates in a cosmic vacuum and accumulates an exclusive mutuality of meaning. The form is repeatedly emptied, imploded, ravaged, or eclipsed by a slow fade. The biologic facts created are experiential facts of form and style—continual outrage, dismemberment, and violation. All perception, we discover, is a polar opposition in which perceiver and perceived are violently permutated through each other. What's folded in is you and me. "Everybody splice himself in with everybody else. Communication must be made total. only way to stop it" (TX 166).

For Burroughs, total communication becomes either grotesquely funny or grotesquely hideous—the nightmare of an angel wounded in its loins. His humor, which many readers will not acknowledge, exists in the same context as the horror: "it's knowing at any second your buddy may be took by the alien virus it's happened cruel idiot smile over the corn flakes . . You gasp and reach for a side arm looking after your own soul like a good Catholic . . too late . . your nerve centers are paralyzed by the dreaded Bor-Bor he has slipped into your Nescafé . . He's going to eat you slow and nasty . . " (TX 5). Burroughs' inescapable nightmare landscapes needn't be quoted. But amidst "screaming glass blizzards of enemy flak" (NE 67), Burroughs suddenly inserts a tranquil poetic language, so original and unexpected that it hints at the existence of another universe:

> Two Lesbian Agents with glazed faces of grafted penis flesh sat
> sipping spinal fluid through alabaster straws. (NE 68)

> soft mendicant words falling like dead birds in the dark street (T 15)

> From an enormous distance he heard the golden hunting horns of the
> Aeons and he was free of a body traveling in the echoing shell of sound
> as herds of mystic animals galloped through dripping primeval forests,
> pursued by the silver hunters in chariots of bone and vine. (TX 86)

These passages of lyrical violence occur only in moments of ultimate confrontation. Duplicating the novel's juxtaposition of the two halves of the body, reader and text react at the limits of language. The cumulative effect, as "Pieces of murder fall slow as opal chips through glycerine" (NL 232), is to overload the flesh script. We can no longer process the novel through our association blocks. Its only relevance is to the naked moment of perception in which we read it. In this terminal landscape, where "one assumes that anyone close to him or her is there precisely to kill" (NE 104), where "every encounter quivers with electric suspicion" (NE 104), the intersection between the reader and the printed page enacts the end of language.

"Globe is self you understand," Burroughs writes, "until I die" (NE 109). His novels create a radical perceptual situation in which the reader can no longer maintain his sense of temporal continuity, in which the self we know does die. Internalizing Burroughs' language, the reader finds it incompatible with his own speech. Yet the novels have entered the reader's experience; their language now exists in his body. Attempting to exert his sense of personal continuity, the reader rejects this violated body in a primal act of self-assertion. But his own language now becomes inoperable, for the body controls the structure of his verbal identities.

As the word script is randomized, the body too dissolves: "no more word scripts, no more flesh scripts" (NE 186); "Every part of your translucent burning fire head shut off" (NE 173–74); "Legs and genitals lost outline careening through dream flesh" (NE 170). "So?" asks Burroughs. "What is word?—Maya—Maya—Illusion—Rub out the word and the image track goes with it" (TX 145). To stop the verbal processing of the environment, to annihilate language, is to witness our bodies dissolving into faded newsprint and randomized tape recordings. Reduced to its intolerably predatory archetype—"Talk, Face"—the flesh script unfolds, emptied of content: "'You and I fading' he said"; "his voice muffled as if I were seeing his face through words fraying breaking focus" (TX 191, 190). When we see through the crack in the double prison of control, the two biologic theaters, planet and body, come to an end: "'All out of time and into space. Come out of the time-word 'the' forever. Come out of the body word 'thee' forever. There is no thing to fear. There is no thing in space. There is no word to fear. There is no word in space' " (SM 162).

The self for Burroughs, like the planet, maintains its sense of historical continuity through the body's influence. Our bodies keep us imprisoned in time. "All out of time," he writes, "and into space." Burroughs perhaps uses more images of body life and internal physical processes than any other author, but his violent imagery does not make us at home in our bodies. His radical space destroys the self as a structure continuous in time by ravaging and irreversibly transforming our biologic existence. "The hope lies in the development of non-body experience and eventually getting away from the body itself, away from three-dimensional coordinates and concomitant animal reactions of fear and flight, which lead inevitably to tribal feuds and dissension" (ART 47). Burroughs rejoices in the end of the body. As inexplicable and intolerable as this statement will be to his readers, he literally intends the end of the human body as we know it.[6] He invokes a radical silence that follows the explosion of the body outward into space. Silence, for Burroughs, is unspeakable.

To his own vision of infinite space, Burroughs deliberately opposes the need to enclose radical experience in protective frames.[7] He himself prefers an image of the astronaut's vulnerable body about to explode into the universe. The "space-suits and masturbating rockets," traditional technological images of the human body, are for him overburdened containers of aggressive energy: "'All out of time and into space' [. . .] 'the naked astronaut.' And the idiot irresponsibles rush in with space-suits and masturbating rockets spatter the city with jissom" (SM 162).

The texture of Burroughs' vision, like the imagery that reaches toward it, suggests an infinite space in which any experience is immediately and wholly available. "Nothing Is True—Everything Is Permitted" (NE 157), but each encounter achieves its total form in an instant, and there is no guarantee it will be successful. "We are still quite definite and vulnerable organisms—Certainly being without a body conveyed no release from fear" (NE 103). The organism's experience is its total intersection with the present; it has no continuity in time. To achieve any possibility, we must be utterly open to it. "This means that the mediating life forms must simultaneously lay aside all defenses and all weapons" (NE 136).

We are left with a tentative image of "the naked astronaut free in space," who found "that he could move on his projected image from point to point—He was already accustomed to life without a body" (NE 103). The novels themselves do not contain that vision; they offer a violent encounter with a mock-Darwinian eschatology that Burroughs calls "the final ape of history." Simultaneously comical and demoniacal, the novels taunt us with an outrageous planetary self ecstatically exploding in space: "I still mushroom planet wide open for jolly" (NE 55).

## Notes

1. William S. Burroughs' works are abbreviated as follows and documented internally: APO—*APO–33 Bulletin: A Metabolic Regulator* (New York: Fuck You Press, 1965); ART—"The Art of Fiction," *Paris Review* 9:35 (1965); CEN—"Censorship," *Transatlantic Review* 11 (1962); E—*The Exterminator* (San Francisco: Auerhahn, 1960); I—"Introduction to Naked

Lunch The Soft Machine Novia Express," *Evergreen Review* (Jan.–Feb. 1962); NE—*Nova Express* (New York: Grove, 1964); NL—*Naked Lunch* (New York: Grove, 1962); SM—*The Soft Machine* (New York: Grove, 1966); T—*Time* (New York: 'C' Press, 1965); TX—*The Ticket That Exploded* (New York: Grove, 1967).

Burroughs considers typographical errors to be fortuitous accidents and preserves them; all curiosities of syntax, spelling, and punctuation in the quotations are his. In block quotations single quotation marks have been changed to double however. Ellipses in brackets indicate my omissions; all others are Burroughs'.

2. Tony Tanner, "The New Demonology," *Partisan Review* 33 (1966): 564.

3. Tanner, 565. Compare: "in the first part of this work, which is by far the most effective, the cut-up method is used cannily and sparingly. [. . .] In his later trilogy, however, Burroughs worked more wildly." Ihab Hassan, "The Subtracting Machine: The Work of William Burroughs," *Critique* 6 (1963): 10. Similarly, "if Burroughs rejected his relentless obsession with literature-by-chance he could quite possibly produce some excellent, effectively original writing again." Richard Kostelanetz, "From Nightmare to Serendipity: A Retrospective Look at William Burroughs," *Twentieth Century Literature* 11 (1965): 130.

4. Hassan, "The Subtracting Machine," 22, rationalizes this fear as a failure of love: "he offers less than the major writers of our century [. . .] not because his scope and knowledge are less than theirs, which is indubitably true, but because his love is also smaller. [. . .] and love is the energy of the soul, the will to life. . . ."

5. Leonard Cohen, *Songs of Leonard Cohen,* Columbia Records, 1967.

6. Burroughs believes the human organism can rapidly evolve beyond the need for its slavish fleshly structures; his vision is of consciousness freed from the flesh script, from the sound and image track we know as the human body. In addition to biologic changes induced by the reading situation, Burroughs dreams of rationally and scientifically planned human mutations: "Science eventually will be forced to establish courts of biologic mediation, because life forms are going to become more incompatible with the conditions of existence as man penetrates further into space. [. . .] We will simply have to use our intelligence to plan mutations, rather than letting them occur at random" (ART 46).

7. Like many of Burroughs' contemporaries, Marshall McLuhan finds hope in the possibility that the body can provide an effective frame for an immensely widened perceptual field: "The totally designed environment necessary to life in the space capsule draws attention to the fact that the astronaut makes the spaces that he needs and encounters. Beyond the environment of this planet there is no space in our planetary or 'container' sense. [. . .] the astronaut must have his own environment with him. [. . . .] Strong indications are given to the astronauts that objects, as well as people, create their own spaces. Outer space is not a frame any more than it is visualizable." Marshall McLuhan and Harley Parker, *Through the Vanishing Point* (New York: Harper & Row, 1968): 25. McLuhan suggests elsewhere that Burroughs wants "to turn the human body itself into an environment that includes the universe." "Notes on Burroughs," *Nation* (28 Dec. 1964): 517. McLuhan's phrase accurately describes Brown's *Love's Body* and perhaps Susan Sontag's novels, but Burroughs believes the body is already the vessel for a universe of birth and death. In his *Paris Review* interview, Burroughs answered McLuhan's description by suggesting an alternative to making the body an environment: "What I want to do is to learn to see more of what's out there, to look outside, to achieve as far as possible a complete awareness of surroundings. Beckett wants to go inward. First he was in a bottle and now he is in the mud. I am aimed in the other direction—outward" (ART 23).

# 15

# Listening to
# Burroughs' Voice

## Neal Oxenhandler

> The artist's privilege is to liberate himself from his
> personal obsessions by incorporating them into the fabric
> of life, by blending them so thoroughly with other
> objects that we too are forced to become aware of them,
> so that he is no longer alone, shut up with his anguish
> in a horrible tête-à-tête.
>
> —Claude-Edmonde Magny

> The "grumus merdae" (heap of feces) left behind by
> criminals upon the scene of their misdeeds seems to
> have both these meanings: contumely, and a regressive
> expression of making amends.
>
> —Sigmund Freud

William Burroughs' five major novels[1] overwhelm us with a chaos of metamorphosing shapes and forms which constantly destroy themselves and rise anew. The novels pulse and glow weirdly with hallucinating lights, they emit strange electronic hums and shrieks. The first impression is of a chaos in eruption, but slowly a sense of design emerges. Burroughs is a poet who knows something about language he can never forget, something about form that he can never eradicate. And he *tries*. He tries to wipe out order which appears in the chaos, tries to strangle his own voice. But there is something in the work itself which resists and defeats him. He *cannot* destroy the integrity of his work, even though he tries with maniac frenzy. He tries by disguising it as science fiction, as vaudeville, as travelogue; he forces us to wade through endless pages of gibberish where random accumulations of speech blend with dreams and fantasies that have the ring of

Neal Oxenhandler, "Listening to Burroughs' Voice," *Surfiction: Fiction Now . . . and Tomorrow*, ed. Raymond Federman (Chicago: Swallow Press, 1975): 181–201. Copyright © 1981 by Ohio University Press/Swallow Press. Reprinted by permission.

authentic experience. Constantly, he tries to keep us from learning the truth which he simultaneously *wants* us to know.

Burroughs' claim to originality as a novelist rests on the technique known as the fold in or cut in:

> Pages of text are cut and rearranged to form new combinations of word and image—In writing my last two novels, *Nova Express* and *The Ticket That Exploded,* i have used an extension of the cut up method i call "the fold in method"—A page of text—my own or some one elses—is folded down the middle and placed on another page— The composite text is then read across half one text and half the other—The fold in method extends to writing the flash back used in films, enabling the writer to move backwards and forwards on his time track—For example i take page one and fold it into page one hundred—I insert the resulting composite as page ten—When the reader reads page ten he is flashing forwards in time to page one hundred and back in time to page one—The deja vu phenomena can so be produced to order—(This method is of course used in music where we are continually moved backwards and forward on the time track by repetition and rearrangement of musical themes—
>
> In using the fold in method i edit delete and rearrange as in any other method of composition—I have frequently had the experience of writing some pages of straight narrative text which were then folded in with other pages and found that the fold ins were clearer and more comprehensible than the original texts—Perfectly clear narrative prose can be produced using the fold in method—Best results are usually obtained by placing pages dealing with similar subjects in juxtaposition—[2]

Burroughs never tells us *why* he uses the method, preferring to justify it by pointing out analogies with music and insisting that, after all, it doesn't make the work unintelligible. In this he is correct. Although the fold in method does throw irrelevances into the narrative stream, the fact that they return at regular intervals converts them into a kind of refrain. They become the steady bass chord (like an imbecile voice muttering inanities) that counterpoints the deeper rhythm.

Or rhythms. For there are many rhythms, many voices shouting, screaming, weeping, yearning, cursing, coughing in the junk-sick industrial dawn through Burroughs' polyphony. The reader listens as best he can, as long as he can bear it. Long enough at least to know that he is Burroughs' *hypocrite lecteur,* his *semblable,* his *frère,* that in this voice the dark side of our nature stands revealed. For Burroughs (who may not be a great social critic or satirist as some make him out to be) reports on the archetypal night of hell. It doesn't matter that this hell sometimes resembles "a kind of Midwestern, small-town, cracker-barrel, pratfall type of folklore, very much my own background";[3] it is still the *real* hell, the one Virgil, Dante, and Rimbaud visited.

This is not a personal world of tics or neurotic compulsions, it is more universal than that. Burroughs goes beyond the neurotic and individual to attain the universality of the madman's dream, the prophet's frenzy. There is a deep paradox in this, that in psychosis or delirium—a state in which the individual seems most cut off from others—there is often the expression of profoundly universal dreams, terrors, desires. And so, no matter how strange, Burroughs' voice speaks with a rhythm that we hear as familiar, as somehow *déjà vu*.

The fold in or splice in technique is an effort to destroy form (and despite the disclaimers it comes close to doing this in the later novels), but even more importantly, it is an effort to *conceal*. Burroughs, who seems to be telling us "everything" is the most secretive of persons. The ambivalence or bipolarity of his work first becomes apparent in the tension between the desire to hide and the desire to reveal. The fold in method hides, under an accompaniment of irrelevances, the dark truths that the other side of Burroughs wants to reveal.

Burroughs, for many years a drug addict, insists on the state of anomie and withdrawal produced by drugs. The addict in terminal state has need of no one and of nothing except junk: "I did absolutely nothing. I could look at the end of my shoe for eight hours. If a friend came to visit [. . .] I sat there not caring that he had entered my field of vision [. . .] and not caring when he walked out of it" (NL xli).[4]

If the addict withdraws from the external world, it is because he has no need of it, except as supplier of junk. Junk itself gives him everything he needs. Intoxication, according both to Burroughs and psychoanalytic authorities, becomes a sexual aim; the addict attains what Sandór Radó calls "pharmacotoxic orgasm."[5] Distinguished from genital orgasm, this is a state of "euphoria, stupefaction and exhilaration." In this form of "metaeroticism" the need for the genital apparatus disappears. With the genital primacy demolished, the pregenital organizations come into their own. In other words, there is regression to infantile stages of development. The fantasies of violence and perversion which are the substance of Burroughs' novels have the arbitrary power of visions released from the id-world. A purely aesthetic account of them would be inadequate; and yet, at the same time, a psychocritique must be severely circumscribed.

First, it must be clear that any judgments I make about the novels will touch Burroughs, the man, only obliquely. The data is not clinical but literary—hence incomplete, deceptive, arranged. We can only guess at the genesis of the strange emotional configurations that repeat themselves from book to book. But we can, through a discussion of repetitive scenes and symbols, show how they connect with each other, setting up a pattern of reciprocal relations, with a specific emotional charge and certain human implications. To attempt more than this would be to minimize the complexity of human personality and to ignore the specificity of the literary work.

\* \* \*

Burroughs' novels are like a movie screen on which flash repetitive images. These images compose a scene which is deeply sadomasochistic. The scene, characterized by magical role changes, in which now one character, now the other becomes the central figure, usually involves hanging with subsequent orgasm or anal intercourse, or both with variations. A complete reenactment of the scene can be read beginning on p. 96 of *Naked Lunch*.

The scene begins with "Johnny impaled on Mark's cock." Mark is mocking and cool. Johnny reaches orgasm, here typically associated with vertigo and premonitions of death: "Johnny scream and whimper. . . . His face disintegrates as if melted from within. . . . Johnny scream like a mandrake, black out as his sperm spurt, slump against Mark's body an angel on the nod."

The scene then changes to another room, like a gymnasium, in which we are going to witness some sexual acrobatics. "Johnny is led in, hands tied, between Mary and Mark." Johnny sees a gallows which has been set up, and at the sight of it, reaches orgasm again. Now Mary and Mark push Johnny up to the gallows. Mary pulls Johnny off the gallows platform and has intercourse with him while he swings. The hanged boy reaches orgasm, Mark cuts him down, Mary then begins to cannibalize him: "She bites away Johnny's lips and nose and sucks out his eyes with a pop. . . . She tears off great hunks of cheek. . . . Now she lunches on his prick. . . ." At this point, Mark kicks her away from the corpse and attacks her. "He leaps on her, fucking her insanely . . . they roll from one end of the room to the other, pinwheel end-over-end and leap high in the air like great hooked fish." Now it is Mary's turn to be hanged. While she struggles, Mark pulls her brutally to the gallows, executes her, entering her at the same time. "He sticks his cock up her and waltzes around the platform and off into space swinging in a great arc. . . . 'Wheeeeee!' he screams, turning into Johnny. Her neck snaps. A great fluid wave undulates through her body. Johnny drops to the floor and stands poised and alert like a young animal."

Wilhelm Steckel, the great authority on sadomasochism, tells us that every sadist has a basic scene which is indefinitely repeated in his fantasy life. This scene reproduces, through displaced and disguised images, a period of the child's early existence when he experienced intense jealousy and hate. While some later writers on sadomasochism disagree, Steckel follows Freud in insisting that masochism is the obverse of sadism; that is, hostile feelings, originally directed against a person in the family environment, are introjected and turned back against the self. The basic scene may thus very well have both masochistic and sadistic components—this constant shift between the two neurotic solutions is, for Steckel, the chief source of the bipolarity typical of the sadist.

In these fantasies the Narrator may identify himself with the active or the passive figure in the fantasy, or with both.

Sadistic behavior originates both in the oral and the anal stages. In the oral stage, it is associated with the appearance of the milk teeth and aggression against the breast. In Burroughs' fiction we find a certain amount of orally-regressed imagery. Willy the Disk has a powerful sucking apparatus:

> If the cops weren't there to restrain him [ . . . ] he would suck the
> juice right out of every junky he ran down. (NL 7)

> The Sailor's face dissolved. His mouth undulated forward on a long
> tube and sucked in the black fuzz, vibrating in supersonic peristalsis
> disappeared in a silent, pink explosion. (NL 52)

The alternative to junk is alcohol:

> At first I started drinking at five in the afternoon. After a week, I
> started drinking at eight in the morning, stayed drunk all day and all
> night, and woke up drunk the next morning. (J 108)

Radó states that "the psychic manifestations of oral eroticism are always present
in a marked form even in those cases of drugmania in which the drug is not taken
by mouth at all. One received the impression that some mysterious bonds exist
between the oral zone and intoxication. . . ."

Orality and sucking imply a mother who supplies breast or bottle. For the junkie
this is the Connection. The Connection, however, is a mean refusing mother who
always makes the baby wait:

> Sometime you can see maybe fifty ratty-looking junkies squealing
> sick, running along behind a boy with a harmonica, and there is The
> Man on a cane seat throwing bread to the swans, a fat queen drag
> walking his Afghan hound through the East Fifties, an old wino
> pissing against an El post, a radical Jewish student giving out leaflets
> in Washington Square, a tree surgeon, an exterminator, an advertising
> fruit in Nedick's where he calls the counterman by his first name. The
> world network of junkies, tuned on a cord of rancid jissom, tying up
> in furnished rooms, shivering in the junk-sick morning. (NL 6)

Since the refusing mother is unconsciously remembered, she can take any form but
her own. In the following quote she appears as a man with strongly maternal
characteristics:

> So this man walks around in the places where he once exercised his
> obsolete and unthinkable trade. But he is unperturbed. His eyes are
> black with an insect's unthinking calm. He looks as if he nourished
> himself on honey and Levantine syrups that he sucks up through a
> proboscis [. . .]. Perhaps he stores something in his body—a
> substance to prolong life—of which he is periodically milked by his
> masters. He is as specialized as an insect, for the performing of some
> inconceivably vile function. (J 100)

Here, in the storing up of a vital substance which the junkie baby desperately needs,
is a transparent identification with the mother. Burroughs may even speak of himself
as a baby: "suddenly food needs of the kicking addict nursing his baby flesh" (NL
8).

But if the mother does feed her junkie baby, it may be poison. There are many references to junk cut with Saniflush: "Well, I guess one hand didn't know what the other was doing when I give him a jar of Saniflush by error . . ." (NL 173). Or food may be poisonous or repulsive: *"The Clear Camel Piss Soup with boiled Earth Worms* [. . .] *The After-Birth Suprême de Boeuf, cooked in drained crank case oil,"* etc. (NL 149).

Images of orality are few in number compared with the abundance of images from the anal stage of libido development. It is here that the regression seems to stop and attain a degree of stabilization. Freud associated sadism with anal eroticism and traced it to the child's resentment at being forced to give up the symbolic penis represented by the fecal mass. The delight in excrement and repulsive objects and the celebration of aggressive acts of anal intercourse appear as the emotional core of the novels. The following quotation is a finger exercise in mixing repellent motifs:

> "Stole an opium suppository out of my grandmother's ass."
> The hypochondriac lassoes the passer-by and administers a
> straightjacket and starts talking about his rotting septum: "An awful
> purulent discharge is subject to flow out . . . just wait till you see it."
> [. . .]
> "Feel that suppurated swelling in my groin where I got the
> lymphogranulomas. . . . And now I want you to palpate my internal
> haemorrhoids." (NL 41)

A variety of causes for the anal fixation may be posited, but since we are not in a therapeutic situation, it is difficult to speak genetically. The child may identify with the mother and wish to be anally penetrated by the father; this is the "negative oedipus" complex. Or he may identify with the pre-oedipal infant who is penetrated by bottle or feces. Or there may be memories of enemas or whippings which are masochistically revived. All we can know here is that we are in the presence of a pronounced anal fixation.

References to anal intercourse are numerous, explicit, pornographic. Various personae for the Narrator are on the receiving end—Johnny, Johnny Yen, Bill Lee, etc. Since one participant is always a boy, the act is heavily laden with narcissism. The narcissism can be taken as corroboration for the view that this is a pre-oedipal scene: mother feeding baby. The passive partner is the baby, the active the mother.

Often these boys are inhuman and reptilian:

> The green boy's penis, which was the same purple color as his gills,
> rose and vibrated into the heavy metal substance of the other—The
> two beings twisted free of human coordinates rectums merging in a
> rusty swamp smell— (TTTE 7)

Whenever sexual contact occurs there is the suggestion of something repellant, poisonous, or viscous—so the green boy moves in swirls of poisonous vapor. The sex act produces images of messing or smearing:

> Later the boy is sitting in a Waldorf with two colleagues dunking
> pound cake. "Most distasteful thing I ever stand still for," he says.
> "Some way he makes himself all soft like a blob of jelly and surround
> me so nasty. Then he gets wet all over like with green slime. So I
> guess he come to some kinda awful climax. . . . I come near wigging
> with that green stuff all over me, and he stink like a old rotten
> cantaloupe." (NL 16)

This fascination with smearing or dirtying is commonly associated with anal-sadistic regression and expresses less the impulse to dirty the object than the autoplastic desire to play with excrement. There is an undeniable playfulness and enjoyment in the imagining of filthy messes with which Burroughs entertains us. The psychoanalytic belief that the literary production may be associated with feces, the first "production" of our chronological lives, seems less absurd when we read Burroughs. It is not only the pleasure with which he revels in "dirty" subjects, but the very method he has hit upon (of chopping things up and shifting them about) seems to represent an aimless stirring or messing or playing around, delighted in for its own sake. Why indeed resort to a method of production that so threatens coherence both of meaning and emotional effect, if it were not gratifying, more gratifying indeed than the mere writing of a story?

Sometimes the smearing may spread from the anal region to absorb the entire body:

> When I closed my eyes I saw an Oriental face, the lips and nose eaten
> away by disease. The disease spread, melting the face into an
> amoeboid mass in which the eyes floated, dull crustacean eyes.
> Slowly, a new face formed around the eyes. A series of faces,
> hieroglyphs, distorted and leading to the final place where the human
> road ends, where the human form can no longer contain the crustacean
> horror that has grown inside it. (J 112)

Several other elements typical of the anally-regressed individual are apparent. These are traits of what Erich Fromm calls the necrophilious individual who is fascinated with corpses, killing, and death.[6] The scene in which Mary eats Johnny's face is only one of many examples. The necrophile is an anal type—he loves the dead mass of his own excrement which normally becomes repugnant and an object of shame. The necrophiles are cold, distant, remote—as are indeed the characters Burroughs creates. They are "driven by the desire to transform the organic into the inorganic, to approach life mechanically, as if all living persons were things." They are in addition "devotees of law and order." There is, throughout the novels, a constant preoccupation with law and order, especially of an authoritarian kind. Mary McCarthy has stated that Burroughs is a moralist. But the competing authority systems in his novels—the Nova Mobsters, Islam Inc., the Liquefactionist Party, the Factualists, the Divisionists, etc.—have no ideological content. They represent the tightening and compressing impulse, typical of the anal-sadistic type; or they may be defenses against guilt feelings; or efforts to control the sadomasochistic drives. Certainly they have nothing to do with any recognizable system of ethics which depends on a stable notion of human nature and behavior. Punishment there is however, enough to revenge all the crimes of the Marquis de Sade.

The anal-sadistic dumbshow occupies center stage in the novels, but for this very reason, were we trying to understand the author of the novels, we would search for deeper, repressed meanings against which the anal-sadistic regression is a defense. But they are not clearly evident, and it would be presumptuous to claim to know what lies *behind* the horrendous scenes we witness. There are, however, a few clues pointing to what lies even deeper than the anal-sadistic regression and, using the viewpoint of Edmund Bergler as an analytic tool, it is possible to speculate on some of these secondary implications.

The explicit role played by women in Burroughs' fantasies is very small, although they often appear in disguise. The Connection is only the first of these disguises. One explicit appearance is of the chopping or castrating woman. There are many references to vaginal teeth or the castrating vaginal grip:

> He was torn in two by a bull dike. Most terrific vaginal grip I ever
> experienced. She could cave in a lead pipe. It was one of her parlor
> tricks. (NL 91)

The flippant tone masks a terror that goes back to an infantile misapprehension. "It takes a long time," says Edmund Bergler, "before the young child perceives his mother as good, generous, and loving. Before this impression has been formed, the child builds up a 'septet of baby fears' in which the mother plays the role of a cruel witch. Fantastic as it may seem, the very young child considers himself the innocent victim of a wicked witch who is capable of starving, devouring, poisoning, and choking him, chopping him to pieces, and draining and castrating him."[7]

I think it likely that the giant crabs and centipedes who loom up and attack male victims are images of the enveloping or choking mother. She seems to press upon the infant like "the monster crab with hot claws" (NL 29). There is a whole zoology of such creatures in the novels, who might well be the infantile mother.

The infantile response to the giantess of the nursery is, first, the masochistic takeover of the terrors inflicted by her, so that they seem to stem from the self rather than an outside force. Passive suffering now becomes active suffering, and the child is well on his way to the masochistic use of pain. The writer frees himself from the pre-oedipal mother by becoming his own mother and feeding himself with words. This is illustrated by Burroughs who *invents* images of poison, suffocation, absorption, etc. Maintaining the self-sufficiency of the womb state, and at the same time transmuting passive reception of pain into active enjoyment of it, he feeds himself (and us) with poison words:

> The "Other Half" is the word. The "Other Half" is an organism. The
> presence of the "Other Half" a separate organism attached to your

nervous system on an air line of words can now be demonstrated
experimentally. [. . .] The word may once have been a healthy neural
cell. It is now a parasitic organism that invades and damages the
central nervous system. (TTTE 49)

If for "Other Half" we read "mother" and for "word" we read "milk," then this
curiously archaic passage duplicates the pre-oedipal situation described above: the
baby is attached to the poisoning mother and blames her for the damage (castration)
to his body.

Explicit attacks on women represent a defense against the masochistic desire to
submit and be overwhelmed by the infantile mother:

Mary the Lesbian Governess has slipped to the pub floor on a bloody
kotex . . . A three-hundred-pound fag tramples her to death with
pathetic whinnies. . . . (NL 127)

Two male homosexuals "know happiness for the first time" when
"Enters the powers of evil. . . ." a wealthy woman. Brad announces
that "Dinner is Lucy Bradshinkel's cunt saignant cooked in kotex
papillon. The boys eat happily looking into each other's eyes. Blood
runs down their chins." (NL 129–30)

The traumatic discovery of early childhood, so important for the development of
castration terror and the flight from women, is parodied in fag talk:

"Oh Gertie it's true. They've got a horrid gash instead of a thrilling
thing."
    "I can't face it."
    "Enough to turn a body to stone." (NL 150)

These episodes mean: I don't really want to be overwhelmed by mother. Look how
much I hate women! But, as in the typical homosexual pattern, the element of
psychic masochism remains the fundamental psychic fact.

The earliest response to the giantess is aggression in the form of breast-biting;
but there is little breast imagery in Burroughs. All interest in the breast has been
transferred to the male organ (which gives "milk" and can be sucked). This accounts
for the intense aggression directed at the penis:

Every night round about eight-thirty he goes over into that lot yonder
and pulls himself off with steel wool. . . . (NL 175)

Descent into penis flesh cut off by a group of them. [ . . . ] The boy
ejaculates blood over the flower floats. (SM 115)

> The penis canal was a jointed iron tube covered by sponge rubber—
> Pubic hairs of fine wire crackled with blue sparks—The dummy cocks
> rose in magnetic attraction of the wall symbols. [. . .] The dummy
> that was precisely *me* penetrated him with a slow magnetic
> movement—Tingling blue fire shot through his genitals transfixed by
> the magnetic revolving wall symbols—The vibrator switched on as the
> other watched—idiot lust drinking his jissom from screen eyes—
> Sucking cones of color that dissolved his penis in orgasms of light—
> (TTTE 76–77)

The third quote shows the connection between genitality and machines that appears throughout Burroughs' work. The machine adds an element of impersonal cruelty to the onanistic act. There are many other examples of cutting, chopping, breaking, or otherwise attacking the penis.

The role of masturbation is, not surprisingly, an important one. This happy event takes place in the Eden of childhood:

> Wooden cubicles around a hot spring . . . rubble of ruined walls in a
> grove of cottonwoods . . . the benches worn smooth as metal by a
> million masturbating boys. (NL 117)
>
> . . . his plan called for cinerama film sequences featuring the Garden
> of Delights shows all kinds of masturbation and self-abuse young boys
> need it special its all electric and very technical you sit down
> anywhere some sex wheel sidles up your ass or clamps onto your
> spine centers and the electronic gallows will just kill you on a
> conveyor belt [. . .] (TTTE 3)

Or masturbation may appear in symbolic disguise. Here the hand is obviously referred to under the circumlocution "Sex Skin":

> [. . .] I remember this one patrol had been liberating a river town and
> picked up the Sex Skin habit. This Sex Skin is a critter found in rivers
> here wraps all around you like a second skin eats you slow and good.
> (TTTE 4)

Masturbation, according to Freud, always has an incestuous as well as a masochistic component. Hence, it is accompanied by feelings of guilt and desire for punishment. One of the most unusual punishments devised in Burroughs' chamber of horrors is found in the passage where we see men changed into "penis urns":

> Carl walked a long row of living penis urns made from men whose
> penis has absorbed the body with vestigial arms and legs breathing
> through purple fungoid gills and dropping a slow metal excrement like
> melted solder [. . .] a vast warehouse of living penis urns slowly
> transmuting to smooth red terra cotta. (SM 112)

Obviously this is only poetic justice for the abuse of an organ—the organ takes over the functions of the entire body! This same form of punishment occurs in other passages, where it is the mouth that takes over, or even the anus. This seems to be a situation in which instinctual drives, related to one particular organ, emerge victorious from an internal conflict with the ego; this is a classic neurotic solution.

Perhaps now some pattern may be seen to emerge. First, I have insisted on the sadomasochistic flavor to many scenes. Suffering inflicted and received takes many forms, but seems to appear most often in the image of the hanged boy. In the sadomasochistic situation it is the explosion of affect that changes pain into pleasure. Hence, these death scenes are explosively written. The hanged boy's orgasm produces a spurt of pleasure that erases the element of pain. This intoxication of affect is a repetitive element in the novels. It produces a mixed reaction in the reader who reads about disagreeable incidents presented with relish and enjoyment; the same bafflement occurs when we encounter images of smearing and messing. The insistence on slimy, viscous, ectoplasmic contacts is a sign of anal regression dramatized more explicitly in scenes of anal intercourse. Most often enacted between two boys, this scene draws its emotional charge in part from the negative oedipus—the desire to be overwhelmed by the father. Yet since the protagonists are usually boys, it seems to insist on another, deeper component. This is a rehearsal of the nursing scene. The participants are nursing mother and nursed baby, penis being substituted for bottles and anus for mouth.

Finally, some clues suggest a mechanism described as "psychic masochism," different from the sexual masochism that demands acts of physical violence. This complex arises from the infantile misapprehension about the mother who appears as the "giantess of the nursery." Its identification is probably the most speculative or doubtful aspect of this analysis of Burroughs' works.

These various components form a field of emotional forces set up by the books' narrative flow, such as it is. Within this field there is a strong sense of polarization, a pulsing rhythm, a purposeful ambivalence which never relents and comes to be the central fact about Burroughs' novels.

We have already seen ambivalence in the duality of sadomasochism, a duality which resolves in the explosive fusion of affect which accompanies the sadomasochistic scene. Ambivalence also takes other forms in Burroughs' work. Early in *Naked Lunch* we meet a character whose physical shape is unstable or ambivalent:

> The physical changes were slow at first, then jumped forward in black
> klunks, falling through his slack tissue, washing away the human
> lines. . . . In his place of total darkness mouth and eyes are one organ
> that leaps forward to snap with transparent teeth . . . but no organ is
> constant as regards either function or position . . . sex organs sprout
> anywhere. . . . rectums open, defecate and close . . . the entire
> organism changes color and consistency in split-second adjustments.
> . . . (NL 9)

A more purposeful change takes place in the case of the man with the talking anus:

> After a while the ass started talking on its own. [. . .] Then it
> developed sort of teeth-like little raspy incurving hooks and started
> eating. He thought this was cute at first and built an act around it, but
> the asshole would eat its way through his pants and start talking on the
> street, shouting out it wanted equal rights. It would get drunk, too,
> and have crying jags nobody loved it and it wanted to be kissed same
> as any other mouth. [. . .] After that he began waking up in the
> morning with a transparent jelly like a tadpole's tail all over his
> mouth. [. . .] So finally his mouth sealed over, and the whole head
> would have amputated spontaneously—[. . .] except for the *eyes* you
> dig. That's one thing the asshole *couldn't* do was see. It needed the
> eyes. But nerve connections were blocked and infiltrated and atrophied
> so the brain couldn't give orders any more. It was trapped in the skull,
> sealed off. For a while you could see the silent, helpless suffering of
> the brain behind the eyes, then finally the brain must have died,
> because the eyes *went out,* and there was no more feeling in them than
> a crab's eyes on the end of a stalk. (NL 132–33)

This brilliant anecdote, which shows Burroughs' tremendous power of improvisation, actually illustrates the genetic development of the negative oedipus as defense against psychic masochism. There is, first, the struggle between the oral impulse and the anal impulse. The anal is seen as sadistic and searching for dominance which it eventually achieves. The face (the seat of orality) is sealed off by a wall of tissue, and finally "goes out," i.e., masochistic attachment to the giantess of the nursery becomes completely unconscious. The domination of anal eroticism then seems complete. However, this domination is only apparent. The buried oral material retains its power and reappears in the forms shown.

Another form of ambivalence is the male-female dualism. The hermaphrodites, the men who become women and vice versa, are probably representations of the couple as witnessed by the child in the primal scene:

> A penis rose out of the jock and dissolved in pink light back to a
> clitoris, balls retract into cunt with a fluid plop. Three times he did
> this to wild "Olés!" from the audience. (SM 73)

The fact that the scene is being witnessed suggests the spying child of the primal scene. There are many other examples of characters who change their sex:

> They say his prick didn't synchronize at all so he cut it off and made
> some kinda awful cunt between the two sides of him. (SM 78)

> The Commandante spread jelly over Carl's naked paralyzed body. The
> Commandante was molding a woman. Carl could feel his body
> draining into the woman mold. His genitals dissolving, tits swelling as
> the Commandante penetrated applying a few touches to face and
> hair— (SM 109)

Here, the psychic mechanism seems clear: it is submission to the father image (the Commandante) which transforms him into a woman (identification with mother).

The psychological tension is exteriorized—he images a war between the sexes:

> The war between the sexes split the planet into armed camps right
> down the middle line divides one thing from the other—[. . .] (SM
> 157)

But the battle is really inside the divided child, torn between two psychic "strata"—the oral stratum, with its submission to the mother; the anal stratum, with its submission to the father. To this there can be no solution except maturity, a solution Burroughs does not seem to envisage.

All writers are exhibitionists of their fantasy experience, Burroughs more so than most. Even when he puts us on and invents polymorphously perverse scenes out of Krafft-Ebing, he is making complicated demands on us. The demand to reject and revile him, the demand to accept him. Once again we return to the inherent ambivalence of Burroughs' psychic experience; if we can focus our attention on it, it will become clear that this is the source for the pulsing rhythm of his prose and the strange flickering alternation of his vision.

\* \* \*

Any appreciation of Burroughs has to answer the question: does he belong in a major literary tradition. I believe that the preceding analysis aligns Burroughs with novelists, such as Kafka and Beckett, whose major theme is ambivalence and indeterminacy. Like these writers Burroughs has created an aesthetic which permits him both to affirm and deny. His characters are simultaneously men and women, simultaneously masochistic and sadistic, simultaneously anal and oral, simultaneously dependent and autarchic, and so on. All psychic phenomena are overdetermined, that is, can never be traced to a single cause; and psychic mechanisms have a way of changing into their opposites, due to the censoring activity of the superego which forces them to assume disguises. The only kind of equilibrium to be found in the emotional world of such writers as Kafka, Beckett, and Burroughs is an equilibrium of alternation, in which emotional states constantly reform opposing patterns. Here the law of contradiction does not apply—an event may be itself yet not itself at the same time. Nothing can ever be affirmed once and for all; no stable emotion, no stable value can be established. The only law is that of flux, and flux is the essence of Burroughs' novelistic style.

Burroughs' use in his later novels of the fold in method contributes both to the indeterminacy of his work and to its basic two-cycle rhythm. Not only does it create a counterpoint or beat, but it produces junctures and discontinuities which are points at which the two-cycle rhythm can shift. Hence, a theme is always prevented from too-lengthy development by a break in continuity which carries the reader off on an opposite current. In this way the powerful ambivalencies of the work are maintained.

Burroughs' novels of ambivalence represent the first truly American contribution to this literature. But this is not all. Far more original than Albee, Burroughs is our only writer of the absurd. Some of his straw hat routines are as American as apple pie. In his wild meanderings across the world, the ubiquitous tourist stopping at American Express to change his traveler's checks into pounds or pesos or piastres so he can buy junk, Burroughs' picaresque hero is a wanderer more cynical and lost than Bellow's Hertzog or Augie March, and he sees deeper into the split psyche that has grown up in this country within sight of the suburban lawns and the progressive schools. Burroughs seems to absorb the environments through which he passes, and like some weird machine of his own invention, his voice modulates with a thousand accents and intonations, producing a style so much no-style that it is entirely his own.

No influence that has affected Burroughs seems to me as important as Rimbaud. Not just the Rimbaud who recounts for us his season in hell. Nor just the Rimbaud of the *Illuminations* whose brilliant discontinuous style Burroughs at his best sometimes attains to. I am thinking rather of the Narrator of "Bateau ivre" who, after his wild, hallucinating journey, suddenly grows tender and yearns for Europe and the contained world of childhood:

> If I desire European waters, it's the puddle
> Black and cold where toward the fragrant evening
> A child crouches full of sadness and sets free
> A paper boat that's frail as a butterfly in May.

There are many moments of such pathos in Burroughs too, moments when he remembers: "that stale summer dawn smell in the garage—vines twisting through steel—bare feet in dog's excrement" (SM 127). Or again: "One morning in April, I woke up a little sick. I lay there looking at shadows on the white plaster ceiling. I remembered a long time ago when I lay in bed beside my mother watching lights from the street move across the ceiling and down the walls. I felt the sharp nostalgia of train whistles, piano music down a city street, burning leaves" (J 107). No more than he has been able to destroy the form of his novels has he been able to destroy that pathos, that tenderness which in an unexpected moment will flash back at us from the page. Instead, just as with Rimbaud, we know that the work grows out of that moment of childish reverie. The work has its genesis there, and even the most violent and aggressive outbursts have something childlike about them.

Like many American writers searching for greatness, Burroughs does not have the stature of Kafka and Beckett, those prototypical writers of the Absurd. There is some intellectual deficiency in his work; and he does not carry as do these two, counterweight to his negating vision, the sense of what the tradition of the West means. There are other crippling limitations. Beckett and Kafka are controlled artists but Burroughs cannot escape—or allow us to escape—from the obsessive monotony of his hallucinations. But a great artist must affirm not only man's bondage but his freedom. Burroughs, returning from the Night with blistered oedipal eyes, crustacean eyes, tender adolescent eyes spewing hate and mistrust, eyes of a sick junkie coughing in the industrial dawn, is unable to free himself from the horror of what he has seen. Conrad's Kurtz died with the words "The horror! The horror!" on his lips; but Conrad threw himself into the hostile element and with his hands and feet kept himself up. Burroughs, carried off on that same tide, turns and shouts over his shoulder the excuse for every unimaginable act ever committed—"Wouldn't *you?*"

## Notes

1. *Junkie* (New York: Ace Books, 1953); the following published by Grove Press: *Naked Lunch* (1962); *Nova Express* (1964); *The Soft Machine* (1966); *The Ticket That Exploded* (1967).
2. *New American Story* (New York: Grove, 1965) 256–57.
3. William S. Burroughs, interview by Conrad Knickerbocker, *Paris Review* 36 (1965): 31.
4. Titles are abbreviated to initials throughout.
5. Sandór Radó, "The Psychic Effects of Intoxicants: an attempt to evolve a psychoanalytic theory of morbid cravings," *International Journal of Psychoanalysis* 7 (1926): 396–413.
6. Erich Fromm, *The Heart of Man* (New York: Harper, 1964) 40–41.
7. Edmund Bergler, M.D., *Homosexuality: Disease or Way of Life?* (New York: Collier, 1956) 36.

# 16

# The Broken Circuit

John Tytell

Society everywhere is in conspiracy against the manhood
of every one of its members.

—Ralph Waldo Emerson
"Self-Reliance"

J ack Kerouac, Allen Ginsberg, William Burroughs, and a group of other
writers, artists, and mavericks of inspiration like Neal Cassady, formed a
"movement" which began near the end of the Second World War, found its voice
during the fifties, and became especially influential in the sixties. Though the
movement lacked any shared platform such as the Imagist or Surrealist manifestoes,
it cohered as a literary group. While the work of one informed the approach and
style of another—in the way that Kerouac's prose line and aesthetic of spontaneity
affected Ginsberg's poetic—the mutuality among these men developed more as a
result of a mythic outlook on their own lives and interactions.

In 1952, Jack Kerouac listed the chief members of the movement in a letter to
Ginsberg, explaining that the crucial motivation for their union was the ability to
honestly confess each other their deepest feelings. Such open revelation of private
matters contradicted the spirit of the age, but led to aesthetic and intellectual
discoveries. The Beat movement was a crystallization of a sweeping discontent with
American "virtues" of progress and power. What began with an exploration of the
bowels and entrails of the city—criminality, drugs, mental hospitals—evolved into
an expression of the visionary sensibility. The romantic militancy of the Beats found
its roots in American transcendentalism. Their spiritual ancestors were men like
Thoreau with his aggressive idealism, his essentially conservative distrust of machines and industry, his desire to return to the origins of man's relations to the land;
or Melville, with his adventurous tolerance of different tribal codes; or Whitman,
optimistically proclaiming with egalitarian gusto the raw newness and velocity of

John Tytell, "The Broken Circuit," *Naked Angels: The Lives and Literature of the Beat
Generation* (New York: McGraw-Hill, 1976): 3–15. Copyright © 1976 by John Tytell.
Reprinted by permission of the author and by permission of Grove Press, a division of
Wheatland Corporation, and by permission of Berenice Hoffman Literary Agency.

self-renewing change in America while joyously admiring the potential of the common man.

Beginning in despair, the Beat vision was elevated through the shocks of experience to a realization of what was most perilous about American life. One of the images that best captures the motivating energy of this search is the nakedness that was expressed aesthetically in Jack Kerouac's idea of the writer committing himself irrevocably to the original impulses of his imagination, in Ginsberg's relentless self-exposure in a poem like "Kaddish," in Burroughs' refusal in *Naked Lunch* to disguise the demonic aspects of his addiction. But for the Beats nakedness did not exist simply as an aesthetic standard, it was to become a symbolic public and private stance, making art and action inseparable: thus Allen Ginsberg disrobed at poetry readings, and Kerouac once wrote that he wanted to be like the medieval Tibetan scholar-monk Milarepa who lived naked in caves—and as a supreme final statement Neal Cassady was found naked and dead near a railroad track in Mexico. This emphasis on baring the body and exposing the soul was an intuitive reaction to a betrayal the Beats felt because of mass acceptance of demeaning changes in the American idea of self-determination. Nakedness signified rebirth, the recovery of identity.

The Beats saw themselves as outcasts, exiles within a hostile culture, freaky progenitors of new attitudes toward sanity and ethics, rejected artists writing anonymously for themselves. Seeking illumination and a transvaluation of values, they deified Rimbaud who had exclaimed in *Une Saison en Enfer:* "Moi! moi qui me suis dit mage ou ange, dispense de toute morale . . ." Messengers of imminent apocalypse, the Beats believed that they were the angels of holocaust—like Kerouac's portrayal of his friend Neal Cassady as a "burning, frightful, shuddering angel, palpitating across the road." The angel image reappears in Kerouac's writing as it does so frequently in the work of all the Beats. In one of Gregory Corso's letters to Allen Ginsberg, there is a drawing of an angelic Virgin cradling William Burroughs in her arms while Ginsberg and Kerouac hover like desolate cherubim—the picture of a brooding reminder of the messianic and reformist impulses of a movement that was steeped in sorrow while yearning for beatitude.

Foundlings of the fifties, the Beats were like a slowly burning fuse in a silent vacuum. The postwar era was a time of extraordinary insecurity, of profound powerlessness as far as individual effort was concerned, when personal responsibility was being abdicated in favor of corporate largeness, when the catchwords were coordination and adjustment, as if we had defeated Germany only to become "good Germans" ourselves. The nuclear blasts in Japan had created new sources of terror, and the ideology of technology became paramount; science was seen as capable of totally dominating man and his environment. And the prospects of total annihilation through nuclear explosion, of mass conditioning through the media, only increased the awesome respect for scientific powers.

Few periods in our history have presented as much of an ordeal for artists and intellectuals. In *The Prisoner of Sex,* Norman Mailer has wondered how he survived those years without losing his mind. What Allen Ginsberg has called the Syndrome of Shutdown began in the late forties: the move toward a closed society where all decisions would be secret; the bureaucratic disease that Hannah Arendt has characterized as rule by Nobody where ultimately, as in Watergate, there is no final authority or responsibility; the paralysis caused by the use of technological devices that invade privacy; the increasing power of the Pentagon with its military bases designed to contain a new enemy supposedly (and suddenly) more threatening than the Nazis. The hysteria of rabid anticommunism was far more damaging, as Thomas Mann told the House Un-American Activities Committee, than any native communism; the patriotic blood-boiling became a convenient veil assuring a continued blindness to domestic social conditions that desperately needed attention. An internal freeze gripped America, an irrational hatred that created intense fear and repression, and since any repression feeds on oppression as its necessary rationalization, the red witch-hunts, the censorship of artists and filmmakers, the regimentation of the average man, began with unparalleled momentum and design. The contamination caused by this psychic and moral rigidity has been discussed by Allen Ginsberg in his *Paris Review* interview:

> The Cold War is the imposition of a vast mental barrier on
> everybody, a vast antinatural psyche. A hardening, a shutting off of
> the perception of desire and tenderness which everybody *knows* . . .
> [creating] a self-consciousness which is a substitute for communication
> with the outside. This consciousness pushed back into the self and
> thinking of how it will hold its face and eyes and hands in order to
> make a mask to hide the flow that is going on. Which it's aware of,
> which everybody is aware of really! So let's say shyness. Fear. Fear
> of total feeling, really, total being is what it is.

With the exception of the Civil War period, never before had the sense of hopefulness usually associated with the American experience been so damaged.

In the late forties and early fifties, the axioms of the upright in America were belief in God, family, and the manifestly benevolent international ambitions of the nation. Americans still conceived of themselves as innocent democratic warriors, protectors of a holy chalice that contained a magic elixir of progress in technology, cleanliness, and order. The middle-class American had become Kipling's white man burdened by a tank that he kept confusing with a tractor. Yet the national consciousness and the face of the land had been inevitably altered by the war effort. Fascism, as Susan Sontag has observed, was not a monstrously sudden growth excised by the war, it is the normal condition of the modern industrial state. As Herbert Marcuse demonstrated in *One Dimensional Man,* productive apparatus tends to become totalitarian to the extent that it determines individual needs and aspirations, and results in a "comfortable, smooth, and reasonable democratic unfreedom." The social goal becomes efficiency; the toll, privacy and freedom. As the war machine of industry became insatiable, the inevitable result was the convenient fiction of the Cold War and the cost of perpetual rearmament. Henry Miller realized the ensuing paradox:

> Never has there been a world so avid for security, and never has
> life been more insecure. To protect ourselves, we invent the most
> fantastic instruments of destruction, which prove to be boomerangs.
> No one seems to believe in the power of love, the only dependable
> power. No one believes in his neighbor, or in himself, let alone a
> supreme being. Fear, envy, suspicion are rampant everywhere.

The "war on communism" created an atmosphere of coercion and conspiracy. The nation's legacy of individuality had been changed to a more standardized expectation of what constituted "Americanism." Traditional tolerance of ideological difference had been subverted to a passion for organization and political similitude. It was a bitter and ironic distortion of our history: the character of the country had always been as various as its topography, and the lack of homogeneity meant that Americans had to work to develop a national consciousness resilient enough to embrace the aspirations of multitudes. Suddenly, there was an alleged contagion of treasonous spies, a mania for internal security, a repression that fostered anxiety and discouraged dissent. Some vital ingredient of the "American Dream" was warped and out of control.

What was the effect on a generation of such a politics of infidelity, such a time of false securities and mistrust? C. Wright Mills saw the emergence of a "mass society" composed of isolated units, formed by media, encouraged only to consume, never to decide. Other social critics noted the development of a mentality that refused to question authority. *Death of a Salesman* dramatized, in the passive victimization of Willy Loman, the immolation of the American soul in the impersonal abstractions of money for its own sake. Even worse, the psychology of the McCarthy era made truth itself suspect; it became something manipulated by "credible" authorities. As Yale chaplain William Sloan Coffin, Jr., observed, students in the fifties agreed their way through life. Education was a means of earning an income, no longer a way of stimulating critical inquiry or deepening sensibility. Novelist Philip Roth has admitted that he belonged to the most patriotic generation of American schoolchildren, the one most willingly and easily propagandized. For those who had reached their majority during the war, the indignity was greater. William Styron claimed that his generation was "not only not intact, it had been cut to pieces." While the end of the war brought with it an enormous sense of relief and a dull weariness, Styron wrote:

> We were traumatized not only by what we had been through and
> by the almost unimaginable presence of the bomb, but by the
> realization that the entire mess was not finished after all: there was
> now the Cold War to face, and its clammy presence oozed into our
> nights and days.

The cosmos seemed unhinged to Styron's generation as it confronted the "ruthless power and the loony fanaticism of the military mind."

The Beats were part of this besieged generation. At first, political consciousness was dormant: politics, Blake had maintained long before, was an objectification of "mental war." The violence, tyranny, and corruption of world leaders, as the Buddhist notion of karma explained, was only the realization of every individual's carelessness, deliberate ignorance, and uninvolvement. But young men like Kerouac were sensitively aware of the disappearing landmarks of regional diversity, the end of that special adaptability that had for so long invigorated the American character. The Beats could still nostalgically recall the time when one could bargain for an article purchased in a general store, when one bought land rather than paper shares in huge corporations, when radio and the airplane represented occasions of tremendous excitement. Kerouac's friend, novelist John Clellon Holmes, reflecting on the late thirties and early forties, saw that it was then—both because of the Depression and the anticipations of the war—that a great fissure had occurred in the American psyche, an uprooting of family relationships, of the sense of place and community that was compounded by a fear of imminent devastation. It was a shared premonition that the entire society was going to be changed in a major way, and that young men were to be particularly sacrificed. In a dream that he recorded, Kerouac noted that somewhere during the war he lost his way and took the wrong path. Holmes offered the image of a broken circuit to suggest the lack of connection to the immediate present felt by the members of his generation. It was as dangerous a condition as a hot electrical wire discharging energy randomly into the universe without a proper destination. The philosophical cause was not so much the horrible fact of the war, as it had been for the Lost Generation of the twenties, but the emergence of the new postwar values that accepted man as the victim of circumstances, and no longer granted him the agency of his own destiny: the illusion of free will, the buoyantly igniting spark in the American character, had been suddenly extinguished.

Simultaneously in Europe, a similar merger of bitterness and idealism resulted in Existentialism. Like the Beats, the Existentialists began by negation, refusing to accept the social given. While the Beats agreed with the Existentialist argument that man defines himself through his actions, they also shared a Spenglerian expectation of the total breakdown of Western culture. The Beats danced to the music of the absurdity they saw around them. When Ginsberg's friend Carl Solomon sent him an unsigned postcard reading simply "VANISHED!" it was a token of an irrepressible anarchic gaiety, but also an ominous warning of the totalitarian potentials of the age—a writer could hobo on the road or be kidnapped to the mental wards, the new concentration camps.

It is now clear that during the forties and fifties the Beats were operating on a definition of sanity that defied the expectations of their time, but proved potently prophetic. In other words, it was not only their writing that was important, but the way they chose to live. As Longfellow once remarked about the transcendentalist utopians, it was a "divine insanity of noble minds." In a culture that suspected mere difference in appearance as deviant behavior, or regarded homosexuality as criminal perversion, Allen Ginsberg maintained that "my measure at the time was the sense of personal genius and acceptance of all strangeness in people as their nobility." In the face of the asphyxiating apathy of the fifties, the Beats enacted their desires, seeking a restoration of innocence by purging guilt and shame. The model was Blakean, but it was never a path of easy irresponsibility. Gary Snyder, keeping a journal while working as a fire lookout on Sourdough Mountain in 1953, wrote:

> Discipline of self-restraint is an easy one; being clear-cut, negative,
> and usually based on some accepted cultural values. Discipline of follow-
> ing desires, *always* doing what you want to do, is hardest. It
> presupposes self-knowledge of motives, a careful balance of free
> action and sense of where the cultural taboos lay.

In the terms of their time, the Beats were regarded as madmen, and they suffered the consequences of the reformatory, the insane asylum, public ridicule, censorship, even prison. But what would seem defeat in the eye of ordinary experience simply instigated them to further adventures. The Beats were attracted to "madness" as a sustained presence; a lucid, singular, and obsessive way to illuminate the shadows of the day. Was William Blake, for example, acting madly when he read *Paradise Lost* with his wife while both sat naked in their garden? Melville had once perceived that the difference between sanity and insanity was analogous to the points in the rainbow where one color begins and another ends. As the eye could not distinguish any demarcation, a subjective value judgment was necessary. In the nineteenth century, madness became interpreted as unusual behavior, an affront to agreed social codes—so as long as Blake remained naked in the privacy of his garden, he was merely eccentric. But like the European Surrealists, the Beats wanted their Blake to dance naked in the public garden, and this was interpreted as a threat to public dignity. In the fifties, the Beats were still not quite as overtly political as the Surrealists had been, but they certainly paid for whatever self-assertions they managed with great psychic costs. There is no accident in the lament of the first line of "Howl": "I saw the best minds of my generation destroyed by madness." The Christian mystic Thomas Merton understood the spirit of revolt that inspired the Beat redefinition of sanity:

> We equate sanity with a sense of justice, with humaneness, with
> prudence, with the capacity to love and understand other people. We
> rely on the sane people of the world to preserve it from barbarism,
> madness, destruction. And now it begins to dawn on us that it is
> precisely the *sane* ones who are the most dangerous.

Recognizing that madness was a kind of retreat for those who wanted to stay privately sane, the Beats induced their madness with drugs, with criminal excess, and the pursuits of ecstasy. They used "madness"—which they regarded as naturalness—as a breakthrough to clarity, as a proper perspective from which to see. At times temporarily broken by the world for their disobedience, they developed, as Hemingway put it in *A Farewell To Arms,* a new strength "at the broken places." As

Edmund Wilson argues in "The Wound and the Bow," there exists an inextricable relationship between genius and disease in modern artists who have so precisely predicted and reflected the general insanity surrounding them. The acting out of repressed inhibitions and taboos relieves binding public pressures to conform, and the artist as scapegoat/shaman creates an alternative with his very being.

In three works particularly, *Naked Lunch,* "Howl," and *On the Road,* the Beats reacted to the embalming insecurities that had quelled the spirit of a generation. Each of these works represented a major departure in literary form as well as a courageous response to the dominating passivity of the age. In retrospect, these books can be seen as the confirmation that America was suffering a collective nervous breakdown in the fifties, and that a new nervous system was a prerequisite to perception. In these three works, then, we will find the key to the cultural disorder of an era.

Nowhere was the fear of institutional power more pronounced than in the nightmarish collage of *Naked Lunch.* Burroughs pictured a future possibility far more dismal and terrifying than Orwell's *1984* or Huxley's *Brave New World,* a dystopia where technology strangles all vestiges of freedom, a police state where the human attributes of love and community are stripped away and defiled. *Naked Lunch* is a hallucinatory vision of the very worst expectations of the fifties. Burroughs' central figure is the junkie, the weakest, most despised and vulnerable of citizens, a Western version of India's untouchable caste. Ginsberg has written that to be a drug addict in America is like having been a Jew in Nazi Germany, and Burroughs reflects this idea of fascist control, magnifying its horror through the distorted lens of the junkie. Burroughs' image of the faceless addict counterpoints his view of a society that controls all its parts while remaining invisibly undetectable. The view of the drug experience is harshly antiromantic. Clinical, detached, almost scientifically cinematic, *Naked Lunch* is an educative warning against the horrors of addiction. It relentlessly parodies our institutional life, and at the same time makes apparent the deconditioning effects of drugs, which, like Dr. Benway's cures, are an end in themselves. Rarely has any novelist managed so explosive a struggle between the demands of total control and the nihilistic impulse to defeat those in control. The ensuing combat is so ferocious that the voice of the novelist, ordering experience, seems distant and lost, especially to the reader already distracted by Burroughs' experimental bias.

If there is an intellectual center in *Naked Lunch,* it will be found in a pervasive suspicion of the dangers inherent in technological organization:

> The end result of complete cellular representation is cancer.
> Democracy is cancerous, and bureaus are its cancer. A bureau takes
> root anywhere in the state, turns malignant like the Narcotics Bureau,
> and grows and grows, always reproducing more of its own kind, until
> it chokes the host if not controlled or excised. Bureaus cannot live
> without a host, being true parasitic organisms. (A cooperative on the
> other hand can live without the state. That is the road to follow. The

building up of independent units to meet the needs of the people who
participate in the functioning of the unit. A bureau operates on
opposite principles of *inventing needs* to justify its existence.)
Bureaucracy is wrong as a cancer, a turning away from the human
evolutionary direction of infinite potentials and differentiation and
independent spontaneous action to the complete parasitism of a virus.

This passage—anticipating the cancer metaphor in Mailer's *An American Dream*—exaggerates a social awareness into a political ideology. It is important because it is one of Burroughs' rare projections of anything that might resemble an ideal, for his usual mood is a disgust so intense, so voluptuously vicious as to make any ideal seem false and impossible, and American ideals, especially, precariously incompatible with the realities of world power.

Burroughs' disdain for future possibilities and his staunch antiromantic bitterness make him an exception among Beat writers. He represents a logical fulfillment of the despair of T. S. Eliot's "The Waste Land." Curiously enough, the backgrounds of the two writers are similar: both were born in St. Louis, both were descendants of old American families, and both attended Harvard. Both writers, especially in "The Waste Land" and *Naked Lunch,* share a destructive attitude toward form and structure. Conrad Aiken was the first to notice that the critics who took such great pains to discover the links and continuities of "The Waste Land" were misreading a poem that intended to reveal dissonance and kaleidoscopic confusion through violently contrasting fragments; Burroughs' discontinuity—his microcosmic focus on what frequently appear to be unrelatable experiences—is part of a similar attempt to deny the organic unities of nineteenth-century structure in poetry and fiction. Burroughs' use of the "cut-up" method—an arbitrary juxtaposition of randomly selected words and phrases—is part of an attempt to restructure the grammar of perception; the new linguistic order that Burroughs invents initiates the Beats' assault on the conditioning influences of language.

Burroughs takes the motif of the unreal city from "The Waste Land" and compounds it with a nauseating imagery of hideous physical disintegration and degradation that promises a state of future plague. His hanged-men episodes in *Naked Lunch* are grotesque parodies of the talismanic material Eliot himself parodied with the grail legend in "The Waste Land." Burroughs presents these horrors with an unsettling calm, a cold earnestness reminiscent of Swift, a view of the psychological transformations latent in fantasy close to Kafka, and a picture of a man as helpless victim that reminds us of Sartre, Beckett, and Genet. Entering the absolute nadir of existence, Burroughs' fiction defines a purgatory of endless suffering—Beat in the sense of beaten, oppressed, and dehumanized. Yet Ginsberg's and Kerouac's pathway to beatitude stemmed from Burroughs' nightmare of devastation.

Burroughs' affinity with Eliot's objectivity and impersonality raises an aesthetic issue that is crucial for the Beats; because of this affinity, Burroughs once denied belonging to the Beat movement, and emphasized the differences in form among writers he considered more as friends than as literary compatriots. The effect of

Burroughs' vision on Ginsberg and Kerouac—who both frequented Burroughs' apartment near Columbia University in 1944–45—cannot be denied; Kerouac, for example, makes Burroughs an oracular source of the wisdom of experience as Bull Lee in *On The Road*. But Burroughs' fiction, while capable of diagnosing what the Beats saw as threatening about American values—especially the worship of technology—did not project a sense of self strong enough to counter the debilitating apathy of the culture. Burroughs clarified his aesthetic of narrative near the end of *Naked Lunch:*

> There is only one thing a writer can write about: *what is in front of his senses at the moment of writing.* . . . I am a recording instrument . . . I do not presume to impose "story" "plot" "continuity." . . . In sofaras I succeed in a *Direct* recording of certain areas of psychic process I may have limited function. . . . I am not an entertainer. . . .

In this respect, Burroughs is in accord with Eliot's notion that the artist's progress is measured by how well he transcends personality and private emotion.

# 17

# On *The Last Words of Dutch Schultz*

### Eric Mottram

**B**urroughs' work frequently transposes cinematic methods into prose and poetic structure, and since the tetralogy much of his writing has been imagined and composed virtually in scenario forms. In this he is, of course, part of that decision to work in the interface of traditionally separated artistic procedures which has become increasingly the common case in this century. As Truffaut and Godard take the story off the plot of fiction in order to move film further from its origins in linear prose narrative, and Eisenstein committed himself to a montage procedure he related to both the ideogrammatic form of Noh drama and to certain epic methods in *Paradise Lost,* so Burroughs composes through cinematically descriptive prose scenario, image montage, and the treatment of reality as a reel of film or sound tape. The wider contemporary context which shows him by no means isolated in his methods can be found in the French collections of *Approches* magazine, and in the American *Experiments in Prose,* whose editor, Eugene Wildman, draws attention to the new methods in his introduction:

> The tape-recorder makes potential really new structural ideas. . . .
> For the first time now the memory is liberated: formulaic structure can
> become a choice rather than a necessity.

Speech becomes a basis of art in a sense hitherto unused, in the transcription of one or more people talking, in dialogue, separately or simultaneously. Language can be used "in conjunction with other visual material, producing a visual-semantic myth" (the form of Burroughs' *The Unspeakable Mr Hart* and *The Book of Breee-thing*). Categories cease to be binding. In his introduction to *Breakthrough Fiction-eers,* Richard Kostelanetz lists five main ventures in "post-realist, post-symbolist"

Eric Mottram, *WILLIAM BURROUGHS: The Algebra of Need* (London: Marion Boyars, 1977): 238–51. Reprinted by permission of the author and Marion Boyars Publishers, Ltd.

composition: Burroughs' collage and cut-ups; "the mixing of physically separated words and images pioneered in America by Kenneth Patchen and extended by Donald Barthelme (in some recent works), R. Crumb, and other counter-cultural comix"; "the flat, scrupulously uninflected, absurdity-haunted prose of Samuel Beckett and his artistic successors"; the deranged, picaresque first-person narrators in Faulkner, John Hawkes, and Barthelme; and "the ironic psuedo-scholarship of John Barth, Jorge Luis Borges and Vladimir Nabokov." The edited arts of film and videotape are steadily teaching the page-turning literary arts how to be nonsequential and remain coherently related, an inventively linguistic field which provides "experiences and perceptions that are simply not available in other technologies of communication." In Artaud's terms they avoid "the idolatry of fixed masterpieces which is one of the aspects of bourgeois conformism."

*The Last Words of Dutch Schultz* (1970) is presented as a film and begins with a cover, by R. B. Kitaj, which transforms a newspaper photograph of the gangster Schultz into an image in shades of brown, through which the grain of canvas shows, making the connections simultaneous to perception between newspaper, portrait, and book, and between newsprint-image, drawing on canvas, and book-cover introduction. Inside, the text begins with four full-page images of a man shot in a street, the original movie shot sequence reduced to a minimum graphic immediacy of violence. Then the words begin: "SPECIAL FEATURES OF THIS FILM," so that the media of presentation are fully given as an initial proposition of the work. Film analyzes the object; reproduction analyzes the image; words analyze the image.

In 1872, the twenty-four cameras of Eadweard Muybridge made a running-horse image to prove that all four hooves left the ground at a point in gallop. Technology thereby extended and arrested a peculiarity in human perception: that persistence of vision through which the eye retains a visual image for approximately one-tenth of a second after it has gone from sight. (The significance of Muybridge in this instance can be quickly gauged in Siegfried Giedion's *Mechanization Takes Command*, which also accurately draws attention to the relationship between analyses of the image in Muybridge's *Athlete Descending a Staircase* and Duchamp's *Nude Descending a Staircase*.)

While transforming a bus into a hearse in the Place de L'Opéra, through the happy accident of a jammed camera (in 1896), Georges Méliès ended theater mimesis in the art of cinema—the audience became conscious that they were watching expression through a particular medium. In twentieth-century arts, the medium became increasingly part of the meaning.

Burroughs' Survival Artist had shown the history of religion as an erotic power film, and throughout *The Wild Boys* the characters move through movie sets as if performing roles in a perpetual historical present. The opening of *Dutch Shultz* overtly describes the technique:

> The sets are presented first and the sets draw character. This is
> done by preparing film loops for the three main periods covered by the
> film: 1902 to 1919, the 1920s, the 1930s. The film loops consist of

> typical films of the period—(these are for the most part made up)—
> typical characters and scenes of the period real or imaginary. The loop
> turns, wheels interlock and the character is drawn on set.

The puns within the last sentence indicate the multiplicity of Burroughs' inference: the loop is in the camera and the projector; the wheels of the film machinery move into each other and so do those of choice, determinacy, and narrative art; the character is depicted through the historical scene's circumstances, and is also drawn into his relevant text, just as we are drawn by the procedures into the set-character ourselves. Dutch Schultz is given as part of a mobile interface of intersections from the past placed in the present. The method can be related to those of Lucien Febvre, the historian of total history conceived rather as Artaud imagined a "theatre of cruelty": "what is needed is a continuous harassment of contemporary man by means of history" by means of a reconstruction of "l'outillage mental," the mental abilities and instruments through which we order experience, both limiting and comprehending it, in each culture. Artaud spoke of resisting any "artistic dallying with forms" and acting instead "like victims burnt at the stake, signaling through the flames":

> This concrete physical language to which I refer is truly theatrical only
> to the degree that the thoughts it expresses are beyond the reach of the
> spoken language . . . it is addressed first of all to the senses instead of
> being addressed primarily to the mind as is the language of words . . .
> a poetry and a space which will be resolved in precisely the domain
> which does not belong strictly to words . . .
>
> The true theatre, like poetry as well, though by other means, is born
> out of a kind of organized anarchy after philosophical battles which
> are the passionate aspect of these primitive unifications.

Later in *The Theatre and Its Double*, Artaud writes of "a kind of total creation in which man must reassume his place between drama and events."

The scenario form incorporates nonverbal forms, structures not necessarily related to traditional verbal syntax, into a new verbal construction based on memory of film. Literacy is extended by our experience of film which has become habits of art experience generally, cutting across boundaries of form which in turn have become standard twentieth-century procedures in order to place examined environment. It is unnecessary for prose and poetry to be restricted to the linear logic of sentences as the sole determining method of composition. Discontinuity, parataxis, and collage have become standard twentieth-century procedures in order to place our information more accurately in ordered space. Scenario draws on film also in its ability to present dramatically without the intervention of continuous explanation and motivation. It resembles a newspaper without editorial explicitness controlling its juxtaposed columns and blocks of print and pictures on the page. Scenario is a mosaic of events in space and time. The sound track is built back silently into the reader's aural imagination while he reads within the orbit of his memory of films (or even of

reading a book-of-the-film registration); the rapid presentation of image he might
even reactivate from the habit of reading "Ode to a Nightingale," "Le Bateau Ivre,"
or *Finnegans Wake,* strip cartoons or *Mad* magazine. He knows the conventions.
Stream of consciousness technique can in these ways be released from the logic of
Indo-European linguistic imposition, and writing can communicate as (in Marshall
McLuhan's terms) "the visualization of acoustic space" into which all dimensions
work simultaneously. The very discontinuity of form is the product of an analysis
of the whole field of the subject (chapter one of Eisenstein's *The Film Sense*—
"Word and Image"—provides some of the theory and practice of such procedures).
[. . .]

In Burroughs' work Dutch Schultz's "mob," the federal government's power in
G-men, Treasury Department tax investigators, Lepke's Syndicate, certain "neutral"
characters, and the Teacher, Albert Stern, move in a continuous sphere of action
within the monologue of the dying gangster, a deathbed "last words" under police
interrogation, transcribed by a police stenographer, which itself hallucinates a time-
less present for the actual sequentiality of a lifetime. In addition "all the characters
take more than one part": the judge who sentences Schultz to a reformatory is Lepke
Buchalter; the doctor who delivers him is Stern, who appears as his teacher at Public
School 12. The effect is to involve the audience in the "set" effect and to imply the
involvement of all characters, together with the audience, in a field of crime, justice,
punishment, and socioeconomic determinism.

But Schultz's last words were delivered under the release of delirium and their
form recalls some of Burroughs' own styles of rapid movement from shot to shot in
order to notate simultaneities in space and time: the document reveals the Dutchman
as a potential artist. Rarely has the feeling of witnessing death been more vividly
communicated. The black and white film breaks into color "for scenes involving
bloodshed and death" but it is in the delirious words that "the secrets of life and
death" are suspended. The film becomes a mystery play written as a scenario of
collages; the very opening gives the complexity to follow: as Schultz recalls his
mother and a detective interrogates with "Who shot you?" the scene dissolves to a
distant door, the sound track contains the cry of a newborn baby, Stern appears as
the delivery doctor with blood (in red) on his hands, and the scene dissolves to
Schultz washing his hands in the Palace Chop House washroom immediately before
his assassination—and dissolves again back to the hospital room and the detective
asking "Who shot you?":

> Cut to back room of The Palace Chop House . . . broken beer
> glasses, bloody account sheets, an adding machine, a smoking cigar
> with chewed end, three men sprawled on the floor. Abe Landau
> heaves himself up off the floor and staggers to the doorway.

Burroughs then inserts a recurrent scene from his own work:

> Cut to room with rose wall paper in colour. Rising sun lights red
> haired boy naked on bed. (Mrs Murphy's rooming house remember? I

> was new to the game and like all young thieves thought I had a
> licence to steal. . . . )

The scenario is controlled by the director, who appears here autobiographically, and, in the prefatory passage to the book, as the selector of destiny controls, an ambivalent Bradly Martin or Faulknerian Dark Diceman:

> This is not just a film about Dutch Schultz. It is a film about Dutch
> Schultz and the sets in which he lived and operated. Success in any
> line is a question of being on set. The Director looks around the set
> and says "I need you and you and you but you don't belong on this
> set. . . . The sets are the medium in which the characters live that
> inexorably mould their actions. When a character is no longer on set
> he is finished.

Stern is on set by mistake: the police suspect him of the Dutchman's murder— "there is no reason to believe he ever shot anybody but himself." The sets are historical necessity with which a man may actively intersect to form character in action. In this sense character is fate, and fate is role on set. The rise and fall of Schultz is a graph whose plot is inexorable. The film's monochrome is the limitation of the plot, a power-world in which blood alone has the dimension of color—the rest is the field of Schultz as successful industrialist "drawn inexorably into the 1920s gangster film." Heroin addicts appear as part of the junk scene of capitalist democracy in the 1920s and 1930s, itself part of interwar addictions of power which moved towards the Wall Street Crash, the Depression, the Spanish Civil War, World War II, and onwards into the twentieth century, still repeating the stale movie of junk. In the reformatory, the guards, homosexual prisoners, and junkies dance in a single stylized ballet of control; when the music of *Der Fliegende Holländer* accompanies released prisoners on a Manhattan ferry, it is no casual pun, since the opera dramatizes the inexorable. The psychopathic criminal haunts Western consciousness once the idea of damnation by necessity grips the imagination of authority. Whether he lives a living death as eternal wanderer or dies in fact, he is imprisoned. None of Burroughs' characters are free. *The Last Words of Dutch Schultz* is part of his developing myth of hell, extermination, and imprisonment which reaches right through to his most recent work:

> [Dutch] and other passengers on the boat might be under different
> circumstances of birth. It is in a sense a book of the dead, a
> suspended interval between prisons.

But once the actors are not "on set," they grow bored; they are addicted to determinist performance.

Schultz's rise begins when he realizes "it is more profitable to give wages than to receive them." So he enters the demonology of capitalism—it includes such figures as the White Bear, who hibernates between crashes, and Hetty Green, the

Witch of Wall Street, and a number of other instances of centralizing control, like the archaeologists excavating the tomb of Tutankhamen and thereby moving into "The Curse of the Pharaohs" (Burroughs will take up this theme in *The Book of Breeething*). The Crash of 1929 is given as part of an inevitable movie which includes Dutch, Legs Diamond, the FBI, Wyatt Earp, and a Mexican pistolero (out of *The Wild Boys*). Burroughs rapidly cuts together shots from his whole action to demonstrate the vile order of chaos:

> An axe still quivers in the door. Coll and Fats open up with
> machine guns. The mobsters fall across the Monopoly board clutching
> their model properties in dying fingers.

The control world of electric technology, guns, magic, and the Mayans swerves into the diagram of Owney Maddon's club, HQ for exterminating Vincent Coll:

> A technician wearing steel rim glasses and headphones is making
> adjustments at a switch board. This is the same actor who plays the
> police stenographer.
> Technician: (removing headphones) "I'm getting the whole block."
> He removes plugs filing the insulation off wires with a knife. Bo
> Weinberg reads a tabloid. The red haired gun is reading Weird Tales.
> On the cover of Weird Tales stands a priest with elaborate Mayan
> head dress wearing a loin cloth his hands raised in prayer or
> invocation. A tentacled monster is pushing his way out of his entrails.
> The priest's face wears an ambiguous expression of dedication, horror,
> and pain mixed with the ecstacy of child birth. Flickering silver words
> hang in the air.
> "Abhooth the Dark, Abhooth the Unclean, I conjure you by the
> Great Black Rock of Kassim, by the Emerald Crown of Luxor, by the
> Luminous Sword of Iblis, by Ormuzd and by Sh'hina come forth."
> "Killed when two cars crashed head on" . . . newspaper picture of
> car wreck . . . screech of brakes, crack of metal, breaking glass,
> blood, shoes, oil on the street, police sirens . . . "critically injured"
> . . . grunting groans of pain pushed out through broken ribs.
> "Now this infinitely vile thing was coming out of its lair" . . .
> (phone rings)

These and related materials intersect with "on the spot documentaries of Harlem in the thirties." Coll is murdered at 23. A Negro hurries off to phone in his policy slip number—23. "The number 23 hangs in the air"—a skull-faced porter's number, a lottery ticket, and the D.A. who later demands the death penalty for the attacker of an old watchman beaten over the head "not once but *23 times.*" The vortex is a deterministic example of number control in the universe. Out of the whirling montage of violence is heard Billy the Kid's cry "Quien es?" (heard again, with the Dutchman, in *The Wild Boys*) across the American decades. The kaleidoscope subsides into the Treasury Department chief's office where agents are briefed to hunt down inland revenue cheats. This is cut into the chairman of the Syndicate briefing *his* men, which is cut into a T-man checking the books of a rancher. The scenes are released in a fast-moving simultaneity of numbers rackets of various kinds, monopolies, and the connected media of radio, film, telephone, and automobiles, registered as a single cultural action and a sardonic criticism of the business of America. Figures, times, durations, and laws are fused into a single control system. Mr Bradshinkle's office investigating a firm's subsidiaries is cut with a queen wounded in a Turkish bath—"a crime of passion" in the passionless chaos of American business rackets—and the headline: "DUTCH SCHULTZ INDICTED FOR TAX EVASION."

Schultz's mansion is, like Herman Teppis' mogul office in *The Deer Park*, a transposition of historical power images and objects into the inheriting American system. Over the gas logs is a bronze replica of "The Thinker" and above that "a painting of Venice involving Nubian gondoliers, a red canopy, aristocrats trail languid hands in the water" (the Nubians recur in *The Wild Boys*). Pictures of Greek gods and Ovidian metamorphoses jostle a Renaissance statue of a naked youth on a column: "Whole scene suggests the ante room of an elegant ambiguous brothel in the international zone of Shanghai" (a thematic scene which, shifted to "Hongkong," Alain Robbe-Grillet exploits to parallel effect in *La Maison de Rendezvous*). Dutch is also associated with *The Life of Napoleon*, which lies on a table next to a decanter labeled SCOTCH, and with the film of magic and priestcraft developed earlier:

> an ornate embroidered dressing gown gives him a curiously majestic
> and mysterious aura like the high priest of a devil worshipping cult in
> some forgotten film.

In his operations room the circled numbers on a board labeled "Harlem" resemble "Cabalistic signs used to invoke spirits." The rapid shots which follow show his mob in action: forms of extreme violence for money. Some are humorous in the wild party or carnival manner of *The Naked Lunch:*

> Waiter: "Voilà le Suprême of Guinea Hen Bonne Chef Specialty of the
> House . . . " (He lifts a silver cover to reveal the bloated corpse of a
> huge sewer rat cooked in axle grease and garnished with rotten
> garbage).

In fact Schultz's organization and its festivities is a version of A.J.'s Islam Inc. and his later orgy in *The Wild Boys*—grotesque scenes of consumption, eating, sexual rampage, and sinister control in the international arena of the rich. Schultz is an archetype of the wealthy, unlike them only in being *overtly* transferred to the world of crime: "I gotta have control." Parallel to these scenes, the strike of Schultz's numbers racket runners parodies union workers' meetings ("some of the strikers are singing Joe Hill and You Can't Scare Me I'm Sticking To The Union"), except that these figures are more militant, openly revealing the injuries to their bodies sustained

from the Dutchman's henchmen. Schultz surrenders to them at the same time as he
surrenders to the government in order to stand trial. Released on 75,000 dollars'
bail, he plans a new cover under the name of Arthur Flegenheimer, a rare books
collector, and donor to libraries. That is, he enters another notorious investment
area of the capitalist system. Aided by The Whisperer, his publicity agent, he
organizes another political network, this time mainly in the rural regions. By projections of film, he is shown merged, first with Abhooth, and then with historical scenes
of control—"the Reichstag Fire, Hitler Youth burning books, the cool grey face of
Ivar Kruger the Match King," and cops beating up a Negro. The madness of power
appears as a contemporary form of an eternal Bradly Martin assimilation as Schultz
murders his treacherous accountant:

> Dutch has lost all human resemblance. Acting in this scene is done
> with all stops removed. The tone is utter insanity.

> Jules Martin falls screaming and moaning to the floor. His
> screaming bloody face, smoke coming out of his mouth, the horrible
> gristly groans from his torn throat flicker on the Dutchman's snarling
> ugly face and something uglier behind the face is *eating* Martin's
> moans.

The cutting montage which follows demonstrates America's cultural involvement
in crime. The jurors at Dutch's trial "clack like ventriloquist dummies" as they indict
the inland revenue agents rather than the mobster:

> Jurors 3, 4, 5: (jumping up) "The Dutchman's trouble could be
> yours or mine . . . " (Dutch's face projected onto the jurors). . . .

> Cut to newspaper headline: DUTCH SCHULTZ ACQUITTED ON
> TAX CHARGES . . . Judge upbraids jury . . .

Then Burroughs moves his routines into a parody of "fighting D.A." films, but
with both the lawyers' and the jurors' power-mania exposed:

> Now something else creeps in feral and furtive intent on its prey.
> He is demanding the death penalty for the killer and two look outs in
> a robbery. . . .
> The Jury: "GUILTY. FRY THEM ALL . . . Fearless fighting D.A.
> can you get us tickets? We want to watch them fry."

The next section superimposes the insane faces of the D.A. and the jury on the
head of the electrocuted youth—"smoke curls out from under the hood and rises to
the ceiling." As in the tetralogy, execution is a major center of mad control, but
Burroughs is not here concerned with repeating the erotic charge of his earlier work,
but rather with the inexorable pattern. Got up in the wealthy class's rig of riding

clothes, standing in a grotesque "horsey rumpus room"—"two toilets one labelled MARES and the other STALLIONS"—Schultz sobs out: "That D.A. He's my NEMESIS." But the D.A. is exterminated in a classic series of shots in an archetypal drugstore, while Dutch and Lepke discuss "territorial terms"; it is 1935 but the parallel might be Stalin and Churchill deciding on territorial claims in Europe at the end of World War II.

Burroughs gives the killers of Dutch Schultz a parodic dimension in order to place them within the mean history of tragedy and the gods. Charlie The Bug Workman in "twilight blue suit," and Jimmy the Shrew (also in *The Wild Boys*) in "a tight peagreen suit and grey fedora," are "spectral actors in future time" as they drive into the Holland Tunnel and appear at the Palace Chop House:

> The workman's cold metallic eyes, his curly hair and pale face.
> The Shrew, smooth poreless red skin drawn tight over the cheek
> bones, lips parted from long yellow teeth the colour of old ivory, his
> black eyes shining. The tunnel lights ring their heads with an orange
> halo. They are angels of death . . .
> [The Shrew's] arms are pipe stems, his wrists and hands smooth
> and hairless as scar tissue. . . .
> They are creatures from another world, Gods of Death.

Under hospital morphine Schultz experiences "a rush of pictures in the brain as if seen from a speeding train. The pictures are dim, jerky, grainy like an old film." In fact, the film of the scenario would here include "arbitrary sequences" from earlier sections cut into scenes from Schultz's life—a childhood attack by a boy in the street, traumatic incidents with his mother, a priest, various crimes, his reading of *Kim*—and from the external history of his time: Hearst's Yellow Peril cartoons, anti-Semitic cartoons from the Nazi paper *Der Völkische Beobachter*, and shots of a city after atomic blast:

> The camera plummets into a slum of metal rubbish heaps, dry heat
> a terrible bright sun. Boys gather around the camera faces scarred with
> hatred evil and despair. They are in rags flesh streaked with coal and
> metal dust. They hold shards of blistered metal in their outstretched
> hands.

This field is deepened by the presence of "a gum chewing tech sergeant [who] sticks his head out of a crippled space ship," Dutch shooting Martin in the mouth, Abhooth who "turns green with fear at the sight of the atomic street boys," and Albert Stern.

Throughout the action, Stern has appeared as doctor, baby-deliverer, and teacher. It seems that although he did not kill Schultz, he is in many ways responsible for Schultz's career, could have delivered him, and could have redeemed the lost boy: "All the actors drain into the face of Albert Stern." But there is no question of blatant psychological or sociological apologetics for the mobster. The book concludes with the "Transcript of Dutch Schultz's Last Words" in which words surface in the coherence of his delirium as a multidimensional précis of his life as he experienced it—that is, including its suppressed anxiety, the reiterated cry of "Please!" which hardly recurred in the life we have witnessed, and the confused desire for both conflict and an end to conflict focussed on his ambiguously kind and brutal mother: "Mother is the best bet and don't let Satan draw you too fast." His last words are, "I want to pay. Let them leave me alone." The scenario is part of Burroughs' analysis of the impositions of the supposed necessity of conflict in making a man and the deep effects of matriarchy, twin major forms of imprisonment in this "book of the dead." His dream of a self-regulatory freedom, some kind of autonomous life entailing choice is constant. His concern for survival is profoundly related to those twentieth-century feelings and circumstances given in Bruno Bettleheim's *The Informed Heart: Autonomy in a Mass Age:*

> To survive, not as a shadow of the SS but as a man, one had to
> find some life experience that mattered, over which one was still in
> command . . . To have some small token experiences of being active
> and passive, each on one's own, and in mind as well as body—this,
> much more than the utility of any one such activity, was what enabled
> me and others like me to survive . . . Those prisoners who blocked
> out neither heart nor reason, neither feelings nor perception, but kept
> informed of their inner attitudes even when they could hardly ever
> afford to act on them, those prisoners survived and came to understand
> the conditions they lived under. They also came to realise what they
> had not perceived before; that they still retained the last, if not the
> greatest, of human freedoms: to choose their own attitude in any given
> circumstance.

Burroughs writes out of his own understanding of the erosion of choice in the twentieth century. The differences between the provincial gangster world and the global action of politics and economics are negligible.

# 18

# "Cut-Ups"
## *A Synema of the text*

### Anne Friedberg

n one of his dadaist manifestos, Tristan Tzara commands:

> Take a newspaper
> Take some scissors

He then directs the making of a dadaist poem: A newspaper article is cut into its constituent words. The words are placed in a paper bag. The paper bag is shaken. The poem is "constructed" by copying the words in the order they are pulled from the paper bag. Full of chance juxtapositions, the dadaist poem foregrounds the process of combination and arrangement. The scissors become a cardinal tool for the creation of modernist art:

> Take the heritage of dadaist collage and futurist sound
> plays.
> Take fifty years of technological sophistication of the
> scissors.

The "cut-up" techniques of William Burroughs echo much of the dadaist fervor against rationality and much irreverence for bourgeois life and art-making. In their simplest conception, "cut-ups" are nothing more than the random graphic rearrangement of words and phrases.

The recently published collaborative effort of William Burroughs and his painter-friend, Brion Gysin, *The Third Mind,* is a synergist manifesto: an exposition of Burroughs and Gysin's "cut-up" and "fold-in" techniques of assemblage and a treatise on the process of collaboration, itself a sort of mental *découpage:*

Anne Friedberg, " 'Cut-Ups': A *Synema* of the text" *Downtown Review* 1.1 (1979): 3–5. Reprinted by permission of the author.

> The third mind is the unseen collaborator, the superior mind con-
> structed when two minds are put together.

Burroughs frequently collaborated with more than one other mind. In fact, in the late fifties and early sixties, he was a writer working closely with a small syndicate of experimentalists: a painter (Brion Gysin), a sound engineer (Ian Sommerville), and a filmmaker (Antony Balch). One wonders about the algebra of such collective experimentation: Is there a fifth mind? Does the effect of "superiority" expand in multiple collaborations?

Burroughs, a self-declared demagogue of the future, was never reluctant to rely on artificial or mechanical aids to the creative process. In a 1965 interview in *Paris Review,* he claimed: "Most serious writers refuse to make themselves available to the things technology is doing."

His collaborative association with Gysin, Sommerville, and Balch shows his eagerness to explore these concerns with other artists. This group of media specialists desired to experiment with the mechanisms of *coupage* and *découpage* specific to their own mediums: painting, sound, and film.

Gysin, a poet and painter who met Burroughs in his "L'Hôtel Beat" days in Paris in the late fifties, is credited by Burroughs for the initial inspiration for the "cut-up" technique, the collage poem, "Minutes To Go," written in 1959.

Ian Sommerville, a British computer programmer and recording engineer, sug- gested many of the tape-splice experiments which Burroughs incorporated into his early sixties' novels, *The Soft Machine* (1961), *The Ticket That Exploded* (1962), and *Nova Express* (1964).

Antony Balch, a British filmmaker who met both Gysin and Burroughs in Paris, is credited for proposing the film-splice extension of the tape recorder experiments. Both Sommerville and Balch are acknowledged at the beginning of *The Ticket That Exploded*.

One of the more curious intrigues to preoccupy the four men was an investigation of the "copulative" nature of montage. While Eisenstein has refered to the "copula- tive" quality of the Chinese ideogram and suggested a rather tame analogy to film editing, this quartet took the metaphor for "copulation" to a more literal degree.

Many of the film and tape-splice experiments (described in *The Ticket That Exploded*) were designed to produce strong erotic results: "Splice your body sounds with the body sounds of your best friend and see how familiar he gets." "Everybody splice himself in with everybody else." On the side of audio-copulation, an audio- bionic birth is proposed: "Biologists talk about creating life in the test tube. All they need is a few tape recorders."

Of course it is difficult to measure if these experiments were taken as anything more serious than metaphoric. Gysin tried projecting his paintings on a human subject and claimed to observe the same effects as produced in the orgone accumulator as Wilhelm Reich. In *The Soft Machine, The Ticket That Exploded,* and *Nova Express,* Burroughs proposes an analogy between film-tape montage and the montage of bodies and combinative possibilities of the sex act.

The "cut-up" technique offers an implicit analogy to film editing—the optical recombination of images. Although film is an art form which combines a multiplicity of codes—music, photography—there has always been a tendency to force an equation between film editing (the construction of a sequence of shots) and verbal language (the construction of a phrase, a sentence, a paragraph). But a myriad of dis-analogies erupt when the film theorist has to derive a grammar and decide whether a cinematic unit (the shot or the frame) contains more than a word, a phrase, or a sentence.

Burroughs' style is an intensely ungrammatical chain of phrases produced by random optical recombinations of various texts. The novels *The Soft Machine, The Ticket That Exploded, Nova Express* form a loose trilogy, cutting-up and folding-in on themselves. They share the metaphoric structures of the "virus" and the "film." To Burroughs, the "word is a virus," an infective agent and powerful instrument of control. Burroughs' own corrosion of syntax is intended to dismantle the mechanisms of control. Within the viral metaphor, "inoculation can only be effected through exposure" (*Ticket*). Words and images must be used, but only in recombinative patterns.

Film is also a metaphor for total control, a "reality studio" which must be challenged and subverted by the same use of recontextualized words and images. *Example:* In *The Soft Machine,* the time traveler travels back to Mayan civilization to destroy the Mayan control calendar. Only the Mayan priests had a knowledge of such a calendar with which they could calculate and command the exact dates required for each process in the agricultural cycle, including festival days, etc. Burroughs compares this form of agricultural fascism over illiterate Mayan farmers to the Luce Empire's complete control of word and image. In any case, the calendar had to be destroyed. The time traveler, equipped with a vibrating camera gun, tape recorder, and transistor radio hidden in a clay pot, is sent to pull such a caper.

He first makes tape recordings of festival music, thus obtaining a sound track, but has greater difficulty obtaining an image track. He prostitutes himself to a Mayan priest so that he may be transferred to the job of janitor in the Mayan temple. As janitor, he has access to the Holy Board Books, which he photographs:

> Equipped now with sound and image track of the control machine I
> was in the position to dismantle it—I had only to mix the order of
> recordings and the order of images and the changed order would be
> picked up and fed back into the machine—

The time traveler programs the machine to destroy itself and kills the priest with his camera gun. This task is accomplished with great ease because the priests "were nothing but word and image, an old film rolling on with dead actors." One of the concluding phrases of *The Soft Machine* is: "Storm the Reality Studio and retake the Universe."

Reality, if seen as a film, offers the recombinative potential to deconstruct its "control" of word and image by unhinging the order of things, by removing the word from its referent, the sound from its image.

Burroughs may have first experienced such a radical restructuring of reality in his junkie days, but he claims, "Anything that can be done chemically, can be done in other ways."

2

In 1963, filmmaker Antony Balch made two films which attempt to provide a cinematic equivalent to Burroughs' writing. *Towers Open Fire* and *Cut-Ups* were made at a time when there was virtually no experimental filmmaking in Britain, whereas 1963 was a landmark year for experimental filmmaking in the United States, a year that produced Kenneth Anger's montage masterpiece *Scorpio Rising* and Andy Warhol's long take epics *Eat, Sleep, Kiss, Haircut,* and *Blow-Job.* It wasn't until after Jonas Mekas' 1964–65 New American Film tour that the seeds for experimentation sprouted a whole movement of experimental British cinema.

Balch began his film career at an advertising house in London in 1956, the year that commercial television first took hold in Britain. His assignments in those days required him to make complete tightly edited commercial spots. He had to shoot, direct, and edit each short film-piece. He later worked as an editor of foreign-language film trailers and then as a subtitler.

Although he apparently made one unfinished film in Paris in 1959, *Towers Open Fire* was actually his first complete film, and an illustration of his expert skill as a *montagist-extraordinaire. Towers* is an eleven-minute assemblage of rapidly cut shots with a narration sound track by Burroughs. There is no discernable structure—the shots are spliced together to follow the "cut-up" strategy of disjunction. *Towers* begins with a straight-on shot of Burroughs in his usual uniform of "banker's drag" (died-in-the-three-piece suit, starched shirt, tie, and black-framed glasses). The Burroughs deadpan is counterpointed by his droll non-sync voiceover of phrases taken, interchangeably, from *The Soft Machine, The Ticket That Exploded,* and *Nova Express.* The texts are punctuated by sound collage elements of machine noise and wind sounds.

*Towers* offers many shots of Burroughs: Burroughs pawing through a stack of film cans, Burroughs staring into a video monitor on vertical roll, Burroughs shooting up. Anyone familiar with his novels will recognize these commands:

> "Shift linguals—Cut word lines—Vibrate tourists—Free
> doorways—Photo falling—Word falling—Break through in
> Grey Room—Towers, open fire"

In Balch's film this decree is accompanied by the images of three-piece-suited "board members" convened around a board table arrayed with large open books which prominently display ink hieroglyphs. A young man in a gas mask and military fatigues "zaps" each board member with a ray-gun device. The "zap" is executed by a video effect which makes each member consecutively disappear, leaving merely an empty boardroom and the books. Balch probably found it appropriate that the room he used in *Towers* was the boardroom of the British Film Institute, the major organ of censorship and control of film in Britain.

*Cut-Ups* has a more precisely planned structure for the cinematic transposition of the "cut-up" technique. Balch cut the original film into four pieces and hired an editor to perform the mechanical task of taking one foot of film from each roll (1–2–3–4). The one-foot segments were joined in consecutive and repeated 1–2–3–4 fashion. The only variation in shot length occurs when there is a shot change within the foot-long section.

The soundtrack, made by Sommerville, Gysin, and Burroughs to the twenty-minute and four-second length, consists of four phrase units, read at different speeds, but always in the same order:

> Yes. Hello.
> Look at this picture.
> Does it seem to be persisting?
> Good. Thank you.

Although *Cut-Ups* proceeds as a fast montage which at points seems indecipherable, the images are describable: Gysin and Burroughs sit at a table with an umbrella; a young man walks through city streets with hieroglyphs mounted on his back; a young boy in underwear lounges in a hotel room; an optical device is placed in front of a subject's face. The four parts continue in loose progression: Burroughs, alone, lurks in front of the Burroughs Building; the young man with hieroglyphs continues down a street; the boy in underwear unrolls a Gysin painting, which, shot from overhead, calls brief attention to the two-dimensionality of the film screen; the optical device flickers on. The total effect of such rhythmic alternation of shots is mesmerizing. Both films, *Towers Open Fire* and *Cut-Ups,* rely on sound-and-image montage strategies which defy any sense of spatial or temporal unity.

3

> You control what you put into your montages; you don't really control what comes out.

All of Burroughs' ideas hover along the boundaries of science and fiction. The actual *effects* of the "cut-up" montages, of the recontextualization of a phrase, an image, a sound, are difficult things to measure. To propose a *synergism,* a third, fourth, or fifth mind, seems to be a notion most suitable for evolutionary metaphors and experimentalist manifestos.

But the vestiges of such investigation remain. The films of Balch, since they have been rarely seen, have been slighted by the superintendents of the avant-garde. If nothing else, they are specimens of Burroughs' own synthesis of the cinema: they offer a *syne*ma of Burroughs' texts.

# 19

# Beckett, Proust, and Burroughs and the Perils of "Image Warfare"

Nicholas Zurbrugg

> The points of intersection are very important. [. . .] In
> cutting up you will get a point of intersection where
> the new material that you have intersects with what is
> there already in some very precise way, and then you
> start from there.[1]

A s this quotation from the novelist and professional wicked uncle of postmodernism, William Burroughs, suggests, one of the central concerns of the twentieth-century writer is the function of those "points of intersection" where different clusters of words and images interact. Burroughs' work may best be introduced anecdotally, in terms of French poet Henri Chopin's observation that when visiting Burroughs one finds that "the television is characteristically switched on, with the sound turned off, while images flicker by." Chopin perceptively adds that Burroughs is "above all an observer, who subsequently imagines cut-ups, thanks to this flood of images."[2]

Burroughs has himself discussed the attraction of flickering "old movies," avowing that "when talkies came in and they perfected the image, the movies became as dull as looking out the window."[3] This fascination for the ambiguous flickering image, as opposed to the "perfected" image, is by no means as eccentric as it might appear. In precisely the same way, pioneer film-maker Sergei Eisenstein insisted upon the "distinct non-synchronisation" of sound and visual imagery, arguing that "only a contrapuntal use of sound in relation to the visual montage piece will afford

Nicholas Zurbrugg, "Beckett, Proust, and Burroughs and the Perils of 'Image Warfare,'" *Samuel Beckett: Humanistic Perspectives,* ed. Morris Beja, S. E. Gontarski, and Pierre Astier (Columbus: Ohio State University Press, 1983): 172–87. Copyright © 1983 Ohio State University Press. Reprinted by permission.

a new potentiality of montage development and perfection," and that "every adhesion of sound to a visual montage piece increases its inertia."[4] In his very last interview, Eisenstein elaborated these ideas, remarking: "Art begins the moment the creaking of a boot on the sound-track occurs against a different visual shot and thus gives rise to corresponding association."[5] Briefly, both Burroughs and Eisenstein appear preoccupied with the ways in which discordant combinations of images, words, and sounds generate what Eisenstein terms "corresponding associations." In Burroughs' terms: "I've been interested in precisely how word and image get around on very, very complex association lines. [. . .] Cut-ups establish new connections between images, and one's range of vision consequently expands."[6]

In the context of this comparison of Beckett's, Proust's, and Burroughs' use of the image, it is essential to make a fundamental distinction between Eisenstein's and Burroughs' responses to "contrapuntal" images. Both agree that such images augment art's development and perfection; in Burroughs' opinion, "cut-up [. . .] enriches the whole aesthetic experience, extends it."[7] To this extent, Eisenstein's and Burroughs' experiments simply confirm the modernist creator's infatuation with surprising links between disparate sensations, which is best expressed by "Breton's law": "The value of the image depends upon the beauty of the spark obtained; it is consequently directly proportional to the difference in potential between the two conductors."[8] Put another way, in symbolic rather than surrealist terms, the value of the image is directly proportional to the sensitivity of the "superior man" who alone:

> can walk as master in the fantastic temple

>> Whose living pillars
>> Sometimes give forth indistinct words

> while the imbecile human flock, duped by the appearances that
> lead them to the denial of essential ideas, will pass forever blind

>> Through forests of symbols
>> Which watch him with familiar glances.[9]

These lines from Aurier's "Symbolism in Painting: Paul Gauguin" (of 1891), with their quotation from Baudelaire's poem "Correspondances," clearly assert that the poet *may* make sense of "indistinct words" and "forests of symbols," in a world in which "Les parfums, les couleurs et les sons se répondent [Perfumes, colors, and sounds answer one another]."[10] Eisenstein's reference to "corresponding associations" resulting from contrapuntal images and sounds similarly implies that his materials finally "answer" one another in what he termed " 'synthetic' combinations of tonal and overtonal montage."[11] The crucial distinction between this predominantly modernist response to the contrapuntal and Burroughs' essentially postmodern response resides in Burroughs' preoccupation with disparate words, images, and sounds that *refuse* to answer one another, and that rather than resolving their differences in "synthetic combinations," clash all the more violently in states that might perhaps be thought of as *image warfare*.

In other words, whereas such modernists as the symbolist poets, the surrealist poets, and Eisenstein combined contrasting images in order to generate new dimensions of artistic *unity*, Burroughs seems most interesting as an author exploring the social and political potential of the word and image as a "virus" propagating chaos. Burroughs has set forth his ideas on this subject in his book entitled *Electronic Revolution* and in his interviews with Daniel Odier collected in *The Job*.[12] The latter volume reprints Burroughs' early essay entitled "The Invisible Generation" (1966), in which Burroughs introduces his theories, first, in terms of experiments with one's own responses to words and images, and second, in terms of the potential public application of these experiments. The essay begins:

> what we see is determined to a large extent by what we hear you can
> verify this proposition by a simple experiment turn off the sound track
> on your television set and substitute an arbitrary sound track
> prerecorded on your tape recorder [. . .] you will find the arbitrary
> sound track seems to be appropriate and is in fact determining your
> interpretation of film track on screen people running for a bus in
> picadilly with a sound track of machine gun fire looks like 1917
> petrograd.[13]

With these admittedly somewhat dubious propositions in mind, Burroughs speculates:

> you want to start a riot put your machines in the street with riot
> recordings move fast enough you can stay just ahead of the riot
> surfboarding we call it no margin for error recollect poor old burns
> caught out in a persian market riot recordings hid under his jallaba and
> they skinned him alive raw peeled thing writhing there in the noon sun
> and we got the picture do you get the picture.[14]

With the entry of the anecdote about "poor old burns," Burroughs' theories drift into fiction and back again, as Burroughs proposes that this picture of "poor old burns" might itself be used subversively in an analogous context. Consistently illustrated and exemplified by the most grotesque fictions, Burroughs' ideas tend to defy credibility, especially when uttered by such freaks as the "death dwarf" from *Nova Express,* who informs his captors:

> Images—millions of images—That's what I eat—Cyclotron shit—Ever
> try kicking *that* habit with apomorphine?—Now I got all the images of
> sex acts and torture ever took place anywhere and I can just blast it
> out and control you gooks right down to the molecule.[15]

Although the comic genius of Burroughs' writing resides precisely in the death dwarf's subsequent antics: his repetition of the words "My Power's coming—My Power's coming—My Power's Coming," and his duplication of "a faith healer routine rolling his eyes and frothing at the mouth" (antics made all the more explicit in Burroughs' reading of this passage),[16] the most interesting factor here seems to be the emphasis upon the way in which images of sex and violence may disorient the dwarf's victims when "cut" into their habitual lifestyles, and thereby "control" them "right down to the molecule." For Burroughs, such "control" inevitably implies the provocation of some sort of humiliating and disordered reaction. Thus *Electronic Revolution* suggests that:

> A mike secreted in the water closet and all his shits and farts recorded
> and scrambled in with stern nanny voices commanding him to shit,
> and the young liberal shits in his pants on the platform right under Old
> Glory.[17]

Burroughs' undeniably idiosyncratic visions of image "warfare" offer a remarkable model for the kind of confusion experienced by the Beckettian hero, a coincidence that is best introduced in terms of the distinction that Burroughs made between their respective concerns when reflecting:

> What I want to do is to learn to see more of what's out there, to look
> outside, to achieve as far as possible a complete awareness of
> surroundings. Beckett wants to go inward.[18]

At the risk of indulging the intentional fallacy, this statement may be read as a valuable indication of Burroughs' interest in the role of images in the context of the "outside" or problems of *social control,* as opposed to Beckett's "inward" preoccupation with conflicting images of the self. To extend this distinction, it might be argued that whereas Burroughs enthusiastically contemplates ways of precipitating image "warfare" within society (by causing riots, for example), Beckett's characters seem the reluctant victims of the rioting images within their own minds—rioting images, moreover, that they would do anything to calm.

*Malone Dies* thus depicts the torments of Lemuel, who is "flayed alive by memory, his mind crawling with cobras, not daring to dream or think and powerless not to," whose only solution is to strike his head with a hammer.[19] Malone himself is similarly tormented. Describing his anguish in terms remarkably reminiscent of those of Burroughs, he comments:

> Words and images run riot in my head, pursuing, flying, clashing,
> merging endlessly. But beyond this tumult there is a great calm, and a
> great indifference, never really to be troubled by anything again.[20]

Malone's complaint, and that of the majority of Beckett's heroes, is that they seldom attain, let alone retain, this ideal calm. This essential dilemma utterly subverts the ideals that most Beckettian critics associate with Beckett's heroes.

The greatest confusion in Beckettian criticism almost certainly results from the repeated identification of Proustian virtues with Beckettian virtues. Nowhere has this identification been more misleading than in the case of Beckett's suggestion, in his study of *A la recherche du temps perdu* entitled *Proust,* that:

> The artist is active, but negatively, shrinking from the nullity of
> extracircumferential phenomena, drawn in to the core of the eddy. He
> cannot practice friendship because friendship is the centrifugal force of
> self-fear, self-negation. [21]

Taken in tandem with Beckett's subsequent reference to the Proustian artist's contempt for "the grotesque fallacy of a realistic art—'the miserable statement of line and surface,' and the penny-a-line vulgarity of a literature of notations" (76), the above statement has persuaded critics that Beckett's heroes similarly probe the "eddy" of the self, reject the "extracircumferential," and despise the superficiality of "line and surface." It is arguable that these ideals inspire certain Beckettian heroes, such as Murphy, at the beginning of their careers. But it is equally evident that by the end of their respective books, Beckettian heroes suffer so intensely from introspective "words and images run riot" that they retreat from what *Murphy* terms the "fly in the ointment of Microcosmos" to the relative safety of macrocosmic mathematics, such as Molloy's sucking-stone calculations. [22]

By the end of *Murphy,* Murphy confronts what he terms a "spool" of disturbing autobiographical images, or rather fragments, as "scraps of bodies, of landscapes, hands, eyes, lines and colours" rise in front of him; yet instead of descending to the "eddy" of these images, he decides that his experience "should be stopped . . . before the deeper coils were reached." [23] Both Beckett's subsequent *Film* and the more recent *A Piece of Monologue* dramatize this retreat from deep autobiographical reality even more explicitly, the former depicting the "scene of inspection and destruction of photographs," the latter depicting the "Speaker" red-handed, as it were, at the scene of the completed crime, avoiding all photographic and verbal "intersections" between his present condition and his past, and relating "Pictures of . . . he all but said of loved ones. . . . Down one after another. Gone. Torn to shreds and scattered. Strewn all over the floor." [24] Far from avoiding friendship, in order to facilitate introspective centripetal activity, most Beckettian heroes, such as the narrator of *Company,* deliberately evade centripetal introspection by following the centrifugal impulse to acquire the fictional friendship—or "company"—of imaginary, nonautobiographical data. Thus the narrator of *Company* expressly defines his dilemma as that of "the craving for company . . . In which to escape from his own." [25] This is, of course, the very reverse of the Proustian strategy of composing fiction to assist self-knowledge; and it is perhaps no coincidence that Beckett annotated Marcel's final wish to offer his readers "le moyen de lire en eux-mêmes" or "the means of reading themselves" with the incredulous, and doubtless disapproving, rejoinder: "Balls."[26]

This curious hostility to introspection seems especially bizarre, coming as it does from an author who quite plainly admires the Proustian hero's rejection of the "nullity" of habitual, macrocosmic reality. What made Beckett reject the Proustian virtues? The answer would seem to be: the Proustian vices. Or more accurately, Beckett's preoccupation with modes of intolerable "image warfare" in Proust's novel appears to have been far more enduring than his dutiful account of the way in which involuntary memory transforms image warfare into perpetual victory asserting the positive permanent reality of the self. Beckett's analyses of moments of image warfare in *A la recherche du temps perdu* are especially rewarding, for they not only point to a neglected dimension of Proust's novel but also indicate the way in which Beckett's critical priorities define his vision as being substantially different from that of Proust.

The two most interesting sections of Beckett's *Proust* concern incidents in which Marcel's images of others and himself cause considerable anguish, rather than resolving themselves and harmoniously responding one to the other, as terms of the symbolist salvation of involuntary memory. Beckett tellingly dubs the first of these— the incident when Marcel, leaning to unbutton his boots, both remembers his dead grandmother, and suffers excruciatingly from her absence—as "perhaps the greatest passage that Proust ever wrote" (39). Diagnosing this as a "poisoned" variant of involuntary memory, Beckett comments: "This contradiction between presence and absence is intolerable" (42), and in identical terms analyzes the way in which Marcel's hopelessly infatuated and hopelessly jealous responses to Albertine constitute "a multiplicity in depth, a turmoil of objective and immanent contradictions over which the subject has no control" (47).

Few phrases could better describe the perceptual chaos afflicting Beckett's subsequent heroes. And with but a shuffling of negatives, few phrases could better describe the Beckettian hero's antidote to such profound perceptual torment: the antidote of "a multiplicity *without depth,* a turmoil of objective and immanent contradictions over which the subject *has control*"—in Molloy's terms, *"dutiful confusions."*[27] Beckett's analysis of Marcel's agonizingly *un*dutiful confusions focuses upon its key crisis: the occasion when, having associated Albertine both with the beauty of the sea, and with a disquieting vision of lesbian love glimpsed at Montjouvain, Marcel not only can no longer differentiate between these conflicting versions of Albertine, but also can no longer enjoy the sea as an object of beauty in its own right, since it has become permanently associated with Albertine and with her disturbing lesbian proclivities. A victim of his own associations, Marcel has—to use Burroughs' terms—inadvertently "cut-up" a "sex" image and a maritime image, finding that "the sea is a veil that cannot hide the horror of Montjouvain, the intolerable vision of sadistic lubricity," and envisioning his subsequent life as "a succession of joyless dawns, poisoned by the tortures of memory and isolation" (52–53).

The concept of memory as a source of "intolerable vision" and of something

"poisoned" duplicates the key adjectives in Beckett's analysis of the previous incident, and partially anticipates his surprising subsequent suggestion that the perceptual
miracle of Proust's novel— involuntary memory—is notable as a source of *"intolerable* brightness" (70).[28] This passage also describes Marcel's revelation more positively, as a source of "felicity." But the suspicion that Beckett would imply that
*all* intense introspective perceptions—poisoned or unpoisoned—are intolerable is
substantially confirmed by Beckett's avowal that Proust's wisdom consists of "the
ablation of desire" (18), and "in obliterating the faculty of suffering" (63). At the
beginning of *Proust,* Beckett quite properly distinguishes between the Proustian
notions of the habitual and the inhabitual, or in Beckett's morose formulas: the
"boredom of living" and the "suffering of being"—a state in which man experiences
the "free play of every faculty" (19, 20). To achieve the supposedly Proustian ideal
of obliterating the faculty of suffering, man must therefore obliterate "being," halt
the free play of every faculty, and limit existence to the very "boredom of living"
constituted by the "nullity of extracircumferential phenomena." This is certainly not
the wisdom of Proust's heroes, who employ their every faculty during the triumphant
existential struggles that Elstir defines as "un combat et une victoire" (1:864)—a
combat and a victory. The ablation of desire, and self-immersion in the extracircumferential *is,* however, the negative wisdom of such nihilistic Proustian characters as
Marcel's *tante* Léonie, who cherishes "l'inertie absolue [absolute inertia]" (1:50);
and it would also appear to be the wisdom of such Beckettian archetypes as Estragon
and Vladimir, who find the habitual "a great deadener."[29]

Despite the fact that Marcel suffers from the intolerable and poisoned memories
and confusions that Beckett analyzes so impressively in his *Proust,* his experience
does not culminate in the Beckettian wisdom of the ablation of desire. Rather, in
the face of considerable evidence to the contrary, Marcel finally concludes that
man's desires *are* worthy of realization. A key phase in the evolution of his conclusion occurs when Marcel meditates upon some pear trees and cherry trees, finding
them to symbolize:

> Custodians of memories from the golden age, witnesses to the promise
> that reality is not what we suppose it to be, and that the splendour of
> poetry and the marvellous radiance of innocence may shine within it,
> and may be the reward that we should make every effort to merit.
> (2:161–62)[30]

As Beckett himself implied, when admiring the "dualism in multiplicity" of the
"Proustian equation" (11), Proust's vision is perhaps most impressive of all in terms
of the ways in which it elaborates the "dual," or positive and negative, potential of
every experience. Although perceptual salvation in Proust's novel results from the
symbolist aesthetic of sensations that both correspond and respond to one another,
Proust's exemplification of "poisoned" memories and associations also probes the
reverse of such perceptual felicity. If few critics apart from Beckett have elucidated
this neglected dimension of Proust's novel, few authors apart from Beckett have

created a life's work based primarily upon such "poisoned" perceptions. The disadvantage of this elaboration of the "poisoned" is, of course, that Beckett cannot (and indeed does not) make any claim to emulate the extraordinary *multiplicity* of Proust's *dualistic* vision. Few trees blossom in Beckett's fiction, and even those that do cause disgust or confusion. Perched under a hawthorn (Marcel's favorite flora), Molloy grimly comments: "The white hawthorn stooped towards me, unfortunately I don't like hawthorn."[31] Waiting next to their solitary tree, Estragon and Vladimir bicker over its identity, finding it both "a bush" and "a shrub."[32]

It may be argued that Beckett's vision *is* nevertheless dualistic, since works like *Waiting for Godot* abound in binary oppositions of words and characters. This is undeniable, yet at the same time the *content* of the binary oppositions in Proust's fiction and those in Beckett's fiction is immensely different. Proust's binary oppositions operate on three distinct levels—between the habitual and the unpoisoned inhabitual; between the habitual and the poisoned inhabitual; and between the poisoned and the unpoisoned inhabitual. Beckett's binaries inhabit a world without unpoisoned inhabitual experience. His characters fluctuate between the boredom of the deadeningly habitual and the intolerable anguish of almost invariably poisoned inhabitual perceptions. At best they occasionally lose consciousness altogether before inevitably boomeranging back into boredom or intolerable anguish.

Caught between the ever increasing perceptual disadvantages of the perceptual frying pan of habit and the perceptual fire of the inhabitual, it is scarcely surprising that Beckett's characters attempt to avoid introspection by absorbing themselves in the ritualistic pastimes of gestures, dialogues, and endlessly invented fictions. At most, their recognition of identity occurs in carefully censored fragmentary monologues, such as those of *Not I, Company,* and *A Piece of Monologue,* in which every effort is made either to avoid the expression of autobiographical data or at least to minimize the anguish accompanying its expression by repetitive and circumambulatory narration. Considered collectively, these recent variations on autobiographical fragments occasionally add to the reader's knowledge of Beckett's own biography. For example, *Company* alludes to a childhood game of jumping from the top of pine trees: an odd pastime only mentioned previously by secondary sources in Deirdre Bair's biography of Beckett.[33] One might surmise that, almost despite himself, Beckett is gradually revealing, and perhaps thereby nullifying, painful autobiographical details, a tendency akin to that which Allen Ginsberg has attributed to William Burroughs' cut-ups. Ginsberg comments:

> In fact, the cut-ups were originally designed to rehearse and repeat his
> obsession with sexual images over and over again, like a movie
> repeating over and over and over again, and then re-combined and cut
> up and mixed in; so that finally the obsessive attachment, compulsion,
> and preoccupation empty out and drain from the image. . . . Finally,
> the hypnotic attachment, the image, becomes demystified. . . . *He can
> finally look at it at the end of the spool;* he can look at his most
> tender, personal, romantic images objectively, and no longer be
> attached to them.[34]

Although the specific content of Burroughs' and Beckett's "most tender, personal
. . . images" are very different, it is perhaps not too wild a suggestion to proprose
that such Beckettian heroes as Krapp might be deemed to be repeating, cutting up,
and demystifying certain highly tender and personal images so as to defuse their
painfully explosive content. In other words, Krapp's repeated reference to his taped
account of his haunting moments with a girl in a punt might be interpreted as his
attempt to come to terms with his poisoned memory of love that he ironically rejected
for a career he now no longer cares for. In Ginsberg's terms, Krapp is trying to
reach the point when he can relatively painlessly "look at it at the end of the spool."

Ginsberg's statement not only provides a helpful method for an understanding of
the introspective strategies of such Beckettian heroes as Krapp but also places
Burroughs' writings in a wider context. Despite Burroughs' suggestion that he is
primarily interested in "outside" reality, it seems clear that to some extent at least
his cut-ups reiterate "inward" imagery, be this to demystify and placate sexual
obsessions, as Ginsberg suggests, or to provoke sexual stimulation (a possibility
that, as Harold Beaver remarks, Burroughs himself implies in his maxim "Any
writer who has not masturbated with his own characters will not be able to make them
live on paper").[35] Whether Burroughs' texts serve or served Burroughs personally as
pornographic intoxicant or disintoxicant is perhaps beside the point, or at least very
secondary to their decisive difference from pulp pornography in terms of their
exploration of the cut-up as both a literary device and as a subversive weapon for
the verbal-visual urban guerilla. To acknowledge this function of Burroughs' writing
is neither to deny its pornographic content nor to accept blindly the frequent eccentric
formulations and exemplifications of its variously convincing theories. It is, however, to suggest the shortsightedness of such evaluations of Burroughs' ideas as
George Steiner's reference to their "childish conceit of a loose-leaf book—to be put
together at random or at the reader's will,"[36] and to argue for Burroughs' validity as
a theorist who has fascinatingly explored the subversive potential of *contrapuntal*
intersections of words and images, and whose work additionally evokes the perfect
concept for the confusion of Beckett's heroes: the concept of *image warfare*.

Located in the perceptual context of rioting words and images, the Beckettian
hero's retreat from painful centripetal confusion to relatively painless centrifugal
confusion is much easier to understand. For too long, critics have misleadingly
attempted to interpret Beckett by *comparing* instead of *contrasting* Proust and
Beckett. Beckett is not Proust (and is not Burroughs), nor was meant to be. But
when considered halfway, as it were, *between* Proust and Burroughs, as a writer
whose concerns are partially Proustian, insofar as they examine poisoned (but not
unpoisoned) involuntary memories, and as a writer who is partially Burroughsian,
insofar as he examines inward (but not outward) manifestations of image warfare,
Beckett can at least be approached within the general parameters of his *own* priorities.
This contextualization plainly takes no account of the different qualities of Beckett's,
Proust's, and Burroughs' writing, but it does perhaps avoid the prevailing myth that
Beckett's and Proust's responses to the autobiographical image—or the image of
the self—are somehow susceptible to the same "law."[37] This is patently not the case;

indeed, it is arguable that writers such as Beckett, Proust, and Burroughs are most fascinating and most satisfying precisely in terms of the ways in which they elaborate and explore diverging—and at times incompatible—approaches to the image of the self.

Proust, for example, provides an exemplary instance of the predominantly optimistic literary experiments of the modernist writer, both in terms of his confident, all-inclusive, telescopic sentences, and in terms of his belief in the perceptual salvation of involuntary memory. By contrast, the respectively "inward" and "outward" texts of Beckett and Burroughs both bear the two hallmarks of the postmodern writer: a pessimistic obsession with incoherent, confused, fragmentary observations, and a more optimistic approach to the creative potential of the new technology of the recording studio, television, and cinema.[38] The originality of Proust, Beckett, and Burroughs lies not so much in any apparent overlap between their ideas in such texts as Beckett's *Proust*, as in the *differences* between their pre-technological and part-technological verbalizations and dramatizations of complex "intersections" between different images of the self. To reduce their originality to any single "law" is to lose sight of their contrasting achievements, and yet to juxtapose their ideas is a useful means of revealing their individuality. As Beckett warned the reader some fifty years ago, "The danger is in the neatness of identifications."[39]

## Notes

1. William Burroughs, *The Job,* interviews by Daniel Odier (London: Cape, 1970) 16–17.

2. Henri Chopin, *Poésie sonore internationale* (Paris: Place, 1979) 136. My translation. ("Il est caractéristique en allant chez lui de voir la T.V. branchée, mais muette, tandis que l'image défile. . . . Burroughs est d'abord un regardant, il imagine ensuite, grâce à ce flot d'images, des *cut-ups*.")

3. William Burroughs, interview by Conrad Knickerbocker, *Paris Review* 35 (1965): 42.

4. S. M. Eisenstein, V. I. Pudovkin, and G. M. Alexandrov, "A Statement," in Sergei Eisenstein, *Film Forum: Essays in Film Theory,* ed. and trans. Jay Leyda (New York: Harcourt, 1949) 258. First published in Leningrad in *Zhizn Iskusstva,* 5 Aug. 1928.

5. Sergei Eisenstein quoted by Ilya Veissfeld, "Mon dernier entretien avec Eisenstein," *Cahiers du Cinéma* 208 (1969): 21. Translated by Stephen Heath in Roland Barthes, *Image Music Text,* ed. and trans. Stephen Heath (Glasgow: Fontana, 1977) 61–62. ("L'art commence à partir du moment où le craquement de la botte [au son], tombe sur un plan visuel différent et suscite ainsi des associations correspondantes.")

6. Burroughs, *Paris Review* interview, 21, 25.

7. Burroughs, 27. Burroughs defines the cut-up process in William Burroughs and Brion Gysin, *The Third Mind* (New York: Viking, 1978) 25–33. Walter Veit has interestingly noted that a variation of the cut-up, the cross-reading (or the process of interlinking lines in consecutive columns), served eighteenth-century newspaper readers as a means of "connecting wittily the unconnected" ("Intellectual Tradition and Pacific Discoveries of the Function of Quotations in Georg Forster's *Voyage Round the World,*" in *Captain James Cook Image and Impact: South Seas Discoveries and the World of Letters, 2, The Pacific Syndrome: Conditions and Consequences,* ed. Walter Veit [Melbourne: Hawthorn, 1979] 117).

8. André Breton, "Manifeste du surréalisme" (1924), in *Manifestes du surréalisme* (Paris: Gallimard, 1966) 51; my translation. ("La valeur de l'image dépend de la beauté de l' étincelle obtenue; elle est, par conséquent, fonction de la différence de potentiel entre les deux conducteurs.")

9. G.-Albert Aurier, "Le Symbolisme en peinture: Paul Gauguin," *Mercure de France* (Paris) 2 (1891): 161. Translated by H. R. Rookmaaker and Herschel B. Chipp in *Theories of Modern Art: A Source Book by Artists and Critics,* ed. Herschel B. Chipp (Berkeley: U of California P, 1968) 91.

("L'homme supérieur . . . seul sait . . . se promener en maître
dans ce temple fantastique
Oú de vivants piliers
Laissent parfois sortir de confuses paroles . . .
alors que l'imbécile troupeau humain, dupé par les apparences qui
lui feront nier les idées essentielles, passera éternellement aveugle
A travers les forêts de symboles
Qui l'observent avec des regards familiers.")

10. Charles Baudelaire, "Correspondences," *Les Fleurs du mal,* collected in *Oeuvres complètes,* ed. Marcel A. Ruff (1857; rpt. Paris: Seuil, 1968) 46.

11. Eisenstein, "The Filmic Fourth Dimension," *Film Form,* 68.

12. William Burroughs, *Electronic Revolution,* collected in *Ah Pook Is Here and Other Texts* (1971; rpt. London: Calder, 1979) 123–57.

13. "The Invisible Generation," collected in *The Job,* 159–60.

14. "The Invisible Generation," 165–66.

15. William Burroughs, *Nova Express* (1964; rpt. London: Panther, 1968) 43.

16. Burroughs reads from this section of *Nova Express,* subtitled "Inflexible Authority," 42–46, on the phonograph recording *Call Me Burroughs* (Paris: English Bookshop, 1965). Burroughs' impressive readings are more readily available on the double recording *William Burroughs/John Giorno* (New York: Giorno Poetry Systems, 1975), GPS 006–007.

17. *Ah Pook Is Here,* 135.

18. *Paris Review* interview, 23.

19. Samuel Beckett, *Malone Dies* (London: Calder, 1956); collected in *Molloy, Malone Dies, The Unnamable* (London: Calder and Boyars, 1959) 268–69.

20. *Molloy, Malone Dies, The Unnamable,* 198.

21. Samuel Beckett, *Proust* (1931; rpt. London: Calder, 1970) 65–66. All subsequent page references to this edition are given in the text.

22. Samuel Beckett, *Murphy* (1938; rpt. London: Calder and Boyars, 1970) 124. *Molloy* (Paris: Olympia, 1955). Collected in *Molloy, Malone Dies, The Unnamable,* 68–74.

23. *Murphy,* 172.

24. Samuel Beckett, *Film* (1969; rpt. London: Faber, 1972) 36; *A Piece of Monologue, Kenyon Review* ns 1 (1979): 2.

25. Samuel Beckett, *Company* (London: Calder, 1980) 77.

26. All references to Marcel Proust's *A la recherche du temps perdu* refer to the three-volume edition edited by Pierre Clarac and André Ferré (Paris: Gallimard, Bibliothèque de la Pléiade, 1954). Beckett's annotated copies of *A la recherche du temps perdu* (1917–27; rpt. Paris: Gallimard, Editions de la Nouvelle Revue Française, 1925–29), are located in the Beckett Collection of the University of Reading Library, England. Beckett's annotated

comment "Balls" appears in *Le Temps retrouvé*, 36th ed. (1927; rpt. Paris: Gallimard, Editions de la Nouvelle Revue Française, 1929) 240 (3:1033).

27. *Molloy, Malone Dies, The Unnamable*, 15. My italics.

28. My italics.

29. Samuel Beckett, *Waiting for Godot* (1956; London: Faber, 1977) 91.

30. My translation. ("Gardiens des souvenirs de l'âge d'or, garants de la promesse que la réalité n'est pas ce qu'on croit, que la splendeur de la poésie, que l'éclat merveilleux de l'innocence peuvent y resplendir et pourront être la récompense que nous nous efforcerons de mériter.")

31. *Molloy, Malone Dies, The Unnamable*, 27.

32. *Waiting for Godot*, 14.

33. Deirdre Bair, *Samuel Beckett: A Biography* (London: Cape, 1978) 15.

34. Allen Ginsberg quoted by Harold Beaver, "Saint William of Tangier," *Times Literary Supplement* (22 July 1977): 893. My italics.

35. Burroughs quoted by Beaver, "Saint William of Tangier."

36. George Steiner, *Language and Silence* (1967; Harmondsworth: Penguin, 1969) 343.

37. See John Fletcher and John Spurling, *Beckett: A Study of His Plays* (London: Eyre, 1972) 28. Here Spurling maintains that Beckett's *Proust* functions as "a table of the law for any student of either Proust, or Beckett."

38. Both Beckett and Burroughs have worked with most of these new technological genres. Burroughs has made such films as *Towers Open Fire* (1963) and *The Cut-Ups* (1967) with Antony Balch, and has also made recorded texts such as "Valentine Day Reading," available on Revue-Disque OU, No. 40–41 (Ingatestone, 1972). Beckett has made *Film* (1964), with Alain Schneider; plays involving tape-recorded monologues for the stage, such as *Krapp's Last Tape* (1958) and *That Time* (1976); as well as radio plays such as "All That Fall" (1957), and television plays such as "Ghost trio" (1977).

39. Samuel Beckett, "Dante . . . Bruno. Vico . . Joyce," in *Our Exagmination Round His Factification for Incamination of Work in Progress* (1929; London: Faber, 1972) 3.

# 20

# Freedom through Fantasy
# in the Recent Novels of
# William S. Burroughs

Jennie Skerl

A lmost all of the serious criticism of William S. Burroughs has been devoted to *Naked Lunch* (1959) and the three related novels that he published soon after that seminal work, *The Soft Machine* (1961), *The Ticket That Exploded* (1962), and *Nova Express* (1964).[1] Several critics have thoroughly explicated the technical innovations in this series of novels: the addiction metaphor, the creation of a mythology (the Nova conspiracy), the use of a montage structure, and the cut-up technique.[2] Very little critical attention, however, has been given to Burroughs' more recent novels, which also constitute a series, beginning with *The Wild Boys* in 1971 and including *Exterminator!* (1973), *Port of Saints* (1975), and *Cities of the Red Night* (1981). Consequently, no critic has pointed out that these works inhabit a different metaphorical world from the earlier series and that Burroughs' technique has changed as well, even though he himself announced a new departure in an interview in 1972.[3] Lack of attention to Burroughs' recent work has also been accompanied by lack of appreciation; recent reviewers have tended to complain that Burroughs' latest work is repetitious and boring.[4] This current assessment unfortunately encourages readers to ignore a body of work that exhibits continued energy and innovation by the self-styled "cosmonaut of inner space."

The four major novels published from 1971 to 1981 create a second metaphorical world which replaces the Nova mythology of Burroughs' earlier work. This second mythology repeats Burroughs' perennial themes: criticism of the social structures that threaten individual freedom, the biological trap of sex and death, and the quest of the writer to free himself and his readers from bondage to social and biological

Jennie Skerl, "Freedom through Fantasy in the Recent Novels of William S. Burroughs," *The Review of Contemporary Fiction* 4.1 (1984): 124–30. Copyright© 1984 by *The Review of Contemporary Fiction*. Reprinted by permission.

control. But the emphasis on politics, on fantasy, and on the writer's power is new in these recent novels, as is the attention given to man's positive potential for autonomy, regeneration, and creation. Whereas the Nova mythology stressed that "To speak is to lie—To live is to collaborate"[5] and that "free men [ . . . ] don't exist in human bodies,"[6] Burroughs' second mythology, which I call "freedom through fantasy," expresses more hope for the individual and for change through "utopian dreams."

Burroughs' second mythology, like the Nova myth, is constructed from autobiographical experience and popular culture, but he makes use of new materials from both sources. The most significant new biographical material in the later works is childhood memories, and, in particular, the sexual fantasies of adolescence. Thus sexuality becomes the central metaphor of the later works, replacing the earlier addiction metaphor. In the recent fiction, pleasure and freedom through fantasy balance the experience of repression, bondage, and death that the earlier works had emphasized. Sexual fantasy is linked to artistic creation as a source of and model for fiction—a different but powerful formulation of Burroughs' recurrent thesis that art can be made by everyone and that everyone is an artist. At the same time, Burroughs attaches greater importance than before to the ability of the *writer*, more than any other artist, to create new worlds, and to writing as an art form that cannot be replaced by other media, whereas his earlier work had been antiliterary in its attack upon the *word*.

As in the earlier novels, Burroughs continues to incorporate new materials from popular culture. Important new additions are allusions to popular political movements (especially extremes of right and left), youth movements, utopian science fiction fantasies, and fascinations with the occult. But Burroughs' most significant use of popular culture in the later works is his imitation of the simple narrative style of popular fiction, especially the pulp fiction he read in his youth. By using the narrative style as well as the characters, images, and actions of the pulps, Burroughs merges his personal fantasies with mass-media fantasies that reach a large public. Thus, for his own subversive purpose, Burroughs appropriates the fantasies of freedom and escape found in the pulps, and, at the same time, develops a style that is more accessible than the prose collage created by cut-ups.

Just as the Nova mythology informed all of Burroughs' fiction in the 1960s, Burroughs' second mythology informs all of his fiction from 1971 to 1981. In this second metaphorical world, however, the myth is developed through narrative rather than through cut-ups. For each of those three major themes—social criticism, the biological trap, and the writer's quest—Burroughs creates a fantasy that becomes one of the major narrative lines in the recent fiction and a metaphor in the myth.

In the recent works, Burroughs' social criticism is conveyed through utopian alternatives to the present social order so that his satirical fantasies now consist of both utopias and dystopias in conflict with each other, whereas his earlier fiction had contained extensive portrayals only of dystopias. Burroughs' utopian vision begins in *The Wild Boys* with the futuristic fantasy of "the wild boys": an adolescent, all-male hunting society that conducts a guerrilla war against our social system. This creation evolves throughout the fiction of the next decade, as Burroughs incorporates the wild boys into various utopian and dystopian fantasies. Finally, in *Cities of the Red Night,* the wild boys are subsumed into an anarchist's republic, founded by eighteenth-century pirates, called a "retroactive utopia" by Burroughs.

In the recent novels, Burroughs again takes up the theme of the biological trap that makes humanity susceptible to manipulation by power structures and incapable of transcending the concepts of reality that reinforce social power relationships. He again equates death with sexuality, but the dream erection replaces the orgasm-death of the hanged man as the central image and thus gives the basis for visions of transcendence as well as bondage. Burroughs proposes an occult fantasy in which, through conscious control of sex and death, an individual can enter a dream state of immortality. He can free himself from time, the body, and the individual ego. Within this fantasy, orgasm produces transformations in identity which can be controlled by adepts. Metamorphosis thus can be positive or neutral in contrast to the predominantly negative metamorphoses of the earlier works. This occult fantasy enables Burroughs to link all of his characters and narratives together through transformations of identity.

The theme of the writer's quest in the later works is conveyed by autobiographical images of Burroughs himself as a writer. Burroughs draws from earlier parts of his biography and creates an important new character—Audrey Carsons—a version of himself as a child-writer that replaces the Lee persona, Burroughs' alter ego in the Nova myth. Like Lee, Audrey plays many roles within the metaphorical world of the later novels. As a character created by Burroughs, he is at times a victim of dystopian forces or at other times a wild boy who attacks social evil or evades the biological trap through metamorphosis. As a version of Burroughs the author, Audrey is often identified as the all-powerful creator of the narratives in which he appears, yet also as a powerless creature manipulated by Burroughs himself. Audrey represents the ambivalent and contradictory status of the writer in Burroughs' second mythology: he has more importance *as* a writer because only writers create stories, and all fantasy is story; yet he is most aware of the limitations of fantasy. Whereas he has total power over his characters, his power over readers is limited to example, and he has no power to free himself from his individual consciousness, history, or death.

The plot of Burroughs' second myth, like the first, is an eternal battle between good and evil, but the opposing forces are now more clearly separated and polarized than in the earlier fiction, leading to simpler images and action, and also leading to more violence as mutually exclusive realities attempt to destroy each other. More weight is given to the power of utopian fantasy to conquer dystopian reality. The wild boys, for example, can finally destroy a repressive civilization simply by ignoring or forgetting it. The individual can enter and control his dreams and thus free himself from his past, his socially controlled ego, and his body. Art can produce individual and social freedom, and everyone is an artist in that everyone can create his own fantasies or stories. The persona of the writer, however, qualifies the myth's simplicity. The consciousness that creates fantasy-story-art remains self-conscious and thus aware that utopian dreams are not themselves actions. Thus Burroughs' utopian fantasies are always placed in the past or in the future as alternative realities that can prompt change in the present, but they are never portrayed as existing in present time.

*The Wild Boys* consists of eighteen relatively brief "routines" (satirical fantasies) that contain more narrative and fewer cut-up passages than Burroughs' previous novels. *The Wild Boys* explicitly tells the reader that the book is a film montage in style and structure, thus clarifying and simplifying the film metaphor that Burroughs has used in the past. Every scene is defined as an ephemeral "set"; every narrative is a "script"; every point of view is a "camera angle"; and every character is an "actor" who frequently changes identities from one narrative sequence to another (as if one film were spliced into another). In addition, greater simplicity of character and image establishes parallels with popular narratives such as comic books.

The story of the wild boys is the dominant narrative in the novel and thus makes revolt the dominant theme. The wild boys story is a science-fiction fantasy set in the near future in which Burroughs imagines a breakdown of the current social order. Large portions of the Western world have reverted to savagery and chaos, and what remains of our civilization exists within walled enclosures where an elite rule through a totalitarian police state. The character of the future dystopia is based on the middle-class, middle-aged Midwestern America of Burroughs' youth, represented by the interminable racist bore Colonel Greenfield. This dystopia is opposed by the wild boys, who are a utopian force: a tribe of youth without a hierarchy and whose cult practices make them immortal. They are both an escape from a repressive civilization to a fantasy world of endlessly gratified desire, and a worldwide guerrilla force that recruits and trains youth to fight the totalitarian social order. The wild boys are intentionally regressive psychologically and socially in order to evade the social controls that underlie our civilization: concepts of God, country, family, and sexuality. As the wild boys' manifesto says:

> We intend to march on the police machine everywhere. We intend to
> destroy the police machine and all its records. We intend to destroy all
> dogmatic verbal systems. The family unit and its cancerous expansion
> into tribes, countries, nations we will eradicate at its vegetable roots.
> We don't want to hear any more family talk, mother talk, father talk,
> cop talk, priest talk, country talk, or party talk. To put it country
> simple we have heard enough bullshit.[7]

The imagery and actions of the wild boys define them as embodiments of demonic energy; and it is as energy that they are best understood, not as characters. They are utopian as a *force,* not as literal images of the ideal community. (Within the total fiction of this novel and the works that follow, they are a force that combats totalitarian repression.) The wild boys represent the release of demonic energy in conscious fantasy, which Burroughs believes is a means of human liberation—both personal and social. By bringing the unconscious, irrational desires of the individual and the group to consciousness and by playing with these forces in artistic structure, Burroughs seeks to free, understand, and regulate man's irrational desires. From this conscious playing with demonic energy, Burroughs believes a new human and a new society can evolve. *The Wild Boys,* however, does not describe this new world: it ends on a note of conflict and disintegration as an unidentified narrator attempts to break conventional time barriers and join the wild boys in the fictional future.

Burroughs' next major work, *Exterminator!*, continues in the style of *The Wild Boys:* more narrative, fewer cut-ups, explicit use of the film metaphor, greater simplicity of action and characterization. The major theme throughout is the writer's quest for freedom, and *Exterminator!* is largely devoted to developing this story line within the second mythology. The autobiographical Audrey Carsons plays a major role as the child-writer whose fiction expresses his fantasies of power and freedom.

In *Exterminator!* the writer takes on the destructive role played by the wild boys in the previous novel. The writer is equated with a (vermin) exterminator, a job that Burroughs once held, and as exterminator he kills off all of his characters and destroys their worlds. The "extermination" is singularly mild in its impact upon the reader, however, because the explicit film metaphor and the cartoon level of characterization distance us from the characters and the acts of violence. Each character is an ephemeral image, not a fixed identity, an actor in the film the author has created from his own consciousness and whom he can painlessly destroy. The ease with which the writer creates, transforms, and destroys his fictions encourages the reader to view "self," "reality," and "time" as equally transitory and illusory fictions which we have the power to destroy or change. Fictional transformation is equated with immortality. But the writer cannot finally disappear into his fictions. In the final routine called "The End," Burroughs portrays a writer whose film is running out, but who cannot imagine a life outside the film. Similarly, Burroughs the man is tied to his temporal, physical existence and cannot be free of his own historical self. *Exterminator!* shows the power of the writer to create and destroy, and thus the power of consciousness to play with the structure of reality, but bondage to "present time" remains.

*Exterminator!* also uses the film metaphor for satirical analysis of social evil. The image of the film running out is used to warn of the imminent collapse of Western civilization which has been repeating the same script of power and control over the centuries. Both the victims and the controllers have begun to lose faith in the repetitious old film. As Burroughs stated in the chapter entitled "The Coming of the Purple Better One," a routine about the 1968 confrontation between the Chicago police and youthful demonstrators:

> I have described the Chicago police as left over from 1910 and in a
> sense this is true. Daley and his nightstick authority date back to turn-
> of-the-century ward politics. They are anachronisms and they know it.
> This I think accounts for the shocking ferocity of their behavior. [. . .]
> And what is the phantom fuzz screaming from Chicago to Berlin,

from Mexico City to Paris? "We are REAL REAL REAL!! Real as
this NIGHTSTICK!" As they feel, in their dim animal way, that
reality is slipping away from them.[8]

The style of Burroughs' satire in *Exterminator!* returns to the broad humor and
outrageous obscenity of his earliest routines, such as "Roosevelt After Inauguration"
(originally part of "In Search of Yage," written in 1953). Some of his oldest
characters and images reappear: the virus, the baboon, the repressive policeman,
the man-become-monster. Burroughs' piece on the 1968 Democratic Convention,
for example, makes brilliant use of the baboon character (with which Burroughs had
attacked Roosevelt's lust for power) in order to satirize the 1968 election and to link
his past and present political satire. This return to an earlier style and imagery
reinforces Burroughs' point that the power structure is endlessly repetitious in its
methods and its goals. Burroughs' satire can only repeat itself, exposing the same
lies, attacking the same outrages.

*Port of Saints* shows Burroughs returning to narrative as the basic form of the
novel, for *Port of Saints* consists entirely of stories. Although some of the stories
are typical Burroughs routines (satirical fantasies), most are nonsatirical narratives
set in an imaginary past or future. For the first time, Burroughs becomes a storyteller
who develops his imaginary world entirely through narrative transformation (that
is, storytelling) rather than through juxtaposition (cut-ups). These stories are not,
however, whole narratives. They tend to be episodes that are part of an implied,
but not completed plot. Also, the stories in *Port of Saints* are not narrated in a
straightforward, conventional manner. Burroughs has fragmented the stories into
very short passages and shuffled them together.

In *Port of Saints*, Burroughs further develops his second mythology by creating
new stories from new and old material and by linking the stories together. He
continues to develop themes, images, characters, and plots from *The Wild Boys* and
*Exterminator!*, the most important being stories about Audrey Carsons and the wild
boys. He resurrects old characters from his earlier fiction, such as Brad, Greg, and
A.J., and he creates many new characters who become important in the mythology:
the boys in Harbor Beach, Captain Opium Jones and his crew, and Jerry the carnival
boy. Stories are linked as characters from one story enter another and as Burroughs
gradually suggests that one of the characters, Audrey the child-writer, is the author
of all the stories. Audrey is a reader of pulp fiction (*Amazing Stories, Weird Tales,
Adventure Stories*) whose stories imitate his reading. Thus the source of the stories
explains their episodic structure and their popular style.

The most important plot development in *Port of Saints* is the merger of the Audrey
Carsons and the wild boys stories in a plot to rewrite history. In *Port of Saints*,
Audrey becomes a wild boy and is part of a guerrilla action by the wild boys to
"rewrite all the wrongs of history" through time travel, identity change, immunity
from the cycle of birth and death, individual control of sex and dreams, and
technological creativity. An example of how to rewrite history is given in the second
chapter, "Numero Uno." The wild boys travel to a West Indian island in the year

1845 and act as technical advisers to black guerrillas fighting Portuguese and British colonialists. Using raw materials, technology, and knowledge available at the time, the wild boys invent new weapons with which the guerrillas defeat the European troops. The wild boys' intervention in the West Indies changes not only political history but also technological history: science fiction changes the present by changing the past. This new plot development in *Port of Saints* prepares the way for the retroactive utopia of Burroughs' next major novel.

*Cities of the Red Night* is a culmination of Burroughs' second mythology of freedom through fantasy. Burroughs attempts in this novel (the longest he has ever written) to expand his mythological narratives to include the entire earth, all of its peoples, both sexes, and all of human history. The book's three interrelated plots thoroughly develop the three major themes of the second mythology. A retroactive utopia founded by eighteenth-century pirates is the basis for Burroughs' social criticism. A story about the dystopian "Cities of the Red Night" focuses on the theme of the biological trap. And the writer's quest is conveyed through a contemporary detective story in which a private investigator finds he must rewrite history to "solve" his case.

*Cities of the Red Night* creates a science-fiction myth that explains all of human history as we know it and an alternative history that shows the power of fantasy. The "Cities" of the title are an imaginary, prehistoric civilization portrayed in a science-fiction mode that satirizes contemporary Western society. The Cities are a dystopia set in the past but mirroring the present. These prehistoric Cities are also the source of the B–23 virus, a metaphor for the biological trap of sex and death. This virus in present time sets in motion a contemporary detective story that is gradually transformed into the writer's attempt to free mankind from bondage to the past. Burroughs contrasts his dystopian vision of the Cities of the Red Night and their disastrous legacy to the present with a retroactive utopia that universalizes the wild boys' fantasy. He transforms the wild boys plot to rewrite history into the story of a libertarian pirate society in eighteenth-century South America which overthrows Spanish rule and changes the course of history. The citizens who subscribe to the "Articles" of liberty fight a continual guerrilla war against the nation-state and its methods of control. They create a society of small communes, loosely federated to share technology, expertise, and defense. This anarchist utopia, perhaps Burroughs' true political ideal, is projected into present time, based on its imaginary historical origin. Thus Burroughs' dystopian Cities and utopian communes are placed in conflict in the present as metaphors for opposing forces in contemporary society, and the writer-detective must resolve the conflict.

Burroughs is not content with simply telling a story, however. Rather, he wants to show the reader the power of storytelling, and, in particular, the power of fantasy in all senses of the word. Although book one begins the novel in a relatively conventional manner by introducing the three plot lines and developing each one separately, Burroughs never goes on to complete these stories. In books two and three, plot development becomes episodic, fragmented, and chaotic. Story lines remain unfinished as Burroughs merges his three narratives in order to emphasize their fictionality, implying that these particular stories are only a few of the infinite possibilities in the field of consciousness. The point is that Burroughs wants to stimulate readers to create their own stories, rather than passively consume his creations. Just as the Nova mythology showed the reader how to destroy old myths with cut-ups, *Cities of the Red Night* shows the reader how to create alternative realities with the basic human ability to dream and tell stories. But, as always, the power of freedom through fantasy is qualified by Burroughs' farewell at the end of the book:

> I have blown a hole in time with a firecracker. Let others step
> through. Into what bigger and bigger firecrackers? Better weapons lead
> to better and better weapons, until the earth is a grenade with the fuse
> burning. [. . .] A few may get through the gate in time. Like Spain, I
> am bound to the past.[9]

As in all of Burroughs' major works, the cosmic conflict remains unresolved: the author, narrators, and reader are left with the need for eternal vigilance and struggle.

In his fiction from *The Wild Boys* to *Cities of the Red Night,* Burroughs continues to be an innovator who combines prophetic visions and experimental technique. He creates powerful imaginary worlds that critique present reality and that show the reader how to alter his consciousness and thus his world. The creation of a second mythology and the return to narrative in his recent novels show his continued vitality as an artist who places the highest value on psychic exploration: "This is the Space Age. Space is a dangerous unmapped area. It is necessary to travel. It is not necessary to live."[10]

## Notes

1. Dates of publication in this paragraph refer to first publication. Several novels were first published abroad; hence, publication in the United States occurred later.

2. Detailed explication of the early series of novels may be found in Eric Mottram, *WILLIAM BURROUGHS: The Algebra of Need* (London: Boyars, 1977); Cary Nelson, *The Incarnate Word: Literature and Verbal Space* (Urbana: U of Illinois P, 1973) 208–29; Donald Palumbo, "William Burroughs' Quartet of Science Fiction Novels as Dystopian Social Satire," *Extrapolation* 20 (1979): 321–29; and Tony Tanner, *City of Words: American Fiction, 1950–70* (New York: Harper, 1971) 109–40. Also see my own "William S. Burroughs: Pop Artist," *Sphinx* 11 (1980): 1–15.

3. Robert Palmer, "William Burroughs," *Rolling Stone* 11 May 1972: 52.

4. See, for example, Thomas Disch's angry review of *Cities of the Red Night:* "Pleasures of Hanging," *New York Times Book Review* 15 Mar. 1981: 14–15.

5. William S. Burroughs, *Nova Express* (New York: Grove, 1964) 15.

6. Quoted in Daniel Odier, *The Job* (New York: Grove, 1970) 23.

7. William S. Burroughs, *The Wild Boys* (New York: Grove, 1971) 139–40.

8. William S. Burroughs, *Exterminator!* (New York: Viking, 1973) 97.

9. William S. Burroughs, *Cities of the Red Night* (New York: Holt, 1981) 332.

10. William S. Burroughs, *The Retreat Diaries* (New York: City Moon, 1976) n. pag.

# 21

# Burroughs' Theater
# of Illusion
## *Cities of the Red Night*

Steven Shaviro

C*ities of the Red Night,* like all of William Burroughs' fiction, is characterized, on one hand, by the narrowness of its obsessive repetitions, and, on
the other hand, by an astonishing freedom of invention. Scenes of rape and
torture, disease and mutilation, addiction and withdrawal, cynical manipulation and
vicarious gratification: all are relentlessly renewed. Yet these repetitions correspond
to no coherence of narrative, no integrity of character, no stability of milieu. Each
recurrence is also a fresh start, random and unpredictable. Burroughs' theater of
illusion comprises nothing more than the action which it depicts. This action is not
the representation of an independent reality, nor does it take place in any preexisting
scene. Its repeated movement is always one of violation and disintegration, but there
is no norm in comparison to which it could be judged a transgression. No ideal is
posited, and no law is enunciated. What is repeated obsessively is not any identity
of form or content, but only the violence of continual metamorphosis. For Burroughs'
discourse encompasses contradictory exigencies of obsession and freedom, replication and mutation, disaster and utopia, satire and celebration, unity and duality,
reality and illusion, death and life. Each of these terms is conditioned and contaminated by its supposed opposite.

Consider death. In *Cities of the Red Night,* the experience of dying is neither
authentic nor final. It does not offer release, but only transmutation. The nihilistic
will is baffled, as even nothingness turns out to be an unattainable illusion: "This
was the basic error of the Transmigrants: you do not get beyond death and conception
by reexperience any more than you get beyond heroin by ingesting larger and larger

Steven Shaviro, "Burroughs' Theater of Illusion: *Cities of the Red Night,*" *The Review of
Contemporary Fiction* 4.1 (1984): 64–74. Copyright© 1984 by *The Review of Contemporary
Fiction.* Reprinted in this volume in revised form by permission.

doses. The Transmigrants were quite literally addicted to death and they needed more and more death to kill the pain of conception. They were buying parasitic life with a promissory death note to be paid at a prearranged time" (157).[1] The Transmigrants are unable either to experience death or to "get beyond" it. For the death which they seek to master has no proper being, but instead assumes multiple, phantasmagoric forms. It is a process without a beginning and without an end, aptly figured by opium addiction or by the anarchic proliferation of the Red Plague, Virus B–23. An addiction or plague suspends present time; its temporality is that of an eternal recurrence, a feverish nightmare in which nothing ever really happens, but everything has already happened and everything is about to happen again. The novel's obsessive repetition of certain horrible scenes, in particular that of ejaculation at the moment of death by hanging, reflects this logic, in which "nothing is true, everything is permitted."

If there is no conclusion, there is also no origin. In the beginning, there is only the replication and alteration— the viral mutation—of a history already in progress. The "portentous event" which sets Virus B–23 in motion is singular, unknown, perhaps even unknowable, "what modern physicists call a black hole" (155). We can neither assert that the virus is "produced out of thin air" and for the first time, nor identify its presence prior to the event which alters it (24). It cannot be differentiated from the host to which it attaches itself; unlike any ordinary virus, it does not merely invade, from the outside, an otherwise healthy organism: "Are not the symptoms of Virus B–23 simply the symptoms of what we are pleased to call 'love'? [. . .] We are all tainted with viral origins. The whole quality of human consciousness, as expressed in male and female, is basically a virus mechanism. [. . .] any attempts to contain Virus B–23 will turn out to be ineffectual because we carry this virus with us. [. . .] Because it is the *human virus*" (25). The host ("human consciousness") has no existence prior to the virus which it harbors. To be "tainted with viral origins" is to discover that one's interiority is always already contaminated by external forces. For life feeds on previous death, and the agonies of death are also the proliferation of new life: "Bright red nipples of flesh about an inch in height, growing in clusters, covered his chest and stomach and sprouted from his face and neck. The growths looked like exotic plants. He noticed that they were oozing a pearly juice that ate into the flesh, leaving luminescent sores" (14). The plague is also a wet dream, an erotic frenzy, a phenomenon of "spontaneous orgasms" (19) and the dissemination of sperm.

"Human consciousness," then, is "basically a virus mechanism," whether in benign or malignant form. The plague breaks out when, "After many thousands of years of more or less benign coexistence, it [the 'human virus'] is now once again on the verge of malignant mutation" (25). In its "more or less benign" state, the virus reproduces itself more or less exactly. Precise replication makes possible the suppression of individual difference, the uniform functioning of control, but it also constitutes the identity of any individual organism. The malignant form of the virus, however, is nothing more than an acceleration of the benign form. Sexual compulsion is a mechanism of repetition and control, but when sexuality reaches a certain pitch of feverish intensity, reproduction erupts into spontaneous mutation. The virus then kills or alters the host, instead of preserving it. Exact replication is only mutation at an exceedingly slow rate; the process of conservation is also a potential force of radical alteration. The same mechanism, internal and external to its host, at once determines identity and difference, continuity and change, life and death. "Benign" and "malignant" are merely relative terms, and reflect no qualitative distinction.

Burroughs' writing thus affirms the violent and ineradicable interpenetration of death and life, control and freedom, repetition (replication) and alteration (mutation). This parasitic structure does not conform to the canons of binary logic. Exact repetition is at once the self-preservation of existing life and the deadly cancer of changelessness and total control. Radical alteration, similarly, is at once the proliferation of new life forms and the sterility of destruction and death. Repetition is violently conditioned by the unpredictability of prior mutation; but alteration functions as a power only insofar as it is forever replicated in the movement of the plague. Life is generated and determined by death, but dying is a movement in which no repose, no terminal state, can ever be attained. The process of life is the process of death, but this process is nothing but an all-encompassing illusion.

The ubiquity of illusion is the key to Burroughs' extended discussion of power, violence, freedom, and control. The violence of political and personal struggle is interminable, like death itself. Every Burroughs protagonist is "A Cowboy in the Seven-Days-A-Week-Fight" (175). There is no haven, no security, no escape. History is a nightmare from which we cannot be awakened, a fatality in which everything ceaselessly recurs. This is what makes the image of revolution so necessary for Burroughs, and yet so problematic. His celebration of liberatory violence quickly collapses into the cynicism of conspiracy and manipulation: "I soon see that there is more here than just a spontaneous explosion of overcrowded poverty-ridden slums. The whole scene has been staged from above to point up the need for a strong police force, and some of the mob ringleaders turn out to be agents of big money" (227). Images of radical revolt can easily be transformed into those of a Hitlerian putsch. Revolution is staged as a theatrical spectacle, channeling energies so that they remain caught within the machinations of politics and "big money," of one system of control merely replacing another. After the revolt in Tamaghis, the forces of Yass-Waddah merely give way to those of Ba'dan (identified with "present-day America" [158]), but business as usual continues: "The Ba'dan Hilton and American Express arrive in a cloud of pop stars" (233). Power is as endless as the resistance which it encounters; itself violent, it feeds on the violence which it provokes. The spontaneity of revolt is only a calculated, illusory effect of its operations.

How then does power work, and what is its relation to death? Power abstracts death from life, in order to create need and instill fear. Such a practice at once belittles death by employing it as a mere means, and inflates it into a fearful absolute. The purpose of such maneuvers is to make death into something efficacious and "real": "Death requires a random witness to be real and a public hanging is real because of random witnesses. In the Garden of Eden, God left Adam and Eve alone to eat the fruit of the Hanging Tree and then popped back in like a random house dick who just happened to be passing in the hall when he heard amorous noises" (224). The old police trick of entrapment imprisons its victims within a spurious "real." A random witness is paradoxically required to register the presence of what is otherwise meaningless. Such a "perfect witness" must take everything in, but respond to nothing and alter nothing; he must be "a sort of camera from which a film could be withdrawn and developed" (80). Control makes death "real" by prerecording it as a film strip and sound track to be endlessly and literally repeated. This is the cycle of orgasm, of heroin addiction and withdrawal, and ultimately of all life from conception to death and back: "The alert student of this noble experiment will perceive that death was regarded as equivalent not to birth but to conception and go on to infer that conception is the basic trauma. In the moment of death, the dying man's whole life may flash in front of his eyes back to conception. In the moment of conception, his future life flashes forward to his future death. *To reexperience conception is fatal*" (157). Since every beginning is really "reexperience," life is always "fatal," and to enter existence is already to be given over to death. There is no security, not even in the fantasy of return to the womb: "If [. . .] conception is the basic trauma, then it is also the basic instrument of control" (166). Control enforces a closed economy of death in which desire is simply short-circuited; the victim is enslaved to a pleasure which has no positive qualities, but denotes only the release from unbearable tension. Any movement of liberation merely reenacts the pattern from which it is trying to escape.

This paradox is inverted in the utopian fantasies of *The Wild Boys* and Burroughs' other writing of the early 1970s. In these works, power is carried to its logical extreme of fragmentation, chaos, and anarchic destruction. Freedom is not the restriction or abolition of power, but its unchecked dissemination beyond all limits. Revolution does not dispense with control, but appropriates the technology of power for its own ends. The youth gangs running rampant in *The Wild Boys* have their parallel in the eighteenth-century pirates of *Cities of the Red Night,* who promulgate Captain Mission's Articles while perfecting techniques of biological, economic, and guerrilla warfare. Cynicism here becomes a revolutionary weapon: "I reflected that the exercise of power conveys a weird sensation of ease and tranquility. [. . .] To turn this mechanism [of power invented by the Inquisition] back on the Inquisitors themselves gives me a feeling of taking over the office of fate. I am become the bad karma of the Inquisition. I am allowing myself also the satisfaction that derives from a measure of hypocrisy, rather like the slow digestion of a good meal" (189–90). There is no question of the means corrupting the ends; for the liberating end in view is nothing other than the unrestricted ability to use such means. The flaw lies elsewhere. Such a process of liberation can never be completed; the revolutionary movement of destruction precludes the building of new institutions. The very triumph of the revolution renders it helpless: "I pointed out that holding a single fortified position—as Hassan i Sabbah did at Alamut—is no longer possible, owing to improved weapons that I have already perfected and which will inevitably, in the course of time, fall into the hands of our prospective enemies" (133). Burroughs continues to endorse revolutionary violence; there is simply no viable alternative.

But when the forces of metamorphosis are unleashed, nobody can hope to stabilize or control the outcome.

A similar dilemma marks Clem Snide's position as master detective. In his relaxed yet attentive distance from the mechanisms of control, Snide is a self-proclaimed Satanic figure: "I am a man of the world. Going to and fro and walking up and down in it" (35). This makes him a mirror image of God as "random house dick": Snide also stands outside hotel rooms, "waiting for the correspondent to reach a crescendo of amorous noises" (35). He has no programmatic opposition to the apparatus of power, but is concerned only to use it rather than being used by it: "I use any methods that help me to find the missing person. If I can locate him in my own mind that makes it easier to locate him outside it" (38). Such pragmatism accounts both for his interest in recording methods and in magic, and for his refreshingly casual attitude toward such technologies of control: "Back at the loft we decide to try some sex magic. According to psychic dogma, sex itself is incidental and should be subordinated to the intent of the ritual. But I don't believe in rules. What happens, happens" (76). Snide refuses to subordinate the "incidental" random-ness of sexuality and magic to the demands of immediate efficacy. His method works around the aleatory margins of consciousness and control: "I played the tape back at low volume while I watched an Italian western with Greek subtitles, keeping my attention on the screen so I was subconsciously hearing the tape" (47). Yet he also justifies his procedure by holding with Castaneda's Don Juan "that nothing is random to a man of knowledge: everything he sees or hears is there just at that time waiting to be seen and heard" (44). Snide is a man who knows the smell of death (35); but this familiarity, this faith that everything has its proper time, will lead only to his being cheated by death, as he walks into a hotel room to discover, not the anticipated scene of lovers caught *in flagrante delicto,* but rather "a real messy love death" (35).

This disappointment prefigures Snide's loss of identity as a victim of soul transfer later in the book. Subjected to this operation, he quickly progresses from "feeling very relaxed and comfortable in Jimmy's body" (211) to finding his own memories submerged by those of the body in which he has been placed. The erstwhile "private asshole" (35) is unable to protect his personal identity from the pressures of alien control systems. His alert independence, attractive as it is, is insufficient to maintain the detachment of a space "in my own mind" which reflects and yet keeps its distance from what takes place "outside it." He is drawn into the violent scenes which he first only imagines, the "legends" which he initially believes he can keep separate from the "facts" (167).

A similar fatality shadows any use of the cut-up method, Burroughs' most famous innovation in literary practice. Snide, in his tape-recorder experiments, expects a pattern to emerge out of randomness: the location of the missing person, the truth of the crime. But the cut-up may also be used to escape from the obsession of pattern, to unleash the randomness which already haunts any control mechanism. In either case, the rearrangement of existing discourses serves to disrupt their power of repetition and conditioning. But in *Cities of the Red Night,* even a cut-up and randomized rerecording is still a playback, and therefore still manipulative. The cut-up method remains in solidarity with the mechanism against which it is directed: "Changes, Mr. Snide, can only be effected by alterations in the *original*. The only thing not prerecorded in a prerecorded universe are the prerecordings themselves. The copies can only repeat themselves word for word. *A virus is a copy.* You can pretty it up, cut it up, scramble it—it will reassemble in the same form" (166). To insert randomness is already to prerecord, to escape from control only by reasserting it. The cut-up method destroys old associations only by establishing new ones; the alteration which breaks repetition becomes the basis of a new repetition. The metamorphosing effect of randomness takes hold in the form of a virus, a new, alien pattern of control; and to cut up, scramble, or randomize a virus is simply to allow it to "reassemble in the same form." Changes can only be made in the original, but in *Cities of the Red Night* there are no originals, only copies.

Such is Snide's experience as he fabricates a series of lurid comic-book fantasies of life in the cities of the Red Night. He is ostensibly being paid to find the originals of the Red Night material, originals which "may contain the truth, which these books cover with a surface so horrible and so nauseously prettified that it remains impervious as a mirror. [ . . . ] And as misleading" (168). But there is no "truth" beneath the sickening surface, just as the books are copies for which there is no original. "I had already decided to fabricate the complete books if I could find the right paper. In fact, I felt sure that this was exactly what I was being paid to do" (170). In perpetrating this forgery, Snide loses control over his production. The power which he exercises is not his own. His activity as an author leads directly to the appropriation of his labor, as he is absorbed into his own script.

All of Burroughs' strategies for opposing control are thus finally recuperated within the space of control. It is impossible to escape from a power which is nowhere and everywhere at once. But power itself remains as indeterminate as any attempt to overturn it. When the police forge evidence, or when Hollywood manufactures images, then the police and Hollywood also fall victim to the illusory power of forged evidence and fascinating images. In the latter portions of the book there is such a proliferation of competing images that the scene explodes into "screaming hurricanes" (304) of carnivalesque confusion: "As the sun climbs higher, the square looks like Hollywood gone berserk" (302). The movement of illusion evades all efforts to contain it. Snide perpetually "run[s] into more death than the law allows. I mean the law of averages" (35). Every law is founded upon death, but death itself knows no law. Even the law of averages, the statistical regularization of randomness, is exceeded by death.

It is at this point, however, that the illusiveness of death may be radically *affirmed:* celebrated in its immanence, rather than being manipulated for ulterior goals. Virus B–23 is not only a violent imposition, but also a new possibility of freedom. Since nothing is true, everything is permitted. Change is always possible, as long as you are able to pay the price of foregoing your own identity, of willing no longer to be yourself. In the face of the Red Plague, "the whole human position is no longer tenable" (25). But the radical, metamorphosing drive of Burroughs' fiction opens the possibility of abandoning the present "human position," and of discovering new, perhaps inhuman, forms of affirmation. There is then no resolution, but instead a joyous multiplication and spectacularization of death's paradoxes. Everything is viewed from a new perspective in which "real" experience is seen to be already permeated with illusion. Such a new affirmation perverts and parodies, rather than subsuming or overcoming, the fascist cult of death and Burroughs' own nihilistic obsession with weaponry and violence. Power is not so much opposed as it is dissolved into its own unreal image, as when the rioters "prance around a dying policeman and mimic his death throes" (227). In affirming death, we celebrate, by means of theatrical simulation, its very irreality and inauthenticity. The book traces a parodic journey through the six cities of the Red Night, from a state in which "everything is as true as you think it is and everything you can get away with is permitted," to one in which "nothing is true and *therefore* everything is permitted" (158–59).

Such a journey is proved to have been unnecessary once its goal has been reached. The revelation towards which the book moves is that there is in fact nothing to reveal, no epistemological foundation beneath the parodic play of illusion. Instead of communicating a prior and external truth, the text dramatizes the indeterminate processes of its own production. Scene after scene is described as a movie set or an engraving, "a sepia etching onscreen" which "slowly comes alive" (27). Events never transpire in a pure present; they are always repeated or anticipated, and must be represented before they can be lived. As Noah Blake remarks at one point, "this day presents itself to my memory as a series of paintings" (93). Noah's fictional representation of the revolution in his diaries is even more important than his activities as a gunsmith (91). Textuality is not only a control mechanism which creates the imprisoning illusion of the "real," but also a liberating movement whose only reality is that of illusion.

The penultimate chapter of *Cities of the Red Night* affirms illusion even more radically, as the book's entire contents fold into phantasmagoric reminiscences of a high-school play (319–30). There is no unveiling of any supposed "truth" which could have generated all these fictions. Even the author is merely an effect of the spectacle. Since the "real" is always already illusory, fiction does not replace reality; rather it is poised, like the fever, "at a point where the line between illusion and reality breaks down" (167). No particular plot level can be privileged in relation to the others. The fiction, like death, lacks a consistent self-identity, and is incapable either of closing in on itself or of indicating a beyond. Precisely because there is no beyond, there is also no inside, no interiority.

The closest the book comes to a conventional climax is in the violent shock of Audrey Carsons' negative epiphany: "Audrey felt the floor shift under his feet and he was standing at the epicenter of a vast web. In that moment, he knew its purpose, knew the reason for suffering, fear, sex, and death. It was all intended to keep human slaves imprisoned in physical bodies while a monstrous matador waved his cloth in the sky, sword ready for the kill.

From the depth of his horror and despair, something was breaking through like molten lava, a shock wave of uncontrollable energy" (309). This "vast web" of torture and conspiracy follows a horrifying circular logic. The purpose of "suffering, fear, sex, and death" is "to keep human slaves imprisoned in physical bodies"; but the only point of such an imprisonment is to maintain its victims in a state in which they are still able to suffer, fear, desire, and die. The entire system is an appalling but empty tautology: its purpose is merely to have a purpose, and thereby to dissimulate its actual purposelessness. The illusion in which "human slaves" are trapped is only the illusion that there is such a trap. The "monstrous matador" can never complete the action which he forever threatens; if he were ever actually to swoop down for the kill, he would obliterate the "human slaves" whose fear and continuing capacity for death is the source of his power. Audrey's insight is the phantasmal parody of a revelation, and its appropriate culmination is to be entirely forgotten: "He felt calm and relaxed. He must have had a nightmare. He couldn't remember what it was and it all seemed very remote and unimportant" (310).

The delirium of "incandescent force," when "the pure young purpose blazes like a comet" (305), is always shadowed by its obscene counterpart, the "appalling expression of idiotic ecstasy as [Adam] bites into the apple" (306). But the "horror and despair" of utter powerlessness breaks forth into a new violence of "uncontrollable energy," an explosive intensity entirely divorced from purpose. Audrey's violent outburst changes everything and yet accomplishes nothing; he awakens into another, equally illusory scene to find himself a hospital patient vainly destroying his pillow. The moment of disaster is simultaneously apotheosis and anticlimax, the most intense point of metamorphosis and of illusion. The space of compulsion, fixation, and obsessive repetition is *at the same time* a space of radical fragmentation, of difference and discontinuity, of illusion and parody. It is not by negating or transcending its horrors and obsessions, but rather by affirming them even to excess, in a tireless movement of repetition and intensification, that Burroughs' survey of contemporary atrocities achieves a tone which is sarcastic and exuberant, and never anguished or despairing.

The book's subversive strategy is not to critique and exclude, but to efface limits and undermine identities by including everything, beyond any possibility of order or coherence. As Burroughs states in an interview: "If we realize that everything is illusion, then any illusion is permitted. As soon as we say that something is true, real, then immediately things are not permitted."[2] This is why the addiction to death, rather than being taken in a spirit of high seriousness, is degraded to the status of fashion. After the riots in Temaghis, the new order does not break the addiction to death, but now "the fashionable thing is to look for the answers or the questions behind sex and death" (230). Such a search will be endless because "every time you find an answer you find six questions under it, like leprechauns under a toadstool" (225). In the academies of Waghdas, "all questions are answered in terms of what can be expressed and understood," and "complete permission derives from complete understanding" (158). But expression and understanding are dissolved into the larger economy of illusion. It is as impossible as it is unnecessary to decide where satire and criticism end and affirmation begins. Death is affirmed in its phantasmal multiplicity, as a force both of repetition and alteration, both of sterility and proliferation. Burroughs refuses the search for ultimate answers, and instead delights in an anti-metaphysical flippancy: " 'Perhaps it was just the basic mystery of life, Skipper,' Audrey said cheekily. 'Now you see it—now you don't' " (316).

The theatrical narrative of *Cities of the Red Night* wanders back and forth in time, linking different realities and fictions, but also dissolving its own suggestions of correspondence. The various plot lines do not so much merge into one another as they interfere with one another. The movement of time travel is inconstant and dangerous, that of the uncontrollable impulsions of orgasm, death, and desire: "I want to learn how to travel in time. [. . .] It is necessary to travel. It is not necessary to live" (246–47). The aim of the book, as of the weapons manufacture and other activities depicted within it, is to "have blown a hole in time" (332); the tyranny of "present time" is broken in the universal affirmation of illusion. Yet such an accomplishment has its own price, that of Clem Snide's traumatic loss of identity, or Noah Blake's alienation at the very moment the revolution appears headed for triumph: "I am the eternal spectator, separated by unbridgeable gaps of knowledge [. . .] torn with an ache of disembodied lust and the searing pain of disintegration. [. . .] I am standing in the empty ruined courtyard hundreds of years from now, a sad ghostly visitant in a dead city, smell of nothing and nobody there" (197). No achievement, no possession, can survive the disruption of presence; not even the achievement of dispossession. Travel through time does not mean liberation from time; or rather, the violence of liberation is also a temporal estrangement productive of nostalgia. There is always something left behind, "a rank musky ozone smell, the smell of time travel" (249). A residual illusion of lost presence is the aftereffect of dislocation.

The nostalgia for a missing concreteness, for a lost freshness of sensation, and especially for the bliss and innocence of adolescent sexual discovery, is continually evoked in Burroughs' work. Yet the radical affirmation of illusion does not allow for any recovery. Nostalgia refers less to that which has been lost than to the repeated experience of loss itself. The attraction of the past is a function of its inaccessibility. Nostalgia is a movement, not of possession and containment, but of expenditure and excess; its economy is best delineated in the fantastic terms of Burroughs' erotic pharmacopoeia: "A Firsty Pop is the hyacinth smell of young hard-ons, a whiff of school toilets, locker rooms, and jockstraps, rectal mucus and summer feet, chigger lotion, and carbolic soap—whiffs you back to your first jackoff and leaves you sitting there on the toilet—if you don't keep flying speed. Never linger over a Firsty" (233). Such an experience can be savored only in retrospect, and would lose its evocative power if one were actually to return to the time of that "first jackoff." To find the past is dangerously to be lost in it. Nostalgia is predicated upon the very distance which it endeavors to overcome. What is most palpable about the lost moment is its evanescence, the play of pungent odors skimmed over at "flying speed." Any realization of this nostalgic impulse would also be its destruction. "Never linger over a Firsty."

In a similar pattern of estrangement, Noah Blake feels "from earliest memory" that he and his friends "came from another world and have been stranded here like mariners on some barren and hostile shore"; there is no answer to his questions "where I come from, how I got here, and who I am" (60). Memory refers to a time before memory, which cannot be brought even into a remembered present. The only "home" Noah can imagine is a transient one: "I feel as if this ship is the home I had left and thought never to find again. But the voyage will end of course, and what then?" (61). There is no potential belonging to contrast with his alienation. It is only in the impermanence of a voyage that he finds a home, just as it is only as an alien that he obtains recognition.

The utopian elements of Burroughs' fiction, the rubbing out of the word, the unified community of the wild boys, the anarchist society under Captain Mission's Articles, are similar to the projections of nostalgia: they also open a prospect of communication and communion, only to remove it beyond any possibility of presence. The preface to *Cities of the Red Night* gives an odd sort of historical concreteness to such unrealizable projects. On one hand, "The liberal principles embodied in the French and American revolutions and later in the liberal revolutions of 1848 had already been codified and put into practice by pirate communes a hundred years earlier" (xi). On the other hand, "Your right to live where you want, with companions of your choosing, under laws to which you agree, died in the eighteenth century" (xv). These rights vanished at the moment of their inauguration, and can be imagined only in the form of a "retroactive Utopia" (xiv), at once anticipated and remembered, but never present, nowhen as well as nowhere. The first stirrings of liberation are lost in much the same way as the first stirrings of sexuality. The revolutions which later seek to generalize these "liberal principles" already take place too late. The utopian impulse, like that of nostalgia, is a movement never to be consummated, but also, in its perpetual incompletion, recurrent and unavoidable. *Cities of the Red Night,* in its incessant jumps backwards and forwards, but without any ultimate issue, may be likened to one figure of the catastrophe which it recounts, "a black hole, a hole in the fabric of reality, through which the inhabitants of these ancient cities traveled in time to a final impasse" (26).

This figure is in turn the subject of a parodic theophany in the phantasmagoria of the penultimate chapter. The supposed author of the spectacle is transformed into an imploding, spinning asshole into which "naked bodies are sucked inexorably forward," and which is thereby identified as a "BLACK HOLE!!" (329). This grotesque image, parodically deflating the recognition which it affords, exemplifies the way in which every escape concludes in an impasse, but every impasse unleashes a new power of metamorphosis. In its illusive, affirmative force, Burroughs' work destroys every finality, the finality of escape no less than the finality of imprisonment. Nostalgia is implicated in this process of dissolution, as a movement of expenditure without limit or recompense: the nonachievement without which the book would not be sufficiently complete, the nonclosure which is its radical mode of inclusion. Every resolution only leads to fresh difficulties, every liberation is also an estrangement, every victory is also an irreparable disaster. "It's too easy. [. . .] The easiest victories are the most costly in the end" (332). When nothing is true and everything is permitted, then also nothing can be avoided. The spectacle of illusion can neither be contemplated from a safe aesthetic distance, nor manipulated by an exertion of the will. The book opens by mocking the self-defeating gestures of detachment and refusal: "Farnsworth, the District Health Officer, was a man so grudging in what he asked of life that every win was a loss" (3). But it ends by ungrudgingly affirming both wins and losses. The unconstrained promise of the future cannot be separated from the imminence of catastrophe or from the fatality of the past. *Cities of the Red Night* affirms even disaster and failure, the pathos of loss, opening itself to a limitless play of violence and death: "I have blown a hole in time with a firecracker. Let others step through. Into what bigger and bigger firecrackers? [. . .] A nightmare feeling of foreboding and desolation comes over me as a great mushroom-shaped cloud darkens the earth. A few may get through the gate in time. Like Spain, I am bound to the past" (332).

## Notes

1. All quotations are from William S. Burroughs, *Cities of the Red Night* (New York: Holt, 1981).
2. *The Job* (New York: Grove, 1970) 90.

# 22

# Burroughs' Western

## David Glover

The coloured wilderness of the West is a place of vast
silence.

—Paul Coates

A ppropriately enough, William Burroughs first publicly mooted the idea of
writing a western during a brief visit to his midwest hometown of St.
Louis in 1965. "I've thought about this for years," he told an interviewer for the
*Paris Review,* and had apparently accumulated "hundreds of pages of notes on the
whole concept of the gunfighter" in the process.[1] Yet it was to be a further nineteen
years before *The Place of Dead Roads* (1984) appeared, finally bringing this project
to completion.

Or does it? Certainly *The Place of Dead Roads* has been heralded as Burroughs'
"long awaited western," and it is indeed "a sort of cowboy story."[2] But it is also far
from being the "straight western" of which Burroughs spoke in 1965. According to
the author's own account this projected novel would have simply transposed the
characters and concerns of *Nova Express* (1964) into a Texas or New Mexico setting,
whilst subjecting them to a much stricter genre treatment than his previous use of
SF. The few fragments to survive from this period seem to bear this out. In "The
Coldspring News" we find Bradley Martin, Burroughs' all-purpose evil spirit ("God
of Arbitrary Power and Restraint, of Prison and Pressure") inserted into two stock
western situations: the lone gunman riding into town, and the accusation of rustling
leveled by one cattle rancher against another. These confrontational episodes are,
however, curiously anticlimactic. In the second, for example, Martin's accuser is
stared down by the arch-villain's "gray eyes . . . cold as metal glinting to a distant
point," and merely turns away without speaking. Characters come up against each
other, but inconclusively: nothing actually happens. It is as if Burroughs has slowed
time down almost to a stop. In the first episode it is the silence of the frontier town,
its setting and its inhabitants, which realizes this effect. The "twilight like heavy
blue dust . . . falling from the mountains" when Martin rides into Blue Junction is
echoed by the final moments of the rustling face-off in which "Martin just stood

David Glover, "Burroughs' Western," *Over Here: An American Studies Journal* 6.2 (1986):
14–23. Reprinted by permission of the author.

there . . . not saying anything and there wasn't anything to say—just cigarette smoke drifting in the still afternoon and Martin's pinpoint metal eyes looking through the smoke."[3] This may have been faithful to Burroughs' concept of the western gun duel as "a real spiritual contest like Zen swordsmanship," but, despite the exceptionally vivid writing, it leads nowhere; the narrative stasis Burroughs creates seems to block any further development of the story line, and the remaining sections of the text slide back predictably into the cut-up techniques he had evidently hoped to leave behind.

What happened to this original idea is unknown. It is hard to see how a heavily freighted figure like Bradley Martin, who serves in Burroughs' early work as both source and symbol of the dualistic mentality vitiating human life and as a vehicle of global conspiracy and planetary destruction, could have been successfully adapted to a western context without these highly condensed layers of meaning being flattened out or lost. In any case, the raw material of the western was no longer available on the old terms. Notwithstanding his desire "to do something different—almost a deliberate change of style," Burroughs was in fact experimenting with a literary genre which was going rapidly into decline. At about the same time Elmore Leonard, arguably the last outstanding writer in this idiom, was abandoning his first love for the thriller as the market for westerns dried up. In film, too, the western was beginning to fall from prominence. The early sixties saw the breakup of the classic western formula and although the innovations that followed might have been expected to attract Burroughs' interest, particularly the new accent on violence in the work of Peckinpah and Leone, he seems not initially to have been drawn to this rich source. As with his many other attempts at "writing something completely different" which "haven't really worked out"—including commercial bestsellers—the project just lapsed.[4] Burroughs continued to be fascinated by the concept of the gunslinger, however, and this theme surfaces in the portrait of the Mexican *pistolero* Tio Mate in *The Wild Boys* (1971). The description of this calculating virtuoso gunman replays exactly that of Bradley Martin six years earlier, as "the gun glints in his eyes a remote mineral calm."[5] But the novel has substituted the Saharan "Blue Desert of Silence" for the silence of "the wall of blue mountains," and western references are only minor ingredients here.

When the gun duel reappears in *The Place of Dead Roads*[6] its significance has been completely transformed. To be sure, the shoot-out in the opening chapter is indeed a kind of Zen contest, a mental exercise in bluff and counterbluff as Burroughs' hero, Kim Carsons, tries to make his opponent see "a phantom gun in an empty hand" by shouting "BANG! YOU'RE *DEAD*," words that are thrown "like a stone," in order to lead him to miscalculate (7). But it functions as an enigma, a central mystery which the text poses for solution. A double mystery in fact, for the first chapter puzzlingly supplies two different versions: an initial newspaper account in which we learn that both Kim and his adversary Mike Chase have inexplicably been shot before firing their own guns, "killed by single rifle shots fired from a distance" which "nobody heard" (3), and a second present-tense description in which Kim shoots Mike Chase down and then proceeds to shoot "a hole in the sky" which is revealed as merely part of a "reality film." Kim has provided an escape route "for others to slip through" and the scene ends in confusion as the film's director frantically calls "ABANDON SHIP, GOD DAMN IT . . . EVERY MAN FOR HIMSELF!" (9). Like all good mysteries, the conundrum of how we are to make sense of the shoot-out is not resolved until the end of the book.

In between what we are given is a typical Burroughs mélange, typical, that is, of his later post-*Wild Boys* work. Part-western, part-science fiction, part-spy thriller, the novel plays with ideas and clichés drawn from all these genres and more, each done out with postmodernist tricksiness. There is, as we have now come to expect from Burroughs' recent writing, a narrative of sorts, but it is a fitful one, moving restlessly through time and place, circling around the author's characteristic obsessions. There is far less of the momentum achieved through the complex interweaving of plots in *Cities of the Red Night* (1981), for example, and the solution to the opening mystery soon starts to seem to have little urgency to it. For the most part the text offers what are quite literally a series of guerrilla raids on favorite Burroughsian targets—Christians, rednecks, mafiosi, establishment politicians, financial wheeler-dealers and the like—the whole paraphernalia of "an increasingly creaky social structure" (216). The agents of these attacks are a reincarnation of the Wild Boys, a gay outlaw gang called "the Wild Fruits" whose sexualized violence presages a radical mutation of the human life form. While there is nothing here which resembles the extraordinary vision of homosexual birth rites in *The Wild Boys* (surely amongst Burroughs' finest and most disturbing writing) the scenes of sex magic and "phantom sexual partners" display once again the familiar preoccupation with immortality and regeneration. When Burroughs mockingly offers his own highly idiosyncratic version of *Beau Geste* at the end of the first part of the book, the dead "crumpled bodies" of the fifty Wild Fruits that lie "strewn about the courtyard" of Fort Johnson have been replaced by clones, "actual biologic cuttings stored in refrigerated vaults" (108–13). If, as Burroughs again posits here, human reality is simply a "prerecorded and prefilmed universe," then this is another assault on "the master film" and "One hole is all it takes. With the right kind of bullet. . . ." (219). The film is being rerun one more time with predictable variations, and we meet an already well-worn cast of characters—even Tio Mate takes a bow. It is all enormously stylized and self-referential and eccentrically true to form. And yet . . .

One indication that this is not quite the usual Burroughs performance comes from the carefully modulated reworking of western motifs. In the nineteen years since he first declared an interest in it this genre has virtually exhausted itself (so that even a latter-day example like Clint Eastwood's *Pale Rider* [1985] has a curiously ironic and stagy feel to it),[7] and Burroughs, with his sharp eye for the vicissitudes of popular forms, is clearly well aware of this. The film critic Paul Coates has recently gone so far as to suggest that "the Western is less a genre than a scene within which a multitude of contradictory stories intersect," and, whether this is true or not, it is certainly an apt description of its role in Burroughs' work. For Burroughs combines the violent "male dream of escape" into the "vast silence" of the West's wide open spaces[8] with elements of a modern *Bildungsroman,* a reprise of boyhood alienation from school and community. In the story of Kim Carsons' adolescence, dreams, genre, and reality merge indissolubly as Kim grows up inside the fantasies he has created for himself. "Kim Carsons" is, unsurprisingly, the pen name of one William Seward Hall, a writer of western stories, and it is noteworthy that Burroughs primarily locates the novel in the country surrounding his native St. Louis (rather than Arizona or New Mexico as he originally envisaged), pointedly including a map of the area for his readers. If these displaced recollections and overheated imaginings are mediated through the formulae of pulp fiction, they are also held together by the brooding presence of what Jennie Skerl has recently called "the Burroughs legend," the finely judged persona of the interviews and the semiautobiographical essay "My Name is Burroughs."[9] Time and again the authorial voice undercuts the images of sexual euphoria and erotic outlaw solidarity to reveal only "a cameo of memory floating in dead stale time" (107). Narrative fantasy is compromised by a growing sense of death and disintegration quite unlike the apocalyptic planetary doom found in much of Burroughs' previous writing. Each of the book's three main sections closes with a sudden vivid evocation of death, and even where recuperation seems possible the Wild Boys are rumored to have "disbanded and scattered" (110).

Not the least of the merits of Jennie Skerl's excellent new book on Burroughs is her recognition that, because the author deliberately blurs the line between life and art "his most important 'work' may be his legend, which exists somewhere between the realms of fact and fiction, partaking of both."[10] Moreover, as she acutely points out, "much is known about the Burroughs legend and little about the man himself."[11] One of her most interesting arguments is that behind the apparent continuities in Burroughs' writing, the sense that, as he once remarked, "all my books are one book," there exist distinct shifts and breaks, and that in the later books we can see a new "metaphorical world" emerging. Replacing the Nova mythology of Burroughs' earlier work is "a second mythology" she terms "freedom through fantasy" which takes as its primary material "childhood memories, and, in particular, the sexual fantasies of adolescence." When interlaced with popular media forms this results in a fiction which is at once more personal and more utopian than the pessimistic social criticism of the Nova mythology where the controlling metaphor of addiction tended to overwhelm any positive content the texts might have. Thus "the wild boys are a metaphorical construct made up of private and public fantasies," and through them utopias and dystopias battle for supremacy.[12]

Whilst much of this is plausible and convincing as an account of the general direction Burroughs' work has taken, Jennie Skerl is forced to end her book at *Cities of the Red Night* so that it is intriguing to see how well her thesis fits the more recent texts. The utopian vision is still clearly present in *The Place of Dead Roads*, but it seems to me rather more strained than was formerly the case. Burroughs' pursuit of immortality as a writer whose dreams and fantasies live on in his readers "is to be taken literally" and it "is the only goal worth striving for." But, although this "saga will shine in the eyes of adolescents squinting through gunsmoke," what it can achieve is only "a measure of immortality" (42). When Burroughs writes in his essay on "Immortality" that "art serves the same function as dreams" he is also aware that "dream lines" can be cut and the dreamer destroyed, just as the white man did to the Indian in order to claim the new frontier.[13] This is not solely the dystopian dismantling of utopia, for Burroughs' remarks on utopias in *The Place of Dead Roads* are querulous and critical. Obligingly quoting Nietzsche's dictum that "Men need play and danger. Civilization gives them work and safety," Burroughs asserts that "utopian concepts stem from a basic misconception as to our mission here," a search for "victory without war" that is "the flaw in all utopias" (237). Fiercely combative to the last, Burroughs' paranoiac view ("my general theory since 1971") that "the Word is literally a virus"[14] (implanted through a set of injections in *The Place of Dead Roads*—see 206–9) means that his commitment to the world-making possibilities of language is always undermined by his struggle against its powers and compulsions and his drive to break through to its utmost limits. And it is this, in the end, which destabilizes any consistent utopia in Burroughs' work, giving it a strong autodestructive undertow.

Indeed, as a counterpart to this, one of the most recurrent motifs in all his writing is that of flight. "Where am I going in such a hurry?" he writes to Allen Ginsberg in *The Yage Letters* (1963):

> Appointment in Talara, Tingo Maria, Pucallpa, Guatemala, Mexico City? I don't know. Suddenly I have to leave right now.[15]

One thinks too of the chase scenes at the beginning of *Naked Lunch* and the aimlessly peripatetic *Junky*. His most recent book, *Queer* (1985), the story of a hopelessly unsuccessful homosexual affair, actually written in 1952 but suppressed by the author until now, shares this same itinerant quality. Explaining his preference for Mexico City or New York, Burroughs says "you are not stuck there; by the fact of being there at all, you are travelling." By contrast "in Panama, crossroads of the world, you are exactly so much aging tissue."[16] And as Burroughs also makes plain in the 1985 introduction to *Queer*, what motivates both the writing and his protagonist Lee's futile attempts "to escape with frantic flights of fantasy" is death, epitomized by "the Place of Dead Roads: a dead, meaningless conglomerate of tin-roofed houses under a continual downpour of rain," for Lee "the end of his line."[17]

Looking back upon *Queer*, Burroughs painfully reaches "the appalling conclusion" that his "lifelong struggle" as a writer had its genesis in the accidental shooting and killing of his wife, Joan, in September, 1951, an incident from which he now exculpates himself by claiming to have been in the grip of some overpowering, unknown, malevolent force, "the Ugly Spirit" of his fictions. However morally dubious this might sound, it is undeniable that his work centers around "the constant threat of possession, and a constant need to escape from possession" and that his own mortality is at stake here.[18] *The Place of Dead Roads* is, then, a sustained meditation upon death, and it comes as no surprise to learn that "whole sections came to me as if dictated, like table-tapping."[19] Michel Foucault in a remarkable essay, "Language to Infinity," once suggested that not only is writing a postponement of death ("writing so as not to die"), but that death is the "limit to which language addresses itself and against which it is poised." What marks out the literature of modernity, however, is that the transcendence of death through the immortality of art now seems unthinkable; and, beginning with de Sade and the Gothic, "language turns back upon itself," transformed into a self-devouring language whose characteristic tropes are mirrors, doubles, and a claustrophobic perception of "the black wall of death." Despite Burroughs' earnest avowals of immortality, it is precisely this sense of unease which haunts *The Place of Dead Roads,* just as the deep mistrust and ambivalence towards language itself has haunted all his work. And when Foucault writes of "these languages which are constantly drawn out of themselves by the overwhelming, the unspeakable, by thrills, stupefaction, ecstasy, dumbness, pure violence, wordless gestures," his words seem peculiarly applicable to Burroughs' fiction.[20]

I suggested earlier in this essay that in Burroughs' western the gun duel which opens the book is posed as an enigma, and I have argued that the specter of death— sometimes actually embodied in phantoms, succubi, and incubi—shadows the fantasies the author so painstakingly constructs. In the last main section of the novel the narrative appears to break free of its western pretensions and the Wild Fruits themselves are left behind as we move quickly forwards in time and space, taking in Tangier, Venus, London, Paris, and finally Mexico. Again, the theme of death is disquietingly sounded in a line that brings the eerie double of Burroughs' own legend into play: "it is said that every man sees the flotsam of his own past here . . . Cottonwoods along an irrigation ditch at Los Alamos Ranch School" (281). From Mexico a journey by river into the depths of the jungle (a description strikingly reminiscent of Conrad's *Heart of Darkness,* a writer often identified by Burroughs as a precursor), reveals the dead roads to be not "roads that are no longer used," but "roads you will never use again" (283–85). All at once the narrative starts to gather speed as the "master film" is remorselessly run back to the Midwest in preparation for the replay of the original shoot-out in Boulder, Colorado, September 17, 1899:

> Perhaps you have just seen the same Stranger too many times, and suddenly it is time to be up and gone.

Despite the "urgency about moving westward" and despite dissatisfied screams from the film's director, there is pause for sad reflection. Kim now knows that "he really can't be reborn anywhere on this planet" because "he just doesn't *fit* somehow" (304). This time, when the final shoot-out comes, there is no escape through a hole in the film's sky; instead, Kim is brutally shot in the back, "blood in his mouth . . . can't turn . . . the sky darkens and goes out" (306). It is a death he can neither anticipate nor control. A brief glance at the very first chapter reminds us that the youthful Kim Carsons was but the pen-name of the sixty-five-year-old writer William Seward Hall. And perhaps this should also remind us that William Seward Burroughs once took the name Bradley Martin from William Golding's *Pincher Martin,* a novel in which a man re-creates an entire world in the split seconds it takes him to die.[21]

# Notes

1. William S. Burroughs, "Interview" (1965), reprinted in *Writers at Work:* Third Series, ed. Alfred Kazin (London: Secker, 1968) 163–65.

2. See Victor Bockris, *With William Burroughs from the Bunker* (New York: Seaver, 1981) xix; and Nicholas Zurbrugg, "Burroughs, Grauerholz, and *Cities of the Red Night:* An Interview with James Grauerholz," *Review of Contemporary Fiction* 4.1 (1984): 22.

3. William S. Burroughs, "The Coldspring News" (1965) in *The Burroughs File* (San Francisco: City Lights, 1984) 67–71.

4. Gerard Malanga, "An Interview with William Burroughs," in *The Beat Book,* eds. Arthur and Glee Knight (California, PA: the unspeakable visions of the individual, 4, [1974]) 103. See also Bockris, 27.

5. William S. Burroughs, *The Wild Boys* (London: Corgi, 1973) 16.

6. William S. Burroughs, *The Place of Dead Roads* (London: Calder, 1984). All references appear in the text.

7. According to one recent survey of the western film "currently critics and industry seem agreed that the era of large-scale and popular production of westerns is over." See Christine Gledhill, "The Western" in *The Cinema Book,* ed. Pam Cook (London: British Film Institute, 1985) 71.

8. Paul Coates, *The Story of the Lost Reflection: The Alienation of the Image in Western and Polish Cinema* (London: Verso, 1985) 57–60.

9. Reprinted in William S. Burroughs, *The Adding Machine: Collected Essays* (London: Calder, 1985). Unfortunately this is by no means a complete edition of Burroughs' essays. For the missing material the reader should consult the two-volume French-language collection, William S. Burroughs, *Essais, tome I* (Paris: Bourgois, 1981) and *Essais, tome II* (Paris: Bourgois, 1984) which includes the important "Rock and Magic."

10. Jennie Skerl, *William S. Burroughs* (Boston: Hall, 1985) 2.

11. Skerl, Preface.

12. Skerl, 77–81.

13. "Immortality" in *The Adding Machine,* 136.

14. "Ten Years and a Billion Dollars," *The Adding Machine,* 48.

15. William S. Burroughs and Allen Ginsberg, *The Yage Letters* (San Francisco: City Lights, 1963) 46.

16. William S. Burroughs, *Queer* (London: Picador, 1986) 119.

17. "Introduction," *Queer,* 14–15.

18. "Introduction," *Queer,* 18. This once more raises the difficult question of the "otherness" of women for the Beats in general, a question which has hardly yet been tackled; but see Joyce Johnson *Minor Characters* (London: Picador, 1983) and Catharine R. Stimpson, "The Beat Generation and the Trials of Homosexual Liberation," *Salmagundi* 58–59 (1982–83): 373–92.

19. "Introduction," *Queer,* 15.

20. "Language to Infinity," in Michel Foucault, *Language, Counter-Memory, Practice: Selected Essays and Interviews* (Oxford: Blackwell, 1977). On Burroughs as modern-day Gothic, see David Punter, *The Literature of Terror* (Harlow: Longman, 1980) 387–89.

21. See Gregory Stephenson, "The Gnostic Vision of William S. Burroughs," *Review of Contemporary Fiction* 4.1 (1984): 47.

# 23

# The Postmodern Anus

## *Parody and Utopia in Two Recent Novels by William Burroughs*

### Wayne Pounds

T o speak of a postmodern asshole is to raise the question of a predecessor, a modern asshole, of which I will mention three. In the first of the Hell Cantos, Canto XIV, Pound shows the usurers orating through their fundaments:

> Faces smeared on their rumps, wide eye on flat buttock
> Bush hanging for beard,
> Addressing crowds through their arse-holes. (14.61)[1]

As a good modernist, Pound uses Dante as his authority for the scatological details of his hell.

The second example I take from the Calypso section of *Ulysses*. Bloom at his morning elimination, "asquat on the crapstool," leisurely folds out his newspaper and enjoys a kingly repose. Momentarily, he is monarch of the conflicting impulses of the self, now centered on the pleasures of elimination. "Quietly he read, restraining himself, the first column and, yielding but resisting, began the second. Midway, his last resistance yielding, he allowed his bowels to ease themselves quietly as he read, reading still patiently. . . . Hope it's not too big to bring on piles again. No, just right. So. Ah!"[2] Bloom's anal pleasures will return to him in the Circe section in an extreme and masochistic form when the Sins of the Past, in chorus, denounce his predilection for anal delights.

The third is from Georges Bataille, from a short novel called *The Story of the*

Wayne Pounds, "The Postmodern Anus: Parody and Utopia in Two Recent Novels by William Burroughs," *Poetics Today* 8.3–4 (1987): 611–29. Copyright© 1987 by *Poetics Today*. Reprinted by permission.

*Eye.* The novel as such is a surrealist fantasy in which sexual appetite is stimulated by the sight of excretory processes and the mutilation of corpses. Bataille added an autobiographical frame to subsequent editions of the work, which allows the whole to be read as a confession and permits the reader to see the equation of the eye/I, the anus, and the Father. The world of the story's action is imaged as the father's chamber pot, and the transgressions which make up the action are only meaningful as transgressions because they take place under the eye/I of the Father.[3]

As a genealogical aside, it should be noted that Bataille's obsession with his father's anus links directly with the immediate sources of Freud's 1911 essay on paranoia—namely, the autobiography of Judge Schreber, whose father's solar beams energized the anus of his son.[4] And the obsession finds its conceptual expression in Bataille's brilliant essays on eroticism, through which it links with de Sade, Ur-father of Burroughs' obsessive images of sexual climax through hanging.

These three examples of the modernist asshole may be characterized as inversions of traditional norms for quite specific purposes: in the instance from Pound, satire, though that is perhaps too mild a word for the paranoid hatred of the passage; in the instance from Joyce, the comedy of the centered self of modernism; and, in the instance from Bataille, a surrealist fantasy within the framework of a psychoanalytic introspection.

An example from Burroughs will produce a major distinction. I begin with a familiar passage, the notorious Talking Asshole routine from *Naked Lunch,* and I would like the reader either to listen to or imagine Burroughs' recorded reading of the passage.[5] Recall that this is a monologue spoken by Dr. Benway, a medical expert in the engineering of consent, who earlier in the novel characterizes himself when he announces, "I deplore brutality. It's not efficient."[6] Benway believes it is possible to increase the efficiency of human physiology by uniting the body's orifices in a single, polypurpose orifice:

> Did I ever tell you about the man who taught his asshole to talk? His whole abdomen would move up and down you dig farting out the words. It was unlike anything I ever heard.
> This ass talk had a sort of gut frequency. It hit you right down there like you gotta go. You know when the old colon gives you the elbow and it feels sorta cold inside, and you know all you have to do is turn loose? Well this talking hit you right down there, a bubbly thick stagnant sound, a sound you could *smell.* [ . . . ]
> After a while the ass started talking on its own. [ . . . ] Then it developed sort of teeth-like raspy incurving hooks and started eating. He thought this was cute at first and built an act around it, but the asshole would eat its way through his pants and start talking on the street, shouting out it wanted equal rights. It would get drunk, too, and have crying jags nobody loved it and it wanted to be kissed same as any other mouth. Finally it talked all the time day and night, you could hear him for blocks screaming at it to shut up, and beating it with his fist, and sticking candles up it, but nothing did any good and

the asshole said to him: "It's you who will shut up in the end. Not me. Because we don't need you around here any more. I can talk and eat *and* shit."

After that he began waking up in the morning with a transparent jelly like a tadpole's tail all over his mouth. This jelly was what the scientists call un-D.T., Undifferentiated Tissue, which can grow into any kind of flesh on the human body. He would tear it off his mouth and the pieces would stick to his hands like burning gasoline jelly and grow there, grow anywhere on him a glob of it fell. So finally his mouth sealed over, and the whole head would have amputated spontaneous [. . .] except for the *eyes* you dig. That's the one thing the asshole *couldn't* do was see. It needed the eyes. The nerve connections were blocked and infiltrated and atrophied so the brain couldn't give orders any more. It was trapped in the skull, sealed off. For a while you could see the silent, helpless suffering of the brain behind the eyes, then finally the brain must have died, because the eyes *went out,* and there was no more feeling in them than a crab's eye on the end of a stalk. (*Naked Lunch* 131–33)

The context here, mad Dr. Benway discussing medical efficiency, draws attention to what Burroughs' own performance makes obvious (or would have made obvious, had the reader heard it): this is full-blown parody, a parody of the discourse of scientistic, behaviorist human engineering.[7] As parody, it implies a utopia: Benway's monologue describes an experiment designed to further the creation of an engineering-efficiency utopia, which the parody shows to be a dystopia. A primary force of Burroughs' writing is precisely this telos: the building of utopia. Parody necessarily implies utopia, an ideal standard by which the vicious is recognized.[8] The utopian goal in Burroughs' work, as I shall show, becomes increasingly foregrounded and thematized as we move from the early work to two recent novels, which are the focus of the present study: *Cities of the Red Night* and *The Place of Dead Roads*. But first some theoretical considerations.

The very possibility of what I am claiming for Burroughs is called into question in Frederic Jameson's 1984 essay on postmodernism, in which he denies the feasibility of parody in contemporary culture and proposes its eclipse by pastiche. He argues that in the postmodern context, "the disappearance of the individual subject, along with its formal consequence, the increasing unavailability of the personal style, engender the well-nigh universal practice today of what may be called pastiche. . . . In this situation, parody finds itself without a vocation and . . . pastiche slowly comes to take its place."[9] But this argument assumes the highly personal styles of classic modern writers as the object of parody; whereas in Burroughs the object of parody is not an art style but an administrative, bureaucratic style—the style of instrumental rationality that, as the discourse of the state, dominates our age. Jameson would probably allow the parodic force of Burroughs' work since his concept of postmodernism as a "cultural dominant" allows for the coexistence of a range of differing, even conflicting, features.

In an earlier version of the 1984 essay, Jameson sketched a range of positions vis-à-vis postmodernism in which Burroughs' work would be located close to that populist impulse in architecture—for Jameson, the privileged terrain of the struggle of postmodernism. Jameson explains:

> What is meant, in the specifically architectural context, is that where
> the now more classical high modernist space of a Corbusier or a
> Wright sought to differentiate itself radically from the fallen city fabric
> in which it appears . . . postmodernist buildings on the contrary
> celebrate their insertion into the heterogeneous fabric of the
> commercial strip and the motel and fast-food landscape of the post-
> superhighway American city.[10]

In Burroughs the populist impulse is represented by the incorporation of the forms of popular fiction—the science-fiction, police, and adventure genres of the airport bookstall—into his recent novels (a point to which I shall return), marking a distinct development from the episodic fragmentation of *Naked Lunch*.

The most useful of theoretical perspectives on Burroughs' work, however, is Bakhtin's discussions of parody as carnival laughter, a theory which also asserts a populist base.[11] Bakhtin sees parody and its correlative utopian or meliorative impulse as determinative for the development of the novel as a genre, arguing that the novel is born of early Greek and Latin parodic-travestying forms, which liberated discourse from the "authoritarian word" of official culture: "They liberated the object from the power of language in which it had become entangled as if in a net; they destroyed the homogenizing power of myth over language; they freed consciousness from the power of the direct word, destroyed the thick walls that had imprisoned consciousness within its own discourse, within its own language."[12] In Burroughs this historical project to use language for liberation from a fixed authoritarian discourse is wholly self-conscious: "Hell consists of falling into enemy hands, into the hands of the virus power [of the word], and heaven consists of freeing oneself from this power, of achieving inner freedom, freedom from conditioning."[13]

The corrosive, liberating function of parodic language—language as laughter—originates in the popular, chthonian impulse to carnival. Parodic laughter overcomes the prohibitions, violence, and intimidation of the official class culture: "It was the victory of laughter over fear that most impressed medieval man. It was not only a victory over mystic terror of God, but also a victory . . . over the oppression and guilt related to all that was consecrated and forbidden ('mana' and 'taboo')."[14] Its essential principle is degradation:

> Degradation here means coming down to earth. . . . [To degrade is] to
> concern oneself with the lower stratum of the body, the life of the
> belly and the reproductive organs; it therefore relates to acts of
> defecation and copulation, conception, pregnancy, and birth.
> Degradation digs a bodily grave for a new birth; it has not only a
> destructive, negative aspect, but also a regenerating one. To degrade

an object does not imply merely hurling it into the void of
nonexistence, into absolute destruction, but to hurl it down to the
reproductive lower stratum, the zone in which conception and a new
birth take place. Grotesque realism knows no other lower level; it is
the fruitful earth and the womb. It is always conceiving. (*Rabelais*
19–21)

To be sure, Bakhtin distinguishes the vital medieval parody from the "formalist
literary parody of modern times," but herein lies Burroughs' distinctive achievement,
which is neither narrowly literary nor formalistic: Burroughs brings in the third
world to supply a popular base for the action of his novels and thereby revitalizes
parody by restoring its base in the people and in spontaneous forms of carnival.

The grotesque image of the body in Burroughs' work would appear to be an
inheritance from carnival as Bakhtin conceives it. Bakhtin's emphasis here is two-
fold. The carnival image of the body is public and inclusive, in contrast to its classic
(post-Renaissance) and modern forms, which are privatized and exclusive. And the
body of carnival is "a body in the act of becoming. It is never finished, never
completed." For this reason "it outgrows its own self, transgressing its own body,
in which it conceives a new, second body: the bowels and the phallus. [. . .] Next
to the bowels and genital organs is the mouth [. . .] and next is the anus," the
physiological system through which the world is ingested, digested, recreated, and
eliminated. These convexities and orifices have a common characteristic: within them
"the confines between bodies and between the body and the world are overcome. . . .
They can even detach themselves from the body and lead an independent life . . ."
(*Rabelais* 317). The carnival "grotesque image" of the body is closely akin to the
body in Burroughs' work: a deprivatized, communal body everywhere in the process
of dismembering, distributing, and remembering itself.

Bakhtin's theory of carnival explains Burroughs' sexual scandal and cultivation
of bad taste. The anus represents the principle of parodic degradation to the lower
stratum: it functions as metonymy (the human reduced to a biological function or
need), as mouth (voice), and eye/I (point of view). If for the author the asshole
functions as the *"I"* or voice, for the reader it functions as the *eye* or point of view.
As the lowest human function, it stands for the highest creative force and links the
human to the divine: "Gentle Reader, we see God through our assholes in the flash
bulb of orgasm" (*Naked Lunch* 229).

Through the anal orifice Burroughs gives voice to the silent and excluded. To
paraphrase Marx, heretofore the anal had been unable to represent itself; it could
only be represented. Edward Said, writing about the realistic novel and the institution
of criticism, asks "why so few 'great' novelists deal directly with the major social
and economic outside facts of their existence—colonialism and imperialism—and
why, too, critics of the novel have continued to honor this remarkable silence."[15] In
opposition to this massive discourse of exclusion, expressed in the sanctioned
norms of novelistic representation and authorized by the institutions of state culture,
Burroughs parodies the authoritarian word and gives voice to what Said says culture

has excluded: "anarchy, disorder, irrationality, inferiority, bad taste, and immorality."[16]

In Burroughs' work the anus as point of view takes over the function of the eye, and it usurps the functions of coitus and utterance as well. As in the the talking-asshole routine, the asshole becomes the w/hole of everything, the Ur field of anarchy. In *The Place of Dead Roads,* this development culminates in black orgiastic ceremonies which celebrate "The creation of ANUS, the foundation of chaos,"[17] the fecund principle of destruction and creation. For all Burroughs' celebration, however, the anus has its ambivalences, already suggested in the homonyms "whole" and "hole": it is both hell and heaven, chaos and order, destruction and creation. Two principal sets of antinomies, utopia-dystopia and the life-death of the author, provide a guide to Burroughs' recent work.

To get at the first set of antinomies it may be asked which way the utopian-dystopian balance tips. Or, to put it country simple, the question is whether the boys' camp of Burroughs' earthly garden of delights is one any of us would want to spend a summer in—not to mention a lifetime. More specifically, it should be asked whether even the most charitably allegorical reading of the boys' camp utopia, with its sexist exclusionism, can save it from falling back into an unredeemed mechanism indistinguishable from the systems of control it is meant to subvert.

The first thing that must be said is on the positive side of the balance: Burroughs' two most recent novels do imagine utopia—the Paradiso that Pound, for example, could never imagine, and they do so by taking into account Said's major social and economic facts, colonialism and imperialism. *Cities of the Red Night* proposes utopia retroactively, in an eighteenth-century pirate commune; and then, with the fluent schizoid technique acquired from decades of cutting out and folding in, Burroughs translates the pirate commune into a future in outer space. The novel's preface explains that the eighteenth-century pirate commune in Central America, upon which the utopia is based, was called Libertatia and was placed under articles which are a clear forecast of the revolutions that close the century. The articles provide for a democratic electorate, the abolition of slavery for any reason including debt, the abolition of the death penalty, and freedom of religious practice. A chain of colonies under the articles was to have acted as a guerrilla force to free Central and South America from their Spanish rulers: "The land would belong to those who used it. No white-man boss, no Pukka Sahib, no Patrons, no colonists. The escalation of mass production and concentration of population in urban areas would be halted. [. . .]"[18]

Historically, the opportunity, if that's what it was, was missed, and Burroughs addresses the reader: "Your right to live where you want, with companions of your choosing, under laws to which you agree, died in the eighteenth century. [. . .] Only a miracle or a disaster could restore it" (*Cities* xv). The novel then proceeds to imagine the necessary disaster, as comic-book Nazi-like scientists undertake biological experiments to control world population. The experiments are referred to collectively as "the pickle factory," a term used to designate the CIA. They take place in South America, and their aim is to destroy the threat of expanding Third World populations while preserving a white gene pool of Hitler *Jungen* for future repopulation and domination. The war between the libertarian pirate communes and the genocidal scientists of the pickle factory makes up the subplot of the novel.

Formally, the pirate adventure story takes place within a larger, open-ended narrative, a detective story whose many-faced hero introduces himself with hard-boiled bravado: "The name is Clem Williamson Snide. I am a private asshole" (*Cities* 35). The name Williamson designates the presence of one of the avatars of the author, and the qualification, in which "private asshole" substitutes for "private eye," asserts that all occurs under the fatherhood—the eye/I—of the asshole. The god-like function of Snide, predictably, is to create the reality of the novel—that is, to write the story we read, including the stories of the pirate commune and the eponymous myth of the Six Cities of the Red Night. The myth explains the origin of the virus of language and the war between the sexes, those twin disasters which for Burroughs have ever since determined the conflicts and course of history.

If *Cities of the Red Night* tries to institute utopia through the imagination of disaster, *The Place of Dead Roads* seeks to imagine it through miracle, the turning back of time to a point in capitalist development when the possibility of building utopia had not yet been lost. A similar miracle occurs in *Cities,* as the story returns to the eighteenth century, but in that novel a whole genocidal conspiracy has also moved back in time and blocks the utopian potential. In *Dead Roads* there is less jumping across expanses of time—the events occur between 1899 and sometime in the mid 1920s—and consequently the utopian force is allowed to develop and work out its fate battling the systems of control. The novel is notable for the concrete detail in which it imagines a string of utopian communities inhabited by ageless all-male families called The Johnsons. The preface, in which Burroughs explains that the original title for the novel was "The Johnson Family," makes it clear that they represent a workers' utopia. (A similar community exists in *Cities,* but its role is much less emphatic.) The Johnsons represent "Potential America," and their objectives are "the realization of our biologic and spiritual destiny in space" (*Dead Roads* 154). "The Johnson Family is a cooperative structure. There isn't any boss man. People know what they are supposed to do and they do it. We're all actors and we change roles. Today's millionaire may be tomorrow's busboy. There's none of that ruling-class old school tie. [ . . . ] We are showing that an organization and a very effective organization can run without boss-man dog-eat-dog fear" (*Dead Roads* 114–15). That is, the Johnsons represent a society of decentered, nonhierarchical socialist democracies with a communal economic base in agriculture and useful industry.

The two novels are not only utopian in content but also in their semiotic structure. The novels' irreducible utopian dimension lies precisely here: the primacy of the asshole, as point of view and as sexual organ, rewrites the symbolic code—that is, the patriarchal code—by restructuring its fundamental oppositions. In *S/Z* Barthes shows that the symbolic code inscribes into literary texts antitheses which are central to the organization of the cultural order to which they belong.[19] The symbolic code is entrusted with the maintenance of the order of dominant binary oppositions, chief

and most sacrosanct among which is that between male and female subjects.[20] This
is why in *S/Z* Barthes takes Balzac's "Sarrasine" as his text: because that story,
in the hermaphrodite figure of Zambinella, challenges precisely this fundamental
antithesis. Similarly, Burroughs' homosexual Wild Boys, moved from the wings of
earlier novels to center stage in his recent work, oblige the symbolic code to operate
in the absence of sexual determinants.

Like Balzac's "Sarrasine," Burroughs' novels articulate the usual conflict between
the terms "active" and "passive," and "castrating" and "castrated," but they abolish
that between "male" and "female." In the process they show that the symbolic field
transcends biological difference/sameness—that lack, where lack means "desire for
the phallus," designates a potential *jouissance* located in the male subject. For the
androgynous males of the Johnson Family, enjoyment of the female role in coitus
requires no sacrifice of the attributes of the Father, for "mommy—and—daddy" are
absent. Their absence is fully explained by cloning, eliminating the need for sexual
reproduction, and by the democratic exchange of roles, whereby any one individual
can and does play either role, active or passive, as the mood takes him and his
partner.

Symbolic attributes are distributed not along gender lines but according to a
tripartite structural metaphor of parasitism. Parasitism divides first into a controlling
elite of parasites and a controlled mass of hosts. The two compose a symbiosis
which contrasts with the nonexploitive grouping of the boys' camps, whose members
know the facts of the parasite symbiosis and withdraw from the game of control.
Expressed in this way, the three groups are distinguished by their relation to knowledge. The mass of hosts simply don't know and are helpless. The parasitical elite
know, but they are driven to exploit their knowledge. In the usual master-slave
pattern, they are dependent on their hosts for their continued existence. The Wild
Boys know, but they are not driven to exploit. Their knowledge frees them, and in the
full consciousness of their freedom they choose perpetual war against the parasitical
system of control which would enmesh them as well as the faceless billions of the
hosts. Given Burroughs' assimilation of popular narrative genres, it is worth noting
that a recent study of the western movie has found this same triple set of binary
oppositions in westerns in the transnational period of late capitalism. The three
sets of characters are the professional heroes, Burroughs' Wild Boys; the villains,
Burroughs' parasites; and society, Burroughs' hosts.[21]

Other elements to be placed in the scale have a dystopian weight, and chief
among these is the exclusion of women. Burroughs' misogyny[22] is too well known
for me to need to discuss it; however, while I certainly do not mean to defend it, in
fairness to Burroughs his own justification should be noted. Like the gnostic Blake,
he sees history as determined by a primordial fall from an androgynous unity into
a strife-ridden duality whose chief expressions are language and sexual difference.
Burroughs' rewriting of the symbolic code and his valorization of homosexuality
attempt to transcend this ancient duality, the base of the oppressive reality he dreams
of escaping. As he writes in *Dead Roads*, "Sex forms the matrix of a dualistic and
therefore solid and real universe. It is possible to resolve the dualistic conflict in a

sex act, where dualism need not exist" (172). Needless to say, this would-be transcendence is hardly satisfactory if it consigns the female half of humanity to outer darkness; and such seems to have been Burroughs' original design for utopia. To his credit, Burroughs has relented in late years, and he now allows that women should build their own utopia. Indeed, it has been argued that there is no intrinsic reason why sexual segregation in itself should degrade women: in classical Greece it was at Sparta, with its homosexual military organization, that "women had freedom and dignity, while the women of the Athenian patriarchal family were degraded into nonentity."[23]

Another indication of this mellowing, if that's not too hopeful a word, is the presence in *Dead Roads* of what must be Burroughs' most positive female character. She is Salt Chunk Mary, spiritual "mother of the Johnson Family," a woman of firm mind who doesn't hesitate to say "no," and "none of her no's ever meant yes" (122). As "salt" she represents the superfluity of fertility conceived as sexual production, and as Mary she is the mother of Christ the Author, the male God who replicates into male disciples who take over history. Salt Chunk Mary is a single exception in an otherwise all-male novel, but in a society based on cloning, it should be borne in mind, the one can very quickly produce the many.

In terms of the utopian-dystopian balance, what Burroughs loses for sexist exclusion he at least partially recuperates through racial inclusion. The original Wild Boys come from the Third World, and as the fictional utopia develops in the later fiction it quickly incorporates all ethnic groups, re-creating Melville's democratic vision of the crew of the *Pequod:* "an Anacharsis Clootz deputation from all the isles of the sea, and all the ends of the earth."

The last element to be weighed in the balance, the relation of knowledge to destructive technology, is dystopian. Drearily enough, knowledge and the technology of destruction correlate as highly in Burroughs' world as in the West generally. It is also chilling to observe how love relations between men replicate the machine analogy which rules the rationalized world of capitalism. Guns in particular are fetishized, and in scenes of sexual activity the same language describes pistols and penises. The equation is anything but unintentional on Burroughs' part, as *Dead Roads* makes plain: "[The boys] handle their bodies like their guns, as artifacts, with the knowing caressing fingers of connoisseurs" (213). To extenuate this fetishization of the body as machine, with its unfortunate resemblance to the glorification of the machine in such proto-facsisms as Italian Futurism, it would be necessary to read these scenes allegorically as satires of the larger society. If such an allegorical reading does not convince, it should at least be noted that the love of weaponry in Burroughs has a human dimension absent from that in the military-industrial complex. For Burroughs' Wild Boys, weapons function only in person-to-person combat, and killing is, to that extent, a personal affair. Mass slaughter is a technology that belongs exclusively to the enemy, the parasitical elite of controllers.

A more radical point of view might argue the eternal warfare of the Wild Boys is necessary. The memory of mass slaughter in our own century is ubiquitous in Burroughs' novels, and a close reading soon discerns that the odor of putrefaction that permeates them emanates from the death camps. Given the destructive control exercised by the parasites and the absence of viable political recourse, guerrilla warfare may seem the only answer. The war is not one the Wild Boys expect to win; war, rather, becomes a way of life. "It is always war," we read in *Dead Roads;* "Planet Earth is by its nature and function a battlefield. Happiness is a by-product of function in a battle context: hence the fatal error of utopians" (116–17). This, however, is only one line of the fictional argument; a happier line suggests that the ultimate medium of control is the image, and that the conscious artist may be the determinative origin of his or her own production. As in the period of modernism, so in the postmodern present, through art an alternative discourse can be established. The second set of antinomies, which deals with the putative life and death of the author, will reveal the sense of this assertion.

This set of antinomies questions the status of the existence of the author, since he is both dead and quite alive. The author's death, in Burroughs' case, is part of the larger utopian project, one with striking Christian overtones, by which the death of the one gives eternal life to the many. As in Bakhtin's carnival, the private body becomes public; and the aging body of the man Burroughs is cloned into the eternally youthful bodies of the Wild Fruits: he gives himself to death that they might have life more abundantly. His death is figured in the fiction by the near disappearance of the autobiographical persona of *Naked Lunch*. His life, at the same time, continues in at least three forms: the communal body comprising the brotherhood of the Wild Boys; the image conveyed through print, visual, and aural media; and the unmistakable parodic voice of the artist as performer of his work.

The idea of immortality through cloning is one whose growth can be traced through Burroughs' work in clearly marked stages, from its seed in *Naked Lunch,* with the violent episodes of identity absorption and transference, to its ripe harvest in *Dead Roads,* where the cloning is taken for granted and the remaining problems are those of strategy—how best to take immortality from the parasites and give it to the deserving minority of the boys' camps. If *Naked Lunch* carries the seeds of the immortality project, *The Wild Boys* is its sprouting season. The authorial persona discovers his identity with the guerrilla gangs of healthy young men who spring up to oppose the police states which, under the pretext of drug control, have been set up throughout the West (the year, prophetically, is 1988). This realization is mediated by the liberating effect of two fictional techniques: the cut-up and fold-in method; and "god's little toy," as Paul Bowles called it,[24] the tape recorder, which replaces scissors and paste with high-speed production. Wild-boy guerrilla units form an army of liberation to free the United States: "Gangs of boys with portable tape recorders record riots from TV. They are dressed in identical grey flannel suits." They play back their tapes in the streets and create riots at will. The anonymous narrator explains, "I have a thousand faces and a thousand names. I am nobody I am everybody. I am me I am you. I am here and there forward back in out. I stay everywhere I stay nowhere. I stay present I stay absent."[25]

The fruit of Burroughs' tree of life matures in his latest novel, the western *The Place of Dead Roads,* where it reaches a stage of critical self-consciousness, problematizing the nature of immortality. Burroughs wants to take immortality from the parasitical exploiters, represented by the Egyptian pharaohs, and give it to the Wild Boys, the workers who make it possible. The Egyptian system of mummification comes under virulent attack for its elitism. "Mummies are the arch-conservatives" (193), we read; and "The Western Lands [the Egyptian paradise] was a vampiric mirage kept solid with fellahin blood" (192). The Egyptian afterlife correlates with social exploitation, for the epithet "Western Lands" instructs us to read this scenario as an allegory of developments in the Americas, which of course existed in the mind of Europe for millennia as a mythological Western Paradise before navigation made them available for actual conquest and exploitation. The privileged interests which have governed their development are represented by the parasitical structure of the Egyptian afterlife.

The critique of elitist immortality is embodied in the following routine from *Dead Roads,* and the reader is again invited to listen:[26]

> The most arbitrary, precarious, and bureaucratic immortality blueprint was drafted by the ancient Egyptians. First you had to get yourself mummified, and that was very expensive, making immortality a monopoly of the truly rich. Then your continued immortality in the Western Lands was entirely dependent on the continued existence of your mummy. That is why they had their mummies guarded by demons and hid good.
>
> Here is plain G. I. Horus. . . . He's got enough *baraka* to survive his first physical death. He won't get far. He's got no mummy, he's got no names, he's got nothing. What happens to a bum like that, a nameless mummyless asshole? Why, demons will swarm all over him at the first checkpoint. He will be dismembered and thrown into a flaming pit, where his soul will be utterly consumed and destroyed forever. While others, with sound mummies and the right names to drop in the right places, sail through to the Western Lands.
>
> There are of course those who just barely squeeze through. Their mummies are not in a good sound condition. These second-class souls are relegated to third-rate transient hotels just beyond the last checkpoint, where they can smell the charnelhouse disposal ovens from their skimpy balconies. [. . .] "Might as well face facts . . . my mummy is going downhill. Cheap job to begin with . . . gawd, maggots is crawling all over it [. . .]"
>
> And here you are in your luxury condo, deep in the Western Lands . . . you got no security. Some disgruntled former employee sneaks into your tomb and throws acid on your mummy. Or sloshes gasoline all over it and burns the shit out of it. "OH . . . someone is fucking with my mummy . . ."
>
> Mummies are sitting ducks. No matter who you are, what can happen to your mummy is a pharaoh's nightmare: the dreaded mummy bashers and grave robbers, scavengers, floods, volcanoes, earthquakes. Perhaps a mummy's best friend is an Egyptologist: sealed in a glass

case, kept at a constant temperature . . . but your mummy isn't even
safe in a museum. *Air-raid sirens, it's the blitz!*
    "For Ra's sake, get us into the vaults," scream the mummies,
without a throat, without a tongue.
    Anybody buy in on a deal like that should have his mummy
examined. (43–44)

Burroughs' primary complaint against the Egyptian system, I repeat, is that it is
elitist, and his populist hatred fuels the parody of inefficiency. *Dead Roads* offers
as an alternative a decentered string of communities of kindred spirits who are
recognizable as clones of the author. Burroughs disposes completely of the bourgeois
family, which to him is the source of the self-righteousness virus, the belief so
characteristic of our national policy that our business is to mind the business of
everyone weaker than ourselves. The bourgeois family is replaced by the Johnsons,
and the upshot of a Johnson takeover, the preface makes clear, will be a workers'
utopia, a united planet behind a "united space program."
    *Dead Roads* shows how Burroughs' immortality system works. The hero of the
novel, Kim Carsons, is one of ten clones derived from Kim Carsons (113), and he
is identical with William Seward Hall, "the man of many faces and many pen names,
of many times and places" (115) whom we recognize as William Seward Burroughs.
In body, Hall is "a sedentary middle-aged man," but his face is "alert and youthful"
(116), and his body is the deprivatized, communal body of Bakhtinian carnival,
establishing its immortality through the life of the community it fathers. Carsons/
Hall's "thought patterns live in a number of different brains and nervous systems,
his speech and genital patterns, all of which are distinctive. [. . .] The clones exist
in a communal mind in which the bodies are at the disposal of all the others, like
rotating quarters" (113). Hall is also the ghost writer of Kim Carsons' book, entitled
"QUIEN ES?" (Readers nurtured on westerns will recall that "Quien es?" are the
last words of Billy the Kid in the dark bedroom where Pat Garret kills him.) Carsons/
Hall's book, which is also Burroughs' book, embodies an immortality, or at least
an entrance thereto, for we read, "No one can apply unless he breathes in a writer's
prose hills and faraway Western Lands . . ." (202).
    The question the book asks—identity—is one of the most banal questions of the
North American hermeneutic, but its answer is jolting: Death. Kim Carsons teaches
his men to identify with Death (95), a populist god to whom all have ready access.
Unlike Life, "Death belongs to anyone who can pick up a frying pan."[27] In this
context, anal intercourse is a sacred act, and as such it often takes place in black
ceremonies notoriously (but not necessarily) involving hanging. The ceremony is
implied as early as *Naked Lunch* in the sentence quoted earlier: "Gentle Reader, we
see God through our assholes in the flash bulb of orgasm" (22). In *Dead Roads* death
is part of a religious rite celebrating "The creation of ANUS, the foundation of
chaos" (94)—an imagery that draws into its associations the flashes of Hiroshima
and Nagasaki as well as the literal level of the novel, in which Kim learns "to shoot
right from his opening asshole" as "a powerful magic." His pistol knocks a black

hole (64) into the paper-thin sky of the media-created universe (5–9)—that is, the celluloid universe produced in the reality studios of the police state.

This exploration of the body of death out of which Burroughs' utopia grows has arrived now at the question of the image—which is to say the kind of life which the author has in the death his fiction declares. It seems appropriate that Burroughs, for whom the image has always been the all-powerful creator of reality, should find his own present life and future immortality given through images. Print, the first medium of this immortality project, is now supplemented through popular, nonprint media. Burroughs, as is well known, is now a media person in his own right—his image projected through countless public performances since the early seventies, when he returned permanently to the United States. Burroughs' experiments with the tape recorder, of course, go back to the early fifties, but his media image is a product of movies, records, public readings, and nightclub appearances which began in the seventies, and this image is now being multiplied through technological advances in audio and videotape.[28]

These media convey not only an image of the author but the audiovisual presence of the author in performance of his work. His intense life in this arena, indicating that reports of his death are greatly exaggerated, would hardly have surprised Barthes, who has laid the groundwork for an affective theory of performance. In an essay called "The Grain of the Voice," Barthes proposes that in a musical performance the listener enters into a "relation to the body of someone who is singing" that is not judged "according to the rules of interpretation . . . but according to the image of the body."[29] Contemplation of "the grain of the voice" creates a relationship between the listener and the performer, rather than between the decoder and the "tissue of quotations" which textuality comprises.[30] In the case of Burroughs (and, *mutatis mutandis,* in that of many other performing authors), this thesis can be pushed further to argue that there is no more mistaking the personal style of his prose than there is mistaking the midwestern, sour, heavy-metal twang of his reading voice. While all art in its aestheticized mode is readily cooptable today—witness the institutionalization of high modernism—the personal experience of Burroughs in performance before a receptive audience can never be coopted or shorn of its subversive power. The crucified and dead author of the novels is resurrected in the authorial performance of the text.

In conclusion, a progressive reading of Burroughs, a charitably allegorical one of the sort I have offered, should read him as one response to Jameson's call for a "social cartography"—that is, for the cognitive mapping which he sees as "one possible form of a new radical cultural politics" made necessary by postmodern space in the era of late capitalism ("Postmodernism" 89). This spacetime grid is the schizoid contemporary world that Burroughs has been mapping for over three decades. In its political dimensions, specifically in its incorporation of Third World and U.S.-ghetto youth into the author's communal body, Burroughs displays that grasp of the totality which, following the argument of Hegel and Lukacs, is available only to the oppressed. His work thus contributes its allegories to the mapping of the cultural imperialism of the first world.[31]

Mapping is a principal function of Burroughs' work. On several occasions he has referred to himself as "a map maker, a cosmonaut of inner space,"[32] and *Dead Roads* in particular calls attention to itself as a mapping exercise in new space:

> The guide traces the area on the map with his finger. [. . .] "The
> Place of Dead Roads, *señor*. This does not mean roads that are no
> longer used, roads that are overgrown, it means roads that are dead.
> You comprehend the difference?"
> "And how can this area be reached?"
> The guide shrugged. "It is usual to start in a City of Dead Streets.
> . . . And where is this city? In every city are dead streets, *señor*, but
> in some more than in others. New York is well supplied in this respect
> . . ." (283)

Any U.S. metropolis may be an image of the postmodern space whose interior leads into the jungles of Central and South America, where the pickle factory's experiments in population control continue. Burroughs' mapping is of course not mimetic in the traditional sense, but it does pose the analysis of representation on a complex level where the artist becomes responsible for his production—for the force of his images and the cultural energies which speak through him. Burroughs puts it plainly: "Every writer must stand behind his words."

Terry Eagleton has charged that "postmodernism mimes the formal resolution of art and social life attempted by the avant-garde, while remorselessly emptying it of its political content," and that the postmodern image is "a dark parody of anti-representationalism."[33] But the image in Burroughs seeks not to mimic a reality drained of political content but rather to recharge the image by revealing its political source, which is to say its function as ideology. In Burroughs' fiction the repressive forces in charge of the Reality Studios produce reality. Allegorically, they produce ideology, in the Althusserian sense, an imagined relation to real conditions. Burroughs' Reality Studios are the scene of our most intimate everyday battle to produce alternative discourses. As Bakhtin asserts of Rabelais, Burroughs' "basic goal [is] to destroy the official picture of events. . . . He summon[s] all the resources of popular imagery in order to break up official lies and the narrow seriousness dictated by the ruling classes" (*Rabelais* 439).

The Althusserian formulation of ideology opposes a realm of abstract knowledge to an existential realm, and these two categories, Jameson suggests, correspond to the Lacanian Imaginary and the Real but omit the Symbolic ("Postmodernism" 91–92). In this last dimension, I would argue, Burroughs' rewriting of the sexual code under the sign of the asshole has its progressive value. It exemplifies the author's power to rewrite the symbolic codes and helps establish an alternative discourse, and in so doing it takes a necessary step toward the building of a socialist democracy. To this achievement it must be added that Burroughs' recent novels, in bringing forward the Third World as a popular base for parody, give voice to cultures excluded by the hegemonic discourses of Western humanism. Like Bakhtin's study of Rabelais in the context of Stalinist repression, Burroughs' work celebrates the potential of an invigorated relation among body, language, and political practice. Symbolically, the ensuing carnival of the asshole envisions utopia, the medieval "feast for all the world."

## Notes

1. Ezra Pound, *The Cantos* (New York: New Directions, 1972).
2. James Joyce, *Ulysses* (London: Bodley Head, 1960) 83–84.
3. Georges Bataille, *The Story of the Eye*, trans. Joachim Nengroschel (1928; New York: Urizen, 1977). This discussion was written before I discovered a parallel treatment of the eye metaphor in Roland Barthes, "The Metaphor of the Eye," *Critical Essays*, trans. Richard Howard (Evanston: Northwestern UP, 1972) 239–47.
4. Gilles Deleuze and Félix Guattari, *Anti-Oedipus: Capitalism and Schizophrenia*, trans. Robert Hurley et al. (Minneapolis: U of Minnesota P, 1983) 2.
5. The passage is recorded on *Call Me Burroughs* (Paris: English Bookshop, 1965).
6. William S. Burroughs, *Naked Lunch* (New York: Grove, 1962) 21. Subsequent page references will appear in the text.
7. I am not the first to observe that Burroughs parodies the language of officialdom. See, for example, R. G. Peterson, "A Picture Is a Fact: Wittgenstein and *Naked Lunch*," *The Beats: Essays in Criticism*, ed. Lee Bartlett (Jefferson, NC: McFarland, 1981) 36. And Robin Lydenberg has preceded me in focusing on the Talking Asshole routine from *Naked Lunch* in "Notes From the Orifice: Language and Body in William Burroughs," *Contemporary Literature* 26 (1985): 62. But Peterson's reference to parody is not developed, and Lydenberg argues for a duality of body and mind which strikes me as misleading.
8. This insight is developed by Robert C. Elliott in *The Power of Satire* (Princeton: Princeton UP, 1960) and *The Shape of Utopia* (Chicago: U of Chicago P, 1970).
9. Frederic Jameson, "Postmodernism, or The Cultural Logic of Late Capitalism," *New Left Review* 146 (1984): 64–65. Subsequent page references will appear in the text.
10. Frederic Jameson, "The Politics of Theory: Ideological Positions in the Postmodernism Debate," *New German Critique* 33 (1984): 63–64.
11. Other critical schools argue other positions for parody. Margaret A. Rose asserts that, "though once in the periphery of the literary canon, parody has come to dominate the norms of literary theory through the use made by Viktor Shklovsky and other Russian formalists," in "Parody Revisited," *Comic Relations: Studies in the Comic, Satire and Parody*, ed. David Petre et al. (Frankfurt: Peter Lang, 1985) 187. Pierre Macherey argues a still more central role for parody as a characteristic of all literary work in *A Theory of Literary Production*, trans. Geoffrey Wall (London: Routledge, 1978) 59–60.
12. M. M. Bakhtin, *The Dialogic Imagination*, trans. Michael Holquist (Austin, U of Texas P, 1981) 60.
13. Cited in Tony Tanner, *City of Words: American Fiction, 1950–1970* (New York: Harper, 1971) 110.
14. M. M. Bakhtin, *Rabelais and His World*, trans. Helene Iswolsky (Bloomington: Indiana UP, 1984) 90. Subsequent page references will appear in the text.
15. Edward W. Said, *The World, the Text, and the Critic* (Cambridge, Harvard UP, 1983) 177.
16. Said, 11.

17. William S. Burroughs, *The Place of Dead Roads* (New York: Holt, 1984) 94. Subsequent page references will appear in the text.

18. William S. Burroughs, *Cities of the Red Night* (New York: Holt, 1981) xiv. Subsequent page references will appear in the text.

19. Roland Barthes, *S/Z*, trans. Richard Miller (New York: Hill, 1974) 19–20.

20. Kaja Silverman, *The Subject of Semiotics* (New York: Oxford UP, 1983) 270.

21. Will Wright, *Sixguns and Society: A Structural Study of the Western* (Berkeley: U of California P, 1975) 85 ff.

22. For Burroughs' discussion of the accusation of misogyny and the offending passage in *The Job* in which he described women as a "biological mistake," see "Women: A Biological Mistake?" in *The Adding Machine: Selected Essays* (New York: Seaver, 1986) 124–26. Burroughs mitigates his offense by enlarging the category of biological mistakes to include dinosaurs ("a noble experiment") and "the whole human race" (124).

23. Norman O. Brown, *Love's Body* (New York: Vintage, 1966) 13.

24. Cited in Daniel Odier, *The Job: Interviews with William S. Burroughs* (New York: Grove, 1974) 162.

25. William S. Burroughs, *Three Novels: The Soft Machine, Nova Express, The Wild Boys* (New York: Grove, 1980) 138 ff.

26. Burroughs reads this passage on *Life is a Killer* (New York: Giorno Poetry Systems, 1982).

27. William S. Burroughs, *The Burroughs File* (San Francisco: City Lights, 1984) 19.

28. Nicholas Zurbrugg, "The Limits of Intertextuality: Barthes, Burroughs, Gysin, Culler," *Southern Review* 16 (1983): 251.

29. Roland Barthes, *The Responsibility of Forms: Critical Essays on Music, Art, and Representation,* trans. Richard Howard (New York: Hill, 1985) 276–77.

30. Zurbrugg, 250–52.

31. Frederic Jameson, "Third World Literature in the Era of Multinational Capitalism," *Social Text* 15 (1986): 87 n. 26.

32. Eric Mottram, *WILLIAM BURROUGHS: The Algebra of Need* (London: Boyars, 1977) 13.

33. Terry Eagleton, "Capitalism, Modernism and Postmodernism," *New Left Review* 148 (1984): 61.

# 24

# 'El Hombre Invisible'

Robin Lydenberg

[Review of William S. Burroughs' *The Western Lands*]

I n Tangier in the 1950s, an exotic outpost for writers and artists and a lively marketplace for drugs and sex, William S. Burroughs was known by the locals as "el hombre invisible," the invisible man. Despite his shadowy presence and conservative dress (he later called it "banker's drag"), Burroughs' life did not long remain obscure. Mythologized in the early fiction of Jack Kerouac, Burroughs became a Beat legend even before he made his mark as a writer. The legend was a paradoxical one. Both Allen Ginsberg and Kerouac credit Burroughs as a "great teacher" who introduced them to modern thought from psychoanalysis to Céline, but he also brought them in touch with the marginal world of outcasts and petty criminals in New York City.

Behind the high drama of the Beat myth and the cultivated anonymity of his actual life, however, Burroughs was composing the routines that would be assembled into his still-outrageous novel, *Naked Lunch*. When the first excerpts appeared here in 1959, a legal battle began that was fought all the way to the Massachusetts Supreme Court where *Naked Lunch* was eventually acquitted of obscenity charges.[1]

*Naked Lunch* set off literary as well as legal controversy, and Burroughs' early admirers and defenders—among them Mary McCarthy, Norman Mailer, and John Ciardi—were countered by those who found his depiction of an underworld of drugs, sex, and violence offensive and his narrative innovations unreadable.

While the critics and the courts debated the merits of *Naked Lunch*, Burroughs had already moved on to more radical stylistic ground with what he called the "cut-up" technique. *The Soft Machine*, *The Ticket That Exploded* and *Nova Express*—the trilogy of novels in which he employed this difficult and disjointed style—found fewer admirers than *Naked Lunch*, but many continued to defend Burroughs as a serious artist, a scientist of the word.

Now in his mid-seventies, Burroughs has achieved critical respectability: elected member of the American Academy of Arts and Letters and a Commandeur de L'Ordre des Arts et Lettres; subject of seven books (four in English, two in French,

Robin Lydenberg, "'El Hombre Invisible,'" *The Nation* (19 Mar. 1988): 387–89. Copyright© 1988 by *The Nation* magazine/The NationCompany, Inc. Reprinted by permission.

and one in German), several bibliographies, dissertations, and a steady flow of scholarly articles. Burroughs' cameo appearances on "Saturday Night Live," in the pages of *Rolling Stone* and *Crawdaddy,* and gliding across the film screen in a ghostly tango with Laurie Anderson have brought him a new generation of admiring readers.

But the Burroughs legend still threatens to mythologize the man and obscure the work. For over thirty years, cultural myopia has prevented many critics and readers from seeing past Burroughs' unconventional life and the extravagant mythology of his novels to the intellectual and aesthetic integrity of his writing. Nevertheless, he has continued to write and evolve. With the 1981 publication of *Cities of the Red Night,* Burroughs entered a new phase in his development, and the novel was praised by many reviewers as his most powerful and organically unified work. The completion of the trilogy—with *The Place of Dead Roads* in 1983 and *The Western Lands* in 1987—provides an occasion for a serious reassessment of the career of "el hombre invisible."

When asked what *he* thought of William Burroughs, Samuel Beckett responded with appropriate minimalist precision, "Well, he's a writer." In his early fiction, Burroughs often casts himself in walk-on roles as junky, con man, carnival huckster, detective, or intergalactic revolutionary agent. Increasingly, however, he has turned up in the more recognizable garb of the writer in solitary combat with language and history. As Jennie Skerl predicted in *William S. Burroughs,*[2] Burroughs' fascination with the writer's power as a storyteller is most explicitly dramatized in his second trilogy. The trilogy begins with the intersecting plots of *Cities of the Red Night,* taking the reader back in time through an ancient plague, through the establishment of a renegade utopian community in the eighteenth century, and into the present and future with a surreal detective story. This sprawling narrative is pulled together by the convergence of the three heroes as writers documenting, forging, and reimagining history. Burroughs' subsequent novel, *The Place of Dead Roads,* also propels the reader back and forth in time, but the narrative is anchored by the single figure of Kim Carsons, nineteenth-century frontier "shootist." Carsons' mission is to "shoot his way out by blasting a hole in reality" before the novel returns to the inevitable moment with which it began: the violent death of his creator, William Seward Hall, who writes western tales under the pseudonym Kim Carsons.

The desire to escape from history, time, and death is still the motivating force in the recently released final novel of the trilogy, *The Western Lands.*[3] But here the extravagant plots and characters of the previous novels are condensed to brief allusions, and the struggle of the writer to create and to keep his creations alive both frames and dominates the narrative. What is unique about the allegory of the writer's struggle in *The Western Lands* is that creativity is no longer depicted as violent aggression, sexual exhilaration, or hallucinatory fantasy—it has instead a peculiarly domestic, almost maternal quality. It is perhaps Burroughs' most intimate self-portrait.

*The Western Lands* opens with a wonderful sequence about "the old writer," William Seward Hall again, living in a boxcar on an abandoned junk heap. Victim of no mere writer's block, Hall is gripped by "a disgust for his words accumulated until it choked him [. . .] like arsenic or lead, which slowly builds up in the body until a certain point is reached and then . . . he hummed the refrain of 'Dead Man Blues' by Jelly Roll Morton." Trying to write his way out of death, Hall relies on dreams and visions to give him access to words not his own. Despite his vigilance, Hall's initial hallucination yields only cryptic fragments, " 'the fate of others' [. . .] 'well almost never' '2001.' " After this halting start, however, the narrative ventures out on what will be a series of attempts to reach the Western Lands, the resting place of the Immortals in the Egyptian mythology that pervades this novel. The pilgrimages take us through ancient Egypt with the scribe Neferti, to the island of the Esmeraldas in search of giant centipedes, and through moments of cataclysmic disaster past and future with Joe the Dead, Kim, and others. But we always return to Hall's mind where these scenarios fade in and out of focus.

Burroughs' fiction has been set on this course since *Naked Lunch,* and the quest for some "way out" of time and into the freedom of bodiless space and silence has led his narratives around the world and into the cosmos. In *The Western Lands* it is finally clear that "There is no transport out. There isn't any important assignment," there is only an aimless itinerary of dead-end excursions.

Somehow this news does not come as a terrible revelation. *The Western Lands* is narrated with a detached irony beyond illusion and thus beyond the pain of disillusionment. While the earlier novels often intone a nostalgic litany of farewells to the past or telegraph urgent messages of an apocalyptic or utopian future, this novel is issued from the present. If Burroughs hasn't made it to the Western Lands, at least he knows where he is and can measure his progress: "a series of modest goals leading to a series of modest achievements which became at some point quite considerable." He concedes with uncharacteristic satisfaction at one point "to be alive at all is a victory."

From this vantage point, Burroughs looks unflinchingly on the panorama of human fears and self-delusions, and he documents this territory with a bleak courage matched perhaps by only that of Kafka or Beckett. Each new pilgrimage is charged with energy and hope, but there is always someone looking to sell immortality cheap, and always the traveler hoping for a shortcut to the Western Lands. So traffickers in illusion drugs hit the market, offering such specialized highs as the "Western Bubble" which gives the buyer a euphoric release from all bodily needs, only to plunge him back into a reality made even bleaker by contrast: "abrasive, dreary, dead-end surfaces where everything is exactly what it seems to be [. . .] no mystery, no magic. [. . .] The unfortunate traveler, having poured all his magic into the bubble . . . POP. . . gritty surface with nothing behind."

While *The Western Lands* documents these painful alternations of mood and energy, Burroughs himself seems less subject to them, or he has learned how to ride them out. Perhaps he has finally achieved in this novel the detached passivity recommended by his dictum "the way OUT is the way IN," the way to escape the horror is to let it in and through. So here, as in all of his work, he generates images of "filth, horror, fear, hate, disease and death." But instead of settling like a heavy fog over these pages, Burroughs' catalogue of "carnival horrors" whirls by in a black tornado "round and round faster and faster," spiraling up into the sky and out of sight. In its wake the world is momentarily cleansed, and glimpses of simple beauty flash out: "a line of trees, then white grain elevators crash into the sky like a painting in the Whitney Museum." The sharpened vision of this book, more pictorial than any of Burroughs' previous novels, yields moments of intense and simple joy set off against the darkened backdrop of horror: "I want to reach the Western Lands— right in front of you, across the bubbling brook. It's a frozen sewer. It's known as the Duad, remember? [ . . . ] Let it flow! My cat Fletch stretches behind me on the bed. A tree like black lace against a gray sky. A flash of joy." These flashes of beauty and joy *are* the Western Lands, and the only mortal error is to cling to them, to try to make them solid like some fool "got his condominium in the Western Lands all picked out and paid for." For Burroughs, the promised land is not a piece of commercial real estate but the self-sustaining and disembodied domain of art: "we will make ourselves less solid. Well that's what art is all about isn't it? All creative thought, actually?"

What makes the Western Lands of art a biological, an evolutionary necessity in Burroughs' mind is the possibility it offers for human contact and continuity. Despite his efforts to escape from memory, emotion, the body; despite an experimental style that has more often repelled than invited readers, the goal of Burroughs' writing has always been to make contact and to leave a legacy. So the "old writer," bereft of family ties and isolated from human companionship, begins to write animal stories inspired by illustrated books: "The writer caresses the pictures as he turns the pages and pulls them toward him as he's seen a mother cat reach out and pull her five kittens to her." But even as he gathers them "gently to his chest, palms crossed" these offspring of the imagination are never meant to be solid. They remain "blueprint hybrids, potentials," each one "the first of its kind, the only one of its kind."

Nothing is solid and irrevocable except the protective and nurturing role the writer is given in *The Western Lands:* the role of Guardian. Biologically bound to his "charge" and with "total responsibility" for its survival, the Guardian is subject to an unbearable intensity of love and pain: "the love for a creature that you have created from your whole being. [. . .] And you do die of it, to lose the only thing your whole life means, every breath, every gesture, all the weariness and pain for this one act." Interwoven with this almost maudlin allegory of the writer's burden are more moving glimpses of domestic reality as the writer obsessively tidies his workspace, making sure that every object has felt his touch.

Despite the tenderness, the precision, and the suffering, there are no guarantees. As Burroughs quipped recently looking back over the years of scandalized reviews of his novels, "Well, in the (last) words of Dutch Schultz, 'So many good ones, and so many bad ones; that's what you get for trying.' "[4]

And Burroughs does keep trying, because he has the "contact habit" and he's still not ready to give up or give up on his readers. So he is always preparing for another pilgrimage, always able to summon the wacky and grotesque humor, the perfect mimicry of American crudeness, the linguistic experimentation and elegaic moments of poetic beauty that make him, as Beckett said, a writer.

## Notes

1. Michael Goodman has meticulously and entertainingly chronicled the entire saga in *Contemporary Literary Censorship: The Case History of Burroughs' "Naked Lunch"* (Metuchen, NJ: Scarecrow, 1981).

2. Jennie Skerl, *William S. Burroughs* (Boston: Hall, 1985).

3. Burroughs, *The Western Lands* (New York: Viking, 1987). All subsequent quotes are from *The Western Lands*.

4. "My Purpose Is to Write For the Space Age," *New York Times Book Review* (19 Feb. 1984): 9.

# 25

# On Burroughs' Art

James Grauerholz

I nevitably, William Burroughs' artwork is considered in terms of his writing, but it may also be considered in terms of his ideas: for what have been influential in his writing, in several fields of contemporary art, are the central ideas in his work. And it is first necessary to put his paintings, qua paintings, in the context of the enormous personal and artistic influence of Brion Gysin, his closest friend. This is as true for his writing as for his painting, so any attempt to "contextualize" Burroughs as a painter must begin with Gysin, who—if we approach the question purely as a matter of art history—was Burroughs' teacher.

Of course the difficulty of "contextualizing" both Burroughs and Gysin in this way is that their work has taken place at the center of a worldwide shift of philosophy, politics, religion, and art: the postwar period in the latter half of the twentieth century, in America and Europe. Burroughs and Gysin were born during World War I, and were mature by the time of the Second World War. Both men traveled the world through their twenties and thirties, along different but intersecting paths, to their first meeting in January 1953, which took place at the gallery in the Rembrandt Hotel in Tangier, where Gysin and Hamri ("the Painter of Morocco") were exhibiting drawings.

Gysin began painting in 1934, at the Sorbonne, in his teens. His circle included Max Ernst, Meret Oppenheim, Valentine Hugo, Salvador Dali, Dora Maar, and Picasso. The story is often told of how his works were removed by Paul Eluard on André Breton's orders in 1935, at Aux Quatre Chemins in Paris, from a show of works by Pablo Picasso, Hans Arp, Hans Bellmer, Victor Brauner, Giorgio di Chirico, Salvador Dali, Marcel Duchamp, Max Ernst, René Magritte, Joan Miró, Man Ray, and Yves Tanguy.[1] This brutal rejection from the pantheon of Surrealists in the 1930s was triggered by Gysin's design for a poster, meant to celebrate the execution of Louis XVI which depicted a huge calf's head in a periwig sitting on a beach, and which Breton apparently felt too closely resembled him. Gysin says he

James Grauerholz, "On Burroughs' Art," in Gallery Casa Sin Nombre catalog (Sante Fe, 1988). Copyright© 1988 by James Grauerholz. Reprinted by permission of the author.

took his pictures out to the sidewalk and exhibited them there. But he felt blackballed, "unhung," and this freed him to renege on the social contract of his middle-class background. At the same time, it caused him lifelong problems with his career, from an economic point of view.

In New York in 1940, Gysin shared a studio with Matta, and saw Arshile Gorky and Jackson Pollock. In the Canadian Army in 1943 he studied Japanese calligraphy, and in 1950, in France, he abandoned his Fulbright to install himself in Tangier, where he would live, on and off, for twenty-three years. There he studied Arabic calligraphy, and learned about magic at first hand from the Master Musicians of Joujouka. The prototypical magic grid of an Arab curse laid on his Moroccan restaurant became a central theme of his art, and his grainy, illusionistic vistas of the desert and the marketplace were precursors to the free, calligraphic abstractions of the late 1950s that are perhaps his finest work.

Another important influence in Gysin's works was the painting of Mark Tobey, whose all-over, calligraphic and gestural figures were arrived at without direct reference to the Dada-inspired Action painting of New York in the 1940s, and were executed in a meditative state (he was converted to Baha'i in 1918). Gysin was very much aware of Tobey's white-line paintings of the early forties. For his part, Tobey's favourite artists included Rothko and Mathieu, even though he paradoxically berated the "abstract academy," saying, "We're getting so abstract that we are practically Arabs. The whole Arab world, outside of Persia, is design in the abstract sense."[2] Ironic, then, that Gysin brought some of Tobey's line to Morocco.

William Rubin pointed out that Tobey's work of the early 1940s, such as *Drift of Summer* (1942) and *Pacific Transition* (1943), "fulfill certain aspects of all-overness in a manner anticipating the classic Pollocks of four years later." Because Pollock himself did not see this "white writing" when it was shown at the Willard Gallery in 1944, his integration of the all-over style "in no way presupposes contact with Tobey." Rubin says that "Tobey arrived at his all-over pictures not via Surreal-ism but through Klee (his 'doodling' and Cubist-influenced grid compositions) and, more significantly (and unfortunately, I believe, for his quality), through Oriental calligraphy."[3] These comments are illustrative of the New York art-establishment prejudice against Tobey, whose large 1961 retrospective at the Louvre was almost completely ignored by *Art News* and *Arts* magazines.

Tobey studied Chinese brush painting in the 1920s, and Zen Buddhism in Japan in the 1930s. He drew a great deal from the work of Paul Klee and Piet Mondrian, the latter a mainstay of l'Ecole de Paris. The School of Paris was the art movement in which Gysin had his roots as a painter, much more than Dada (for all that its iconoclasm and emphasis on revolution and chance were later central to his work), or than Surrealism (from which he was socially and professionally excluded). While living in New York in 1941, he was making *décalcomanies* after Oscar Dominguez's work and talking with Ernst and Matta, all of them Europeans transplanted to the New World. It is possible that Gysin saw Tobey's famous "Broadway," a prime example of the "white writing" series, at the "Artists for Victory" show at the Metropolitan Museum of Art in 1942.

Curiously, Gysin's name is seldom mentioned in standard art-history texts, even in context with the movement whose work comes closest to resembling his own painting. If we consider all the mediums Gysin worked in as his total art, we recognize that his collaboration with William Burroughs took his work into a more radical and conceptual direction. Together they launched an assault on the dividing lines between painting and writing, which would be taken up by waves of succeeding generations of multimedia artists. Pop Art, environmental art, performance art, conceptual art, all drew emphasis away from "oil on canvas," from the patterns of pigment on paper or wood. During the same years, however, painting—as an art not referring directly to any other medium—continued to be made and evaluated, and this is where Gysin was unable to make his true mark.

Gysin has been identified with the Lettristes of the 1960s, and associated with Roberto Altmann, Bernard Heidsieck, Jean-Jacques Lebel and the Domaine Poétique and Poésie Sonore. His sound-poetry work was characterized as influential by George Maciunas in his book on Fluxus, and Gysin spoke of the influence upon his art of the magical "mare's nest" in the chimney of his restaurant, "The 1001 Nights," as "an example of a cabalistic square, which I then began to apply much more directly to my own painting when I returned to Paris in 1958 . . . from 1958 until 1964 I worked out all sorts of different applications of this [approach] directly applied to my painting. . . . And therefore inadvertently became part of that group of writing painters, which is now sort of an historical movement all over Western painting, the people who recognized that writing and painting were somehow related."[4]

Gysin was shown in 1963 at the gallery Valérie Schmidt in Paris with Hans Hartung, Franz Kline, Georges Mathieu, Henri Michaux, Pierre Soulages, Mark Tobey, Zao Wou-ki, Arman, Robert Filliou, Jasper Johns, Jean-Jacques Lebel, Cy Twombly, and others, in an important exhibition called *"La lettre et le signe dans la peinture contemporaine."* Gysin's use of writing in his painting of that time appears as an alien symbology: the glyphs of space and silence, of the desert. Unlike Francis Bacon, who also spent time in Tangier, Gysin "went native" during the 1950s, and his work was presented from a mystical, hallucinogenic stance, suspended in the rectangle of the picture. It was in the "scrapbooks" and other collaborations with Burroughs that Gysin employed the avant-garde forms of montage, appropriation, and juxtaposition, for the first time since his *décrochage* in 1935. In the sixties, these old Surrealist impulses were liberated by the impact of Burroughs' personality on Gysin.

Gysin was never to find a place in the ranks of the group that Michel Tapié called *l'art informel,* with Mathieu, Soulages, Hartung, Wols, and Maria Elena Vieira da Silva (who first painted her abstract architectural grids in the 1940s). The ideas of *tachisme* in Paris, of the unconscious, spontaneous gesture, preceded Action painting in America, where Abstract Expressionism remained transfixed by the heroism of oil and canvas until the 1960s. Even then, the *nouveau réalisme* of Yves Klein, Arman, Jean Tinguely, and others retained clearer echoes of its Dada origins than did its American equivalent, Pop Art.

When he first met Gysin in Tangier, William Burroughs was at a turning point in his life. He was working on what he called *Interzone,* soon to be called *Naked Lunch,* and he wrote in his journals: "I am trying, like Klee, *to create something that will have a life of its own, that can put me in real danger, a danger which I willingly take on myself*" (emphasis his). And he quotes Klee: "The painter who is called will come near the secret abyss where elemental law nourishes evolution"; and Genet: "The creator has committed himself to the fearful adventure of taking upon himself, to the very end, the perils risked by his creatures."[5]

Although as a boy in St. Louis he had been interested in art, Burroughs was imbued by his father and older brother with the idea that he was no good at mechanical things, and could not draw pictures. When he showed up at Gysin's Rembrandt Hotel show in 1953, he had just spent the past year in Ecuador and New York, and his first impression of Gysin and his paintings was not especially charitable. But within a few years he and Brion were inseparable, and they moved from Tangier to Paris at about the same time, in 1959, which was the beginning of the Beat Hotel period and the discovery of the cut-ups.

Burroughs' first participation in visual art may have been his development of his "scrapbook" form, in collaboration with Gysin. These joint works of drawing, photography, typing, clippings, and collage continued from Paris in the mid-sixties through the early seventies, when Burroughs and Gysin moved to Duke Street in London. Burroughs also made a number of collages from the "tourist snapshot" photographs he had taken in South America and North Africa, decorating the margins with heavy brushstrokes in black ink.

After his return to the United States in 1974, Burroughs' scrapbooks evolved in a different, and in some respects more visually austere, direction, but they continued to be used as reference points and resources for his writing. There are perhaps twenty scrapbooks in all, in various hands. These early works, if they are examined, will illustrate the precise interconnections between Gysin's art training and experience and Burroughs' earliest defined conception of the visual art object.

Because of the circumstances of Burroughs' life as an avant-garde novelist, he has been in contact with many painters since the 1950s. In Tangier he knew Francis Bacon, whose masterly studies of madness and alienation greatly impressed Burroughs at the time. They met again in 1982 in London, during the filming of the "Burroughs" documentary, and exchanged cordial observations on death, a central subject for both artists.

In Paris, at the Beat Hotel, Burroughs first met the painter David Budd, a member of the second generation of Abstract Expressionists in New York and Long Island. Budd had worked with Jackson Pollock for a year and a half, but his own painting showed little direct influence from his personal associations with Pollock, de Kooning, and Kline in his choice of thematic elements. His first individual show, in 1956 at the American University in Washington, interestingly included a white-on-white oil painting about four feet square, but he soon developed a distinctive, hypnotic style, based upon countless tiny wave-shaped strokes of the palette knife, defining fields of color and energy. The work partook of the conceptual wing of Abstract

Expressionism's reification of the painting as a record of a sublime activity, i.e., the moment of its creation.

Recently, Jackson Pollock's paint-spattered studio floor has been preserved under plexiglas—and although Pollock clearly was amenable to accident in his pouring drawing, he would never, I think, have accepted an equation of the stains and evidence of his work with the finished paintings. In any case, Budd's work is fastidious compared to Pollock's, and the events recorded by the art are his hours of painting meditation. Burroughs, on the other hand, strives to unleash the forces of random recombination in his work, as he stated in the gallery text for the 1987 exhibition at the Tony Shafrazi Gallery: "The shotgun blast releases the little spirits compacted into the layers of wood, releases the colors of the paints to splash out in unforeseeable unpredictable images and patterns."

Budd had spent years with the circus, wintering in Sarasota, and is, as Gysin was, a great *raconteur*. He and Burroughs became good friends, and Budd was a significant figure in the development of Burroughs' "Dutch Schultz" mythology, as well as his first film script. In March 1964, Budd showed large metal sculptures with words painted on them (many of them taken from the last words of the gangster Dutch Schultz), in a show at Galerie Stadler in Paris called *"Peinture, Poésie, Musique: David Budd, rencontre avec William Burroughs et Earl Browne."*

Gallimard was publishing *Naked Lunch* in French at that time, and a big party with Stadler was planned, but for some reason Burroughs was not sent an airplane ticket from Tangier to Paris and did not show up. The show was notorious nonetheless, with Browne's aleatory music playing continuously and long-haired young proto-hippies lounging around the *très élégant* gallery of Rodolph Stadler (who was also Mathieu's dealer), and writing graffiti on the sculptures. "Stars splash the silver answer back," was Burroughs' gnomic comment in support of Budd's work in the gallery catalog for that show.

Burroughs spent most of 1965 in New York, first at the Chelsea Hotel and then at 310 Center Street. At the Chelsea he came and went through Stanley Bard's famous Pop Art lobby, and during that time he gave a reading in the 222 Bowery loft of Wyn Chamberlain, which was attended by Larry Rivers, Larry Poons, Barnett Newman, Al Leslie, Andy Warhol, Gerard Malanga, Diane Arbus, and Richard Avedon, not to mention Ron Padgett, Ted Berrigan, and Frank O'Hara. Burroughs' biographer, Ted Morgan, called this evening "a quorum of the downtown art scene, a charged, electric, high-energy event."[6] Burroughs read from cut-ups of the Dutchman's last words, then ripped down a white sheet to reveal a giant rubber tarantula on the wall.

It was during this spring that Burroughs first met John Giorno, a poet whose work was then reaching out beyond the printed page to performance, cybernetics (Dial-a-Poem), and art actions. Giorno lived at 222 Bowery, and was closely tied to Robert Rauschenberg, Jasper Johns, and Andy Warhol, and eventually to Brion Gysin. At the same time he was involved in Abbie Hoffman's political circle, and was instrumental in founding the New York School of poetry (predecessor of the St. Mark's

Church group and later the Naropa Institute core faculty, such as Anne Waldman and Allen Ginsberg), so he was a cultural bridge between several important scenes in those years.

While staying a few months on Center Street, Burroughs met David Prentice, a painter from Connecticut who came up in the same generation as Forrest Myers and the late Neil Williams, and who worked with Rauschenberg during the sixties. Prentice showed off his "off-white painting," with its overtones of Malevich's powerful "Suprematist Compositions" of World War I, and Rauschenberg's "Radiant White" unpainted canvases on stretchers, at Ileana Sonnabend in New York in the early seventies. It was Prentice who first introduced Burroughs to Rauschenberg in New York, at around this time. Rauschenberg was working on a poster for "Earth Day," and he picked up on a remark of Burroughs' at the meeting: "They did not fully understand the technique and in a very short time nearly wrecked the planet." This text was emblazoned on the poster, and foreshadowed a later collaboration between them.

Back in London in the late sixties, Burroughs had dinner one night with Jasper Johns at the Connaught Hotel, an event which he mentions in his essay, "The Fall of Art."[7] It is clear from his account that Burroughs did not begin to formulate his "magical" theory of art and writing until after that time, and again his primary influence was Brion Gysin. This essay, as written, makes Burroughs seem a bit the *enfant terrible*, with his art-historically naïve propositions for a conceptually violent, viewer-involving art of exploding pictures and painting potlatches. He seems to have absorbed the work of Arman and Klein without knowing it, but is undeterred nevertheless from exploring this area for himself.

A better example of Burroughs' understanding of art in general, and of Gysin's art in particular, is found in "Ports of Entry," a piece he wrote for a gallery brochure at Gysin's 1973 show at Galerie Weiller in Paris. This piece, essentially a transcription of a conversation between Burroughs and Gysin while looking at Gysin's work, was reproduced in Terry Wilson's *Here to Go* as well as in the October Gallery's catalog for Gysin's 1981 show in London. Here we see for the first time how Burroughs explicitly seeks to "see things" in the work, which he takes as a point of departure for his shifting, vertiginous visions: "The pictures constantly change because you are drawn into time travel on a network of associations."

Burroughs elaborates: "The viewer has to learn how to flicker back and forth between a telescopic and a microscopic point of view while his attention is centered on some small, beautiful scene which may be no bigger than your index fingernail at one moment, and then your attention is suddenly jerked back to a clear long range view of the picture or its allover patterns. What you actually see at any given moment becomes only a part of a visual operation which includes an infinite series of images. This leads you along a certain path, like a row or series of patterns . . . a series of neural patterns which already exist in the human brain."[8]

This is consistent with Burroughs' statement for his show at Tony Shafrazi Gallery fifteen years later, "I am trying to get the pictures to move." There is an interesting distinction, though, between this oneiric approach and Burroughs' earlier slogan, received from Gysin in 1959. "Writing is fifty years behind painting," they said, and applied the montage technique to writing. From the early cut-up experiments, Burroughs developed the idea that painting and writing were originally one, drawing on his studies of Mayan and Egyptian hieroglyphs, as Gysin drew on his knowledge of Japanese and Arabic. They set out to explore this area, and their efforts, being divided among several mediums, must be considered laterally rather than vertically. But this program led them away from the ongoing currents of contemporary art at that time, consigning them, as far as art history, to the "cubbyhole" of Lettrism.

Burroughs' written exploration of the limits of collaboration and the breakdown of boundaries between forms of art reached its expression in *The Third Mind,* which was created with Gysin in 1972–73, but not published until 1978, when it was denatured from its original "scrapbook" format and reduced to a more or less traditional book form. Like Burroughs' later attempt to have a fully illustrated "comix"-format edition of *Ah Pook Is Here* published with illustrations by Malcolm McNeill, this project was ahead of its time. We have since seen the growth of several new forms of popularly published illustrated books with literary or quasi-literary texts, including *Heavy Metal Magazine* and its French counterpart, *Metal Hurlant,* as well as the works of Alex Barbier and the new wave of *bandes déssinateurs,* and the rise of the San Francisco comix scene with R. Crumb, S. Clay Wilson, Moscoso, Spain, Art Spiegelman, Bill Griffith, and many others. And in writing, the "science-fiction" aspects of Burroughs' first trilogy (*The Soft Machine, Nova Express, The Ticket That Exploded*) had a definable influence on the current school of sci-fi known loosely as "cyberpunk"—William Gibson, Bruce Stirling, Clive Barker—all of whom in turn have incorporated elements of film into their work.

Burroughs attempted to make an explicit connection between writing and painting in *The Book of Breeething,*[9] illustrated by Bob Gale, and in the section called "Hieroglyphic Silence" in *The Third Mind:* "So, you see, I take a picture which stands for and, by God, *is* a word and it just naturally opens itself out, feeling for other pictures . . . doing what pictures will do. Just let the words dissolve in the picture. Why listen to one house when you can *see* all the houses? So my words just disintegrate into a Gysin picture."[10]

Again there is the connotation of destruction, a fall: *la chute du mot, la chute de l'art.* This in part reflects Gysin's Surrealist heritage of provocation and revolution, a belief in the power of the manifesto to shock the bourgeois. In time, however, the shock began to wear off, and it became clear that writing and painting could change and intersect in a thousand ways without either one losing its identity, and this is in fact what happened throughout the 1960s. At some point the cut-up philosophy had outlived its usefulness as an approach to visual art—that is, at the point that its principles had thoroughly permeated the world of modern and postmodern art.

Burroughs left London for New York in 1974. His first New York residence was a loft at 452 Broadway, which he sublet from the painter Michael Balog, and it is interesting to note that at the time Balog was working in broken plywood, painted according to the contours of its pith, shattered and framed. This four-month period may have alerted Burroughs to the possibilities inherent in the medium of ordinary plywood, which he would later explore with his shotgun art.

During the seventies and eighties, Burroughs' friend John Giorno continued to expand the range of his poetic media to include record albums, videotape, and rock, as did Burroughs and Gysin—often with Giorno's help. Several performances and tours with Giorno, such as the Nova Convention in 1978, the Red Night Tour in 1981 and the Final Academy in 1982, allowed Burroughs to develop a literary showmanship that drew new readers to the flock. (For several years now Burroughs has been semiretired from performance, however.)

In 1981, after Burroughs had been back in the United States for six years, he worked again with Robert Rauschenberg on a six-lithograph series known as *American Pewter with Burroughs,* produced at Gemini G.E.L. As before, Rauschenberg chose short fragments of Burroughs' text, with a dreamlike cut-up quality, and employed them in his familiar overlaid-image collage works as embossed legends along the side: "We are the language"; "We are here because of you"; "Are they doing mummies to standard?"; "Green is a man, to fill is a boy"; "The sky is thin as paper here."

Later that year, Burroughs moved to Lawrence, Kansas, and lived for nine months in a small rustic nineteenth-century stone house outside the city limits, where he could indulge his lifelong passion for target practice with pistols, rifles, and shotguns. When he first noticed that a load of no. 9 shot ripped through a sheet of plywood like a painter's brush spattering color on canvas, it is doubtful if he was thinking consciously of the gun-art experiments of the painter and erstwhile parfumier Nikki de St. Phalle, or of the personalized lithographic-target series of his friend, the artist and professional marksman David Bradshaw. As always, Burroughs proceeded as an autodidact.

He produced a series of shot and painted works in Lawrence in 1982, about thirty in all. One of these early works, *Gun Door,* was a stark two-sided piece of wood, layered with white and yellow house paint over an old coat of institutional green, and peppered with a splintering blast of birdshot. It was framed in a wood-and-glass box, and was exhibited in New York at Ronald Feldman's "The Atomic Salon" show in 1982, and at the B–2 Gallery, along with paintings by Gysin, as part of the Final Academy in London, later that year. It is now in the Giorno Poetry Systems collection in the Bunker in New York. The work's title, and its eloquent brokenness and purity, testify to one of the themes of Burroughs' latest novel; he mostly suspended his art-making activities in 1983–85, to complete *The Western Lands,* the third book in the Red Night trilogy.

During a 1983 visit to New York for a show at the Tower Gallery, Brion Gysin was introduced to Keith Haring, who had first discovered Burroughs and Gysin at the Nova Convention in 1978. As an artist working in the area then known as "graffiti art," Haring recognized the significance for his own painting of Burroughs' and Gysin's ideas about the conjunction of writing and art. In 1986, taking passages from the penultimate draft of Gysin's last published novel, *The Last Museum,* Haring created a fine edition called *Fault Lines* for Schellman Editions of Munich, with eighty-eight original drawings. At about the same time, the Grenfell Press of New York published *The Cat Inside,* a fine edition of a Burroughs text written toward the end of the composition of *The Western Lands,* with eight haunting drawings of cats by Gysin.

Brion Gysin died July 13, 1986, in Paris. That December, the Galerie de France held a retrospective show, and the catalog essay by Gladys Fabre is a valuable introduction to the formation of Gysin's aesthetic as a painter, as well as his trans-disciplinary forays into music, writing, and performance. The Musée d'Art Moderne de la Ville de Paris now holds the largest collection of Gysin's works, thanks to his having collected them as best he could in his final years, and having left his paintings to the Musée. At some point there will be a major retrospective of Gysin's work in Paris, as part of a move begun with Catherine Thieck's show at Galerie de France in December 1986. There are also plans for a book of Gysin's painting, with numerous color illustrations. Only after this is published will it become possible to assess Gysin's painting.

In early 1987, Burroughs was contacted by Diego Cortez, who subsequently came to Lawrence with Phillip Taaffe to work on a catalog text for the latter's show at the Pat Hearn Gallery. Taaffe and Burroughs ended up making a series of drawings, and Taaffe and Cortez came along for a session of painting and shooting one afternoon. They also taped their discussions while painting together, and this was published as "Drawing Dialogue" in the gallery's brochure for the Taaffe show. Naturally, Taaffe's and Cortez's enthusiasm for works Burroughs had made encouraged him to redouble his efforts, as he had already finished his novel. He began painting in earnest every day, turning one room in his home into a gallery, and another into a studio, gradually filling them with pigments and materials and finished works. These efforts were further encouraged that year by Steven Lowe, a young writer and painter whom Burroughs first met in New York in 1974, and who worked on Burroughs' novel *Cities of the Red Night.*

Cortez eventually helped to arrange Burroughs' debut show in December 1987 at the Tony Shafrazi Gallery in New York. Shafrazi has done a great deal of work with Keith Haring, and the show included Haring's eighty-eight original *Fault Lines* drawings as well as Gysin's pictures for *The Cat Inside.* Exhibited were twenty-nine of Burroughs' works on wood (half from 1982, half from 1987), thirteen newer works on paper, and two works on metal. The show was seriously received, with positive reviews in *Art News, Artforum,* and *Flash Art,* among others.

In his text for the show, Burroughs speaks again of his "ports of entry into the pictures," and his way of seeing as a "creative observer," recalling the viewer-driven aesthetic of Pop Art, into which broad tradition (in part descended from Dada) the critic Jennie Skerl places much of Burroughs' writing. The catalog text ends with the statement that "what emerges from these creations is the testament that everything is alive." We can see that Burroughs has now moved beyond the Surrealist-based "fall-of-art" approach that he took to its limits during Brion Gysin's life.

Also in December 1987, *The Western Lands* was published. The novel ends with these sombre, elegiac words: "The old writer couldn't write anymore because he had reached the end of words, the end of what can be done with words."[11] While it suggests the artist's exhaustion of his postmodern innovation in letters, this is no more fateful than the remarks of certain commentators who could not resist the macabre observation that it might be Burroughs' last book—as if any of the others before it might not have been. It is a notion that takes its resonance from the very fecundity of Burroughs' typewriter since the 1950s, without which such a pause or end in the production of writing would not seem so portentous. In any case, he has continued to write and paint and make art, and is dedicated to go on doing so.

Is William Burroughs a writer transgressing on the territory of painters with his artworks in the 1980s? Or is he an artist of ideas as much as of words, ideas which he has translated into words for thirty years and is now translating into visual images? Despite the subjectivity of his approach, or because of it, the paintings are handmade and good looking, enjoyable for themselves in their visual totality. The work itself is unself-conscious, and unashamed of any perceived lack of context or reference.

Burroughs is an "outsider" only to the extent that he comes to painting late, and without formal training; he is "naïve" only insofar as he does not necessarily produce a stream of theoretical art-talk to accompany his paintings. He belongs to no current "school" of art, but is subjectively exploring art-making techniques according to the literary and artistic ideas he began to develop twenty-five years ago. The challenge of contextualizing his work is a red herring, because the true context is the body of his own wide-ranging work and life.

Jackson Pollock said in 1956, two months before his tragic and unexpected death: "When you're painting out of your subconscious, figures are bound to emerge. . . . Painting is a state of being . . . painting is self-discovery. Every good artist paints what he is."[12] William Burroughs has dedicated himself in the last few years to a new form of expression, and although it is too much to hope that his work will mark a radical innovation of plastic invention, it is not too much to ask that it be considered in its own proper context, as the sincere creation of an artist who refuses to put away his colors with his typewriter, but chooses to "paint what he is." This painting is just what it is, and on its own terms it promises the open-minded viewer a voyage of discovery through the themes and images that Burroughs has developed during a lifetime of making art.

## Notes

1. Terry Wilson and Brion Gysin, *Here to Go: Planet R–101* (San Francisco: Re/Search, 1982) 17–18.

2. Quoted in William C. Seitz, *Mark Tobey* (New York: Museum of Modern Art, 1962) 33.

3. William Rubin, "Jackson Pollock and the Modern Tradition, Part III," *Artforum* Apr. 1967: 27.

4. Wilson and Gysin, 41.

5. William S. Burroughs, *Interzone* (New York: Viking, 1989) 128.

6. Ted Morgan, *Literary Outlaw: The Life and Times of William S. Burroughs* (New York: Holt, 1988) 412.

7. William S. Burroughs, "The Fall of Art," *The Adding Machine: Selected Essays* (New York: Seaver, 1986) 61.

8. Wilson and Gysin, 179.

9. William S. Burroughs and Robert Gale, *The Book of Breeething* (Berkeley: Blue Wind, 1975).

10. William S. Burroughs and Brion Gysin, *The Third Mind* (New York: Viking, 1978) 190.

11. William S. Burroughs, *The Western Lands* (New York: Viking, 1987) 258.

12. Quoted in Francis V. O'Connor, *Jackson Pollock* (New York: Museum of Modern Art, 1967) 73.

# 26

# Cut-Up Closure
## *The Return to Narrative*

### Oliver C. G. Harris

I n 1962 Burroughs looked back on the publication, two years earlier, of *Minutes To Go* and *The Exterminator,* observing of those initial experimental cut-up texts: "A breakthrough that knows exactly what it is breaking through into is not a break-through which is a step in the dark."[1] This understanding of the cut-up enterprise indicated his goal to break new territory, to leave behind both his own past writing and the writing of the past. Some copies of *Minutes To Go* had been issued with a wraparound band that explicitly announced the adversary, as well as exploratory, aim of the cut-up "breakthrough": *"Un règlement de comptes avec la littérature."* Affirming Burroughs' radical positioning of cut-up methods against both the medium and its historical assumptions, this desire to "settle the score" exploited both the necessity of direct, violent and violating, material involvement and the unforeseen nature of the results obtained in cut-up operations. Yet, while the aesthetic outcome could not by the very nature of his techniques be predicted, from the outset Burroughs' practice drew upon, and inevitably defined itself against, the history of prior modernist experiments; cut-ups were not, as Brion Gysin acknowledged in *Minutes To Go,* "a new discovery."[2] Deriving his knowledge largely from his collaborations with Gysin, Burroughs intended to achieve his settling of scores through a renewed interest in the material and technological possibilities offered by the modernist development of collage. Described by George Steiner as constituting "one of the few undoubted revolutions or 'cuts' in the history of the imagination,"[3] those previous avant-garde experiments had been promoted through interdisciplinary movements producing multimedia practices. In the Beat Hotel during the early 1960s, the cut-up movement evolved in the same direction, as Burroughs recalled: "We held constant meetings and conferences with exchange of ideas and comparison of cut-up writing, painting and tape recorder experiments."[4]

Recognizing, with hindsight, that *Minutes To Go* and *The Exterminator* had given such precedence to the material qualities of language that subject matter remained nominal, Burroughs went on to produce cut-up texts whose combination of formal and thematic concerns demonstrated a strategic recuperation of meaning. This phase of cut-up composition was enormously productive; Barry Miles, in his *Catalogue of the William Burroughs Archive,* lists over six thousand pages of manuscript covering the six years between 1958 and 1964. Having exhausted the material drawn from *The Naked Lunch* body of manuscripts to make *The Soft Machine* and *The Ticket That Exploded,* his exploratory work generated an equally large variety of different textual formats and a significant range of cut-up methods extended to other media. But, if the infinite possibilities promised by cut-up techniques appeared to have been realized, 1966 marked a stark literary terminal point; for that year the Burroughs *Catalogue* records a mere twenty-eight pages of manuscript. After his final part of the cut-up trilogy, *Nova Express,* in 1964, it was six years to the appearance of his seventy-page screenplay, *The Last Words of Dutch Schultz,* and another year before the next full-length book, his novel *The Wild Boys.* Varying according to each category of cut-up applications (photomontage, scrapbooks, tapes), this drastic attenuation manifested a common paradox; proliferation of materials and media lead to stasis.

Burroughs first experimented with photomontage in the summer of 1961, culminating in 1964 with extensive illustrations to *Nova Express,* where the method, described as making "a statement in flexible picture language," generates "Juxtaposition Formulae" rather than "alleged content."[5] In "its earliest form," noted one of the technique's pioneers, Raoul Hausmann, photomontage "was an explosive mixture of different points of view and levels."[6] "In its pure form," as the art critic William Rubin observed, the medium's juxtapositions of ready-made materials "entirely eliminated any need to paint or draw,"[7] thus questioning creative hierarchies and purging subjectivity in the fashion Hausmann intended: "We called this process photomontage because it embodies our refusal to play the part of the artist. We regarded ourselves as engineers, and our work as construction: we *assembled* our work, like a fitter."[8] His conception of a "static film" using nonauthorial presentation of diverse material and multiple perspectives, offered analogous functions to cut-up texts. A further related possibility was indicated by Burroughs' alignment, in 1965, of cut-up effects with the "camera eye" sections of Dos Passos' novel *U.S.A.* Montage, according to Dos Passos, allowed him "to distil [his] subjective feelings," aiming "at a total objectivity by giving conflicting views."[9] The key term here for Burroughs' use of photomontage is *distil.* This can be seen to date from his interest, recounted by Gysin, in collaging together "fading snapshots [. . .] of boys from every time and place," which coincided with, and even took precedence over, his efforts to finalize the structure of *The Naked Lunch:*

> Burroughs was more intent on Scotch-taping his photos together into one great continuum on the wall, where scenes faded and slipped into one another, than occupied with editing the monster manuscript.[10]

The visual bias in this autobiographical procedure was developed from a mode of superimposition into a method of distillation. Timothy Leary, drawing on the time he spent with Burroughs as he started to make photomontages in 1961, paraphrased a basic function of his cut-up practices:

> The essence of anything is the cut-up. Cut up words. Cut up pictures.
> Boil it down to the essence [ . . . ]. Paste up all the pictures on a wall
> and take a picture of that—then all the thousand photos are in one
> photo.[11]

This is precisely what Burroughs did, together with Ian Sommerville who arrived in Tangier in 1961 to take "over the technical aspect of montages" (*Adding Machine* 12).

In 1964, two years after making the collage cover to *The Ticket That Exploded*, Sommerville put together "Mr. & Mrs. D," which Eric Mottram describes as "a grid of photographed mirror inter-reflections and permutations, a photocollage which is at once fragmented and a single picture."[12] In *Nova Express* "Mr. D," mocking "those dumb rubes playing around with photomontage," explains the technique's logical conclusion, the "microfilm principle": "smaller and smaller, more and more images in less space pounded down under the cyclotron to crystal image meal."[13] When Burroughs restated the mechanism of cut-ups in *The Job*, he did so in terms of this dual process of concentration and fragmentation: "Carried further we can break the page down into smaller and smaller units in altered sequences" (*The Job* 178).

Burroughs made a great number of photomontages, but soon pushed the principle of abbreviated visual juxtaposition to its limit: "There is a point of diminishing return. I then turned to scrap-books, making layouts and photos to tell a story."[14] As is clear from his retrospective account of the shift from one medium to another, it was the loss of narrative potentials that motivated his move away from photomontage. This was also true for his cut-up texts that applied the same principles of distillation to the point of stasis. Comparing the experience with minimalism in painting, in the mid-1970s he admitted that "one arrives at a point where, cutting a page, you can cut cut and cut it to infinity; but, as one goes along, the results become less and less convincing" (*Colloque* 270). In both the visual and literary cases, Burroughs recognized the futility of pursuing such experiments beyond the point of the texts in *The Third Mind*. In *The Job* he conceded, "I've done writing that I thought was interesting experimentally, but simply not readable" (*The Job* 56). Gysin recollected the extreme difficulty presented by such "image meal" texts: "[Burroughs] came to a sort of *puddle* at the end, called Brownian movement in physics, where it was so . . . so unpleasant, even painful to read, that it gave one psychic pain and he had to admit that he must dismiss it as not readable nor publishable."[15] Burroughs' discovery of cut-up methods in 1959 had brought about a major shift in his writing; from being largely concerned with the extreme offensiveness of its expressive content—to such an extent that he had agonized over its salability—he launched his work on a violent formal offensive directed against the medium of literature itself. Soon, however, Burroughs once again found himself in danger, as he had been up until the appearance of *The Naked Lunch,* of being isolated by being unpublishable.

According to James Grauerholz in a letter to the author (14 October 1986), Burroughs first thought of his scrapbooks as incantatory materials made partly in imitation of Brion Gysin's "intersection points." In his text "Precise Intersection Points," Burroughs promoted the interchangeability of his verbal and visual materials: "words *are* pictures and vice versa" (*Third Mind* 135). His published scrapbook texts solicited the contribution of the reader's own intersections: "Put any picture that fits from your time into this space," he urges in a handwritten instruction next to an empty box under the three-column layout of "Afternoon Tickertape."[16] Confirming his use of scrapbooks as source material, he later observed, "Your own photos or photos in newspapers and magazines may suggest a narrative."[17] In the 1970s Burroughs was still using scrapbooks, now "to overcome writer's block— juxtaposing pictures from newspapers and magazines and other bits of writing that are relevant." However, during the 1960s, his concentration on such collections and collages of material directly affected the form of his experimental texts, with consequences for their production of which he was well aware.

Asked in 1965 about the files of material used for cross-referencing sources, Burroughs' reply indicated the physical restrictions imposed by his methods of construction: "*I need it all.* I brought everything. That's why I have to travel by boat and by train, because, well, just to give you an idea, that's a photographic file. [*Thud*] Those are all photographs and photographs [ . . . ]. Those dresser drawers are full of files. All those drawers are full of files" (*Writers at Work* 162–63). At the literal level of his own mobility, the congestion of accumulated material threatened stasis. In the same year, in his magazine, *Time,* modeled on Luce's "word-and-image" bank with its pictures "reduced to microphotos," Burroughs considered the inevitable financial limitations determining the potential for incorporating grids, hieroglyphs, and photographs: "Now as to presentation on a page within a practical budget."[18] When this and the preceding passages were included in the text of *The Third Mind,* this line was, pointedly, removed.

Although assembled during 1964 and 1965, *The Third Mind,* as the updated manifesto and documentation of Burroughs and Gysin's hybrid collaborations, was not published until 1976 in a French edition, and 1978 in English. Due to the "outrageous prices" that impeded reproduction of its verbal-visual formats, *The Third Mind* represented for Gysin "one of the saddest stories in publishing" (*Rolling Stone* 53). This was, however, a difficulty for Burroughs' development of such texts throughout the decade, the obstacle being one of artistic context. As Barry Miles observed in an interview with the author in December 1984: "One of the main problems was that a lot of the material that Burroughs was working with was just basically not commercial. In the London period he did a lot of scrapbooks which by their very nature, unless you have an art book publisher and spend a fortune, is not a commercial possibility." The long hieroglyphic text that Burroughs modeled on the Mayan codices, *Ah Pook Is Here,* was delayed eight years and printed without the artwork, as he notes in his Preface to the book on its publication in 1979, "owing partly to the expense of full-color reproduction."[19] One consequence of these and previous cases has been the marginalization that has obscured the full extent of Burroughs' experiments in the mid-1960s—so that his recent public venture into visual art appears divorced from its experimental origins. In the 1960s, Burroughs' hybrid development of combined word and image formats was pursued without expectations of artistic exhibition, and publication was restricted, beyond the main-stream of cut-up texts, to only those in three columns or several typefaces. Those using colored inks, more complicated layouts, or pasted materials were neither themselves printed nor useful research for texts that could be published. For different reasons, the scrapbooks which Burroughs had taken up after the diminishing returns of photomontage, led once again to a dead end for his creativity. In 1965, at a time when he was working with Antony Balch on the film *Cut-Ups* and doing "a lot of scrapbook work," he recalled that Gysin "frequently remonstrated" with him "to leave these experiments and write some straight narrative" (*Adding Machine* 13). Instead, as another extension of cut-up practices, Burroughs turned to tape recorders.

From their inception in 1959, cut-ups had been applied to tape by both Burroughs and Gysin. It was, however, several years later that Burroughs made the extensive practical use of them that, beyond exercising theoretical or methodological influence over his texts, came to substitue for writing altogether. When he revised *The Ticket That Exploded* for publication in 1967, the majority of the thirty pages of additional material inserted within the text, as well as that placed in the Appendix, had introduced, developed, or dramatized techniques applying cut-up methods to tape. In 1966 Burroughs informed his literary agent: "Fact is I have not been writing lately but turning all my attention to work with tape recorders and movie cameras." Four months later his research, with a scientific rigor, had eliminated film as suitable for his experiments: "Right now I am working again with tape recorders which seems to me the best possibility of breakthrough."[20] In *The Job* and *Electronic Revolution* he gave a full account of the various functions of tape recorders, specifying the "concept of simultaneity cannot be indicated on a printed page except very crudely through the use of columns and even so the reader must follow one column down"; he noted that "We're used to reading from left to right and then back, and this conditioning is not easy to break down" (*The Job* 15). His efforts to establish new forms of readability by reproducing effects achieved through tape-recorder technology were checked by limitations inherent to the medium. Conversely, Bur-roughs recognized that however interesting the results of tape and film experiments were, they were not applicable to writing.

Like the initial cut-up exercises, Burroughs' technological applications of cut-up methods represented an experimental engagement; unlike the texts of *Minutes To Go* and *The Exterminator,* they did not bear significant literary fruit. As Grauerholz notes, they were "just one logical development" for the cut-up practitioners: "Tape was a natural thing, just as they were using photography for collage [. . .]. In a way, obviously, they're a little bit of a cul-de-sac for the writer."[21] As with photomontage and then scrapbooks, Burroughs' tape-recorder experiments manifested a characteristic multimedia development of collage practices. In the context of collage collaborations, each phase of his involvement was logical and natural, generating new ideas and forms for his cut-up texts. But in leading to literary dead ends, they pointed up his overwhelming need as a writer to resume contact with the reader. This was evident in the direct forms of didactic address and clear narrative prose that marked his response to the double failure to write and be read: "By 1967 [. . .] I had such an overrun on tape-recorders, cameras and scrapbooks that I couldn't look at them, and started writing straight narrative and essays that later found their way into *The Wild Boys* and *The Job*" (*Adding Machine* 14). It was also at this time that he returned to Tangier in order to rework *The Ticket That Exploded,* so completing the progressive revisions of his cut-up trilogy that constituted a further attempt to recover readability by restoring narrative.

While it would be incorrect to assume that Burroughs' revisions were solely concerned to restore or create narrative clarity or stability, his general position was clear: "I felt that there had been too much of the raw cut-ups that went into *Ticket That Exploded* and *Soft Machine,* and that some of that material should come out. I substituted more straight narrative. I, sort of, tightened the structure."[22] In doing so, he also brought about a considerable chronological confusion of their sequence, problematizing the collective structure of a trilogy the autonomy of whose parts was already problematic. But, more significantly, Burroughs' revisions recognized that to maximize the potency of his texts it was necessary to retain a dialectical relation to the conventional prose that defined the norm against which cut-ups were designed to act. His rewriting instigated the restoration of generic conventions that distinguishes his texts from *The Wild Boys* onwards, so clarifying the violation of readerly expectations. In the revised texts of the trilogy, transgressions work towards an effect of infinite possibility by playing off the desired state of spontaneity against the threat of determinism implied by predictability. As a result, the unrevised *Nova Express,* although the last part of the original trilogy, came to be seen as not "in any sense a wholly successful book" (*The Job* 13). The ratio of loss to gain persuaded Burroughs to restore the "dialectical contrary" that Werner Schmalenbach observed Kurt Schwitters had lost touch with in his comparable collage texts fifty years earlier: "Where all is surprise, line after line after line, all sense of surprise is lost."[23] This can be seen from Burroughs' suggestion, made when referring to Claude Pelieu's cut-up text "The Colourless Veins," in 1967: "Try interposing some straight narrative with the cut up material narrative : : cut ups : : narrative continued : : cut ups. This potentiates both narrative and cut ups."[24]

Burroughs' continual reworkings of his cut-up trilogy suggest several interpretations of his situation in the late 1960s. His revisions were, in a sense, entirely consistent with his cut-up methods. In forming new arrangements of the same material while introducing alterations, they violated the norms of a text's defined limits and stable identity, so participating in his "Operation Rewrite." Aware that these books contained "too much rather undifferentiated cut-up material" (*Rolling Stone* 51), his revisons also signaled the importance of those books to Burroughs, to the extent that he was not prepared to leave them in forms he now considered unsatisfactory. The inclusion in *Nova Express* of direct statements explaining the purpose of his writing, the incorporation into *The Ticket That Exploded* of cut-ups of hostile critical reviews, and the addition of essays as appendices to *The Ticket That Exploded* and *The Soft Machine*, give the same impression of trying to clarify or rectify the texts themselves. However, with his failure after 1964 to produce new texts larger than pamphlets, the preoccupation with his trilogy also suggested the lack of other avenues open to him. Asked in *The Job* whether he regarded Joyce's *Finnegans Wake* as "a maginificent literary dead end," Burroughs replied:

> I think *Finnegans Wake* rather represents a trap into which
> experimental writing can fall when it becomes purely experimental. I
> would go so far with any given experiment and then come back; that
> is, I am coming back now to purely conventional straight-forward
> narrative [ . . . ]. It's simply if you go too far in one direction, you
> can never get back, and you're out there in complete isolation. (*The
> Job* 46)

As early as 1965 he had sensed that, in order to continue writing, a change of direction was necessary: "Occasionally I have the sensation that I'm repeating myself in my work, and I would like to do something different—almost a deliberate change of style. I'm not sure if that's possible, but I want to try" (*Writers at Work* 164). Believing that "a writer should be comprehensible to any intelligent reader," he now insisted that he was "not a dadaist" and that he did not believe in being obscure,[25] thereby reasserting the criterion of accessibility against *Minutes To Go*'s aggressive ambition to "rub out the word": "I don't think when I said that I had any clear idea as to what it would involve" (*Rolling Stone* 50). When asked his opinion in 1972 of Marshall McLuhan's thesis of the obsolescence of print, his rhetorical reply was based on a decade's efforts in that direction: "What does he think is going to take its place?" (*Rolling Stone* 50).

Having followed to its logical conclusion his refusal in *The Naked Lunch* to impose narrative, Burroughs conceded in *The Job* that he may have gone too far in his abdication of conventional aesthetic control: "One tries not to impose story plot or continuity artificially but you do have to compose the materials, you can't just dump down a jumble of notes and thoughts and considerations and expect people to read it" (*The Job* 39). Explaining his method of selecting cut-up material, Burroughs concluded that he "would work [it] over into an acceptable form" (*The Job* 16); defined against the forms of his previous cut-up texts, his conception in 1969 of what was "acceptable" and what people might be expected to read had clearly been revised. Referring to the recently written *The Last Words of Dutch Schultz*, Burroughs described his use of cut-ups as "incorporated into the structure of the narrative," claiming, with a certain disingenuity, that the result "is a perfectly straight film treatment, quite intelligible to the average reader, in no sense experimental writing" (*The Job* 16). His concern for the general reader is symptomatic of an

awareness that "purely experimental" work threatened "complete isolation," returning him to the nightmare impasse of emotional and creative energy that had motivated
his epistolary activity throughout the 1950s, and the creation in his letters at that
time of what he later termed the "frantic attention-getting format" of the routine
form.[26] In the late 1960s Burroughs' attention to the viability and availability of his
work confirms the renewed force of the psychological necessity of readers for his
writing. Personal isolation now coincided with aesthetic inaccessibility. As Robert
Adams observes with reference to the "endlessly busy, but almost motionless"
*Finnegans Wake* and its successors: "Atrophy of narrative, ironing out of paper
thin characters, multi-dimensional anti-narrative reading habits—such depletion of
fiction's traditional energies and inertias seems to lead toward a kind of stasis."[27]
Echoing his desire to "do something different" in 1965, nine years later Burroughs
again noted that he had recently been thinking "of writing something completely
different," acknowledging that he had tried but failed: "I've made a number of
attempts that haven't really worked out. I've been thinking of writing a completely
straight-forward novel with a beginning, a middle and an end" (*Beat Book* 103).
Given his exhaustive experimental efforts to transcend a form he found so personally
and ideologically unsuitable, the prospect of the latter course has the extraordinary
effect of appearing radical. It confirms the direction in which Burroughs' attempts
to avoid creative repetition and textual stasis were leading him.

In *The Adding Machine* Burroughs' image of what was involved stresses the
commodification of writing he had set out to oppose in *The Naked Lunch,* and the
writer's inevitable submission to the values of the marketplace: "But a writer has to
do something new, or he has to standardize a product—one or the other. Like I
could standardize the queer Peter-Pan wild-boy product, and put it out year after
year like the Tarzan series; or I could write a *Finnegans Wake*" (*Adding Machine*
29). The change he initiated in 1967 in order to recover motion entailed a conscious
decision to adopt the most traditional sylistic forms of narrative: "I was quite
deliberately returning to older styles of writing," he observed of *The Wild Boys* in
1972: "Quite a bit of it is really 19th century. It's a different style of writing" (*Rolling
Stone* 52). The paradoxical nature of this strategic historical reversal was indicated
in 1970, when, having dismissed the "omniscient author" as an "outworn device,"
he observed: "Unless writing can bring to the page the immediate impact of film it
may well cease to exist as a separate genre. We are no longer living in the 19th
century."[28] The "novelistic form," he noted in *The Job,* "is probably outmoded"
(*The Job* 13).

Having pursued experimental modes of composition that embraced both methodological and technological features borrowed from other art media in order to
"update" writing, he nevertheless saw no inconsistency with borrowing stylistically
from the era of Joseph Conrad. Citing Conrad in *The Job,* he claimed that in his
collaborative work with Ford Maddox Ford "there are passages where he does seem
to be escaping from words, or going beyond words, in a quite conventional, quite
classic narrative form" (*The Job* 46). Burroughs made it clear that his return to
narrative did not mean he had abandoned or transcended the purposes and needs

motivating his original engagement with cut-ups: "But applying what I have learned from the cut-up and the other techniques to the problem of conventional writing" (*The Job* 46). The "*problem* of conventional writing" is an expression that says much about both the impediments from which he had suffered as writer and his sense of the inadequacy of his medium. Given his inability, as he often noted in his letters to Ginsberg and Kerouac during the 1950s, to write anything conventional enough to be acceptable to a commercial publisher, and the lack of previous narratives bearing any stylistic resemblance to Conrad, the "return" to older novelistic styles was not a return at all. Rather it was a breakthrough, a discovery made possible for Burroughs by the cut-up enterprise. Resistance through cut-ups to the tyranny of artificially imposed narrative structures, and of individualistic style, gradually gave way to the use of a plurality of inherited styles. Burroughs' writing strategy became consonant with a key position in current postmodern and poststructuralist theory, as accounted for by Frederic Jameson: in "a world in which stylistic innovation is no longer possible, all that is left is to imitate dead styles, to speak through the masks and with the voices of the styles in the imaginary museum."[29] In the mid-1970s Burroughs observed that he now wrote in several different modes, using not only "fragments of Conrad [but] also the Conrad style" (*Colloque* 270).

While Burroughs continued to use cut-ups, they now either generated ideas for more conventional texts, or were subjected to a more rigorous process of selection. When, in 1965, he speculated about writing a book set in the Wild West, the shift in function was clear: "I'd use cutups extensively in the preparation, because they would give me all sorts of facets of character and place, but the final version would be straight narrative" (*Writers at Work* 164). When he did keep cut-up results in the text, as in *The Wild Boys*, it was only after "sifting through them many many times" (*Rolling Stone* 52), a process which was, however, in service of a quite different strategy from that at work in his earlier method of cutting up. Rather than selecting the most interesting products of the "result message" to construct texts in which their anomalous nature created a largely alienating effect, Burroughs now chose only those elements that did fit and belong. Furthermore, by creating more stable personae, his practice gradually restored the possibility of attributing cut-up passages to the subjective experience of an individual identity. This function, one of several isolated in his redefinition of his use of cut-up methods for *The Wild Boys*, returned them to one of the precursors of their development.

Stating that he used cut-ups "sparingly" for the text, he observed that "there are literary situations in which they are useful, and others in which they are not. [. . .] Now, in recreating a delirium, they're very good, because that is what is happening. In high fever the images cut in, quite arbitrarily" (*Rolling Stone* 52). Introduced as "detailed notes on sickness and delirium," *The Naked Lunch* presented the raw materials of sensual derangement and discontinuity—the author's experience as an addict—that he felt able to approximate more realistically using cut-up techniques than by "artificial reconstruction" (*The Job* 16). Prefacing *The Last Words of Dutch Schultz* in 1970, he described the gangster's deathbed soliloquy as "inspired delirium revealing the Dutchman as a potential artist."[30] Originating in a single consciousness, the cut-up material now resumes a mimetic purpose within a unified fictional frame more characteristic in earlier modernist streams of consciousness than in Burroughs' previous texts. The provision of a motivating framework, as a locus for the arbitrary sequence of images, was not intended to resolve them altogether, as he noted in *The Retreat Diaries:*

> Some of Dutch's associations cannot be traced or even guessed at.
> Others quite clearly derive from the known facts of his life. The
> *structure* is that a man is *seeing a film* composed of past present and
> future, dream and fantasy, a film which the reader cannot see directly
> but only infer through the words.[31]

The ontological incompatabilities of Interzone, and the distancing effect introduced by the only partially translatable mediation of film, are thus anchored in the monological plane of Schultz's enigmatic last words. Burroughs' reference to the biographical detective work of character that can "clearly" fit certain images, if not all, prepares the way for the parallel reconstruction of the author in his subsequent texts.

The film-script format of *The Last Words of Dutch Schultz* indicated, as did *The Wild Boys,* a revised use of the cinematic dimensions of cut-up procedures. Whereas he had previously attempted to translate certain methodological qualities of the medium into literary form, or to engage in actual film production, in these texts Burroughs widely employed the economical rhetorical devices of the shooting script, as in the opening lines of *The Wild Boys:* "The camera is the eye of a cruising vulture flying over an area of scrub. [. . .] The camera zooms up past a red-brick tenement. [. . .] Camera sweeps to the top of the building."[32] In *Port of Saints,* the use of cinematic discourse extends to a sequence of "Flash forward," "Carnival flashbacks," "St. Louis Flashbacks," "Prep School Flashbacks." Despite the modernity of the cinematic notations, and the postmodernity of the *"thematic* function of the interposed ontological level of the film" detected in *The Wild Boys* by Brian McHale,[33] it is the largely retrospective nature of the notations that is most revealing. They no longer function, as in the cut-up trilogy, as technical or metaphoric tropes serving the speculative genre of science fiction, but, in the stylistic context of "19th century" prose, as creative anachronisms. As the generic shift from prolepsis to analepsis suggests, while McHale may be right to see "breaching the ontological boundary" as the escape route from the movie as "a global metaphor for Burroughs' master-theme of control,"[34] the direction of that escape is emphatically backwards in time. It was no coincidence that the historical "return" to the traditional novel form, which Burroughs required to resume narrative composition, should function as the vehicle for the creation of the autobiographical character of his youth. Bound to the past, the adolescent heroes of Burroughs' texts from *The Wild Boys* onwards are products of "paper-thin dreams, 19th century nostalgia," signaling their author's own nostalgia for both a former age of writing, and for an earlier age of his own life as a writer: "And here's your script Audrey [. . .] You're the writer."[35]

# Notes

1. William S. Burroughs, letter to Howard Schulman, 31 Aug. 1962, quoted in Michael B. Goodman, *William S. Burroughs: An Annotated Bibliography of His Works and Criticism* (New York: Garland, 1975) 83.

2. William Burroughs, Sinclair Beiles, Gregory Corso, and Brion Gysin, *Minutes To Go* (Paris: Two Cities, 1960) 42.

3. George Steiner, *After Babel* (Oxford: Oxford UP, 1975) 192.

4. William S. Burroughs, Foreword, *Beat Hotel*, by Harold Norse (San Diego: Atticus, 1983) viii.

5. William S. Burroughs, *Nova Express* (New York: Grove, 1964) 93.

6. Quoted in Hans Richter, *Dada: Art and Anti-Art* (London: Thames and Hudson, 1965) 116.

7. William Rubin, *Dada, Surrealism, and Their Heritage* (New York: Museum of Modern Art, 1968) 42.

8. Quoted in Richter, 118.

9. John Dos Passos, interview, *Writers at Work*, ed. George Plimpton (New York: Viking, 1976) 81.

10. William S. Burroughs and Brion Gysin, *The Third Mind* (New York: Viking, 1978) 43. Subsequent references will be noted in the text. The following essays and interviews by Burroughs also referred to in the text provide the background on Burroughs' aesthetic development during this period: Interview with Conrad Knickerbocker, *Writers at Work*, ed. George Plimpton (New York: Viking, 1967); interviews with Daniel Odier, *The Job* (New York: Grove, 1970); interview with Robert Palmer, *Rolling Stone*, 11 May 1972: 48–53; interview with Gerard Malanga, *The Beat Book*, ed. Arthur and Glee Knight (California, PA: unspeakable visions, 1974) 90–112; *Colloque de Tanger II* (Paris: Bourgois, 1979), translated by the author; *The Adding Machine: Collected Essays* (London: Calder, 1985).

11. Timothy Leary, *High Priest* (New York: College Notes, 1968) 225.

12. Eric Mottram, *WILLIAM BURROUGHS: The Algebra of Need* (London: Boyars, 1977) 85.

13. *Nova Express*, 52.

14. Quoted in Miles Associates, *A Descriptive Catalogue of the William S. Burroughs Archive* (London: Covent Garden, 1973) 266.

15. Terry Wilson and Brion Gysin, *Here to Go: Planet R–101* (San Francisco: Re/Search, 1982) 192.

16. William S. Burroughs, "Afternoon Tickertape," *My Own Mag* 5 (1964): n.p.

17. Miles Associates, 265.

18. William S. Burroughs, *Time* (New York: 'C' Press, 1965) 23.

19. William S. Burroughs, *Ah Pook Is Here and Other Texts* (London: Calder, 1979) 11.

20. William S. Burroughs, letters to Peter Matson, 2 June and 10 Nov. 1966, University of Kansas.

21. James Grauerholz, interview with Nicholas Zurbrugg, *Review of Contemporary Fiction* 4.1 (1984): 21.

22. William S. Burroughs, interview with Allen Ginsberg, *Three Novels: The Soft Machine, Nova Express, The Wild Boys* (New York: Grove, 1980) n.p.

23. Werner Schmalenbach, *Kurt Schwitters* (London: Thames and Hudson, 1970) 234.

24. William S. Burroughs, letter to Claude Pelieu, 4 May 1967, University of Kansas.

25. Quoted in Mottram, 98.

26. William S. Burroughs, "Introduction," *Queer* (New York: Viking, 1985) xv.

27. Robert Adams, *AFTERJOYCE: Studies in Fiction After Ulysses* (New York: Oxford UP, 1977) 169.

28. William S. Burroughs, "Without Your Name Who Are You?" *Mayfair*, Mar. 1970, 52.

29. Frederic Jameson, *Postmodern Culture,* ed. Hal Foster (London: Pluto, 1985) 114.

30. William S. Burroughs, *The Last Words of Dutch Schultz* (London: Cape, 1970) 7.

31. William S. Burroughs, *The Retreat Diaries,* in *The Burroughs File* (San Francisco: City Lights, 1984) 192.

32. William S. Burroughs, *The Wild Boys* (New York: Grove, 1971) 3–4.

33. Brian McHale, *Postmodernist Fiction* (London: Methuen, 1987) 129.

34. McHale, 130.

35. William S. Burroughs, *Port of Saints* (London: Covent Garden, 1975) 60, 22.

# 27

# My Purpose Is to Write For the Space Age

William S. Burroughs

I began writing thirty-five years ago, at the age of thirty-five, in Mexico City after the war. Encouraged by Allen Ginsberg, I set down my experiences from five years of addiction to opiates, sticking close to the facts and using, as Wordsworth put it, "the language actually used by men." *Junky* was published in 1953 as an original paperback, and there were no reviews at the time. After all, the book was presented as an "inside look" at the world of a drug addict, with no literary pretensions.

During the next six years I lived in Tangier, Morocco, then in Paris, and experienced the depression and hopelessness of heavy addiction, a state of which De Quincey gives a good account in his *Confessions of an English Opium-Eater,* under the section entitled "The Pains of Opium"—the numb, despairing feeling of being buried alive. All through this period I wrote long letters to Allen Ginsberg and others, and made many notes and sketches which later became the basis of *Naked Lunch.*

After I took the apomorphine cure with Dr. John Dent in London in 1957, it was as though an inner dam had broken. I felt reborn and was content to spend long hours at the typewriter, transcribing the images and characters of the novel, who took shape as though of their own volition. I had small hopes of publication, and my attempts to place parts of the manuscript were very discouraging. But in 1959 Maurice Girodias decided his Olympia Press should publish *Naked Lunch.* It was assembled in two weeks from a mass of pages, the balance of which were to form the basis for *The Ticket That Exploded, The Soft Machine,* and *Nova Express.* It

William S. Burroughs, "My Purpose Is to Write For the Space Age," *New York Times Book Review* (19 Feb. 1984): 9–10. Copyright© 1984 by The New York Times Company. Reprinted by permission.

was after the publication of *Naked Lunch* that I first had any notion of the various pigeonholes into which critics would try to fit my work.

"The writer of drug addiction" was one. Certainly *Junky* was firmly within this category, and drugs have continued to play a part in all my subsequent work. But from the beginning I have been far more concerned, as a writer, with addiction itself (whether to drugs, or sex, or money, or power) as a model of control, and with the ultimate decadence of humanity's biological potentials, perverted by stupidity and inhuman malice.

Critical reaction to *Naked Lunch* and the other books tended to be immoderate. There were thoughtful and laudatory reviews and comments from Mary McCarthy, Norman Mailer, Terry Southern, John Ciardi, Marshall McLuhan, and others. And of course the outraged shrieks: "Strident and illiterate to its heart of pulp." And the old clichés: "After all, simply boring rubbish." Another eminent critic called *Nova Express* "a book to be left under a stone, allowing free access to rats and other vermin." Well, in the (last) words of Dutch Schultz, "So many good ones, and so many bad ones; that's what you get for trying."

"Nihilism, unrelieved despair and negation, misanthropy, pessimism"—very much the same set of clichés that greeted Louis-Ferdinand Céline's *Journey to the End of the Night,* which to my mind is a very funny book, in a picaresque tradition stretching back to Petronius and to *The Unfortunate Traveller* by Thomas Nashe. I have always seen my own work in the light of the picaresque—a series of adventures and misadventures, horrific and comic, encountered by an antihero. Much of my work is intended to be *funny*.

Another pigeonhole: "experimental" or even "unintelligible." I recall one prissy literary type who sniffed, "As *I* understand it, an experimental writer is one whose experiment has failed." Such comments refer to the "cut-up" technique, which is merely an application of the montage method (in 1959, already old hat in painting, as the painter Brion Gysin pointed out at the time) to writing. In recent years, similar quasi-aleatory methods have been used in music by John Cage and Earle Brown, in film by Nicolas Roeg, and in painting by Robert Rauschenberg, to name only a few. In any event, I moved beyond the "cut-up" in the 1960s and use the technique only rarely in recent works.

*The Wild Boys,* which I started in Morocco, around 1957, inaugurated a new cycle that continued with *Exterminator!, Port of Saints,* and *Ah Pook Is Here.* In these books I am increasingly preoccupied by the themes of space travel and biological mutation as a prerequisite for space travel. A Russian scientist said, "We will travel not only in space, but in time as well." Space travel involves time travel, seeing the dimension of time from outside time, as a landscape spread out before the observer, where a number of things are going on simultaneously—as in the Djemalfnaa in Marrakech: Gnaoua drummers, snake charmers, trick bicycle riders. The image of a vast market occurs repeatedly in later work.

Another theme is tribal societies, not only with different customs from ours, but with different biological designs. *The Wild Boys* could be considered a kind of homosexual *Peter Pan*. And these are four relatively lighthearted books: In *Ah Pook*

*Is Here,* Mr. Hart, the villainous newspaper tycoon, is a rather ineffectual crocodile with a Geiger counter in his belly.

In 1974, when I returned to the United States, I decided to shelve verbal experiments and write a more or less straight narrative. The result was *Cities of the Red Night.* It was while working on this project that I encountered a deadly occupational hazard—writer's block. Suddenly you would rather do anything than sit down and write. When you force yourself, the words seem banal, dead, false, stale, flat, and unprofitable—that is, unpublishable. Writer's block often results from overwriting; the general has gotten too far ahead of his army and finds his supply lines cut. "It just doesn't come anymore!" Hemingway moaned. But I wrote some essays instead, and rode it out.

Mary McCarthy once described me, not unkindly, as a "soured Utopian." That depends on how you see Utopia. In a sense, an ideal society would be a static society, and any such society is an evolutionary dead end. Happiness is a byproduct of function, purpose, and conflict; those who seek happiness for itself seek victory without war.

In *Cities of the Red Night* I parachute my characters behind enemy lines in time. Their mission is to correct retroactively certain fatal errors at crucial turning points in human history. I am speaking of biological errors that tend to block man's path to his biological and spiritual destiny in space. I postulate a social structure offering maximum variation of small communes, as opposed to the uniformity imposed by industrialization and overpopulation. From *Cities of the Red Night:* "Your chance to live in communes of your own choosing, with like-minded companions, died with Captain Mission [the libertarian pirate commander]. Only a miracle or a disaster can restore it."

And the idea of disaster conjures another pigeonhole: "Writer of the apocalypse, prophet of doom." Well, mine is hardly a voice in the wilderness at this point; rather, one voice in a swelling chorus.

*The Place of Dead Roads* is a sequel, clarifying and reiterating similar themes. As I wrote at the beginning of it, "This book postulates that man is an artifact designed for space travel. He is not designed to stagnate in present form any more than a tadpole is designed to remain a tadpole. Man is in a state of arrested evolution." And, drawing the lines of battle: "So our little local war comes down to a struggle between those of us who must go into space or die, and those who, owing to their parasitic needs, will die if we go."

The *Ubermensch* pigeonhole arises here: "A cult of violence." But a concern with biological objectives entails a sanguine attitude toward conflict and violence. There are no second chances in Mother Nature's survival course—"Millions died in the mud flats, only one blasted through to lungs" (*Naked Lunch*).

The novel I am working on is entitled *Western Lands.* This refers to the Egyptian paradise, which is seen as a very real place, reached by a very dangerous road: "Kim had never doubted the existence of gods or the possibility of an afterlife. He considered that immortality was the only goal worth striving for. He knew it was not something you automatically get for believing in some arbitrary dogma like

Christianity or Islam. It is something you have to work and fight for, like everything else in this life or another." And much worse than the false promise of Christianity is the denial of *any* spiritual potentials, as exemplified in the dreary doctrine of Communism.

Perhaps the most basic concept of my writing is a belief in the magical universe, a universe of many gods, often in conflict. The paradox of an all-powerful, all-seeing God who nonetheless allows suffering, evil, and death, does not arise.

"We got a famine here, Osiris. What happened?"

"Well, you can't win 'em all. Hustling myself."

My purpose in writing has always been to express human potentials and purposes relevant to the Space Age.

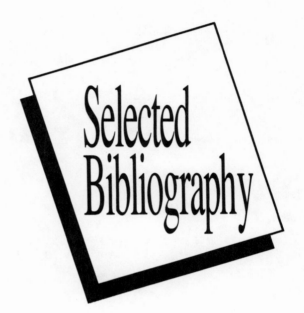

# Selected Bibliography

## Selected Works

Original publication is given first, followed by revised editions, followed by the currently available reprint, if any.

*Ah Pook Is Here and Other Texts*. London: Calder, 1979. New York: Riverrun, 1982.

*Blade Runner: A Movie*. Berkeley: Blue Wind, 1979.

*Cities of the Red Night*. New York: Holt, 1981. New York: Owl-Holt, 1982.

*Cobble Stone Gardens*. Cherry Valley, NY: Cherry Valley, 1976.

*Dead Fingers Talk*. London: Calder, 1963.

*Entretiens avec William Burroughs*. Interviews by Daniel Odier. Paris: Belfond, 1969. Translated as *The Job*, revised and enlarged. New York: Grove, 1970. *The Job*, further enlarged. New York: Grove, 1974.

*Essais, tome I*. Paris: Bourgois, 1981. *Essais, tome II*. Paris: Bourgois, 1984. *The Adding Machine: Collected Essays*. London: Calder, 1985. *The Adding Machine: Selected Essays*. New York: Seaver-Holt, 1986.

*The Exterminator*. With Brion Gysin. San Francisco: Auerhahn, 1960.

*Exterminator!* New York: Viking, 1973. New York: Penguin, 1979.

*Interzone*. New York: Viking, 1989.

*Junkie*. By "William Lee," with *Narcotic Agent* by Maurice Helbrant. New York: Ace, 1953. *Junky*. The complete original text (with revised spelling of title). New York: Penguin, 1977.

*The Last Words of Dutch Schultz: A Fiction in the Form of a Film Script*. London: Cape, 1970. New York: Seaver, 1987.

*Letters to Allen Ginsberg, 1953–1957*. New York: Full Court, 1982.

*Minutes To Go*. With Sinclair Beiles, Gregory Corso, and Brion Gysin. Paris: Two Cities, 1960.

*The Naked Lunch*. Paris: Olympia, 1959. *Naked Lunch*. New York: Grove, 1962. With "Deposition: Testimony Concerning a Sickness" as introduction and "Letter from a Master Addict to Dangerous Drugs" as appendix. New York: Grove, 1969.

*Nova Express*. New York: Grove, 1964. Included in *Three Novels*. New York: Grove, 1980.

*Oeuvre croisée*. Translated into French by Gérard-Georges Lemaire and C. Taylor. Paris: Flammarion, 1976. Published in English as *The Third Mind*. With Brion Gysin. New York: Viking, 1978. New York: Seaver, 1982.

*The Place of Dead Roads*. New York: Holt, 1984. New York: Owl-Holt, 1985.

*Port of Saints*. London: Covent Garden, 1975. Berkeley: Blue Wind, 1980.

*Queer*. New York: Viking, 1985. New York: Penguin, 1987.

*Roosevelt After Inauguration*. San Francisco: City Lights, 1979.

*The Soft Machine*. Paris: Olympia Press, 1961. Revised edition, New York: Grove, 1966. Included in *Three Novels*. New York: Grove, 1980.

271

*The Ticket That Exploded.* Paris: Olympia, 1962. Revised edition, New York: Grove, 1967. New York: Grove, 1987.
*The Western Lands.* New York: Viking, 1987. New York: Penguin, 1988.
*The Wild Boys.* New York: Grove, 1971. Included in *Three Novels.* New York: Grove, 1980.
*The Yage Letters.* With Allen Ginsberg. San Francisco: City Lights, 1963.

## Selected Criticism in English

Ansen, Alan. "Anyone Who Can Pick Up a Frying Pan Owns Death." *Big Table* 2 (Summer 1959): 32–41.
―――. *William Burroughs.* Sudbury: Water Row, 1986.
Bliss, Michael. "The Orchestration of Chaos: Verbal Technique in William Burroughs' *Naked Lunch.*" *enclitic* 1 (1977): 59–69.
Bryan, Jeff. "William Burroughs and His Faith in X." *West Virginia University Philological Papers* 32 (1986–87): 79–89.
Bryant, Jerry H. *The Open Decision: The Contemporary American Novel and Its Intellectual Background.* New York: Free, 1970.
Burgess, Anthony. "Yards and Yards of Entrails." *Observer* 13 Feb. 1966: 27.
Bush, Clive. "Review article: An anarchy of new speech: notes on the American tradition of William Burroughs." *Journal of Beckett Studies* 6 (1980): 120–28.
Carr, C. "Hollow Man." *Voice Literary Supplement* Oct. 1986: 20–22.
Ciardi, John. "The Book Burners and Sweet Sixteen." *Saturday Review* 27 June 1959: 22, 30.
Cordesse, Gérard. "The Science-fiction of William Burroughs." *Caliban* 12 (1975): 33–43.
Didion, Joan. "Wired for Shock Treatments." *Book Week* 27 Mar. 1966: 2–3.
Dorn, Edward. "Notes More or Less Relevant to Burroughs and Trocchi." *Kulchur* 7 (1962): 3–22.
Fiedler, Leslie. "The New Mutants." *Partisan Review* 32 (1965): 505–25.
Friedberg, Anne. "'Cut-Ups': A *Syn*ema of the Text." *Downtown Review* 1.1 (1979): 3–5.
Géfin, Laszlo K. "Collage, Theory, Reception, and the Cutups of William Burroughs." *Literature and the Other Arts: Perspectives on Contemporary Literature* 13 (1987): 91–100.
Glover, David. "Burroughs' Western." *Over Here: An American Studies Journal* 6.2 (1986): 14–23.
―――. "Utopian Fantasy in the Late 1960's: Burroughs, Moorcock, Tolkien." *Popular Fiction and Social Change.* Ed. Christopher Pawling. London: Macmillan, 1984: 185–211.
Gold, Herbert. "Instead of Love, the Fix." *New York Times Book Review* 25 Nov. 1962: 4, 69.
Goodman, Michael Barry. *Contemporary Literary Censorship: The Case History of Burroughs' "Naked Lunch."* Metuchen: Scarecrow, 1981.
Grauerholz, James. "On Burroughs' Art." Santa Fe: Gallery Casa Sin Nombre catalog, 1988. N. pag.
Hassan, Ihab. "The Literature of Silence: From Henry Miller to Beckett and Burroughs." *Encounter* Jan. 1967: 74–82.
―――. "The Novel of Outrage: a Minority Voice in Postwar American Fiction." *American Scholar* 34 (1965): 239–53.

———. "The Subtracting Machine: The Work of William Burroughs." *Critique* 6 (1963): 4–23.

Hendin, Josephine. *Vulnerable People: A View of American Fiction Since 1945*. New York: Oxford UP, 1978.

Hilfer, Anthony Channell. "Mariner and Wedding Guest in William Burroughs' *Naked Lunch*." *Criticism* 22 (1980): 252–65.

Jardine, Alice. *Gynesis: Configurations of Woman and Modernity*. Ithaca: Cornell UP, 1985.

Kazin, Alfred. *Bright Book of Life: American Novelists and Storytellers from Hemingway to Mailer*. Boston: Little, 1973.

———. "He's just wild about writing." *New York Times Book Review* 12 Dec. 1971: 4, 22.

Koch, Stephen. "Images of Loathing." *Nation* 4 July 1966: 25–26.

Kostelanetz, Richard. "From Nightmare to Serendipity: A Retrospective Look at William Burroughs." *Twentieth Century Literature* 11 (1965): 123–30.

Leddy, Michael. "'Departed have left no address': Revelation/Concealment Presence/Absence in *Naked Lunch*." *Review of Contemporary Fiction* 4.1 (1984): 33–39.

Lee, Robert A. "William Burroughs and the Sexuality of Power." *20th Century Studies* 2 (1969): 74–88.

Lemaire, Gérard-Georges. "23 Stitches Taken." In William Burroughs and Brion Gysin *The Third Mind*. New York: Viking, 1978: 9–24.

Lodge, David. *Modes of Modern Writing: Metaphor, Metonymy and the Typology of Modern Literature*. Ithaca: Cornell UP, 1977.

———. *The Novelist at the Crossroads and Other Essays in Fiction and Criticism*. Ithaca: Cornell UP, 1971. London: Routledge, 1971 and 1986.

———. "Objections to William Burroughs." *Critical Quarterly* 8 (1966): 203–12.

Lydenberg, Robin. "Cut-Up: Negative Poetics in William Burroughs and Roland Barthes." *Comparative Literature Studies* 15 (1978): 414–30.

———. "'El Hombre Invisible.'" *Nation* 19 Mar. 1988: 387–89.

———. *Word Cultures: Radical Theory and Practice in William S. Burroughs' Fiction*. Urbana: U of Illinois P, 1987.

McCarthy, Mary. "Burroughs' *Naked Lunch*." *Encounter* 20 (1963): 92–98.

———. "Déjeuner sur l'Herbe." *New York Review of Books* 1.1 (1963): 4–5.

———. *The Writing on the Wall and Other Literary Essays*. New York: Harcourt, 1970.

McConnell, Frank D. "William Burroughs and the Literature of Addiction." *Massachusetts Review* 8 (1967): 665–80.

McLuhan, Marshall. "Notes on Burroughs." *Nation* 28 Dec. 1964: 517–19.

Mottram, Eric. *WILLIAM BURROUGHS: The Algebra of Need*. London: Boyars, 1977.

Nelson, Cary. *The Incarnate Word: Literature and Verbal Space*. Urbana: U of Illinois P, 1973.

Oxenhandler, Neal. "Listening to Burroughs' Voice." *Surfiction: Fiction Now . . . and Tomorrow*. Ed. Raymond Federman. Chicago: Swallow, 1975: 181–201. Athens: Ohio UP/Swallow, 1981.

Palumbo, Donald. "William Burroughs' Quartet of Science Fiction Novels as Dystopian Social Satire." *Extrapolation* 20 (1979): 321–29.

Pearce, Richard. *Stages of the Clown: Perspectives on Modern Fiction from Dostoevsky to Beckett*. Carbondale: Southern Illinois UP, 1970.

Pounds, Wayne. "The Postmodern Anus: Parody and Utopia in Two Recent Novels by William Burroughs." *Poetics Today* 8.3–4 (1987): 611–29.

Russell, Charles. "Individual Voice in the Collective Discourse: Literary Innovation in

Postmodern American Fiction." *Sub-stance: A Review of Theory and Literary Criticism* 27 (1980): 29–39.

Sante, Luc. "The Invisible Man." *New York Review of Books* 10 May 1984: 12–15.

Seldon, E. S. "The Cannibal Feast." *Evergreen Review* Jan.–Feb. 1962: 110–13.

Seltzer, Alvin. *Chaos in the Novel: The Novel in Chaos.* New York: Schocken, 1974.

Sharret, Christopher. "The Hero as Pastiche: Myth, Male Fantasy and Simulacra in *Mad Max* and *The Road Warrior.*" *Journal of Popular Film and Television* 13 (1985): 82–91.

Shaviro, Steven. "Burroughs' Theater of Illusion: *Cities of the Red Night.*" *Review of Contemporary Fiction* 4.1 (1984): 64–74.

Skau, Michael. "The Central Verbal System: The Prose of William Burroughs." *Style* 15 (1981): 401–14.

Skerl, Jennie. "Freedom through Fantasy in the Recent Novels of William S. Burroughs." *Review of Contemporary Fiction* 4.1 (1984): 124–30.

———. *William S. Burroughs.* Twayne's United States Authors Series 438. Boston: Hall, 1985.

———. "William S. Burroughs: Pop Artist." *Sphinx* 11 (1980): 1–15.

Solotaroff, Theodore. "The Algebra of Need." *New Republic* 5 Aug. 1967: 29–34.

Sorrentino, Gilbert. "Firing a Flare for the Avant-garde." *Book Week* 3 Jan. 1965: 10.

Southern, Terry. "Rolling Over our Nerve-endings." *Book Week* 8 Nov. 1964: 5, 31.

Stimpson, Catharine R. "The Beat Generation and the Trials of Homosexual Liberation." *Salmagundi* 58–59 (1982–83): 373–92.

Tanner, Tony. *City of Words: American Fiction, 1950–1970.* New York: Harper, 1971.

Tytell, John. *Naked Angels: The Lives and Literature of the Beat Generation.* New York: McGraw-Hill, 1976. New York: Grove, 1986.

Vernon, John. *The Garden and the Map: Schizophrenia in Twentieth Century Literature and Culture.* Urbana: U of Illinois P, 1973.

Wain, John. "The Great Burroughs Affair." *New Republic* 1 Dec. 1962: 21–23.

Weinreich, Regina. "Dynamic Déjà Vu of William Burroughs." *Review of Contemporary Fiction* 4.1 (1984): 55–58.

Werner, Craig Hansen. *Paradoxical Resolutions: American Fiction since James Joyce.* Urbana: U of Illinois P, 1982.

[Willett, John]. "UGH . . ." *Times Literary Supplement* 3220 (14 Nov. 1963): 919. Correspondence weekly through 23 Jan. 1964.

Zurbrugg, Nicholas. "Beckett, Proust, and Burroughs and the Perils of 'Image Warfare.'" *Samuel Beckett: Humanistic Perspectives.* Ed. Morris Beja, S. E. Gontarski, and Pierre Astier. Columbis: Ohio State UP, 1983: 172–87.

———. "Burroughs, Barthes, and the Limits of Intertextuality." *Review of Contemporary Fiction* 4.1 (1984): 86–107.

Jennie Skerl is Associate Dean, College of Arts and Sciences, West Chester University. The author of *William S. Burroughs* (1985), she has published on Burroughs, the Beats, Beckett, Joyce, and narrative theory.

Robin Lydenberg is Professor of English, Boston College. Her *Word Cultures: Radical Theory and Practice in William S. Burroughs' Fiction* appeared in 1987. She has also published articles on Roland Barthes, Lautréamont, and the collage aesthetic.